PAISLEY

ED MOLONEY & ANDY POLLAK

POOLBEG

A Paperback Original
First published 1986 by
Poolbeg Press Ltd.,
Knocksedan House,
Swords, Co. Dublin, Ireland

ISBN 0 905169 75 1

Editors:
Lorna Stevens
Antony Farrell
Hilary O'Donoghue

Cover design by Steven Hope
incorporating photographs by Derek Speirs
Index by Helen Litton
Map of Free Presbyterian Churches
by Brian O'Donoghue
Typeset from Computer Discs by Typographics
Steeple Lane, Lucan, Co. Dublin.
Printed by The Guernsey Press Ltd.,
Vale, Guernsey, Channel Islands.

ACKNOWLEDGEMENTS

This book could not have been written without the assistance of a great many people, most of whom we are constrained by the ethics of journalism from naming. There are some, however, we can thank personally.

Joan McKiernan spent countless hours transcribing and summarising dozens of tape-recorded interviews. Both Joan and Doireann Ni Bhriain offered loving support and helpful criticism at times of depression and near incoherence, while Ciaran Moloney pluckily endured almost nine fatherless months.

Our friends and former *Irish Times* colleagues, David McKittrick and Fionnuala O'Connor read drafts of the manuscript and gave much needed encouragement and invaluable advice. Any deficiencies in the finished product are, however, entirely our responsibility. David also put his unrivalled knowledge of Loyalist politics and paramilitary affairs freely at our disposal.

We would also like to give special thanks to Clifford Smyth, whose excellent PhD thesis on the Democratic Unionist Party helped to guide us through the maze of Paisleyite politics. Clifford also gave generously of his time and insights, despite the demands of his own book on Paisley, and we are duly grateful. David Taylor's illuminating PhD thesis on Paisleyism was of inestimable value in helping us to understand the inner workings of the Free Presbyterian Church.

Others who were particularly helpful were Wallace Thompson, the Rev. Martin Smyth, William Craig, Richard Reid and Steve Bruce. The staff of the Linenhall library in Belfast gave ungrudging assistance despite our constant demands. Thanks are also due to the NI controller of the BBC,

James Hawthorne, who gave us access to the BBC library in Belfast, and to Jean Gamble for all her help. The photo library of the *Belfast Telegraph* and the staff of Pacemaker were generous with assistance as were the *Irish Times* librarians. Hilary O'Donoghue of Poolbeg Press dealt patiently and good-humouredly with all our problems.

We wrote twice to the Rev Ian Paisley asking for an interview but have yet to receive a reply. Many current and former members of his church and party were, however, less reticent and, although wishing to remain anonymous, gave us their co-operation in researching this book. To them and to members and ex-members of the following groups and organisations with which the Rev Paisley was associated over the years, we extend particular thanks: The National Union of Protestants, Ulster Protestant Action, the Protestant Unionists, the Ulster Constitution Defence Committee, the Ulster Protestant Volunteers, the Official Unionist Party, the Ulster Workers Council, the United Unionist Action Council, Vanguard, the Independent Unionist movement, the Orange Order, the Apprentice Boys of Derry, the UDA, the UVF and the Red Hand Commandos. A number of Presbyterian ministers, former Northern Ireland Office Ministers and Unionist Cabinet Ministers also gave us help, as did past and present civil servants and RUC officers.

Ed Moloney
Andy Pollak

Belfast,
August 1986

CONTENTS

To Joan and Ciaran and in memory of my parents
Ed Moloney

To Doireann, Eileen and Claire, and to Val for courage
Andy Pollak

INTRODUCTION

Saturday, 18 January 1986 was a busy day for Rev Dr Ian Richard Kyle Paisley, leader of the Democratic Unionist Party, Moderator of the Free Presbyterian Church, Member of Parliament, Member of the European Parliament and Member of the Northern Ireland Assembly. Although only three months off his 60th birthday, he still kept to a schedule that would have crippled many younger men, often ending a day spent in London or Strasbourg with a gospel campaign in some country church and then a round of late night calls to deal with constituents' problems.

He spent most of that day electioneering in his North Antrim constituency. The following week the Protestant voters of Northern Ireland would be asked to turn out in a series of by-elections to deliver an overwhelming "No" to the Anglo-Irish Agreement. Outraged by the Agreement, which for the first time gave the Irish Government a say in Northern Ireland's affairs, all the Unionist MPs at Westminster had resigned their seats to give their supporters the chance to vent their opposition to it.

The atmosphere was one of crisis and impending conflict. Unionists of all classes, creeds and political tendencies were angry and afraid at this new incursion by the ancient enemy from the South. This was no ordinary election, Paisley told a rally in his home town of Ballymena that afternoon: "a battle for the very freedom of Ulster from rule by a foreign hostile power" was under way. At such a moment of peril all Unionists must stand together, he declared in his usual thunderous crescendo. Sitting beside him on the platform, nodding in agreement, was his erstwhile bitter political rival, Official Unionist leader Jim Molyneaux. Below in the crowd stood ranks of young toughs, clad in the combat jackets of the Ulster Defence Association, the paramilitary cutting edge of Loyalism.

The Unionist family had put aside its past quarrels and been reunited by the age-old threat, banding together for self-protection and looking for a strong man to lead them. To many in the crowd Ian Paisley was not only that leader, but a militant prophet who combined in his massive frame all the divinely-inspired defiance of their past religious and political heroes. "He is a man raised up by God in Ulster's hour of need", said one ardent follower.

But even in the middle of this grave political crisis for his people, Ian Paisley put his fanatical religious faith first. Earlier that day he had added a bizarre touch to an anti-Catholic protest his church was planning for the following week, two days before the by-elections. The former Roman Catholic Primate of Belgium, Cardinal Leo Josef Suenens, was coming to Belfast to preach in the Protestant Cathedral of St Anne's. Paisley could not ignore another opportunity to challenge the Roman antichrist, the same challenge which 40 years earlier had launched his spectacular religious and political career.

His protest was full of the wild extravagance and primitive superstition which had made his name a byword for bigotry long before he attained the respectability of elected office. In a letter to the Church of Ireland Dean of St Anne's, Paisley accused Suenens of having presided in 1970 over a Catholic theological congress in Brussels, largely attended by young women, which had turned into a celebration of sexual potency and fertility worship. He challenged the Dean to say whether the pulpit of St Anne's was a fit place for such an idolator.

Quoting from a Belgian press agency report of the time, Paisley claimed that the congress had started with dancing and a feast of wine and cigarettes, but had quickly deteriorated into outright obscenity when the eyes of the young delegates were drawn towards the altar. There "something was beginning to rise and take on an unbelievable shape. It was at first greeted with gasps, then giggles, and finally pandemonium broke loose as the transparent plastic forming the shape was seen to represent a gigantic penis. The delegates screamed themselves hoarse, feeling it was a challenge to - a recognition of - their virility. It was the sort of climax that had never been imagined and might only figure in the most extravagant of bawdy dreams".

The explanation for this "amazing exhibition of carnal tomfoolery", he said, was the perfidy of Rome. Suenens, like the Pope, was not a Christian at all - both were masters of a heathen temple where "atavistic rites, all with sexual undertones, take the place of religion". He went on: "When the adolescent girls shrieked with delighted embarrassment as the large plastic penis rose up before them, Cardinal Suenens knew perfectly well that they were, as he intended, commemorating the heathen god Baal whose name . . . has several meanings. Among them are lord, master, possessor or husband, while others refer to a controlling male's penis with its forceful boring and thrusting.

"So what the Cardinal arranged for the young, mostly girls, of Brussels was a show of phallic worship, which symbolises the generative power contained in the semen, or life juice, which streamed down upon all life and nature from the mighty penis of Baal."

Paisley was not finished. The then Pope, Paul VI, had used a "praise chant", he claimed, which had the same origins in the pagan worship of the power of semen: "During public displays of mass sexual intercourse, which go by the name of fertility rites, this semen, when ejaculated, was caught in the hands of the officiating priests, who held it up for the approval of Yahweh (Jehovah) and then proceeded to smear it on their bodies".

Three days later, when Cardinal Suenens arrived at St Anne's Cathedral, he was greeted by 200 noisy and abusive placard-waving Free Presbyterians. Inside the cathedral were 50 more, including Paisley's daughter Rhonda, artist and DUP councillor, who was one of the first to interrupt Suenens as he tried to start his sermon. Eventually the shouting Paisleyites were escorted outside by the police.

The protest was an embarrassment both to the Church of Ireland and to Paisley's new Official Unionist allies, an unwelcome reminder of the divisive, disruptive Paisley of old. The Dean of St Anne's called it "an attempt to gain votes" and echoed the worries of respectable Unionism: "Certain people will be impressed by this, but there are plenty of decent, honourable Unionists who will be bewildered by it".

The Dean was wrong. Two days later, nearly 34,000 Unionists in North Antrim voted for the man who claimed that Catholics worshipped gigantic phalluses, the largest Unionist turn-out of the day. They were not the religious fanatics on the pavement outside St Anne's Cathedral, nor were they the hard men of the loyalist paramilitary world - most of them were precisely the kind of solid, decent, respectable Protestants the Dean had referred to.

Why would tens of thousands of such people - even hundreds of thousands in European elections - turn out to support the man who has come to personify Northern Ireland's unenviable reputation as the most impregnable bastion of religious bigotry and bloodletting in the Western world? That is the riddle of Ian Paisley, a conundrum which lies at the very heart of the enduring conflict in Ireland.

Part 1

CHAPTER ONE

A Separate Youth

Come out from among them and be ye separate, saith the Lord,
and touch not the unclean thing.
II Corinthians, chapter 6, verse 17.

Northern Ireland in 1926 was drawing its breath. Five years earlier, in the middle of a bloody 24 months which left over 400 people dead and nearly 1800 wounded, Ireland's six north-eastern counties had been partitioned from the rest of the country. Unionist resistance in those counties had thwarted the age-old Nationalist goal of complete independence and brought into being the truncated, but still British, state of Northern Ireland. It was a state dominated by its Protestant majority. Its Catholic minority accepted it sullenly and unwillingly.

The new creation was the result of over four centuries of struggle between British and Irish, Protestants and Catholics, Unionists and Nationalists. It was the latest and most concrete manifestation of the siege mentality of the Protestant "planters" who had arrived from England and Scotland in the 16th and 17th centuries. Unionists did not emerge from the violent years surrounding its birth as a confident majority, prepared to be generous to their Nationalist fellow-citizens, but as beleaguered and obsessed with their history as ever.

They still looked back to the first great slaughter of their forefathers by the native Irish in 1641. Their celebrations of the victories against Catholicism represented by the 1689 Siege of Londonderry and the 1690 Battle of the Boyne were still the high point of the official year. Their heroes were Oliver Cromwell and King William of Orange, the 17th century scourges of the

7

Catholic Irish, and the Protestant Apprentice Boys who closed the gates of Derry to prevent the traitorous Governor Lundy from dealing with the enemy. Most recently, and potently, tens of thousands of them remembered how a decade earlier they had banded together in the manner of their ancestors into the Ulster Volunteer Force, and under Sir Edward Carson's leadership had defied an attempt by the British parliament and government to impose Home Rule on Ireland. This, rather than the establishment of Northern Ireland, they regarded as their finest hour.

Meanwhile the new state struggled into existence and its people back to some kind of normality. By the end of 1922 the violence was over. Its first prime minister, Carson's lieutenant Sir James Craig, later Lord Craigavon, lifted internment at the end of 1924. In 1925 the first and last Stormont election held under proportional representation returned 20 opposition MPs, the biggest number that parliament would ever see. Nationalist MPs dropped their boycott and started to take their seats, encouraged by a Catholic hierarchy who were worried about the Unionist regime's only attempt at non-sectarian legislation, the 1923 Education Bill.

1925 also saw the securing of Unionism's new frontier. After the Boundary Commission's report was leaked, the London, Dublin and Belfast governments hastily agreed that partition would remain in place exactly as it was. The new state was protected by the draconian powers of the Special Powers Act and a formidable array of overwhelmingly Protestant security forces, including the Royal Ulster Constabulary and the part-time "B Specials" of the Ulster Special Constabulary.

Ian Richard Kyle Paisley became the youngest citizen of this new state on 6 April 1926 in a modest two-storey terraced house opposite the railway station in the little cathedral city of Armagh. He was born into a town which illustrated the Northern Ireland problem in miniature. Just over half its population was Catholic, and the Paisley house was in a largely Catholic area. Armagh's classic colonial lay-out meant that Protestants ran the town's commercial centre in English and Scotch Street, while its southern and western districts, in Irish Street and around their recently-completed cathedral, were overwhelmingly Catholic.

The countryside to the south and west was mixed but mainly Catholic, and to the north and east strongly Protestant. Seven miles north-east of the town was the Diamond, where in 1796 Catholic Defenders and Protestant Peep o'Day Boys fought a battle which resulted in the formation of the Orange Order. Over the following century this Protestant secret society, bringing together in hundreds of "lodges" men of all classes, social backgrounds and denominations, would become one of Unionism's most important weapons in the struggle against Irish Catholicism and Nationalism.

The city of Armagh's one unusual feature was that in the 1920s, before the gerrymandering designs of the Unionists were put into effect, it was run by a Catholic council.[1] The year before Paisley was born its Nationalist councillors had petitioned the Boundary Commissioners to be included in the Irish Free State, if necessary by a narrow corridor to link it to the predominantly Catholic areas of South Armagh and North Monaghan.

The experience of being surrounded by the ancient Nationalist enemy was nothing new to the child's father, James Kyle Paisley, the local Baptist pastor. Known as Kyle, his mother's family name, he was then 34. He came from a long line of staunch Orangemen from the hill country around the County Tyrone village of Sixmilecross, an area of poor land with a long history of conflict between the native Irish and the descendants of Protestant "planters" from lowland Scotland and northern England. The Paisleys and the Kyles had arrived in the townland of Brackey, just outside Sixmilecross, in the first wave of Scottish settlers in the early 17th century.

Members of both families had marched with the Brackey Orange lodge through the neighbouring village of Beragh in the 1830s in defiance of a British government ban on Orange parades. An ancestor of Kyle's mother, John "Belt" Kyle, a leading member of the Brackey lodge, had died from injuries received in a violent brawl between the Orangemen and local Catholics after one such march.

In 1916, on the eve of the Easter Rising, Kyle Paisley's uncle, David, for 51 years Master of the Brackey lodge, was tipped off by the local police inspector that an attempt would be made by Republicans from nearby Carrickmore, reinforced by a force from Belfast, to seize the military barracks at Omagh. According to local loyalist legend he rallied his old Ulster Volunteer Force unit and laid an ambush for the Republicans, successfully scaring them off.[2]

David Paisley was something of an expert at instilling fear into local Catholics, a talent his great-nephew was to inherit. When Catholic children in the area saw the big Brackey farmer approaching them along a country lane, they would take to the fields rather than risk coming face to face with such a dangerous Orangeman.

The young Kyle Paisley had himself served in Carson's Ulster Volunteer Force during the Home Rule crisis of 1912-13. It was a service which his son Ian, conscious of his own lack of experience in the violent front line of Protestant Ulster's defences, would frequently recall in order to boost his credentials as a loyalist leader. Nearly three quarters of a century later Ian Paisley still shows visitors the bandolier his father carried in those days and the wooden rifle he trained with.

Kyle's father Richard was a farmer, shoemaker and member of the Church of Ireland. Like many Ulster members of the established church in the late 19th century, he was an "evangelical": meaning that, like his Presbyterian neighbours, he was suspicious of ritual and dogma and held to a simple faith in the teachings of Christ as laid down in the New Testament. So it was not totally surprising when in 1908 his son, a big quiet-spoken boy, was converted to "born again" evangelical Christianity while working behind the counter of a drapery store in Omagh. Kyle went home to the family farm at Kilcam, outside Sixmilecross, cleaned out an old barn, put seats in it and started to preach to his family and neighbours. He had found his vocation.

A short time later he took his conversion one step further when he was baptised in the river Strule outside Omagh by the Baptist pastor, a famous local character who played the fiddle and doubled as a farmer, creamery manager and postmaster.

Baptists were looked upon as strange people in those days, and were sometimes socially ostracised because of their belief that only people who were re-baptised by total immersion in water could be "saved". But Kyle Paisley did not worry that he might be cutting himself off from family and friends by this new departure. He was "absolutely uncompromising" when he believed something to be right, his son boasted later, and "the more he was persecuted the more he excelled in evangelism". He became an itinerant preacher, a "fire and brimstone" hot gospeller trying to save souls in the prayer meetings held in the farm kitchens, tent missions and open-air pulpits of Protestant mid-Ulster.

In 1915 he moved to Armagh to work in a big drapery store run by a family of strict Plymouth Brethren, an evangelical sect considered ultra-Protestant even by the rigid standards of the north of Ireland. His new employers, the Lennoxes, refused to take on anyone who was not a "born again" Christian.

Here, in October 1918, he was invited to become the first pastor of Armagh's twelve-strong Baptist congregation. They held their services in a tin hut rented from a local Presbyterian minister, who had opened it as a teetotal gathering place for local drunks. Kyle Paisley was a well-liked and hard-working pastor, who did a correspondence course with the Irish Baptist College in Dublin at night while working behind the drapery counter during the day.

He soon became well known in the countryside around Armagh for the fieriness of his preaching. On one celebrated occasion he was returning to the town after a rural mission on his bicycle when he was stopped by an IRA unit. They put him up against the hedge but let him go when they found out that he was only an evangelist. By 1923 he had succeeded in building up his tiny church's membership to 54 souls, with a Sunday morning attendance of twice or even three times that number. In August of that year he married Isabella Turnbull, a 24-year-old railway worker's daughter from Kilsyth, near Stirling in Scotland. He had met her while preaching in the neighbouring town of Lurgan, where she was working as governess to the children of a local doctor. His new wife had been brought up as a strict Bible-reading Presbyterian in a town famous for its associations with the 17th century Presbyterian "Covenanters" and their struggles against successive English monarchs.

At the age of 15 she was converted to "born again" Christianity when she heard a coal-heaver preaching in a gospel hall in Edinburgh, and started going to Baptist services. She had come to Northern Ireland some years earlier following the death of her mother in an influenza epidemic in the Scottish capital.

The new Mrs Paisley was as assertive and abrasive as her husband - outside the pulpit - was gentle and unassuming. At Lurgan Baptist Church she had occasionally preached the sermon, almost unheard-of behaviour for a woman at that time. She held strong views on everything from the leading role a pastor's wife should play to the unseemly behaviour and dress of the younger generation. "Ian got most of his fire and fury from Scotland", someone who knew her in Lurgan once remarked.

In 1924, while the Paisleys were living just outside Armagh in the village of Killylea, their first son was born, and was named Harold Spurgeon after the famous 19th century English Baptist preacher. Shortly afterwards they moved from the Killylea house, noted for the huge biblical text painted on its roof for the enlightenment of passing train passengers, back into Armagh. A member of the Armagh Baptist congregation had donated to the church the redbrick house opposite the station to be used as a residence for its pastor. It was here that the Paisleys' second son first saw the light of day, half a mile away from the splendid new seat of the Irish Catholic Church he was to come to hate with such a venom.

BALLYMENA'S HILL STREET BLUES

But the new addition to the family was to know little of Ireland's ancient religious capital, the place where St Patrick had built his first cathedral. For in May 1928, when he was two years old, his father answered a "call" from the considerably larger Baptist congregation at Hill Street in Ballymena, County Antrim. For the next five years Ian and Harold lived and played in the pastor's spacious house and garden which adjoined the rear of the church, while their father ministered to the spiritual needs of his new 200-strong congregation.

Ballymena in the 1920s was a staunchly Presbyterian town, proud of the puritan traditions it had inherited from its Scots settler founders. In the late 18th century it had briefly been a centre of Presbyterian dissent and even rebellion against the British and their established church. It boasted five Presbyterian churches, including one which had celebrated its 300th anniversary the year before the Paisleys arrived. It had two reputations, both traceable to its founders: its tight-fisted attitude to money and its extremely strait-laced views on everything else.

Its more devout citizens viewed most of the pastimes and styles of the contemporary Western world as sinful. Their list of vices was endless: smoking, drinking and gambling, of course, but also all forms of dancing, from the waltz to the charleston. Girls who wore lipstick, make-up and their hair short in the "bobbed" fashion of the day were regarded as the next worst thing to prostitutes.

Going to the cinema, even when, as in Ballymena, films were shown in the local Protestant hall, was frowned upon. Even attending local soccer matches was discouraged on the grounds that the language of the spectators might be offensive to devout Protestant ears. There was a ditty that parents in the town used to teach to teenagers:

> There is one thing I will not do, I will not stand in a cinema queue. There are two things I do detest, a painted face and a low-backed dress. There are three things I will not do, I will not gamble, smoke or chew.

The religious expression of this puritanism was an old-fashioned evangelical doctrine which emphasised the absolute authority of the Bible and the need for everyone, even those who were already practising Protestants, to be converted to "born again" Christianity and thus "saved" from the hellfire of eternal damnation. The climax of the evangelical movement in Irish Protestantism had come with the "Great Revival" of 1859 - an explosion of religious enthusiasm in which it was claimed that more than 100,000 people had been converted. That revival had started in the Ballymena area and the Hill Street church was a product of it.

The 1920s saw the emergence of a powerful "hellfire" preacher in the 1859 mould, an ex-seaman and reformed alcoholic called W.P.Nicholson who had turned his back on his evil ways to become a Presbyterian evangelist. During the years of sectarian violence which followed the birth of the state, the Northern Ireland Prime Minister, Sir James Craig, had persuaded Nicholson, in the interests of community harmony, not to preach against Catholicism.

He turned instead to exposing the sins of mainstream Presbyterianism. He became notorious for the aggression of his attacks on loose morals, lifeless religious observance and the "bastard theology" of that church's leadership. Although ordinary church members may have found his language shocking, they loved his revivalist message - a lesson Paisley was to take to heart in later years. And once again Ballymena, the most devoutly Presbyterian town in the North, was at the centre of things: during a five week mission by Nicholson in the town in the spring of 1923 over 2,500 people were "saved", more than a quarter of its total Protestant population.[3]

In stark contrast to Nicholson's revivalist tirades was a new spirit of liberal enquiry among a small group of Presbyterian intellectuals, led by Ernest Davey, a young professor at Assembly's Theological College, the church's training college for ministers in Belfast. Davey set out to re-examine a number of key Presbyterian beliefs in the light of contemporary theology. He studied Christ's virgin birth, and the riddle of how He could have been a divine and a human being at the same time. And he asked what Christ's crucifixion signified for 20th century people seeking Christian "salvation'.

His attempt to demystify the birth and death of Christ proved particularly offensive to many of the church's more old-fashioned evangelicals, and sparked off a Nicholson-supported campaign against him. This in turn led to a group of conservative churchmen taking the almost unprecedented step of laying charges of heresy against him. After a brilliant defence he was acquitted, and an appeal to that year's General Assembly, the church's highest authority, was dismissed. A small group of hard-liners quit the church in protest, leaving behind a sizable rump of conservatives, particularly in rural congregations, who were still deeply suspicious of the "modernist" ideas of Davey and his friends. They were to provide Ian Paisley with some of his first followers a quarter of a century later.

It was against this background of evangelical fervour and heresy-hunting that tensions started to develop between Kyle Paisley and some senior members of his new Ballymena congregation. Mrs Paisley was at the centre of most of the storms. Her rigid puritan beliefs, quick temper and fondness for bringing disagreements to a head with a sharp word, seemed to make for discord. In later years she was also to divide the Ballymena St John's Ambulance Brigade, in which she was a superintendent, over her strict interpretation of Sunday observance.

In the Hill Street church Mrs Paisley insisted on rudely displacing the much-loved former pastor's widow at the organ. She got rid of the choir after a row over what kind of hymns should be sung. She had complained that the girls in the choir were wearing their hair short in the current "bobbed" fashion in contravention of St Paul's admonition that women should never be "shorn or shaven". She also claimed that some of the leading men at Hill Street had liberal or "modernist" tendencies.

Although fellow pastors more experienced in dealing with the sensitivities of congregations warned him not to make an issue of such internal disputes, the quiet-spoken Kyle was totally unable to curb his wife's tempestuous nature. "She threw a tantrum if she didn't get her way", recalled one member of the church. "Pastor Forbes, who took over from Kyle Paisley, said they should have thrown a bucket of water over her".

According to Ian Paisley's version, matters came to a head in 1933 when his father preached two sermons denouncing the sale of alcoholic drink and sexual immorality. According to his son, these were aimed at two leading church members: one who owned a plot of land on which there was a pub; the other, the church's treasurer, who was allegedly paying women "large sums of money to keep their mouths closed" about his immorality. Not surprisingly the church's deacons as well as the Baptist Union headquarters in Belfast asked him to withdraw his accusations.[4]

It was not for nothing, however, that Paisley had boasted that his father was "absolutely uncompromising". Kyle Paisley's response was to break away from the Hill Street church together with nearly 80 followers, many of them younger men and women whom he had brought into the church by his tent and gospel hall missions in the countryside around Ballymena. In the autumn of 1933 he started to hold meetings in a room at a local iron foundry.

Within a year the foundation stone for a new "gospel tabernacle" had been laid in Waveney Road on a plot beside the main Ballymena to Belfast railway line. The ceremony was carried out by a Canadian friend of Kyle Paisley's, Dr T.T. Shields, himself the breakaway pastor of a large independent Baptist congregation in Toronto, and a man prominently identified with the fundamentalist movement in North America.

Fundamentalism had been a fast-growing movement in America until the 1920s. It emphasised the literal truth of every word in the Bible about the birth and development of man, in opposition to Darwin's Theory of Evolution and the "modernist" Protestant theology which followed it. In the USA fundamentalists had fought bitter court battles against the teaching of evolution in schools. They became increasingly "separatist", both from other Protestant churches and wider

American society, which they denounced as sinful and ungodly for its indulgence in drinking, dancing and sexual licence.[5]

Separatist fundamentalists followed to the letter St Paul's warning not to have any dealings with "unbelievers", however Christian they might claim to be. Their most sacred text was his message to the early Christians of Corinth: "Come out from among them and be ye separate, saith the Lord, and touch not the unclean thing". It was to become the guiding slogan of Ian Paisley's life.

Kyle Paisley's new congregation was both fundamentalist and separatist: it believed in "the whole Word of God, the Bible, verbally inspired by the Holy Ghost, as the final authority on all matters of Doctrine, Faith, Practice". It aimed to be "a faithful remnant . . . free from compromise", supporting "the supernaturalism of Christianity against the anti-supernaturalism of modernity".[6]

Many of the breakaway Baptists were young farmers from the surrounding countryside, and it was their contributions, together with some help from evangelical circles in Canada, which raised the £1,200 needed to build the little tabernacle. They also provided the unpaid labour to build the plain single-storey structure, an example that his son's congregations were to follow in their more ambitious church-building projects in later years.

Times were hard for the Paisleys. It was the middle of the Depression. Mrs Paisley wanted a daughter, so they adopted the youngest daughter of a cousin of Kyle Paisley's in Tyrone, a small farmer with seven children, all of them girls. They moved into a three-storey redbrick house a few doors down from the new church, but Kyle Paisley never took a regular salary from his congregation, relying instead on the Sunday collection and the generosity of individual members for survival. They were often left with a bare larder and literally praying for enough food to get them through the week.

Once again the farmers came to their aid in the shape of families like the Beatties, dissident Presbyterians looking for "old-style" gospel preaching and the values that went with it. Their son William was later to become a Free Presbyterian minister and Ian Paisley's deputy in the Democratic Unionist Party, while two daughters were to marry leading Free Presbyterian ministers. The Beatties had a farm above Broughshane, northeast of Ballymena towards the Antrim hills, and regularly brought them in eggs, milk, potatoes and vegetables.

Contemporaries of the Paisley brothers at the Ballymena Model School in the 1930s remember them as big ungainly boys, always dressed very neatly in dark suits, collars and ties. Ian had become a "born again" Christian at the extraordinarily young age of six during a children's service conducted by his mother in the Hill Street church the year before the split. He told later how he had been affected by her sermon about the good shepherd and "the little lost sheep". After the service he remained behind and told her: "I don't want to be a lost sheep, I want to be a saved lamb". They knelt down in a pew in the church "and at that spot I found Jesus Christ as my Saviour and Lord".[7] Nearly 50 years later, when the church was being renovated, Paisley asked for and was given that pew: it now adorns the front hall of his home in East Belfast.

Both Ian and Harold were taught that as children of a family and a congregation that had "separated" themselves from the sinful ways of ordinary religious and social life, they had to be very careful whom they mixed with. This meant that they usually played by themselves, never went to the cinema (even for a school-organised educational film) and on Sundays stayed indoors praying and reading the bible while other children were outside playing. As a result of this upbringing Ian was not a boy who mixed well at school: he did not take part in football matches in the school yard, stammered nervously when asked questions by teachers and went off home by himself as soon as the school bell sounded at the end of the day. But as the years passed he started to follow the example of his more confident older brother, and by the time he reached his teens he had a reputation as something of a bully.

One former Model School boy, now a clergyman, remembers Ian, then around 12 years old, punching his 12-year-old brother, knocking his ice-cream out of his hand, and getting a bloody nose for his trouble. However most boys of their age were afraid of the size and belligerence of the Paisley boys and kept out of their way. Other contemporaries remember Ian as a very pious boy. His mother used to claim that at eight years of age he was already reading books of Calvinist theology like the 17th century classic on damnation and salvation, *Death of Deaths*. In his early teens he used to get up at three and four in the morning to pray and read the Bible. Above his bed hung a picture of one of his earliest heroes, the founder of the Salvation Army, General William Booth, and the text "Salvation to the Uttermost". It was a phrase Paisley the preacher would use in later years to glorify the ascent from deepest depravity to transformation through "born again" Christianity - "from the guttermost to the uttermost".

Both Harold and Ian were quite able at school, though not clever enough to pass the scholarship exam at age 12 or the pupil teachership exam the following year which in those days were the only routes by which poor bright boys could get to the local grammar school and on to university or teacher training college.

On the eve of the Second World War, Harold, already the "black sheep" of the family, left home, lied about his age and joined the Royal Air Force. He would go on to spend time in both the Merchant Navy and the RUC, which he left after waving around a gun while under the influence of drink. It was a brief rebellion. By the mid-1940s he had returned to the fundamentalist fold as a Plymouth Brethren evangelist. His views were by now even more extreme than his family's: he refused to allow his mother, as a woman, to join in when he said prayers, and attacked his brother for wearing a priestly dog collar on entering the ministry.

Meanwhile 14-year-old Ian had moved to the local technical college, intending eventually to go to the Greenmount Agricultural College near Antrim. After being told that he would first need a year of practical farming experience, his father arranged to send the boy back to his home village of Sixmilecross in Tyrone to serve his time with a former neighbour called George Watson. Watson was a member of the local "tin hut" mission hall, built by members of the village's three Protestant congregations. It was here, in April 1942, that the tall, skinny 16-year-old with the thick Ballymena accent preached his first sermon on the subject of the good samaritan to a congregation of eight people.

Even he admitted in later years that this first effort was a disaster, lasting less than four minutes. His second attempt, after a month spent working by himself in the outlying fields of the Watson farm, was more successful. It was shortly after this, again while out in the fields harrowing corn, that he says he received his "call" to follow in his father's footsteps and become a minister of religion.

In the autumn of 1942 Paisley travelled to South Wales to enrol in the Barry School of Evangelism, ten miles south of Cardiff. Although only 16 years old, Ian was allowed into the school as a personal favour to his father, a close friend of the principal, Rev S. B. Fidler who, like Kyle Paisley, was a fundamentalist Baptist. Fidler had broken with the mainstream Baptist Union because of its heretical "modernist" leanings. Under him, Barry was known for its fundamentalist theology, but even more for its emphasis on practical evangelism and the art of preaching.

Paisley shared a room there with an Englishman called Dennis Parry, a conscientious objector who had spent three months in Cardiff jail because of his pacifist convictions. Parry later became a missionary and was killed by Simba tribesmen in the Congo. His bust is one of those - alongside Luther, Calvin, Knox and Wyclif - which now line the inner walls of Paisley's Martyrs Memorial Church, giving it its name.

Paisley too had thoughts about being a missionary after the war. A short time afterwards he became friendly with one of the pioneers of the Acre Gospel Mission, a Belfast-based evangelical mission which sent people to that most desolate corner of Brazil's Amazonian jungle. He always took a keen interest in its work, and Brazil would become one of the favourite destinations of Free Presbyterian missionaries in later years.

Although enrolled in Barry for a year's course in preparatory Hebrew, Paisley also acquired there a valuable training in the art of preaching to difficult and often hostile audiences: the tough dockers and navvies of Cardiff and Barry ports; the seamen who sailed into them; and the highly critical chapel congregations of the Welsh valleys. The latter were often less than happy when their preacher turned out to be a gangling teenager with an unfamiliar Ulster accent.

But many of the preachers were away at the war, and the less than a dozen students at Barry had to fill in. Despite his extreme youth, Ian Paisley was soon in great demand for his flamboyant style, his swingeing attacks on the heresies of the mainstream Baptist Union and his already impressive knowledge of the Bible. One of his most effective mentors was a former boxer called Teddy Sherwood, who would gather a large crowd around his soapbox, preach until he was hoarse and then call the young

Ulsterman "into the ring".

It was in such situations that Paisley developed the aggressive preaching style that was to serve him so well in later political arenas. When confronted by hostility he soon learned to turn it to his advantage by the age-old orator's trick of challenging a hostile questioner with a question of his own. In later years he told the story of how, during one sermon to an unruly Welsh crowd, a woman called out "How do you know there is a Jesus Christ?" Paisley recalled what happened next:

> There was a great shout of derision that went up from the crowd. And there I was, a mere stripling . . . and faced with a hostile crowd. I said to the Lord "Lord, give me a weapon that will turn as a boomerang in the face of the Devil". And God gave me the answer. I said "Young woman, I come from Ireland, and an Irishman always answers a question by asking another . . ." "What's your question?", she said. I asked "What day is it?" And then the crowd laughed. She said "It's Sunday". I then asked "Could you tell me what month it is?" She said it was the month of August. I said "I have only one more question. Can you tell me what year it is?" Then the crowd knew what I was getting at. They started to laugh and sneer at her. She said "It is 1942". I said "How could you get that number - 1942 years from where? From where?" And she mumbled and stuttered. I said "I'll help you out. It's A.D.; the year of our Lord. There is a Christ! And, young woman, when you take your diary out and you look at the year, the year stands as a living testimony that there is a Christ!".[8]

The Second World War reached Barry in 1943, and Ian Paisley, like all the students at the school, was out on fire-watching duty during that year's massive wave of German bombing raids on the docks and arms factories of nearby Cardiff. But the young evangelist, unlike his rebellious brother, was more interested in serving his God than his country - leaving himself open to charges in later years that he had dodged the war.

That autumn found Paisley, aged 17, back in Belfast as a guest student at the tiny seminary, or "theological hall", of the Reformed Presbyterian Church of Ireland. Once again his father had interceded for him with a friend who was a Reformed Presbyterian minister and professor at the theological hall,

Rev T.B. McFarlane.

The Reformed Presbyterians were known as Covenanters because of their uncompromising adherence to the Scottish Covenants of the 1640s, which bound the puritan parliaments of England and Scotland "to rule in accordance with God's will". In Ireland they were a small sect with fewer than 40 congregations of God-fearing puritan people who held to an old-fashioned gospel as taught by Calvin and John Knox, with a particular emphasis on the latter's doctrine that kings and governments who trample on the religious liberties of their people forfeit their right to rule.

Their theocratic views led them to reject all 20th century politics. They did not vote, refused to take any oath of allegiance to the British monarchy, and condemned secret societies like the Freemasons and the Orange Order. They were the most conservative of the various strains in Scottish Presbyterianism, and had gone their own way after the rebellion by militant Scottish Covenanters against the Catholic James II in the 1680s. Theirs was a creed that the strict young evangelical Baptist from Ballymena could easily feel comfortable with.

The three year part-time course in the Reformed Presbyterian meeting house on Belfast's Grosvenor Road was not an arduous one. In his final two years Paisley was one of only two students attending classes in Greek, Hebrew, elocution, theology and church history. As the only non-graduate and non-member of the Reformed Presbyterian Church, he was not entitled to receive any of its usual bursaries and prizes. But since he did reasonably well in all his exams, the committee of ministers who ran the theological hall, only too conscious of the potential embarrassment when it came to the annual distribution of awards to the minute student body, gave Paisley a special prize for each of his three years there.

Paisley's real interest, however, continued to be in preaching. Long before he left the Covenanters' seminary he was starting to become a regular fixture in mission halls and on open-air pulpits around Belfast. He was befriended by Rev W.J. Grier, a leading figure in the small Irish Evangelical Church, which grouped together a couple of hundred hard-line evangelicals who had broken away from the Irish Presbyterian Church after the Davey heresy trial of 1927. Grier helped the impecunious theological student financially, and introduced his protégé, already becoming known as "the boy preacher", to the Evangelical Church's half a dozen congregations around Belfast.

Belfast in 1946 was already the "city of religious nightclubs" that the English Methodist leader, Donald Soper, was to be so scathing about many years later. Every Saturday the *Belfast Telegraph* carried advertisements for services the next day at over 200 places of Protestant worship, three-fifths of them held by denominations and sects outside the three main Protestant churches: the Presbyterians, Methodists and Church of Ireland.

Audiences of 6000 people attended revival campaign meetings run by the Irish Evangelization Society at the Kings Hall. In High Street, where German bombs had left a wide open space known as "Blitz Square", evangelical preachers of all sects and sizes rubbed shoulders uneasily with the occasional socialist orator promising a new beginning in the wake of the British Labour Party's overwhelming victory in the 1945 general election.

There was precious little chance of any new beginning in postwar Northern Ireland. Churchill's reflection after the First World War still held as true as ever: the unchanging integrity of the Unionist-Nationalist quarrel and the dreary steeples of religious controversy still dominated the political landscape.

A new Nationalist assault on partition was heralded by the formation in Dungannon in November 1945 of the Anti-Partition League. Two months later the Northern Ireland government refused to follow Britain's example and introduce "one man, one vote" in local elections. The Unionist chief whip, Major L.E. Curran, was brutally frank about the reason for this: it was to prevent "Nationalists getting control of the three border counties and Derry City". Such people, he went on, did not have "the welfare of the people of Ulster at heart", and the best way to prevent them overthrowing the government was to disenfranchise them.[9]

The other burning issue of the next few years would be the bitter campaign by Protestant churchmen against the 1947 Education Act, which for the first time since 1930 allowed teachers in state schools to opt out of giving Bible instruction. A second source of Protestant grievance was the old sectarian bogey of financial aid to Catholic schools, and in particular a proposed increase, from 50 per cent to 65 per cent, in government capital grants.

This was the atmosphere in which Ian Paisley, aged 20, made

his first small entry into Northern Ireland's ecclesiastical and political life. He had been preaching regularly at Irish Evangelical churches in East and North Belfast since his return from Wales, and at gospel hall and tent missions in and around his native Ballymena. In December 1945 he was invited to take a service at the Ravenhill Evangelical Mission Church by an elder, a senior lay member there, who had heard him preach and had been impressed.

The Ravenhill church was a small independent evangelical congregation which met in a tin-roofed hall on a rather grimy working-class street within shouting distance of both the Belfast shipyard and East Belfast's only Catholic district, the tiny enclave of Short Strand. Paisley preached there a number of times over the next eight months and so impressed the church's elders that they invited him to become their pastor the following summer.

It was a congenial appointment for him. The 60-strong congregation, much influenced by W.P.Nicholson's sermons against sins of dress, adornment and hairstyle, had broken away from the Ravenhill Presbyterian Church in 1935 over the issue of girls in the choir - including the daughter of the deeply conservative minister - wearing their hair short and "bobbed" in the style of the "flappers". It was the same issue which had played a minor part in the split in Paisley's father's church two years previously. Three of the Ravenhill elders who broke away had been among those who signed the heresy charges against Professor Ernest Davey in 1927.

Despite some opposition from an extreme puritan element in the congregation who said they wanted no pastor of theirs to wear what they called the "roman collar", Paisley declared his intention of being ordained as a minister. Oddly enough, even five weeks before his ordination on 1 August 1946, he was already being billed as the Reverend Ian Paisley at an Irish Evangelical Church in North Belfast.[10]

His actual ordination was to be the subject of heated debate in Presbyterian circles for the next quarter of a century. Some theologians argued that despite Paisley's claims that the ceremony was firmly in the tradition of evangelical Presbyterianism, it was never valid under Presbyterian rules - although it might be recognised by smaller more congregationally-oriented sects like the Baptists and the

Plymouth Brethren.

Only one recognised clergyman, his father Kyle Paisley, an independent Baptist pastor, actually "laid hands" on him in the traditional Presbyterian manner of ordination, as well as a number of the church's leading lay members, the elders. However three clergymen took part in the service who were all recognised Presbyterian ministers of some kind - Rev W. J. Grier of the breakaway Irish Evangelical Church; Professor T.B.McFarlane of the Reformed Presbyterian Church, who had brought Paisley into his church's theological hall; and Rev Thomas Rowan, an old ultra-evangelical Presbyterian minister who had worked with visiting American revivalist preachers at the turn of the century.

Paisley himself has dismissed the later controversy over his ordination, claiming that he had no great commitment to a specifically Presbyterian ritual, despite his attempt five years later to set up a direct rival to mainstream Presbyterianism. He claims to set more store by the imprimatur he says was given him by the legendary Presbyterian evangelist Rev W.P.Nicholson at the first service after his ordination.

He has repeatedly told his congregations that Nicholson walked up to him after that service and asked him if he had ever seen a cow's tongue. When he said he had, Nicholson asked him what it was like. Paisley replied that it was like a file, and Nicholson lifted his hand and prayed "Lord, give this young man a tongue like an old cow".[11] However, a former Free Presbyterian who was at this service as a child claims that Paisley, always prone to exaggerate stories to his own benefit, turned a passing conversation during Nicholson's only visit to the Ravenhill church into a clinching piece of evidence of his own legitimacy as the inheritor of the true Presbyterian preaching tradition.

AGITATOR FOR PROTESTANT ASCENDANCY

It took Paisley little more than a month to translate his new religious status into political involvement. In late August and September he helped to organise an inaugural series of meetings in Northern Ireland for the National Union of Protestants (NUP), a group of evangelical extremists set up in England in 1942 to combat "Romanist" and high church tendencies in the

Church of England, and whose principal activity appeared to be disrupting Anglican services. Its general director was Paisley's maternal uncle, a fundamentalist Baptist called Rev W. St. Clair Taylor.

At the organisation's inaugural meeting at Belfast's "Blitz Square" St. Clair Taylor was the main speaker and Paisley said that they were looking for 50,000 Protestants from Northern Ireland to join up. At a private meeting earlier Paisley had become treasurer of the NUP's local branch with a young East Belfast Baptist called Norman Porter as secretary. However they soon found that high church practice in the Church of England was not an issue guaranteed to raise the ire of Protestants locally. So Paisley and Porter travelled to London and obtained the NUP's agreement to start their own autonomous organisation, the NUP (Ireland).

This was an altogether more red-blooded body. An early circular made it clear that politics and discrimination in employment, as well as religion, would be its business:

> Roman Catho   are demanding a United Irish
> Roman Cath   Roman Catholics in Northern
> Ireland are   tant farms, houses, land and
> property in t   blish the Papacy in Ulster. The
> NUP has h   mployers to obtain Protestant
> employees   s pledged its determination to
> maintain   the Protestant Throne and
> Constituti   and has opened the door to a
> Protestar   y true loyalist who wants to see
> in North   stant country for a Protestant
> people.

Over the   y built up a minor reputation as
one of   rful speakers. He accompanied
travellin   angelists from America and
conver   iests on tours of the North. He
himse   etings and in Orange and church
halls   pish Tyranny versus Protestant
Tole   ce, the buying up of property by
Ror   nixed marriage and the dangers of
all   to be appointed to state (i.e.
Pr

The atmosphere at such meetings was one of strong and occasionally hysterical anti-Catholicism, sometimes accompanied by a dose of the anti-Communism of the early Cold War years (although Communism was usually seen as the lesser evil and often the result of Catholicism). The speakers were not all extreme Loyalists. For example, at a meeting of the supposedly extremist Ulster Protestant League in April 1948, the chairman was Alderman Kennedy Leacock of Belfast City Council and the vote of thanks was by Senator Joseph Cunningham, the County Grand Master of the Orange Order. The speaker on this occasion - on the subject "Rome or Moscow? A study in dictatorships" - was the Grand Master of the Orange Order in England, Alderman H.D. Longbottom from Liverpool.

Catholic property and Catholic teachers were particularly sensitive issues to those determined to defend the Protestant ascendancy in Northern Ireland. In several speeches in 1948, including a Twelfth of July address to Ballymena Orangemen, Paisley warned against Catholics buying up Protestant property, and supported the Derry Unionist MP, Rev J.G. McManaway, in his scheme to ensure that Protestants were provided with capital to buy houses, farms and businesses in border areas. Later that year he was prominently involved in an agitation mounted in Ballymena against the appointment of a Catholic art teacher to the town's newly-opened intermediate school.

The year 1948 was a particularly busy one for the 22-year-old agitator. He was in constant demand as a speaker at NUP meetings: on waste ground in the fiercely loyalist Shankill Road, in Orange halls and Presbyterian churches in Antrim and Down, and at Belfast's big Wellington and Grosvenor Halls. One evening in May he even found himself at Crossgar Presbyterian Church in East Down, to which he would return three years later in order to divide it and form the first congregation of his Free Presbyterian Church of Ulster.

Paisley was also one of the leading protagonists in the controversy that raged that year (and every year until the early fifties), sparked off by the decision of the Redemptorist priests at the Clonard Monastery in the Falls Road to hold an annual "mission for non-Catholics". This provoked a howl of outrage among Belfast's evangelical Protestants, led by the NUP. An audience of more than 2000 people turned up to hear Paisley and others attack the Clonard priests at one of the first of the NUP's counter-meetings to Clonard at the Ulster Hall in March 1948. Hundreds more who were locked out were addressed by separate speakers in the street outside.

In May 1948 he was one of the speakers at an NUP double protest meeting: against a Corporation proposal (later thrown out) to open Belfast Museum and Art Gallery on Sunday afternoons; and against the heir to the throne, Princess Elizabeth, going racing and dancing on a Sunday during a visit to Paris. The chairman of this meeting, Senator William Wilton, said the Border was a minor matter compared with "the preserving of the Sabbath day".[13]

The young Paisley, however, had already started to take a strong interest in the politics of that Border, and the state on the other side of it. The Protestants of Monaghan, the vast majority of whom were still Unionist in politics, had organised themselves into the Monaghan Protestant Association in order to ensure a voice for themselves on the county council. Three years earlier they had been furious because they suspected two of the three candidates in the 1945 presidential election, Sean MacEoin of Fine Gael and an independent Republican called Patrick McCartan, of having been involved in attacks on Monaghan Protestants during the war of independence in the early 1920s. In 1948 they put up their own candidate for the Dail. Hearing of this, Paisley wrote a vitriolic letter to the secretary of the Protestant Defence Association, a Clones solicitor, offering to come down and lend his support to their election campaign. On the advice of a local Presbyterian minister they wrote back declining his services.

In the event Paisley's first visit to the South as a Protestant controversialist had to wait until the following October when, in the more peaceful surroundings of the Dublin YMCA, he led an "evangelistic service" as part of an NUP initiative to try to set up a branch in the Irish capital. It proved to be his last visit to the Irish capital for 30 years.

The NUP was obsessively interested in the South. In the 1930s Roman Catholic triumphalism in the Irish Free State had reached new heights following the 1932 Eucharistic Congress and the pro-Franco agitation during the Spanish Civil War. The Catholic primate, Cardinal MacRory, had said that Protestants had no right to take part in the 15th centenary celebrations of St

27

Patrick's coming to Ireland, pointing out that their churches were "not even a part of the Church of Christ". Anticipating a fine distinction Paisley would adopt two decades later, he later added that he had no ill-feeling towards individual non-Catholics - it was their churches he was opposed to.

In 1937 the Irish Free State's territorial claim to Northern Ireland and the Catholic Church's teaching on the family, education and property were enshrined in de Valera's new Irish Constitution. This appeared to confirm every Northern Protestant's fear that in a united Ireland their own religion would be totally subordinate to Roman Catholicism.

By the late 1940s the Catholic ethos across the border seemed, if anything, to be growing even stronger. A group calling itself Maria Duce, which attracted large crowds to its rallies in Dublin's O'Connell Street, demanded that the Constitution be changed so that the Roman Catholic Church was recognised as the only true Church. In 1947 the hierarchy backed Galway farmers who were refusing to let a local hunt pass over their lands because its joint master was a divorced Protestant women.

In 1950 came the Tilson case, when the President of the High Court in Dublin ordered three children of a mixed marriage to be taken from their Protestant father and returned to their Catholic mother, thus apparently giving legal recognition to the Catholic Church's contentious rule that Protestant partners had to sign away their rights to bring up their children in their faith. The Catholic Protection and Rescue Society was active in preventing the adoption of Catholic children by Protestants. And finally, of course, there was the long drawn-out "Mother and Child" controversy between Irish Health Minister Noel Browne and the Catholic hierarchy in 1951.[14] That was greeted with predictable glee by Unionists. The Unionist Party published the Dail debate in book form, and the NUP used it to make their case against a united Ireland throughout England and America.

In this atmosphere of cold war between Irish Protestantism and Catholicism, the NUP was only one of a whole plethora of politico-religious pressure groups making up the northern battle line. There was the Protestant Action Society, in which Norman Porter had been involved, formed to combat the rash of Catholic propaganda organisations which had sprung up in Belfast during the previous two decades, and to make sure that Protestant property was not bought by Catholics. There was the more respectable Ulster Protestant Defence and Propaganda Society, whose meetings were chaired by establishment figures like the former Presbyterian moderator, Rev William Corkey, who had led the rearguard action to keep Protestant influence and Bible instruction in state schools; and Orange leader and NUP president Rev Henry O'Connor.

Then there was the once very disreputable Ulster Protestant League (UPL), formed in 1931 to "safeguard the employment of Protestants" during the Depression, and deeply involved in fomenting the sectarian riots of 1935. One of the UPL's supporters was J.W. Nixon, a notorious former RUC district inspector who had led police squads to assassinate Catholics in the Shankill Road area in 1922, and been dismissed for making an inflammatory speech from an Orange platform two years later. Nixon was elected to Stormont as an independent Unionist in 1929. He used to terrify MPs by producing what he called his "black book", which he alleged contained details of their connivance in sectarian attacks during his RUC days.

Paisley, already a fascinated follower of the Unionist-dominated politics of the Northern state, was a friend and admirer of Nixon's. He used to visit Stormont once a week, usually on a Tuesday, driving there with Nixon in his car. He thought him "the most able and effective politician" of those days. Later, in the 1970s and 1980s, when the SDLP were boycotting Stormont and Jim Prior's new Assembly, Paisley remembered Nixon and the independent Unionists who followed him, and declared that Stormont could carry on its business even more effectively when there were no Nationalists present.[15]

Another Ulster Protestant League platform speaker and close friend of both Nixon and Paisley was Senator William Wilton. He was to provide a link to the new generation of Paisleyite extremists. A prosperous undertaker and well-known figure in the Shankill Road, he made his funeral parlours available for meetings of the political groups Paisley would lead in the 1950s and 1960s, Ulster Protestant Action and the Protestant Unionist Party.

THE MAN WHO WON DOCK FOR THE UNIONISTS

Nixon and Wilton were not the only contacts the young Ravenhill minister had in politics. He had joined the Orange Order, first in

North Belfast, later moving to the Mountpottinger Temperance Lodge near his church in East Belfast. This automatically made him a chaplain of both the lodge and the No. 6 East Belfast District which, with 55 lodges, was the largest in Ireland. He shared Orange platforms with the Belfast Grand Master, Senator Joseph Cunningham, and - in July 1949 - with an up-and-coming young Unionist politician called Brian Faulkner. That month he also led 2000 Belfast Orangemen on a demonstration in Motherwell in Scotland.

He was on friendly terms with a wide range of Unionist political figures who had chaired NUP meetings: people like the Westminster MP for Down, Rev James Little; the Mayor of Londonderry, Sir Frederick Simmons; William Morgan, a prominent Presbyterian lay preacher, businessman, Stormont MP and later a cabinet minister under Terence O'Neill; and Dinah McNabb, the hard-line Unionist MP for North Armagh.

NUP Secretary Norman Porter had also introduced him to the Westminster MP for East Belfast, Tommy Cole, yet another speaker on Ulster Protestant League platforms, who would bring him for the first time into the electoral arena. Cole, originally from Cavan, one of the "lost" Ulster counties, was a colourless but extremely wealthy chemist, estate agent and property developer. He had already been defeated twice in Stormont elections but, largely through his generosity to Unionist Party funds, had managed to gain the nomination for the East Belfast seat in 1945. In such an overwhelmingly Protestant area, this meant automatic election.

In January 1949 the Northern Ireland Prime Minister, Sir Basil Brooke, called a snap election for the following month to hammer home Unionist antipathy to the South in the wake of the Dublin Government's declaration of a republic outside the Commonwealth the previous September. It was clearly a single-issue election : Norman Porter, who had been planning to stand as an independent against Education Minister Major Hall-Thompson on the Protestant education issue, was persuaded to stand down in the general Unionist interest.

Paisley was asked by Cole to work in his campaign in the marginal Dock ward, a poor working class area, the scene of sectarian rioting and killing in both the twenties and thirties, which by the 1940s had become the nearest thing in Northern Ireland to a Labour stronghold. In the 1945 Stormont election it had returned

Hugh Downey, a Catholic barman from West Belfast, who defeated Sir George Clark, a wealthy farmer and company director later to become head of the Orange Order. In the municipal elections the following year it sent four more Labour men to Belfast Corporation.

In the event Paisley took over and virtually ran Cole's campaign single-handed. He organised canvassing, speakers, processions and postering with an energy rarely seen before by a local Unionist organisation more used to fleeting visits by Unionist and Orange bigwigs. He worked closely with Unionist party secretary Billy Douglas, who had a notorious reputation for organising personation and vote-stuffing in marginal constituencies. He paid young men like "Buck Alec", the famous Protestant street fighter, to fly-poster even the toughest nationalist streets. The posters were aimed at Downey's ambivalence on the Border: one showed the Labour man as a goalkeeper with the question "Which way will he kick?" and two arrows, one pointing to "Northern Ireland and prosperity", the other to "The Republic and poverty".[16]

Cole was a small insignificant-looking man and a poor public speaker. He looked even less impressive beside the strapping young clergyman from Ballymena, 6 feet 3 inches tall and with a voice to match, who had little problem in identifying with the election's only issue. Gerry Fitt (now Lord Fitt), who was to become Stormont MP for the area thirteen years later, remembers Paisley "roaring like a bull" on a street corner between the Catholic New Lodge and the Protestant Duncairn districts: "Pulling at his clerical collar he shouted - 'This is what you're voting for, you're voting for your Protestantism'".

It was a black and white election even by Northern Ireland's standards, and there was no room for socialist interlopers who might be weak on the Union. The tone had been set by the Southern political parties, who, blatantly ignoring Northern political sensitivities, had organised a church gate collection in the South to raise money for anti-partitionist candidates. This outraged Northern Unionists, confirmed all their worst fears about the new Republic's Catholic ethos, and led to the poll being dubbed the "chapel gates election".

It was also the most violent election campaign since 1921, with Labour and anti-partitionist candidates being beaten up and stoned off platforms, and widespread intimidation. In the small

Catholic New Lodge area Paisley was involved in his first sectarian skirmish when Cole's procession came under fire from stones and bottles in Spamount Street on the eve of polling.[17] Two future cabinet ministers, Robert "Beezer" Porter and William Craig, shared the platform with him that day. At the end of it Cole was presented with a lucky black cat by the Loyalists of East Belfast and a Bible by the workers in Gallahers tobacco factory.

The result the next day was a triumph for the all-class alliance of Unionism and the politics of sectarianism. The Unionists gained three seats, including Downey's in Dock by the margin of 284 votes. The Labour vote was decimated. For the first time since 1925 Stormont consisted entirely of a Protestant government and a Catholic opposition. Cole told friends there was no way he would have won if it had not been for Paisley's organising flair. Although barely 23 years of age, the young extremist from Ballymena had already played his first small part in the movement towards the final violent polarization of Northern Ireland society more than two decades later.

To the working class Unionists of Dock Paisley was a revelation. He spoke their language and understood their concerns: one observer remembers him roaring at a street meeting that disloyal Catholics, by breeding large families, were deliberately exploiting the new family allowance system. This had been recently and reluctantly introduced by the Unionists into Northern Ireland as part of the Labour Government's Welfare State provisions, largely because the British Treasury was underwriting it.

Before one election meeting in the Unionist Labour Hall in York Street, a group of constituency workers asked him why he did not think about standing as a Unionist candidate himself in the next election. Paisley replied that he would go away and give it "prayerful consideration". A few days later he came back and said that he saw his future in the church and not in politics. However, he thought he had seen an easier way to get into politics: by being elected to the Northern Ireland Senate. This body - largely made up of ageing landlords, businessmen and Unionist retainers - was chosen by the newly elected members of the Stormont House of Commons. Tommy Cole lobbied among his fellow Unionists and independents like Nixon to get his young protégé the four votes required for a Senate seat, but in the end without success. Ironically Nixon was doing the same thing for Paisley's colleague in the NUP, Norman Porter, again in vain.

Porter had to wait only another four years, until 1953, to get into Stormont, when he stood as an independent Unionist, once again largely on the issue of Protestant education. Paisley, meanwhile, turned his attention after 1951 to building up his new church. It was to be another 20 years before he ran for Stormont, although he would be deeply involved in politics again long before that.

In any case he already had his eye on another more spectacular road to prominence. One day in the late 1940s he told a colleague as they walked along Belfast's Great Victoria Street after a National Union of Protestants meeting that the only way to get anywhere in Northern Ireland was to go to jail. When this remark was retold to other NUP committee members they treated it as a joke. But it stuck in that colleague's mind for years afterwards: "I said to myself - this guy will go to jail. He'll make it seem that he's been persecuted. That's where his road to success in politics lies. And what happened? He tried for years to get to jail before he got there. And he got there eventually".

MARATHON PRAYERS AND POWER FROM HEAVEN

1950 saw Paisley's first clash with the Unionist establishment in Northern Ireland, in the shape of the Orange Order of which until then he had been such an ambitious member. It was over the issue of temperance, always a sensitive one among strait-laced Northern Protestants. The temperance movement had been a feature of Unionist politics since the 1859 Revival. A "local optionist" group, led mainly by Presbyterian clergymen, had gone as far as putting up three candidates in the 1929 Stormont election on a ticket demanding the right of local authorities to prevent the sale of alcohol in their areas.

In January 1950 the National Union of Protestants called on the "Protestant representatives in the Belfast City Council" to oppose the advertising of alcoholic drink on Belfast Corporation buses and trams. The transport committee, headed by its chairman, the Orange Order's County Grand Master, Senator Joseph Cunningham, ignored this call and recommended that advertising on the buses go to the highest bidder. A heated if intermittent debate on the issue continued throughout the spring and summer of that year.

On 31 August, at an NUP protest meeting on the eve of a crucial city council vote on the issue, both Norman Porter and Paisley bitterly attacked Cunningham for voting "in the company of the Irish Labour Party, a Republican party, for liquor advertisements". The *Irish News* report described the scene:

> Raising his eyes ceilingwards and with outstretched hands, the Rev. Paisley, in a loud voice, declared: "The liquor traffic is a liar. It promises men health but gives only disease; it promises strength but gives weakness; it promises prosperity but brings only adversity. I'm telling you it's a liar. We don't want to see trams and buses used as a signpost to hell. Lord Craigavon coined a slogan—"Not an inch" and we say to the Corporation: "Not an inch of space on the trams for advertising liquor".

The accusations against Cunningham, which Paisley and Porter had incorporated in a handbill published by "a group of loyal Orangemen", caused a furore inside the Order. The Belfast Grand Master tried to have the two men expelled. However, Porter got his own lodge to pass a similar resolution against Cunningham, and the Grand Master retreated. But it was the first sign that Paisley was prepared to make enemies in the high places of Unionism.

In the summer of 1950 he had struck the first tiny blow against a Unionist politician he would spend a good part of the next 20 years reviling. Five years earlier Captain Terence O'Neill, a young Irish Guards officer brought up in England, had been returned unopposed as the Stormont member for Bannside, which included Paisley's home town of Ballymena. On the last Sunday of July 1950 the Catholics of Rasharkin, a mixed village north-west of Ballymena, planned to march with their bands to a local field for their annual parochial sports day. To the outrage of local Orangemen, the route agreed with the RUC took them past a local Orange hall on the townland of Ballymaconnolly, where Protestant Sunday school classes were usually held.

A protest deputation was sent to O'Neill's house in the neighbouring village of Ahoghill, and another, from the County Grand Lodge of the Orange Order, to Home Affairs Minister Brian Maginess, who was something of a liberal in

Unionist terms. It might have been a storm in a teacup, but the teacup was an Orange one, and a County Antrim Orange one at that, and both delegations were received and listened to respectfully at the highest level. They even obtained an audience with the Prime Minister, Sir Basil Brooke, himself. On this occasion, however, neither the police nor the politicians believed that the Catholic procession threatened civil order in Rasharkin, and it went ahead without incident.

Two weeks later, at a protest meeting in the Ballymaconnolly Orange hall addressed by Paisley and leading local Orange luminaries, a resolution was passed calling for the resignation of both O'Neill and Maginess. There was loud applause when the Sunday school superintendent warned that by their attitude on this issue the authorities had "started something in Ballymaconnolly that would go to the ends of Ulster".

Paisley said they were determined, come what may, that never again would a Hibernian procession pass along that road, destroy their Sabbath school meeting, and throw defiance in their faces. This was a Protestant area, he declared, and what they had they were determined to hold. They wanted a leader who could grace their platform by standing up for their principles, but no such leader had come forward. He said that such a man would arise from among themselves, a man who would stand with them in defence of their heritage.[18]

If the 24-year-old Paisley yet saw himself as that leader, circumstances, at least in the immediate future, would dictate that he spent more time on church affairs than on becoming a Protestant political champion. For in June 1949 an event had taken place that radically changed the whole direction of his career. Worried about his Ravenhill congregation's small size and lack of enthusiasm, he had asked four men to join him in an all-night and all-day 36-hour prayer meeting to ask God for guidance. On the second evening of this marathon session, Paisley told his congregation later, he was "anointed with power" by God. He said he had been given a vision that thousands of souls were going to be saved and that the Ravenhill church was going to prove far too small for his ministry. God had told him to finish with politics, because his calling was to preach the gospel and help bring about a spiritual revival in Northern Ireland, he went on. If anyone objected to this they should do it now, because he was quite prepared to leave and proclaim his new message elsewhere: "the canopy of heaven is my roof", one man who was there remembers him declaring.[19]

It quickly became clear that this new divinely-inspired Paisley intended to be the boss in his own church. Suddenly the place became a hive of activity: there were prayer meetings nearly every night; open-air and street meetings in the Ormeau Park, the shipyard and Belfast city centre; drunks were brought in to fill the church on Friday nights and preached to outside the pubs on Saturday nights.

However, their minister's vehement new mixture of hellfire evangelism and intolerance of those who failed to match his fervour did not suit everyone in the church. Particularly unhappy were those respectable former Presbyterian folk who had already been irritated by the amount of time he spent away from it involved in political and NUP affairs.

Over the next few years there were several ugly rows. Following his father's example he sacked the choir. He forced out a leading woman member who had complained to the elders over a sermon about hell which Paisley had preached when her elderly unconverted father was in the congregation. "When you meet a devil wearing trousers it's bad, but a devil wearing a skirt is ten times worse", Paisley would tell his congregations in later years when recounting this tale.

Throughout his career Paisley felt uncomfortable with strong-minded women. The first significant split in the church was to come when a woman stood up to him. There had been discontent with his high-handed ways and growing attacks on other churches for several years after the marathon prayer meeting. It reached a breaking point in the early summer of 1953 when Paisley barred the dissidents from the communion table. Finally, Paisley announced during one Sunday morning service in July that there were people in the church with "sin in their lives", and the congregation would sing the hymn "Would you be free from your burden of sin" while they left.

A woman from one prominent dissident family rose to her feet and called out "What's the sin in my life, Mr Paisley?" "Let your women keep silence in the church", was his only response before he started into the hymn in his usual loud, tuneless singing voice.

On the way out after the service the woman's husband, normally the mildest of men, seized Paisley by his lapels. "If it wasn't for the grace of God, I'd wring your neck", he barked at him. Around 25 people had left the church before that drawn-out dispute was over.

Around this time the Ravenhill minister was also having worries over women in his personal life. In 1951 he had met Eileen Cassells, the 17-year-old daughter of a devout East Belfast Baptist family, in the house of Norman Porter's parents, where he was lodging. Eileen, whose father was a prosperous Baptist shopkeeper, was working as a secretary, and Paisley asked her to take a shorthand note of his speeches for a magazine he was planning to start.

Eileen was a shy and retiring girl, but she took an immediate fancy to the big brash clergyman and they became unofficially engaged on their third evening out together.[20] It would not be the easiest of courtships: Ian Paisley has never been noted for his sensitivity to human feelings, and acquaintances remember her being reduced to tears on several occasions when he stood her up to go to some church meeting or speaking engagement.

The problem arose because until a short time before Paisley had been engaged to another girl in Ballymena, whom he had known when they were teenagers together at his father's church. The Paisley children had been regular visitors to her family's farm on the edge of the Antrim Hills. She had first started going out with Harold Paisley, and then with Ian. After he had been in Belfast for several years he broke off the relationship. But she had held on to the engagement ring and friends remember Ian living in mortal fear right up to his wedding day that she would reappear and threaten to sue him for "breach of promise'.

Ian Paisley and Eileen Cassells were eventually married in October 1956 at the Ravenhill Church. John Wylie, Paisley's number two in the Free Presbyterian Church, was best man.

THE DIVISION OF EAST DOWN

Until 1951 Paisley's minor - but growing - reputation as an anti-Catholic evangelical preacher and National Union of Protestants speaker had made him a welcome guest in many conservative Presbyterian congregations. But in February and March of that year a series of events took place in the Presbyterian Church in the small town of Crossgar in County Down which would change all that. They would turn Paisley into an outcast from, and an angry rebel against, the whole religious establishment of Northern Ireland.

Crossgar was a typically quiet one-street Ulster Protestant town in the prosperous East Down countryside five miles outside the market town of Downpatrick. The local Lissara Presbyterian Church was just as typical. But there were also undercurrents of tension in the congregation which were symptomatic of the strains between liberal "modernists" and conservative "evangelicals" in Northern Irish Presbyterianism. The minister's job at Lissara was vacant, the previous incumbent having retired in the summer of 1950.

One of those who had applied for the vacancy was Rev Geoffrey Chart, a strong conservative with whom Paisley had shared NUP platforms. However, he had narrowly failed to get the necessary two thirds majority in a vote of the church's members. There followed a row over the voting list used in the election, with objections coming from a vociferous group of evangelicals led by an elder called George Gibson, an architect who came from one of the area's most prominent and devout Presbyterian families.

Gibson also ran his own mission hall, inherited from his uncle, a cattle-dealer and lay preacher nicknamed "Hallelujah Gibson" who had shared pulpits with the legendary W.P.Nicholson. His group of evangelicals were much influenced by itinerant "Faith Mission" preachers, who made a fetish of holy living and were fanatically opposed to people who smoked, drank and engaged in other "ungodly" and worldly pleasures.

The previous year Paisley had been invited by Gibson to lead a gospel campaign in Crossgar in February 1951. Since his little hall was too small, Gibson requested and was given permission to use the larger Lissara church hall. However, at the last moment the Down Presbytery, the governing Presbyterian body in the area, ruled that Paisley could not use the hall while the church had no minister. The decision outraged the church's evangelicals. They alleged that the local Presbyterian bigwigs were unhappy about Paisley's mission, not because of any particular fear of Paisley, but because it might boost the campaign of the conservative Chart and get him the votes he needed in a fresh election for the minister's job.

The Presbytery's decision was communicated to Gibson and his friends on the Saturday that Paisley's mission was due to open. Paisley acted immediately. The next morning, as the moderator of the Down Presbytery, Rev William Boland, arrived to read out suspension notices on Gibson and another Lissara elder who had refused to accept its ruling, he was greeted by a noisy and abusive picket led by Paisley and around 30 supporters. The protesters invaded the service with their placards, and afterwards the RUC had to escort Boland to his car, which they discovered had been put out of action by water having been poured into its petrol tank. That night the gospel mission went ahead in Hallelujah Gibson's hall down the road, with Paisley as the preacher.

However, Paisley was now not merely interested in running a gospel campaign. He was looking to seize this opportunity of a domestic squabble within Presbyterianism to launch his own separate denomination. Over the next five weeks there were a number of lengthy meetings between Paisley and the Lissara dissidents at Ravenhill - Paisley claimed later that they were also attended by two conservative Presbyterian ministers, Geoffrey Chart, the candidate at Crossgar, and Ivor Lewis, another Presbyterian minister and NUP stalwart. On 11 March five Lissara elders announced that they were breaking away, with Paisley's backing, to form the Free Presbyterian Church of Ulster.

Their "manifesto" was a mixture of Paisley's recently-found revival enthusiasm, Gibson's obsession with holy living, and their common belief in separation from "the unclean thing" of mainstream Presbyterianism. It was contemptuous of "the dead and stagnant, powerless and fruitless religion of our day". It accused ministers of preferring financial · security, material comforts and worldly pleasures like smoking tobacco to saving the souls of their congregations (the last was a reference to the previous minister at Lissara, who liked his pipe). And it concluded that "clear-thinking people are beginning to realise that the only course to pursue is to save that which is worth saving, and like Sodom and Gomorrah, leave the rest to God's wrath and judgement".[21]

By the following Saturday, 17 March - St Patrick's Day - Hallelujah Gibson's little hall in Killyleagh Street had been transformed into a temporary church building complete with a new stained glass window bearing the emblem of the new denomination, a burning bush and the motto "Christ for Ulster". The name "Free Presbyterian" was at least partly dictated by the terms of Gibson's will, which stipulated that the hall had to be used in conjunction with a Presbyterian church. Paisley's first task that day was to induct the new church's temporary minister, a returned missionary called Rev George Stears from the unheard of and unrecognised "Presbyterian Church of South America". In his sermon Paisley accused the Irish Presbyterian Church of having "sold the past". "We in Crossgar are going back to the old standards", he declared, "and to preach the faith of our fathers".

The breakaway church may not have been planned by Paisley. "It came out of the blue, an overnight decision", recalls one former associate in the National Union of Protestants. "Ivor Lewis said to him jokingly 'Why don't you start the Free Presbyterian Church?'". Paisley had spent the Saturday night before the first protest at Crossgar desperately trying to find someone to stand in for him the next morning at Ravenhill. It would be late April, five weeks after the breakaway, before he could overcome opposition within his own Ravenhill congregation and persuade it, on a split vote, to join the new denomination.

Then, using the same skilful pragmatism that was to govern his later political career, he moved quickly to consolidate the Free Presbyterian Church as a real alternative to established Irish Presbyterianism. Its manifesto not only attacked lifeless religion and godless tobacco-smoking ministers, but also the "modernism" of the Presbyterian Assembly's Theological College and its principal, Ernest Davey, and the mainstream church's "betrayal of the Reformation" through its membership of the ecumenical World Council of Churches, formed in 1948. Its doctrinal statement, which allowed it to carry out adult baptism, was aimed at making it more attractive to those of the Baptist faith Paisley had grown up in.

The reaction of the Irish Presbyterian Church was to express "great sorrow" at the break, and to claim that the breakaway group's St Patrick's Day service was "completely invalid in Presbyterian history, practice and tradition". However, Northern Ireland's largest church, despite its long history of schism, was protected by an astonishing smugness about its own well-being. The same meeting of Belfast churches which discussed the Crossgar split also heard a report that: ". . . people in district after district are simply crowding to church and then spending their entire time during the rest of the week in embodying in their work all the fine Christian exhortations they hear on the Sunday; and in many, many areas not the slightest suspicion of a social blemish is showing itself above the horizon."[22]

The Irish Presbyterian Church was out of touch with its own grass-roots. For in congregations as far apart as South Tyrone and North Antrim there were ugly stirrings and social blemishes that would play right into the hands of Ian Paisley and his little group of fundamentalist troublemakers.

CHAPTER TWO

Building A Church

We know the hells declared for such as serve not Rome.
"1912" by Rudyard Kipling.

*They were determined that Free Presbyterianism
would never get recognition anywhere.*
Orangeman speaking about reaction to
the growth of Paisley's Church in the 1950's.

The village of Pomeroy in County Tyrone is, in all the important ways, Northern Ireland writ small. Set in rolling countryside in the foothills of the Sperrin mountains it is a place where the native Catholic and the planter Protestant populations have lived uneasily together for over three centuries. Although open conflict is rare the village displays its divisions for all to see.

Like so many of Northern Ireland's rural towns and villages, Pomeroy is separated into ghettoes. The western end of the village's one and only main street is Catholic and Republican, as the IRA wall slogans and graffiti amply testify. At the eastern end of the town squats an ugly British Army and RUC post, its walls and roof protected from mortar attack by wire mesh. A few yards away the pavement kerbs are painted red, white and blue and straddling the road is a spindly wooden arch. It is here, every Twelfth of July, that the local Orangemen assemble, ready to parade their politics, their Protestantism and the claim that this part of Pomeroy is for ever theirs.

Pomeroy occupies a special place in Nationalist mythology. It was here in 1951, only 9 months after Paisley had founded the Free Presbyterian Church, that Saor Uladh (Free Ulster), a violent splinter from the IRA, was born. In 1953 Catholics fought the RUC hand to hand in the village when they welcomed home from jail their local MP,Liam Kelly, who had been imprisoned for making seditious election speeches. Two years later Saor Uladh, which was Kelly's brainchild, began a series of bomb and gun attacks that prompted the IRA's own ill-fated 1956 campaign, a campaign that was to have a considerable impact on the course of Unionist politics and the career of Ian Paisley.

Paisley himself was no stranger to Pomeroy. Just as the village was a fertile ground for militant Republicanism so it was for Loyalists and fundamentalist Protestants. In the late 1940s and early 1950s the National Union of Protestants was in the vanguard of that ideology. The NUP's favourite tactic was to parade converted Catholics at their meetings as living proof of the superiority of the Reformation and - by implication - Unionism also. In October 1950 the NUP and Paisley came to Pomeroy to stage one such show.

The star of the NUP rallies in those days was an Australian woman who had been born a southern Irish Catholic. Monica Farrell had, to judge from the advertisements for her meetings in Ireland, made a career out of describing her conversion and the perfidies of Rome. "Thousands attend her meetings in all parts of Australia", trumpeted one newspaper ad which went on to describe how she would address the subject of "Women in chains - Rome's convent laundries" to the faithful in Lurgan, County Armagh.

Monica Farrell and the NUP were given a warm welcome by Pomeroy's fundamentalists in 1950 but Catholics were up in arms. The meeting had been arranged by Richard Reid, a local farmer and evangelical Presbyterian who had become friendly with the NUP secretary, Norman Porter. Eager to hear Miss Farrell's testimony he arranged to hire the local courthouse for the evening but before long local Catholics got to hear of the plans and objected. The RUC sergeant, a Catholic, was worried that the meeting would cause conflict and even violence in the village and he persuaded Reid to move the meeting elsewhere. The local Presbyterian minister duly obliged and his church hall was made available instead.

Monica Farrell's meeting was a big success and passed off peacefully but Reid was surprised to see arriving with the NUP entourage the tall, gangly figure of Ian Paisley. He hadn't been listed to appear and had turned up apparently in anticipation of trouble. "He said he'd come because he'd heard about the objections from Catholics", recalled Reid who has an abiding memory of Paisley and Norman Porter prowling Pomeroy's main street after the meeting looking, in vain, for hostile Catholic crowds.

Monica Farrell was a big hit with the village's Protestants, so much so that Porter asked Reid to arrange a return meeting in early April 1951 with the young Paisley also billed as a speaker. When the time came for the meeting, however, Reid discovered that it wasn't just local Catholics who had objections to the meeting.

Just two weeks before, the traumatic split in the Presbyterian congregation of Crossgar had given birth to the Free Presbyterian Church of Ulster, and the event had received wide coverage in the Unionist newspapers. The scandalous tales of Paisleyites interrupting the service in Crossgar, the images of strident placards and of the RUC having to protect a senior minister from howling pickets had spread throughout the network of Presbyterian churches. Irritated by the unseemly publicity, Presbyterian ministers began closing ranks against Paisley.

The news of Crossgar had also made its way to Pomeroy and there Paisley discovered, for the first time, what the Lissara split would cost him. Presbyterian doors in Pomeroy were barred to him, as they soon would be elsewhere. Reid remembers the reaction of the Pomeroy Presbyterians: "I had hired the church hall again but I hadn't told them that Paisley's name was to be on the handbill. When they found out, two elders came to me after Sunday service and said that we'd either have to remove his name or they wouldn't give permission to hold the meeting in the church hall."

Outraged, Reid left the Presbyterian church and sought out a more fundamentalist gospel elsewhere. He had found Paisley's message and style attractive, however, and when the opportunity arose in later years he became one of Paisley's most ardent supporters. He was a founder member and elder of the Dungannon Free Presbyterian Church and stood successfully as a DUP candidate for Mid-Ulster in the 1975 Northern Ireland Convention until his own acrimonious parting of the ways with Paisley in 1979.

It was discontented, conservative Presbyterians like Reid who were, in its early years, to form the basis for the growth of the fledgling Free Presbyterian church, as Paisley, transformed by Crossgar into the leader of a new denomination, sought out splits in other congregations to exploit.

Only two months after Crossgar he found his first dissident congregation in North Antrim, only fifteen miles from his Ballymena home. In 1951 the minister of Drumreagh Presbyterian church, a parish on the southern outskirts of Ballymoney, was the Rev Billy Hyndman, a liberal cleric with no liking for the evangelicals of Presbyterianism and a man who, as a former colleague recalled, "was fond of a glass of whiskey on a Saturday night".

The Drumreagh congregation had had a recent history of dissension. The minister before Hyndman was John Barkley, a prominent liberal cleric who went on to become Principal of the Assembly's Theological College in Belfast. Barkley had found himself in constant argument with a group of evangelicals in the church led by a local farmer called Sandy McAuley and when Hyndman replaced him, the disputes continued. McAuley had been "saved" by W. P. Nicholson in the 1920s and he and his family shared the same rigid, uncompromising faith.

McAuley's arguments with Hyndman, though, were not just theological. In the spring of 1951 he levelled an accusation against him which was to cause scandal in the area. Hyndman, he alleged, had fathered an illegitimate child by a woman who already had four illegitimate children. She had relatives in the congregation and McAuley made the issue church business. The matter soon deteriorated into violence: Hyndman heard of the accusation, confronted McAuley and floored him with his fists.

The congregation soon split into warring factions and the story came to the ears of Ian Paisley's newest disciple, John Wylie. An electrician from Dundonald in East Belfast, Wylie, already a conservative Presbyterian dissident, had heard the young Paisley preaching at gospel missions. He was immediately attracted by his anti-Catholic, anti-liberal message and decided to join the Ravenhill congregation. That Summer, he was tent-preaching in the Cabra area, near Ballymoney, preparing to enter the Free Presbyterian ministry when the Drumreagh congregation divided.

"Wylie held counter meetings outside the Drumreagh church every Sunday denouncing Hyndman and the Presbyterian church", recollected another local Presbyterian minister. "He also canvassed the district urging people from the congregation and their sympathisers to leave, going to their homes for private chats and generally putting anti-Hyndman propaganda around". Wylie also brought Paisley down to Drumreagh and the two of them intensified the effort to divide the congregation.

Eventually the allegation against Hyndman - which he had always denied and for which there was never a shred of proof - was brought to the Route Presbytery, the governing body of the local Presbyterian church. Hyndman was cleared of the charge, but to save his wife and family further distress he left Drumreagh and emigrated to Canada. That June, between 20 and 30 of the congregation left as well, some to go to other Presbyterian churches nearby, but a handful, led by McAuley and his family, joined the Free Presbyterian Church. It initially met for worship in the upstairs room of a barn until a more permanent building was erected in Cabra a year later with Wylie as the first minister.

Nearby Rasharkin, on the border of Counties Derry and Antrim, was the scene later that summer of the next Presbyterian split and again Paisley's infant church was quick to exploit it. Once more a suggestion of scandal and sexual innuendo was at the centre of the divisions. The minister of Rasharkin was the Rev Ernest Stronge, a very strict evangelical who was married to a local woman, a member of a large family called Wallace, who were both wealthy and influential in the Orange Order. The marriage had never been happy. Although they had children, the Stronges had been incompatible for some years and there were stories of violence and ill-treatment in the home. Early in 1951 they separated. The children left with their mother, and so bitter were relations between husband and wife that the children were forbidden to acknowledge their father when they met him in the street.

Predictably this marital argument spilled over into the congregation. Many Rasharkin Presbyterians took the side of their local friends, Mrs Stronge and her family against their minister. Eventually in the Winter of 1951 the couple were divorced, an almost unheard of event in those days. When the case came to court there were so many ministers in the courtroom eager to hear the scandalous detail unfold that the presiding judge, Lord Chief Justice McDermott, himself a pillar of the Presbyterian establishment, rebuked them for neglecting their spiritual duties.

The divisions in Rasharkin came to the ears of Paisley via the ever alert John Wylie and again the Free Presbyterians moved in in force to take advantage. The tactics were the same as in Drumreagh; noisy meetings were held outside the Rasharkin church during the summer months attacking Ernest Stronge and dissidents hosted private meetings with Wylie. That August some of the congregation split off - Paisley claimed between 200 and 300 - and led by Mrs Stronge's father, Daniel Wallace, the family formed the core of the third new Free Presbyterian church which, to begin with, worshipped in a barn donated by the Wallaces - local Presbyterian loyalists immediately dubbed them "barn-rats".

Only eight months after the Crossgar split, Ian Paisley had brought two new churches into his Free Presbyterian fold - one other church, Mount Merrion in East Belfast had been started in 1951 but this was a poorly attended extension of the original Ravenhill congregation which didn't properly get off the ground until the next year. Only Crossgar, however, could be properly classified as a product of the battle for theological principle.

The significance of both the Cabra and Rasharkin splits was that Paisley's assaults on Presbyterianism there were not centred on his theological criticisms. In each case he seized the opportunities presented by sexual scandal and marital division to woo dissidents away. One of the casualties also happened to be an ally in his battle against liberal Presbyterianism - Ernest Stronge, the Rasharkin minister, was a conservative evangelical and a member of the National Union of Protestants along with Paisley.

An NUP colleague offered this insight into the Rasharkin split and the then widely-held interpretation of Paisley's behaviour: "Old Stronge was a doting old fool of a man but sound as a bell theologically. Paisley could have found no fault there. Stronge and I would sit on the same NUP platform and he would have grunted amen to what I would say and I would do the same with him. Stronge was on our street, in every way he was on our side but he still had a go at him. Paisley would find an issue in those days, it didn't matter what the issue was, if it gave him an opening he was in. He was shrewd enough".

If Crossgar had irritated the Presbyterian church, Cabra and Rasharkin set alarm bells ringing. The message from Paisley and his Free Presbyterians was clear - he had meant what he said about splitting the church from top to bottom and it seemed that it wasn't going to matter how he did it.

The first reverberations from Cabra and Rasharkin were felt in the inter-denominational ranks of the National Union of Protestants. Many in the NUP were already envious of Paisley's impressive preaching style, his popularity with crowds and his phenomenal, photographic memory - "he could read Churchill or he could read Spurgeon, it didn't matter, he could stand on a platform and it would come out of him like water from a tap", recalled an NUP colleague - but his behaviour at NUP meetings had made him an unpopular and resented figure.

"I would go on to the platform of the Ulster Hall like every one else at the start of the meeting but no Paisley. Then just after the opening prayer or hymn, on he would stride to get his own round of applause", complained one NUP official.

Others accused him of over-ambition and egotism: "The day after a meeting he would come into my office and say 'The *Belfast Telegraph's* report is not bad. I see you got 39 lines. I got 54.' He would actually count the number of lines he got in reports of our meetings. Then he would say 'Let's attack the Archbishop of Canterbury, pass a resolution and send it to the press'. I'd say 'You can't pass a resolution, you can't say anything until we call a committee meeting.' But it was no use, he couldn't see the need."

Annoying as these traits were, the Cabra and Rasharkin episodes caused much more concern among Paisley's NUP colleagues, particularly the Presbyterians. It seemed to them that if he was declaring open war on Presbyterian churches all around the country and was ready to take advantage even of Ernest Stronge's difficulties, then none of them could rest easy.

The NUP executive member most disturbed about things was the Rev Eric Borland, a Presbyterian minister from Bangor, County Down, who was vice-president of the NUP and a high ranking Orangeman. His concern was shared by other Bangor Presbyterians; after the Crossgar split Paisley had been banned from preaching in one church there.

That winter at an NUP executive committee meeting Borland brought matters to a head. A fellow Presbyterian minister, the Rev Martin Smyth, now the Official Unionist MP for South Belfast and Grand Master of the Orange Order in Ireland, was a regular speaker on NUP platforms. He remembers what happened next:

> At the committee meeting they were discussing these things and Borland challenged Paisley: "Am I hearing you right Ian? You're saying that if any of us would have any trouble you would come down to try to capitalise on that trouble to build up your cause?" And Paisley said he would. Then says Eric: "Any of us in the ministry can have differences of opinion with our congregations at any time and for any reason, but I have to say I can no longer work with you if that's your attitude to brother ministers".

Other Presbyterians in the NUP shared Borland's concern. Norman Porter intervened to try to avoid the inevitable parting of the ways but to no avail. One of them recalled: "Norman went to Paisley and said 'Look, I'm not worried about you splitting Presbyterian churches, provided you go for modernist churches and if the truth be told neither would anyone else. But if you're making an attack on all Presbyterian churches how can you sit on the same platform as Borland and his people?' He just laughed. I don't know what his motive was but it looked as if he wanted to build up a congregation and it didn't matter what price or what issue".

In February 1952 at the annual general meeting of the National Union of Protestants in Belfast, Borland took his challenge to Paisley a stage further. Addressing the 100 or so delegates Borland gave the membership a simple choice: they could either keep him in the NUP or have Paisley but he was not prepared to stay in the same organisation as Paisley. The NUP rank and file chose Borland, and Paisley was voted off the executive committee.

Paisley stepped up his feud with the NUP. He won the support of the head of the English National Union of Protestants, Arnold Perkins, and with his help staged rival meetings advertised under the label of NUP (England). At some meetings he would launch bitter attacks on former colleagues, particularly Norman Porter who, unusually for a Baptist, was becoming increasingly involved in politics as a hard line Independent Unionist.

"Paisley wasn't interested in politics in those days and when Porter got elected to Stormont, he attacked him at a big rally in the Ulster Hall saying that was no place for a Christian to be. He would also criticise Porter for sharing a platform with Tommy Henderson (the Independent Unionist MP for Shankill) because Tommy was known to take a drink", remembered one NUP member. Criticism like this conveniently ignored his own flirtation with politics in 1949 and was totally forgotten when Paisley later immersed himself in political activity.

Having alienated mainstream liberal Presbyterianism, Paisley now grasped every opportunity to divide and attack his former conservative allies. He was determined to portray himself as the only principled voice of fundamentalist Protestantism and in the Spring of 1954 he showed that he was ready to go to some lengths to do it.

Earlier that year a woman supporter of the National Union of Protestants had died, leaving a sum of money to be divided amongst various evangelical organisations. Among the bequests was £400 for the NUP - a considerable sum for those days - and eventually the money was handed over to Porter. Paisley got to hear about it, contacted Perkins in England and together they decided to challenge the will, on the grounds that the woman had not stipulated which branch of the NUP - English or Irish - was to get the money.

Since the English branch of NUP was the parent organisation, they reckoned they had a good claim and Paisley and Perkins pursued it to court. On the day of the hearing, however, lawyers for Porter and Paisley got together and persuaded the two men to divide the money between them and to drop the action to protect "the good name of Protestantism".

Paisley was delighted with the outcome of the case. "He went to his church and said the NUP is finished, the NUP is gone, he'd wiped it out", recalled a witness. Paisley's victory was sealed at the next NUP committee meeting. The name of the Irish branch of the NUP was changed to the Evangelical Protestant Society, leaving Paisley in sole possession of the title. Right up until the early 1960s, he would use the name National Union of Protestants for many of his protest meetings. He had beaten his old allies.

Despite an encouraging start, the Free Presbyterian Church grew only slowly. There were many other fundamentalist sects around to compete with and by 1959 Paisley had managed to add only four tiny congregations to the Crossgar, Cabra and Rasharkin churches.

More importantly, the reaction against him inside the NUP was repeated on a much more significant level. The Orange Order, the most powerful of all Protestant and Unionist organisations, turned against him. This more than anything else ensured that Paisley would never quite repeat the aggressive church building tactics of the summer and autumn of 1951.

BITTER ORANGE

In the late 1940s and early 1950s Paisley's powerful oratory and his strongly anti-Catholic message had made him a popular speaker on the Orange Order's circuit of arch-opening and marching each summer. Paisley himself was a member of an Orange Lodge, first in North Belfast and then in a Lodge near his Ravenhill church where he became Chaplain. In 1949, after a year in the post, he automatically became one of the Orange Order's Chaplains for No. 6 District, the administrative body for private Lodges throughout the entire East Belfast area, the largest in the Order.

To become a District Chaplain, at least for a Protestant cleric, is an important step on the road to power and influence in the Orange Order and by extension in Official Unionist party politics as well. It confers automatic eligibility for election to one of the seven County Grand Lodges, which govern the Order in each of Northern Ireland's six counties and in Belfast. The membership of the Order's overall ruling body, the Grand Lodge of Ireland, is in turn drawn from the officer boards of the County Grand Lodges.

The Orange Order is still dominated by the Official Unionists and nearly all the Grand Lodge's members are in that party. But the party itself is a shadow of its former self, challenged for Unionist supremacy by Paisley and deprived of considerable power and patronage by British direct rule. In the 1950s and right up until the suspension of the Stormont parliament in 1972, however, the Grand Lodge and County Lodges were peppered with Cabinet ministers, Unionist MPs and party officials. Political power, patronage and influence were synonymous with the Orange Order and the higher one could rise in the organisation the nearer one came to the source of all that power and influence. The Rev Martin Smyth MP, currently a contender for the leadership of the Official Unionist party, rose to power by such a route.

After the Crossgar, Cabra and Rasharkin splits, the hierarchy of the Orange Order moved decisively to block off this route to Paisley and his Free Presbyterian ministers. NUP officials like Eric Borland, who knew Paisley well, sat on the Grand Lodge, as did the Rev Jack Finch of the Church of Ireland, another NUP man and a Chaplain in the senior Orange body, the Royal Black Preceptory. They were worried at the divisive impact Paisley and his ministers could have on the Order. That worry was shared by senior Orangemen of all denominations.

In December 1951, only months after Paisley had stirred up ructions in County Antrim Presbyterianism, the Grand Lodge formalised its rules for the eligibility of Orange Order Chaplains. Prior to that, there had been an understanding that any Protestant minister who was a member of an Orange Lodge would automatically become its Chaplain. As a chaplain, the way was then open to influence and promotion to the County Grand Lodges. Paisley's ministers could thus rise in the Order in the same fashion as other Protestant clerics. But the Grand Lodge drew up a list of Protestant denominations and ordered that only ministers of those denominations could be made chaplains. The Free Presbyterians were deliberately excluded from the list.

The list included the main Protestant denominations - Presbyterian, Church of Ireland, Methodist, Baptist, Congregationalist, the Reformed Presbyterians and the non-subscribing Presbyterians. Even the tiny Moravian sect, which in the 1981 census was outnumbered by Northern Ireland's Muslims, was included - but not Paisley's Free Presbyterians.

Only in those few Lodges that didn't have a Protestant cleric as a member, could the Free Presbyterians have a chance of gaining office as chaplains. The Grand Lodge rules allowed for the election of lay chaplains in such cases but even then the Free Presbyterians could be frustrated by the simple expedient of ensuring that any Lodge which contained a Free Presbyterian minister also included a minister from one of the recognised denominations. The Orange Order's refusal to recognise Free Presbyterianism as a Protestant denomination was a massive snub to Paisley. "Their opposition to the Free Presbyterians was desperate", recalled an Orange colleague of Paisley's. "They were determined that Free Presbyterianism would never get recognition anywhere".

The move against Paisley in the Loyalist establishment wasn't confined to the Orange Order. Paisley had also risen through the ranks of the Apprentice Boys of Derry, the smallest of the three Loyal Orders, but symbolically the most evocative to Protestants. He had impressed the Belfast Apprentice Boys with his oratory and Loyalist convictions in the same way as he had the grass roots Orangemen. They had elected him to the Chaplaincy of the Belfast and District Amalgamated Committee, the ruling body for Apprentice Boys" clubs in the city. But again the Presbyterians in the Apprentice Boys mobilised against him.

The vice-chairman of the Committee at that time was James Smyth, father of the Rev Martin Smyth. In 1952, largely at his urging, Eric Borland was persuaded to stand against Paisley in the annual elections for the Chaplaincy. Borland was successful and Paisley was deposed. He was to leave the Apprentice Boys after that but re-joined in 1971 when the hardline Dromara Apprentice Boys Club in County Down invited him back in. Since then Free Presbyterians have flocked to the Apprentice Boys, a much smaller organisation than the Orange Order, where they can exercise much greater influence.

During the 1950s Paisley's relationship with the Orange Order deteriorated even further. In 1958 a prominent member of his own Mountpottinger Lodge threatened to bring a disciplinary complaint against him under one of the more serious charges possible in the Orange Order - that of "unbrotherly conduct". The complainant was the Rev Warren Porter, who had succeeded Paisley as Chaplain at Mountpottinger. A Presbyterian minister based in Baillieboro, County Cavan, Warren Porter had, until his return to the orthodox fold, been a member of the Irish Evangelical Church, the product of the last division in the Presbyterian church in the 1920s. He had also been a member of the National Union of Protestants and strongly sympathised with its conservative brand of evangelism. But when he left the Irish Evangelical Church to join Presbyterianism, Paisley rounded on him in his magazine *The Revivalist,* calling him a treacherous and compromising "time-server", a "very bitter enemy of the Free Presbyterian Church" who "Like Lot . . . began pitching his tent towards Sodom before he went to reside in the Sodom of Irish Presbyterian apostasy".

According to a member of the Lodge, Paisley had long avoided attending meetings of the Lodge if he thought Warren Porter might show up - he wanted to avoid open confrontation. But one night Porter happened to be in Belfast for a Lodge meeting and so by chance was Paisley. He immediately challenged Paisley over his attacks on him but what followed showed, that in this case at least, Paisley was not eager for a fight.

"Paisley had no answer for him that night but said he would come back the next week to answer Porter's complaints. But in fact he didn't come back. Porter came up from Baillieboro, but Brother Ian wasn't there; instead there was this letter from him requesting a transfer to another Lodge. Porter had threatened to charge him with unbrotherly conduct, it would have been debated on the floor of the Lodge but the most that could have happened to him was a reprimand. I don't think he wanted to face criticism and the possibility that Warren would have won."

Paisley's request for a transfer was granted and he moved over to a Lodge on the Shankill Road led by a political friend called Charlie McCullough. By all accounts he was an infrequent attender there but several times over the intervening years he was to try, without success, to persuade the Grand Orange Lodge to include the Free Presbyterian Church on its list of Orange chaplains.

In September 1962 he finally quit the Order, citing the attendance of the Lord Mayor of Belfast, Sir Robin Kinahan, a Unionist and Orangeman, at the funeral Mass of a Catholic Alderman as the reason. Kinahan was not expelled, as others had been, for breaking this cardinal rule of Orangeism, which forbids attendance at a Catholic Mass. Paisley accused the Grand Lodge of ignoring the offence because of Kinahan's political influence in the Unionist party. He was later to tell his supporters that what angered him most was that Kinahan had brought his mayoral mace-bearer, a lifelong staunch Orangeman, to the Mass and that he had later died of a broken heart.

Whatever he told his supporters, this was not, however, the reason Paisley gave when he handed his resignation in to the Orange authorities. "He resigned because he objected to certain chaplains in the Order, whom he named, having what he called 'a Romeward trend' in their philosophy", recalled a leading Orangeman of the day. "At that particular time he was denouncing anyone who as much as showed friendship towards Roman Catholics. He had his spies out everywhere reporting back to him and then he would have stood up at a ceremony, perhaps the opening of some Orange arch, hold up a slip of paper and roar 'I have proof! I have proof!' But we always suspected that he really resigned because he finally realised that he was not going to get anywhere inside the Order. Being outside also gave him the freedom to attack us as much as he wanted to."

Paisley's quarrels with the Orange Order in the 1950s automatically deprived him of access to political influence within mainstream Unionism - the leadership of both overlapped - and compounded his enmity of Presbyterianism. Almost at the very start of his career he had the three pillars of the Protestant establishment lined up against him and he against them. The rest of his career would be dominated by the battle between them but in that apparently unequal struggle, Paisley would always have important allies.

While the leaders of Orangeism, Unionism and Presbyterianism were united in their hostility towards Paisley, their rank and file would find his anti-Catholic message and his warnings of compromise and sell-outs by their leaders increasingly appealing. Nowhere was this more apparent than in the Orange Order, the body which united all three.

Despite his break with the Order, Paisley was to remain a regular speaker at Orange ceremonies in Belfast and around the country; his popularity with ordinary Orangemen gave him an invaluable platform from which to mount attacks and foment dissension. He was to be a sharp thorn in the Protestant establishment's flesh for years to come.

But in the early and mid-1950s Paisley's chief targets were still the main Protestant churches. During his days with the National Union of Protestants he had established, beyond any shadow of doubt, his anti-Catholic credentials. After Crossgar, however, he directed his hostility as much towards Protestant sects which showed any sign of friendship towards Catholicism or any flexibility in their own theologies.

Membership of the World Council of Churches (WCC), an international ecumenical body set up in 1948 to promote Christian dialogue and unity, or its smaller affiliate, the British Council of Churches, automatically made a church the target for Paisley's invective. The WCC's membership was almost entirely Protestant - the Catholic church had declined an invitation to the inaugural meeting in Amsterdam but the WCC included the Greek Orthodox Church and sects like the Unitarian Hickside

Quakers who were regarded as heretical by Protestant fundamentalists. The WCC - "the Antichrist's bride" - became the focus for Paisley's increasingly aggressive and divisive campaigns.

In April 1952, barely a year after the formation of the Free Presbyterian Church, the British Council of Churches met in Belfast and Paisley seized the opportunity to mount his first large scale protest. Free Presbyterian pickets were placed outside the meeting and Paisley called a rally to explain his opposition.

The annual meeting of the Presbyterian General Assembly the following June saw Paisley lead his flock from Ravenhill into the centre of Belfast where, on the blitz ground in High Street in conscious imitation of Martin Luther burning Papal Bulls nearly 450 years earlier, they burned books and articles written by the hated liberal theologian, Professor Ernest Davey, who had just been installed as Moderator.

During that year and the next, Paisley toured Northern Ireland, sometimes conducting gospel missions to recruit Free Presbyterians from disgruntled rival congregations, sometimes at NUP (England) rallies with his ally, Arnold Perkins.

In April 1955 he published the first regular issue of his monthly church magazine, *The Revivalist,* which was produced with the help of his church secretary, Bob Cleland, who worked in a Belfast printworks. That issue set the tone of the magazine: "Antichrist's Bride Prepares Herself", screamed the headline above a story attacking Presbyterians in Ballymoney who had celebrated the second assembly of the World Council of Churches in the United States by holding an inter-denominational, Protestant service.

On the inside pages of that inaugural issue Paisley, who edited the magazine and stamped it with his own shrill style, castigated the BBC - always a favourite target - as being under the control "partly of Romanists and partly by modernists and infidels", and launched attacks on two other arch-enemies: "the near Communist", Donald Soper, then President of the Methodist Church, and the "blasphemous" Professor Davey both of whom were suspect on the doctrine of the Virgin birth of Christ.[1]

From then on *The Revivalist* was Paisley's main vehicle for launching assaults on theological liberalism in other Protestant churches, and as the years went on, for lambasting the slightest sign of moderation by Unionist politicians. For although Paisley had promised in 1949 to stay out of politics, he always saw theological and political liberalism as the major, twin threats to traditional Protestant values.

The fourth issue of *The Revivalist* showed that clearly. The entire issue was devoted to a thunderous exposure of "the betrayal of Ulster Protestantism - Bible-believing, Bible-defending, Bible - practising Protestantism". The Protestantism which Carson and Craigavon had stood for - the Protestantism which had resisted every conspiracy by Rome from 1641 to 1916 - was being undermined by sinister forces, he cried. It was being undermined by "unfaithful and unregenerate clergy" in the World Council of Churches, some of them Orangemen, who had invited the "Roman Antichrist" to join their ranks, and by compromising Unionist politicians.

There was betrayal in the home where liberal ideas were destroying morals; betrayal in the schools where, thanks to the Unionist government's Education Act, Bible Protestantism had been replaced by the heresy of evolution ; betrayal of the Christian sabbath, desecrated by "Rome's Continental Sunday" and finally political betrayal by Unionists. They, he warned, were "subsidising the enemies of Ulster" by giving grants to Catholic schools and they were planning to spend £300,000 on "a Roman Catholic Boy's Training school built by the Ministry of Home Affairs" in Belfast, complete with an attached Catholic church.

Paisley's advice to his faithful was that it was better "to face the stern facts now than to realise too late our peril when hopelessly wrecked on the reefs of disaster. If we cannot regain what is lost, then we can, alarmed at what is lost forever, make doubly sure that those things which remain are not lost in the same treacherous and subtle manner".[2]

That, simply, was to be Paisley's manifesto for the next fifteen years, a manifesto that was to become increasingly attractive to Northern Ireland Unionists as the movement towards religious and political ecumenism slowly gathered speed.

Subsequent *Revivalist*s continued the assault on all forms of "backsliding compromise" by all denominations. The Presbyterians remained the major target for his criticism - their pews after all were the richest ground for recruits - but they weren't alone. The Church of Ireland was attacked on a variety of fronts - some of them absurd. Selling vacant churches to

Rome, entertaining "Romish" High Anglicans like Trevor Huddleston and the Church's commemoration of the centenary of Guinness" brewery were typical of his assaults.

The conservative and evangelical Irish Baptists, who theologically were on Paisley's side, were also a target. Although not members themselves of the WCC, they were guilty by association because the English Baptists were members - a clever exploitation of the half-truth that was to be Paisley's hallmark later in politics. The Methodists were beyond redemption not just because they too were in the WCC but because they favoured the opening of parks and playgrounds on Sundays or because they nursed in their bosom the viperous Donald Soper.

Individual ministers were also singled out for attack - sometimes *The Revivalist* carried paragraph after paragraph naming them and detailing their offences - usually over some tenuous assocation with the WCC. The Church of Ireland Dean of Belfast, Bishop R. C. Elliot, a senior Orangeman, was a constant target because of his suspected sympathy with the WCC - Free Presbyterians capitalised on the initials of his christian names by chanting "RC Elliot" whenever he spoke on Orange platforms. The slightest gesture of friendship towards Roman Catholics was rank blasphemy - like the Presbyterian Moderator in 1958, the Rev R. J. Wilson who was visited by a Catholic priest during a tour of Donegal: "the massing priest and the modernistic presbyter . . . under the ecumenical umbrella", shrieked *The Revivalist*.

If Protestant liberalism and ecumenism were The *Revivalist's* foes, hatred of Roman Catholicism remained the staple fare for his church services on the Ravenhill Road. There the credulous faithful were treated to a simple message of superstition, Popish plots and distortions.

In July 1959, shortly after a frost-melting visit to Pope John 23rd in Rome by the British Queen Mother and her daughter Princess Margaret - the first contact between British royalty and Rome since the Reformation - the Protestant monthly review *Focus* sent an anonymous writer to report on one of Paisley's services, a service that was typical of the 1950s genre. The article described a semi-fictional service conducted by "a Rev John McIlhagga", a thinly disguised Paisley as *The Revivalist* acknowledged, when it reprinted the piece the following month.

The church was packed out and the writer was half-forced, half-carried by the pressure of people into the small Ravenhill hall. He described the scene that followed:

The Rev Mr McIlhagga appeared and shouted informally down the hall: "Come on up, friends - there's a couple of seats up here!" He was a burly, fairly youthful figure, with heavy full face and cold grey eyes.

The first hymn almost stunned me with the exultant joyous roar of voices concentrated behind me. Rhythmic, with almost rollicking refrains, it released a kind of heart-catching uplift into the air; gaily, yet fervently, indeed almost fiercely, they shouted their happiness in being washed in the Blood of the Lamb. Then the minister prayed. In the plain voice of the people he prayed against Romanism; and in particular, in a tone of sad solemnity, for members of Royalty "now flirting with the Anti-Christ".

The perils of "Popery" were expounded and exposed in a thundering invective which rose from height to height of vehemence to finally come down in crushing denunciation. With hand outflung in furious gesticulation, he hurled his scorn of Rome down the hall. On all sides the murmur of "Hallelujah!" and "God save us!"

The thesis was simple, England was being slowly recaptured by Rome. "Every time an English ruler moved towards the Pope", he cried, plunging into history, "England decayed; every time the English King stood out against the Pope, England prospered. Take William the Conqueror; he resisted the Pope and in his time England ruled more land in France than the French did".

The present Royalty were committing spiritual fornication and adultery with the Anti-Christ, he thundered, and "God will be displeased, and God's curse will fall on England! And look at the tutors appointed for Prince Charles and Princess Anne", he said darkly. "I wouldn't be surprised if they were Jesuits in disguise and paid by the Pope!"

He could quote them hundreds of examples, he went on, of where disaster followed anything to do with the Pope, but here were just a few: The Queen of Brazil was going to have a baby. She sent for the Pope's blessing; the baby was born deformed. The Emperor of Mexico had the Papal blessing; he was shot. The ship *San Spirito* set sail for Naples in 1888, having been blessed by the Pope; it sank with terrible loss of life. "And now that Princess Margaret is after seeing the Pope", he added, "I hear she's got a cold". He smiled grimly at the joke upon his own thesis. Laughter stirred through the church.

In the Belfast of the 1950s Paisley found a natural constituency for that sort of message among the working and lower middle classes, reared in a city where "No Pope Here!" was to be found chalked on many a red-brick gable end and where regular outbreaks of conflict between Protestants and Catholics were part of growing up.

Attendance at his Ravenhill church steadily grew: by the end of the decade he had plans to install an upstairs gallery to accommodate the crowds, and had opened an American-style gospel telephone service, an early sign of the growing influence on him of that continent. His NUP services in the Ulster Hall - Unionism's cathedral, where Carson had ended his anti-Home Rule campaign with a huge eve of Covenant rally - regularly attracted crowds of up to 2,000.

At an institutional level, relations between the Catholic Church and Protestantism in the 1950s by and large mirrored those between East and West at the time. There was very little dialogue between leaders, and on the extreme fringes between the two - as in Ireland - there were occasional outbursts of cold warfare. Paisley's anti-Catholic, anti-ecumenical rhetoric, although bizarre and strident, found a distinct echo in the mainstream.

The Church of England for one still distrusted Rome, as the Archbishop of Canterbury, Dr Geoffrey Fisher demonstrated in October 1953 when he denounced "the oppressions and denials of just liberties which lie at the door of the Roman Catholic Church". He later commended "as a brief but effective reply" to Catholic propaganda a Church booklet which accused Rome of "duplicity, reckless and impertinent propaganda and the wholesale exploitation of simple people's credulity".[3]

Even the faltering moves towards reconciliation between Protestant denominations, as represented by the work of the British and World Councils of Churches were viewed with some anxiety by conventional Irish clerics. "It is sometimes felt that our ecumenical friends exaggerated a little the harm that was done by the fact that the churches were not united", warned the

Presbyterian Moderator, the Rev Hugh McIlroy when the Belfast Council of Churches affiliated to the British Council.[4]

Abroad the persecution of small Protestant communities in Franco's Spain and South America caused concern to Northern Protestants. They saw there warnings of their own possible fate in an all-Ireland Republic - a warning that was amplified when, in 1952, the Republic's census results revealed a half per cent rise in the Catholic population and a 13 per cent drop in Protestant numbers between 1936, the year before de Valera's Constitution gave the Catholic church a special position in the State, and 1946.

The June 1954 Presbyterian General Assembly heard that Spain's 20,000 Protestants encountered "the utmost difficulty and frustration" in practising their faith thanks to Franco's pact with the Vatican. Protestants were not allowed to run their own schools and their churches were forbidden to advertise services or publish literature. In some areas they were not allowed to hold religious services when burying their dead and only close family members were permitted to attend the last rites. They were barred from the armed services and from practising law. Worst of all "only in rare instances can people be legally married, (and only) if one of the two should happen to have been baptised a Roman Catholic".[5]

The plight of Spanish Protestants was raised at Westminster by a Unionist MP in an effort to get the Foreign Office to act. In 1953 the Unionist party published a pamphlet linking the Spanish Protestant experience with their own argument against Irish unity. During these years many of Paisley's Sunday services featured missionaries returned from Catholic South America with blood-curdling stories to tell of similar persecution.

In Belfast the Catholic church and Protestant evangelicals fought guerrilla warfare trying to out-proselytise each other. Norman Porter had organised an Evangelical Catholic Fellowship group partly as an escape route for converted Catholics "saved" by Protestant missioners at factory and workplace gospel meetings. The Legion of Mary aggressively sold Catholic literature from stalls in the centre of Belfast and on the Falls Road; the Redemptorist priests of the Clonard monastery were still running their missions aimed specifically at converting Protestants. Paisley was an occasional attender, loudly disputing theology with Catholic clerics.

Some in the Catholic hierarchy regularly warned their flock of the dangers of mixing with Protestants. Bishop Farren of Derry was one who was particularly concerned by the effects on young Catholics of their "seeking amusement" in non-Catholic dance halls. "If you allow your children to be contaminated by those who are not of the fold", he told Catholic parents in 1951, "then you can expect nothing but disaster".[6]

Protestant intolerance was, however, backed up by political power. In Enniskillen the local Unionist controlled borough council sacked thirteen Catholic relief workers when they attended Mass without permission on New Year's Day 1953. A local Catholic priest protested that the incident "gives us just one more proof that freedom of worship is not recognised by the Protestant bigots who control the jobs in North-East Ulster".[7]

Evangelical Protestants and working class Loyalists on the other hand firmly believed that the Catholic Church, through an organisation called "Catholic Action", was conspiring everywhere to take jobs away from them and to prevent them preaching the gospel. In fact "Catholic Action" was a figment of their imagination; it was a handy name for all those Catholic groups which, in one way or another, seemed to threaten them just by their very existence. But it was a sign of the times. Paisley's anti-Catholicism was an integral part of a tradition that stretched way back into the nineteenth century.

FLAGS AND DRUMS

Protestant-Catholic relations in the religious world were mirrored in politics. The Unionist government showed no signs of relaxing its unchallenged grip on the levers of power. Catholics were either Nationalists or Republicans and by definition enemies. They had deeply held grievances over discrimination in jobs and housing and were deprived of political power in local councils by the Unionist gerrymandering of electoral boundaries.

In addition, draconian legislation like the Special Powers Act was regularly used to suppress even normal political activity. After the war, Nationalists had tried to improve their lot by trying to work the system and by participating in Unionist institutions like the Stormont parliament, but when Unionists refused to respond they moved back to abstentionism. When attempts to highlight their grievances or assert their identity by flying the Irish Tricolour at marches and parades in the early 1950s were met with RUC baton charges they drifted towards violence.

The split in the County Tyrone IRA in 1954 which gave birth to Saor Uladh galvanised the IRA into action and partly to forestall any more defections and partly in response to the growing impatience of Catholics, plans were laid for another campaign - the first stage was to collect weapons and a spectacular raid was mounted on Ebrington barracks in Derry which netted machine guns, rifles and ammunition.

The mood of Nationalists was reflected during the Unionist celebrations for the Coronation of the young Queen Elizabeth II in the summer of 1953. While Nationalist MPs publicly repudiated her right to reign over Northern Ireland, the IRA let off bombs in Kilkeel, County Down, and in Belfast. In Newry, a Border town controlled by Nationalists, the council forbade the use of council property for the flying of patriotic bunting.

In contrast, Protestant areas of Belfast vied with each other to display the largest Union Jacks or the biggest street arches and held street parties and religious services. Catholic Belfast shunned the celebrations.

The flying of bunting in divided areas soon became a political issue. In Cookstown, County Tyrone, Catholics tore down flags and streamers erected by the Unionist council, which promptly replaced them under police guard. Union Jacks were burned in Dungannon and other villages in County Tyrone, while in the townland of Derrymacash outside Lurgan, County Armagh, the police had to intervene to prevent sectarian fighting when Catholics erected Tricolours in reply to two Union Jacks raised by their Protestant neighbours. Peace was restored only when the police persuaded everyone to lower their flags.

In the Nationalist town of Dungiven, County Derry, Loyalist plans for a children's parade on Coronation day were disrupted when a crowd of Catholics gathered with hurley sticks to prevent a notoriously bigoted Orange band, the Boveva flute band, from joining it. Catholics allowed the parade to go ahead only when the Loyalists removed a large Union Jack from one of the floats.

The Unionist government of Lord Brookeborough - he was made a Viscount in 1952 - was largely undisturbed by these signs of growing Nationalist aggression. In July of 1953, to underline Unionism's sense of security, the new Queen paid her first visit to

Northern Ireland and was greeted everywhere by crowds of cheering Protestants. Catholic sensitivities were largely ignored. In the predominantly Catholic city of Derry, 1,300 police, nearly a third of the entire force, were drafted in to make sure the natives made no trouble when the royal visitor made a fleeting visit. At Hillsborough Castle, the Governor's residence, she was entertained after dinner to a display of Lambeg drumming, the huge Orange war drums beaten feverishly with cane sticks strapped to the drummer's wrist till they bleed.

But trouble was brewing for Brookeborough and not just from the Catholics. His own right-wing extremists were stirring. In June 1952, the Minister of Home Affairs, Brian Maginess, had banned Orangemen from parading on the Longstone Road, a Nationalist enclave at the foot of the Mourne mountains near Annalong, County Down. They hadn't marched there for 25 years and their plan was clearly an attempt to parade Protestant triumphalism and was a potentially violent one at that.

The ban was rescinded a month later in the face of Orange protests, but hard line Loyalists had been angered at Maginess' "appeasement" of Catholic sensitivities and they decided to try to unseat him at the next available opportunity. That came in a Stormont general election in October 1953.

Another group of Loyalists, Independent Unionists, whose base until then had been confined to the tough Shankill Road area of Belfast, also decided to mount challenges to the Unionists' monopoly of power elsewhere. They had been angered at the Government's inability or unwillingness to stamp out Catholic disaffection during the Coronation and they also accused the government of "appeasing" the Catholic Church over a decision to increase building grants to Catholic schools. They sensed a betrayal of traditional Unionism by their leaders.

There was also unconscious class antagonism in their opposition - resentment at "Big House Unionists", the landowners and businessmen who controlled the Unionist party and dominated Orangeism - and they demanded more jobs, better conditions and more housing for Protestants. The Unionist party's influence in the Orange Order was a particular grievance - they felt that the Order, like the Unionist party, was falling out of the hands of rank and file Loyalists and into the control of a privileged and increasingly liberal élite.

Seven Independent Unionists stood in the election on a

platform of ultra-Loyalism, anti-Catholicism and social and economic populism. Exactly the same ingredients were to make up Paisley's political manifesto over a decade later. They got mixed results. Norman Porter, Paisley's old rival from their NUP days, won comfortably in Clifton in North Belfast, but Tommy Henderson lost the Shankill seat he had represented since the 1920s.

Maginess's Iveagh constituency, in south-west County Down, was the scene of the most bitter contest. There he was opposed by Willie John McCracken, a poor farmer and a member of the youth branch of the Unionist party. McCracken's manifesto included demands for jobs and better conditions for farmworkers, but he campaigned mostly on Maginess's "appeasing" record as Minister of Home Affairs.

During the campaign, he attacked Maginess for banning the Longstone march, for allowing the RUC to take down Union Jacks at Derrymacash and for "weakness" towards the Catholic enemy - a plan by Catholics to build a church in a town in his constituency was blamed on Maginess. The affair in Dungiven during the Coronation celebrations, when Catholics had stopped the Boveva flute band from parading, quickly became a *cause célèbre*. McCracken's supporters, who included prominent local Orangemen, claimed that the IRA had actually stopped the band and had taken over the town while the RUC stood idly by. That charge, the gravest that could be directed at Unionism, implicated the entire Government.

A worried Brookeborough was forced to come to Maginess's rescue and he addressed election meetings for him. At one, in an Orange hall, he was constantly heckled by 30 to 40 McCracken supporters who threw firecrackers at the platform; one singed Lady Brookeborough's fur coat. Brookeborough defended the Longstone ban, saying that violence could have spread to areas where Protestants were outnumbered, but he shifted the blame for the Union Jack incidents on to the RUC and pledged: "I can promise you that the Union Jack will fly in any part of this country in future".

Maginess survived the challenge but was badly bruised. His vote dropped by over 3,000 and his majority was cut from 7,500 to 1,500. Brookeborough got the message and moved him into the Finance Ministry away from controversy.

The Independent Unionists pressed home their advantage

after the election. In December they formed an Ulster Protestant and Orange Committee and called a huge anti-Government rally in the Ulster Hall for the next month. Their manifesto was simple: "We believe the time has come for the Loyalists of Ulster to awake and to consider their position before it is too late. Ulster is the heritage of our forefathers; Ulster is ours and we mean to hold it come what may. Our motto is still 'No Surrender!'"

At the rally the government was fiercely attacked over the Coronation incidents. The RUC was bitterly criticised for removing Union Jacks in Derrymacash and the Boveva bandmaster, William Douglas, gave a lurid account of the IRA's "takeover" of Dungiven. A vote of no confidence in the government was unanimously passed and, to cheers, Porter called for Brookeborough's resignation.

Faced with this challenge, the Unionist establishment retreated. The Orange Order ordered an enquiry into the Dungiven affair and Unionist MPs from Stormont and Westminster met in emergency session to discuss the crisis. Despite an RUC report which had dismissed the Dungiven allegations as nonsense, the new Home Affairs Minister, G. B. Hanna also ordered a government enquiry.

Eight days after the Ulster Hall rally, on 12 January 1954, the government - as its predecessors had done in earlier decades - surrendered to the pressure from extremists. In the 1960s Paisley would apply the same pressure with the same success.

Hanna announced that new legislation to protect the Union Jack would be introduced. The law, called the Flags and Emblems Act, would make it an offence to interfere with the Union Jack and the police were empowered to remove any other flag whose display might provoke a breach of the peace. This section was aimed at the Irish Tricolour - announcing the new law, Hanna apologised that he couldn't ban the Tricolour outright as this was a matter of foreign policy reserved to Westminster.

Encouraged by their victory the Orange and Protestant Committee formed a new political party called the Ulster Loyalist and Democratic Unionist Association with Independent Unionists as the leaders. Their aim was to extend the electoral challenge to the official Unionists - "every appeaser would be contested" at the next poll, declared McCracken.

These early precursors of Paisley's own Democratic Unionists never really got off the ground. The IRA campaign two years later reunited Unionism and some prominent Independent Unionists were bought off with the promise of official Unionist nominations.

Another serious weakness was their lack of a coherent organisation and grass roots followers, as Willie John McCracken explained thirty years later: "We never had what Paisley had when he started, churches all over the place to give him people to work with".

During all this Loyalist ferment, Paisley was nowhere to be seen - he was still honouring his promise to keep out of the worldly life of politics. He was to keep that promise for another three years, until late 1956, when a bizarre religious controversy involving the disappearance of a young Catholic girl brought him notoriety throughout Ireland and with it an entrée to the world of Loyalist politics.

A RELIGION OF FEAR AND DREAD

In the mid-1950s, Protestant gospel meetings in factories and other workplaces were commonplace; the practice had started in the Belfast shipyard in the 1920s and had spread. Sometimes the workers from two or three factories gathered together in one canteen to hear preaching and to sing hymns as they ate their sandwiches.

The Star Clothing Company on Belfast's Donegall Road, a Protestant area near the fiercely Loyalist Sandy Row and on the fringes of Catholic West Belfast was the regular scene of such evangelizing efforts. Although the workforce was predominantly Protestant, it did include some Catholic women who worked as stitchers. One of them was a 15-year-old girl called Maura Lyons, the eldest of a family of five. The family, all devout Catholics, lived in Iris Drive in the heart of the Falls Road.

In the early autumn of 1956, the Star Clothing Company was visited by missionaries from the Elim Pentecostal church and according to her later, much publicised testimony, Maura was deeply struck by their message: "there was something about them which impressed me. My own religion was a religion of fear and dread, while their religion was so simple and so free from fear".[8]

There were a number of "saved" Protestants in the Star

workforce; one of them was a Free Presbyterian, Joe Walker, and Maura discussed her doubts about Catholicism with him. Walker put her in contact with the Rev David Leatham of the Dunmurry Free Presbyterian Church and through him she met Paisley. She was a guest at Paisley's wedding to Eileen Cassells in the Ravenhill church in mid-October.

On 18 October she joined the Free Presbyterian Church, renouncing her Catholicism and three days later, on the Sunday, she told her parents. Her father was so outraged that he beat her: "He would rather have a traitor than one who was giving up her religion", she said. The next day she returned from work to find two priests in the tiny house. One was her parish priest, a Father Madden, the other a stranger. They pleaded with her to change her mind, to tell God how sorry she was, but as they knelt to say the family rosary, she stubbornly remained on her feet.

Two days later there were three priests in the house when she came home. They demanded to know if she had repented and returned to her faith. "They seemed determined to force me into convent life", she said. Her father had already packed her suitcase, but on a pretence she slipped upstairs, opened her bedroom window and jumped out, making good her escape through the backyard door.

She made straight for Joe Walker's house near the Star Clothing factory and from there was taken by car to Leatham's house. Leatham immediately got in touch with Bob Cleland, the secretary of Paisley's Ravenhill presbytery, and together they decided to approach Norman Porter for help. His Catholic Evangelical Fellowship could provide her with an escape route to a quiet life in England and away from the convent she so feared.

Paisley was in Scotland on honeymoon with his new bride, Eileen, when Maura had made her getaway. But on the night Porter had agreed to handle her case, he returned and intervened to prevent his old rival reaping the kudos. A member of Porter's group recalled: "Cleland told him what had happened but he said 'Porter will have nothing to do with this, I'll handle it'". Maura Lyons, after all, encompassed all the Romish perfidies he had been preaching about - intimidating priests, convent imprisonment and a Church conspiring to deny a young girl the true word of God.

The Maura Lyons case was handed over to Paisley's trusted deputy, John Wylie. Together with another Belfast Free

Presbyterian, Emma Munn, they took Maura to Belfast docks and posing as her parents boarded the ferry to Liverpool. From there they travelled first to stay in the homes of sympathisers in England and then to Scotland where she was deposited in the care of a retired Protestant missionary, Jock Purvis.

The news of her disappearance didn't break until early November but when it did the Belfast newspapers made it a front page story. Soon the whole of Northern Ireland was either fascinated or outraged by this bizarre manifestation of its own religious conflict. Her parents made a public appeal on 5 November, saying they were convinced that she was being held against her will. The RUC started investigations and traced her to Leatham who at first denied any involvement. He later admitted helping the girl, but elsewhere the police came up against a brick wall of silence.

Paisley issued a statement when it emerged that his church was involved: "The missing girl, an RC, attended a lunch hour meeting at her work which was not conducted by my church. She became friendly with a member of my congregation and requested to be taken to see one of my ministers, the Rev David Leatham. While with him she professed salvation and later attended a prayer meeting and two church services. This was before she left home. On the night she did leave she arrived at Mr Leatham's house and he sat praying with her and talking to her. He does not know where she is at present and neither do I."

That version of events, noticeably incomplete as it was, appeared, however, to be accurate in one revealing aspect, as a former church member could testify: "Although, when the police came to see Ian, he could honestly say that he didn't know where she was - and that was true in that he didn't know exactly where she was at that moment - he knew who had her and what was happening. There were some things that happened in the Church that people didn't tell Ian about deliberately. He knew that things were going on, he didn't inquire and they protected him so that he could honestly say that he didn't know."

Those responsible for spiriting Maura Lyons away were guilty of a criminal offence - the law forbade the removal of any child under 16 from the control of her parents even if done voluntarily - but despite the risk, or perhaps because of it, Paisley was unapologetic for the "militant Protestant activities" of his church members, as he called them, and showed himself ready to make as much mileage as possible out of the teenager.

His ten years of preaching anti-Catholicism at NUP rallies and at his own services throughout the North had given Paisley a fine sense of what appealed to his audiences and theatre was always an essential ingredient. On 21 December at an Ulster Hall rally, two months after Maura Lyons' disappearance, he staged his most dramatic spectacle yet.

The adverts for the rally hinted at a personal appearance by the missing girl and the crowds flocked to the Ulster Hall as did the police who mingled in plain clothes with the audience. But that was not to be. Instead a tape recording of her voice, recounting her conversion to Free Presbyterianism and the wickedness of the priests, was played. It had been made by John Wylie who had travelled to Scotland to record her. Paisley's explanation for the tape was ingenious: "I got it when my wife went out for the milk a few mornings ago. It was there with the bottles".

The crowds were not disappointed, though. The *Belfast Telegraph* reported that "several hundred people chanting religious songs queued five deep outside the Ulster Hall", and they gave his performance, albeit minus Maura Lyons in person, a tremendous reception.

Paisley began the rally, the report went on, with a frontal attack on the old enemy: "'There are certain members of the Roman Catholic community who have threatened to create trouble at this meeting tonight', he shouted. 'I can say we are not going to tolerate . . .' At this point his remarks were drowned in a roar of applause from the body of the Hall".[9]

Nine days earlier, the IRA had launched bomb and gun attacks against the police and "B" Specials along the Border and in rural Catholic areas, and Paisley brought this new threat to Protestantism into the performance. He claimed that "he had received two communications saying that the building would be blasted with explosives and that the meeting would be wrecked." It was the first of many claims to be on an IRA hit list.

He went on to issue a challenge to the authorities to prosecute him, but it was a subtly worded challenge which placed his own innocence firmly on the record: "It was suggested to me by a policeman that I was responsible for Miss Lyons going away. I went to the police station and protested against this allegation. They said that they believed I knew where the girl was. I told them I did not know and I tell you the same. If I did know the girl's address tonight, I would never divulge it to any man. Do you think that I, as a Protestant minister, would hand over any girl to a convent of Rome? If I knew where the girl was I would not take her to the police. I am happy that I don't know where she is but if I did know all the policemen in Ireland would not get it out of me. The police say 'You are committing an offence'. Very well, I am committing an offence. I will do time for it. I would be proud to do time for Protestant liberty".[10]

To hushed quiet Maura Lyons' tape was played. Among the audience, listening to her account of her escape from a convent life, were her brother and her father. Hugh Lyons later told the press that he was sure that the voice in the tape recording was not his daughter's. But he was the only one not to be convinced.

Maura Lyons was fast making Paisley a household name. Most people in Northern Ireland date the first time they heard of Paisley to the affair and many Catholics trace their fear and dislike of him back to it also.

The Maura Lyons affair, while upsetting Catholics' religious sensibilities, also took on a political flavour. One Nationalist MP complained in Stormont that while the RUC were able to round up IRA suspects daily for internment, they somehow couldn't manage to trace one young girl.

The RUC had appointed their most senior policewoman, District Inspector Marion McMillan to handle the case, and she had travelled to England in her search. Other British police forces were helping as were the Garda Siochana across the Border. But despite renewed appeals from her parents and from newspapers like the *Belfast Telegraph,* the police got nowhere.

The affair was also exacerbating sectarian tensions. The Republican Labour MP for Falls, Harry Diamond, had named Joe Walker in a Stormont debate, and later Norman Porter alleged that Walker had been intimidated out of his job and had been manhandled by Catholics who threatened to kidnap his son. He had been forced to leave Northern Ireland a frightened man, Porter said. The Government meanwhile insisted that there was "no letting up" in the search and that if evidence came to hand of criminal activity then those responsible would be prosecuted. Nationalists greeted that with scepticism.

Nothing more was heard of Maura Lyons until the following February when her parents received a letter from a Mrs Standage, of the Sentinel Union in Sussex, a refuge for converted

Catholics, offering to return the girl if they agreed to allow her to practise her new religion. The same month an interview with Maura was published in the English *News Chronicle* - Paisley denied all knowledge of it - and that was followed by another flurry of police activity as they hurriedly interviewed the reporter responsible.

The RUC were never to find Maura Lyons. On 10 May 1957 she turned up at 423 Beersbridge Road in East Belfast, the Manse of the Ravenhill Free Presbyterian Church. It was her sixteenth birthday and now she was legally free to go where she pleased. Paisley explained her dramatic reappearance in a statement to the press: "A knock came to the door of my home yesterday. It was Maura Lyons. I did what any public spirited citizen should do. I got in touch with my solicitor and then with the police. I did not delay." His new found public spiritedness contrasted sharply with his Ulster Hall defiance, but no-one seemed to notice.

Maura was reunited with her parents at the RUC City Commissioners' office but didn't go home with them. The police detained her under the Young Persons Act and took her that night to a welfare home until the Attorney-General decided her fate.

She didn't want to return home anyway; by all accounts the brief reunion with her parents was traumatic. Her aunt sprinkled her with holy water, as if to disinfect her of Free Presbyterianism, and tried to embrace her, but Maura objected. Her father tried to hug her as well but Maura shrieked and pulled away; he then knocked Paisley's solicitor to the ground, mistaking him for one of her abductors. Then Maura and her parents shouted names at each other and when her father again pleaded with her to come home she became hysterical and ran out of the room screaming.

Her real fear, it seemed, was of being locked away in a convent, the fate fundamentalist Protestants believed awaited all converted Catholics who fell back into the clutches of the priests. Her parents denied all along making this threat or intimidating her with priests; the fear of a convent, they said, had been put into her imagination by Free Presbyterians. Induced or not, Maura Lyons' fear was real enough.

Paisley appeared to be apprehensive as well about what would happen when Maura Lyons returned to Belfast. Three days before her re-appearance he made an effort to show that when it came to converting teenage girls he could be even-handed. An 18-year-old girl from a Church of Ireland home, Kathleen Kelly, who had worked with Maura Lyons in the Star Clothing Company, had also disappeared and had been converted to Free Presbyterianism. On 7 May, three days before Maura Lyons turned up on his doorstep, Paisley took Kathleen Kelly around newspaper offices in Belfast, trying to stimulate interest in an interview, but with no success. Protestants converting Protestants, like dogs biting men, made poor copy.

The Maura Lyons case came to the Belfast High Court on 20 May before the Lord Chief Justice, Lord MacDermott, on an application from her father to have her made a ward of court. Paisley meanwhile had been working hard to keep her out of her parents" grasp. He approached the Belfast Bible College and asked them to admit her as a missionary trainee but he had often attacked the College for "ecumenism" and they refused. Finally he persuaded Mr and Mrs George Gibson, veterans of the Crossgar split, to offer Maura a home and he brought them to court with him on the day of the hearing.

But it was no use. Lord MacDermott granted Mr Lyons' application and made him her guardian. She was to return to Iris Drive, he ruled, but she was not to be taken out of Northern Ireland. Furthermore she was to be free to practice her Protestantism if she desired and was to be kept out of a convent. Even marriage could only take place with the court's permission.

As he deprived Paisley of his prize, Lord MacDermott took a sideswipe at him. The reports of the Ulster Hall rally, he said, were evidence that "Mr Paisley was in touch with the girl when prima facie she was abducted". Paisley was asked if he was prepared to assist the court by throwing some light on the matter but after consulting his solicitor he refused. Even Lord MacDermott's promise that he wouldn't incriminate himself couldn't budge him.

Maura Lyons returned to her parents and, eventually, to Catholicism. Two years later she got married in a Catholic Church. When he was presented with this proof that her conversion to Free Presbyterianism had been shortlived, Paisley claimed that the wedding was an elaborate fraud.

But she has never spoken of the events that followed her dramatic escape from Iris Drive in October 1956. She kept silent to the police when she returned to Belfast and she is silent today.

Maura Lyons now lives in a beleaguered Catholic ghetto in Belfast, the scene of some of the bloodiest sectarian killings carried out by Loyalist paramilitants during the Troubles. A reporter visiting her home will be closely questioned at the door by one of her three daughters; at the first mention of Paisley's name, it is hurriedly slammed shut.

A FRIEND IS MADE

Paisley's handling of the Maura Lyons' affair had embarrassed many Protestants. Sincere evangelicals with experience at "handling" converted Catholics quietly and with the aim of keeping them converted were disturbed at the way he had shamelessly milked publicity out of the affair with little regard for Maura Lyons" own interests. The Presbyterians had been irritated at the way English journalists easily confused their church with Paisley's and, not for the last time, publicly repudiated the Free Presbyterian Church.

But among hard-line Loyalists, Paisley's activities had struck a chord. The Summer of 1957 saw an outbreak of anti-Protestantism in the Republic for which the Maura Lyons' affair seemed an appropriate response. In the tiny County Wexford village of Fethard-on-Sea, local Catholics started a boycott of Protestants, and Northern Unionists soon saw in it vindication for their own anti-Catholicism. The boycott also justified Paisley's handling of the Maura Lyons affair in many Loyalist eyes, but more significantly it was to bring Paisley together with a man who was to have a significant influence on his career.

The cause of the Fethard boycott was the break-up of a mixed marriage between a local farmer, Sean Cloney and his Church of Ireland wife, Sheila. On their marriage, Mrs Cloney had agreed to abide by Catholic doctrine which stipulated that the children of a mixed marriage should be brought up Catholics. But when the eldest of their two daughters reached school age, Mrs Cloney changed her mind, the couple quarrelled and on 27 April 1957 she left home with the children and fled to Belfast. Fethard Catholics blamed local Protestants for aiding her and, with clerical approval, started their protest. Protestant shops were boycotted and Protestant teachers lost nearly all their pupils.

Three days after Sheila Cloney's disappearance, Sean Cloney had a surprise visitor. A car drew up in his farmyard and out stepped a young Belfast barrister called Desmond Boal who asked to speak to him. Boal was then in his fifth year at the Northern Ireland Bar where he had already established a reputation as a gifted and articulate advocate. He also had a name for uncompromising Loyalism. Born and bred in the tough, working class Protestant Fountain area of Derry, a small enclave on the Catholic side of the city, Boal had brought his politics with him to Trinity College, Dublin where he had helped to start an Orange Lodge. Like Mrs Cloney, Boal was a member of the Church of Ireland.

According to Cloney's later court testimony, Boal told him that he had been in touch with his wife in Belfast and that he had come to offer terms for a settlement which would allow the couple to re-unite. Cloney could have his wife and daughters back, Boal said, if he agreed to sell their Fethard farm, emigrate to Australia or Canada, consent to the children being brought up Protestants and if he himself agreed to consider abandoning Catholicism. Cloney refused and Boal left.

The next day Cloney changed his mind and travelled up to Belfast where he met Boal at his home. He told Boal that he wanted to discuss emigration with his wife and Boal went to fetch her. But he never returned. The following morning Cloney again went to Boal's home where the two men argued. Boal accused Cloney of dishonesty and said that he had closed the door on negotiations with his wife. She wouldn't see him but she might contact him by letter later.

Cloney then applied for a writ of habeas corpus seeking the return of his daughters, and named his wife and Boal as the people who knew their whereabouts. It was conditionally granted but a month later, when an application was made to make it absolute, the High Court adjourned it in the hope that the couple might be reconciled. They were, and the Fethard boycott ended.

The Fethard incident had, though, stirred Loyalist emotions. It was mentioned on virtually every Orange platform that Twelfth of July as evidence of Romish perfidy and Boal's involvement brought him an invitation to address Orangemen in County Donegal. He told them that the boycott weapon "must surely have been forged for the Roman Catholic Church, so enthusiastically had it been used by her to her political advantage in other countries".[12] Other Loyalists singled out marriages between Protestants and Catholics for criticism.

Boal had become involved in the Fethard affair through his friendship with the Rev George Thompson, a Church of Ireland minister who ran the Church's mission in the Republic. Thompson helped to raise funds to alleviate Protestant distress in Fethard and had enlisted the aid of Norman Porter and his Evangelical Protestant Society. Through Thompson, Boal met Porter and soon he was a regular visitor to Porter's Howard Street office in Belfast.

Paisley was also an occasional caller at the office. Although he had broken with Porter during their quarrels in the National Union of Protestants, he still visited him now and then. Porter was on the executive of the right-wing International Council of Christian Churches and Paisley would borrow its literature from him to use in his services. On one such visit Boal was in the office, and Porter introduced them.

It was the start of a strange but productive relationship between the worldly barrister and the hellfire preaching Free Presbyterian Moderator. The two had little in common except their hardline Loyalism and a dislike of the Unionist establishment and the Catholic Church.

In religious matters the two could hardly be more different. Boal has an apparently open-minded attitude to religion and a compelling interest in the bizarre and offbeat - he has been known to spend Summer holidays wandering alone in the Himalayas, the Far East or Africa and once lived for weeks in a Buddhist monastery. Although he neither drinks nor smokes, he loves fast cars and the excitement of the roulette wheel.

The relationship prospered nevertheless, and Boal was to be always at hand with legal and political advice for Paisley. Eventually the two formed the Democratic Unionist Party together but it was to be an unequal relationship; apparently spellbound by Boal's intellect, Paisley invariably deferred to Boal's judgement.

The two stayed together as political allies until 1973 when Boal became a convert to the cause of Irish Federalism. But it was an affable separation. To this day, at the end of what is always an arduous schedule of meetings and speaking engagements, Paisley will often order his RUC driver to go to Boal's house where, sometimes until the early hours of the next morning, the two men will sit discussing politics.

CHAPTER THREE

God, Guns and Politics

We can never relax and if we do, Ulster is doomed.
Lord Brookeborough, Prime Minister of Northern Ireland,
addressing County Fermanagh Orangewomen, 25 April 1958.

At the time that Paisley was hitting the headlines with the Maura
Lyons affair in the Irish papers, there were distinct stirrings in the
underworld of Protestant extremism in Belfast, among those
who a decade later would be dubbed Loyalists to denote their
association with conflict and their flirtation with violence and to
distinguish them from respectable, middle class Unionists. They
would soon provide Paisley with a platform for increasingly
turbulent protests and, by following virtually step by step the
path trodden by the Independent Unionists a few years earlier,
an avenue into electoral politics. From that would follow his
lengthy and ultimately successful campaign against the Unionist
establishment, during which he would establish his reputation
among rank and file Loyalists as one of the most charismatic
leaders ever produced by Northern Protestantism. He would also
come into contact with the more shady and violent side of
Protestantism, an association that dogs him to this day.

Loyalists were stirring because in 1956 Northern Ireland was
expecting a renewed IRA campaign to break out at any moment,
and Protestants feared that it would be the fiercest onslaught
against the State since the early 1920s.

All the signs were there. Aside from the Derry raid, the IRA
had mounted a well-executed sortie against the British Army's
barracks in Armagh in June 1955, netting another massive haul
of rifles and machine guns. A raid on Omagh barracks the

following October had been a fiasco but nevertheless the IRA was arming itself with the weapons of war. In July 1955, a Dublin-based jeweller blew himself to pieces with his own bomb in East Belfast on his way to put government phones out of action in the Stormont parliament. He was a member of a violent IRA splinter group; the other splinter, Saor Uladh, launched a bomb and gun attack on Rosslea RUC barracks in County Fermanagh four months later.

Furthermore, in May 1955, the IRA's violent remedy for their ills was apparently endorsed by the Nationalist population. Its political wing, Sinn Fein, outmanoeuvred the Nationalist party by standing candidates in all 12 Westminster seats at the general election and unopposed, except by Unionists, won 152,000 votes and the Mid-Ulster and Fermanagh-South Tyrone seats. It was the biggest anti-Partition vote since 1921. Northern Unionists braced themselves for a violent campaign which they imagined would be directed at every conceivable target, Belfast included.

In the Autumn of 1956 some Loyalists in Belfast decided that they too would have to prepare for the coming violence. One of them was Ernie Lusty, a lamplighter from the lower Shankill Road who had been a member of the militant Ulster Protestant League in the 1930s and had a name as a gunman. The other was a shipyard worker called Albert Thoburn. Both men were members of the Unionist party.

They contacted other sympathetic Loyalists and in December called a meeting in the Unionist party's headquarters in Glengall Street near the city centre. Their idea was to organise a semi-paramilitary group, partly to defend Protestant areas, partly to retaliate as the old Ulster Protestant Association had done in the 1920s. That group had been deeply involved in an assassination campaign aimed at Catholics. Their imitators in 1956 wanted to be ready to react to the IRA's violence.

As one of the founder members of the group remembered: "We were half convinced that the war was going to be waged against the Protestant community. We felt it necessary to be in a position to take on and destroy the IRA. We would have gone out looking for them, you know, take them on. I think a considerable number of us would have been quite happy to have done that."[1]

Among those invited to the inaugural meeting were some who were to make their mark later, more conventionally, in Unionist and Loyalist politics, and others whose contribution would be violent. A former British Army Chindit from the Shankill Road, Johnny McQuade, was one who straddled both. Charlie McCullough, also from the Shankill and a future Unionist Senator was in the former category as was Frank Millar, a prominent Independent Unionist whose son is now Secretary of the Official Unionist party. Another leading Shankill Loyalist who worked in Belfast Corporation's Transport department as a timekeeper was also invited. His name was Billy Spence. His brother Gusty, then serving in the British Army as an NCO in the Royal Ulster Rifles, was to make his own bloody imprint in Northern Ireland ten years later.

The Maura Lyons affair had earned Paisley an invitation too, and had brought him to the attention of Loyalists who were rarely to be found in church - "He was looked upon as one of the more forthright Protestant clergymen because of Maura Lyons", recalled one of those at that first meeting. Norman Porter, by then an MP at Stormont, also received an invitation but left when he saw Paisley arriving; his NUP experiences had warned him off too close an association with Paisley.

A name for the organisation was chosen at that meeting. Ulster Protestant Action (UPA) was decided upon, the initials suitably evocative of its bloody 1920s forerunner. On the nights of 11 and 12 December 1956, just after that meeting, the IRA launched its much-awaited campaign, Operation Harvest, the brainchild of a young Dublin journalist and ex-Irish Army officer called Sean Cronin. As Border RUC stations were bombed and machine-gunned and bridges mined, UPA's members congratulated themselves that they had acted just in time.

For the first nine months or so of its life UPA meetings were full of discussion of vigilante patrols, barricades, emergency medical services, transport and communications as its members waited for the IRA to strike in Belfast. A smaller group within UPA made its own plans.

They drew up a list of suspected IRA members in Belfast and rural areas, and collected a small cache of handguns left over from the 1920s and 1930s in preparation for a campaign of assassinations.

If it had got to the stage where ordinary Protestants had been murdered by the IRA, there would have been retaliations, there would have been murders committed.

We had a number of volunteers who were prepared to do that sort of thing; they weren't really interested in the discussions we were having, they just sort of sat there at meetings and didn't say much, but they had it in their minds to do that sort of thing and would have spoken about how things had been handled in the twenties and thirties.[2]

But the talk of violence didn't last for more than a year. The IRA threat to Belfast never materialised and its campaign was confined almost entirely to the remote Border areas of Fermanagh, Tyrone and Derry. Even then, swift government reaction on both sides of the Border, primarily through the introduction of internment, had cut swathes into the IRA's personnel and logistical capacity. By the beginning of 1958 incidents were fewer and further between.

Another major factor, not acknowledged publicly by Unionists until 1959, was the lack of Catholic support for the IRA. Although Catholics had voted in huge numbers for the IRA's political wing, a vote repeated on a smaller scale in the Republic in June 1957, the benefits of the Welfare State - grudgingly introduced by the Unionists in the post-war years - and a growing social services gap between North and South, led some Nationalists, particularly those in the middle class, to re-question their political ideals. The Sinn Fein vote was as much, if not more, a protest against Unionist intransigence as a vote for violence. When it came to the bit, Catholics were reluctant to openly assist the IRA.

With Belfast untouched by the IRA, there were small signs of a defrosting in community antagonisms as the decade wore on. UPA members noticed it and were alarmed at the implications:

There were Prods who were drinking in bars, not many bars, but in one or two bars on the lower Falls and RCs who were drinking in the Shankill area with people they worked alongside.

Despite our involvement, despite the IRA's performance, there were people who were just living together and mixing together. The Twelfth of July came and passed without a care. Loyalists cared but there was never any annoyance taken to Orange demonstrations. In fact the vast majority of RCs in our area, you could have seen them right along the route of the Orangemen on the Twelfth morning. They waved at them. Whenever the bonfires were lit on the Eleventh night, a considerable number of RCs were there and mixed. Protestants really didn't want to know about UPA, they didn't want to become involved. If the IRA had opened its campaign in Belfast there would have been a far greater response but they weren't feeling threatened.[3]

Despite this, UPA soldiered on and by the beginning of 1958 had set themselves new goals: the strengthening of Protestantism in factories and the backstreets of Belfast, and resistance to any attempt to dilute or weaken Bible Protestantism. Desmond Boal was asked by UPA to draft a constitution and prominently featured in it was a pledge to work only by "lawful means". All of Paisley's subsequent organisations would contain a similar commitment - something he could always point to as a defence when accused of inspiring violence.

Boal's constitution described UPA as:

ULSTER:
    Its field of activity is Ulster. Its great objectives are the solving of Protestant problems, the strengthening of Protestant bulwarks and the stabilising of new Protestant safeguards in order that our glorious Reformation Heritage may be preserved and our Province delivered from the slavery of a Roman Catholic Republic.

PROTESTANT:
    Its basis and bond of union is Protestantism, the Protestantism of the Bible. It unflinchingly maintains the cardinal doctrines of Christianity as set forth in the Apostles' Creed and uncompromisingly denounces and resists all forms of Popery.

ACTION:
    It is Ulster's Protestantism in Action. It operates by efficient organisation, effective propaganda and eternal vigilance. It resists by all lawful means every activity which would jeopardise our Protestant faith and heritage. Its purpose is to permeate all activities, social and cultural with Protestant ideas and in the accomplishment of this end it is

primarily dedicated to immediate action in the sphere of employment.

As the last of its aims implied, UPA's base was to be found in the Protestant workplaces of Belfast where, as the decade turned into the 1960s, rising unemployment was beginning to affect Protestants, and where the imaginary Catholic Action was thought to be at work ceaselessly striving to take away Protestant jobs to place in Catholic hands.

Branches of UPA were formed in various factories and workplaces, or in Protestant areas of Belfast. Paisley had his own branch formed around his Ravenhill congregation and called, appropriately, the Premier branch. There was also a women's branch which excelled at collecting funds and a branch in Coleraine, County Derry, the only one outside Belfast, led by John Wylie.

But the bulk of UPA's sixteen or so branches, claiming a membership of some 2,000, were workforce oriented. There were branches in the shipyard, in the aircraft factory Shorts, in Mackies engineering works, the docks, Belfast Corporation and the City's gasworks. They were given names like Steadfast, Bulwark, Bible and Crown, Lutheran and Protestant Link. Sixteen years later, in 1974, other Loyalist workers were to unconsciously imitate UPA. Calling themselves the Ulster Workers' Council, they launched a general strike which brought a British government to its knees.

A ruling Executive body was formed with each branch sending along two delegates. Paisley was an ex-officio member and others on the committee were McQuade, Billy Spence, who was chairman, Charlie McCullough, Richard Fenton, Frank Millar, Sammy Verner, later a Major in the Shankill Road UDA, Herbert Ditty who became Belfast's High Sheriff in 1986, Bob Newman, later Belfast's deputy Mayor. From Paisley's Premier branch in East Belfast, came a 16-year-old apprentice printer called Noel Doherty.

Branches met in Orange halls or in Unionist Party rooms across the city. The Executive at first met above a butcher's shop in Woodvale in the upper Shankill area but then moved down the Shankill Road to a room above a pub called the Berlin Arms, which two decades later became a regular haunt of members of the Ulster Defence Association. A member of the UPA can recall the teetotal, fiercely anti-alcohol Paisley sitting down to meetings as other Executive members filed up the stairs with pints of foaming Guinness in their hands.

UPA members sold tin badges around the shipyard and other factories to raise money. That activity alerted the police, who suspected a more sinister use for the money; the Special Branch on the Shankill took an increasing interest in UPA's activities and occasionally raided UPA homes looking for hidden guns.

Some branches, like Protestant Link in the tough and violent York Street area of North Belfast, raised money to keep Catholics out of their areas, an obsession with Unionists even of Lord Brookeborough's social class - he had encouraged similarly motivated organisations in Fermanagh and Derry in the late 1940s. If a house went up for sale and no Protestant family could afford the deposit, Protestant Link would offer them an interest free loan.

UPA's abiding concern, however, was to keep jobs in Protestant hands. That concern intensified in the late 1950s as unemployment in the shipyard and Shorts grew. It attempted to infiltrate the trade union movement and scored a notable success when a UPA member, John Gregg, was elected as a full-time official in the Boilermakers Union in the shipyard. In the docks, where workers were employed on a daily casual basis, UPA persuaded foremen to hire only Protestants. Elsewhere, as the *Irish Times* reported: "The purpose, in any given context, was simply to have a Protestant employed or given over-time, or not sacked rather than a Catholic."

UPA also continued the agitation over flags started in 1953 by the Independent Unionists. Rallies were held at the Ulster Hall demanding that the Union Jack be flown over every public building. After one rally in 1958, Paisley led a large crowd to Henry Street in the mixed Catholic/Protestant Docks area where, with a large force of nervous RUC men looking on, they hoisted a Union Jack over a children's play centre and burned the Irish Tricolour. The agitation paid off in the following year when Belfast Corporation ordered all schools in the city to fly the Union flag.

Paisley soon came to dominate UPA. A former member recalled: "We found we were more and more dependent on Ian Paisley to address rallies and things of that nature. Most of us were working class people who never had to get up and make a speech or anything like that and we left that to Paisley who was a born preacher". He also had the branch most active and keen on protests, and he pushed UPA into confrontational religious protests and, ultimately, into electoral politics. He was swift to exploit even the smallest situation.

Typical of UPA's religious protests was a takeover of a Legion of Mary bookstall in Belfast's Royal Avenue in April 1959. The Legion of Mary had been selling Catholic literature there for years but one Saturday they arrived to find UPA people in their place selling gospel tracts and religious magazines. A crowd gathered and the police hastily moved in to prevent a confrontation. The Legion of Mary never came back.

In August 1957, Paisley's confrontational tactics brought his first brush with the law and his first, but by no means his last, appearance in a courtroom. In Donaghadee, a pleasant seaside town on the north County Down coast, householders on the seafront had objected to the noise made by "beach" preachers - itinerant evangelists who blasted out their gospel message with loudhailers. One Monday they called the RUC in to ask the preachers to turn down the volume. Paisley got to hear about it from John Wylie and the next night the pair travelled to Donaghadee, set up their own loud speakers, and turned the volume on full blast.

It was a clear invitation to the police to take action against them and it worked. This tactic of defying the authorities, inviting them to take action and then denouncing them as traitors to traditional Protestantism if they did, was further refined by Paisley in the 1960s. It was to be an important element in his appeal to hard-line Loyalists for it echoed past Orange heroes who had similarly defied "appeasement".

An RUC sergeant moved in to ask Paisley and Wylie to turn their loudspeakers down. Predictably they refused. Their names were taken and later they were summonsed under a council bye-law for making a public disturbance. Paisley extracted considerable publicity out of the incident in the Belfast papers. Donaghadee councillors were called Romanists and Iscariots, the RUC were taken to task for harassing Protestant ministers when they should have been out fighting the IRA, and Donaghadee Catholics were blamed for making the original objections to the preachers.

The case came to Donaghadee petty sessions on 6 September, with Paisley and Wylie defending themselves. Some 150 UPA supporters packed the courtroom an hour before proceedings started and cheered and clapped when the Magistrate dismissed the charge on a technicality - the summons had been issued before the council had authorised prosecution and no-one could find the relevant minute.

Paisley and Wylie were surrounded by jubilant supporters on the steps of the courthouse, where Paisley reminded them who was really responsible for their success: "We thank God for the victory which He gave and for the many Donaghadee people who stood with us in our stand for civil and religious liberty". Not for the last time, God was invoked as Paisley's personal ally.

ON THE HUSTINGS

Seven months later, in the March 1958 Stormont general election, Ulster Protestant Action decided, at Paisley's urging, to extend their campaign against Protestant "appeasers" to the hustings. It was Paisley's first foray into electoral politics since 1949 and signalled the start of his long campaign against the Unionist Party. The first target was the Independent Unionists' old enemy, Brian Maginess, now the Attorney-General.

Perhaps because his 1949 pledge to stay out of politics was still fresh in some memories, or because some in his church disapproved of his links with the "toughs" of UPA, Paisley resisted all efforts to persuade him to stand. Instead, another evangelical called Albert "Da" Duff, a lay preacher, who ran a gospel mission in Aughrim Street in Sandy Row, was chosen under the party label "Protestant Unionist", the name Paisley later chose for his own party.

Maginess' Unionist credentials had long been suspect and he had been opposed in Iveagh by ultra-Loyalists at four general elections - he was married to a Catholic and "leaned too much to the other side", was how it was put. Duff, with Paisley as his election agent, campaigned on almost the same issues as the Independent Unionists had five years before, and the campaign was as bitter.

Once again the ban on the Longstone Orange march was raised and Maginess was blamed for a government decision to build a training school for juvenile delinquents in West Belfast which would be run by the Catholic de la Salle order. State finance for Catholic schools, in the form of a 65 per cent building grant, was once again an issue - Duff alleged that the 1947 Education Act which had made this obligatory, had destroyed Protestant schools.

Maginess became a focus for all Loyalist grievances against Brookeborough's government and Duff got the support of the County Down Orangemen who had backed McCracken in 1953. A decision to withdraw the Family Allowances Bill, an extraordinary Act which would have penalised Catholics by depriving large families of increased financial aid, was an example, Duff said, of "appeasement" of the Catholic Church. So was the fact that citizens of the Republic were allowed to work in Northern Ireland.

Paisley and Duff, who ran their campaign from Paisley's car, planning their next moves at the roadside, also made unemployment and the cost of living an issue. Billy Belshaw, a long time Paisley disciple and subsequently the DUP mayor of Lisburn, County Antrim, can remember these issues being raised: "Paisley was speaking to a large crowd when someone shouted at him 'Vote Maginess!' He was quick with his reply - for Maginess in parliament had tried to get the bus fares put up and he had voted for dearer coal. So Paisley shouted back, as quick as a flash, 'Yes, vote Maginess and dearer bus fares and dearer coal'".

Once again Brookeborough was forced to come to Maginess' aid - just as he had in 1953 - and spoke for him at election meetings. At one meeting in Gilford Orange Hall, Brookeborough said that he had been disturbed to hear that Maginess' opponents had labelled him a "Lundy", the worst sort of Protestant traitor, and he invoked his own impeccable Loyalist credentials in his defence.

The *Belfast Telegraph* reported Brookeborough as saying that as County Grand Master of the Orange Order in County Fermanagh and the honorary commandant of the "B Special" Constabulary, he could vouch for Maginess' loyalty: "Do you think for one minute", asked the Prime Minister, "that the county Fermanagh Grand Orange Lodge would have elected me to the high office of County Grand Master and would continue to have me as their honorary County Commandant if they thought I was nursing in my bosom a Lundy? Never!"[1]

Another feature of the 1953 campaign was repeated - Maginess was again the target for violent protest. A week after that speech from Brookeborough, Maginess was surrounded by a hostile mob of 200 Loyalists as he left Dromore Orange Hall, booing and jeering as the police struggled to make a passage for him. When he got to his car, he found the tyres had been let down, and then some of the crowd tried to overturn the car with Maginess, his wife and brother in it. He eventually made his getaway but the next morning in Belfast, as he left home to go canvassing, he found that his car tyres had once again been punctured.

Maginess survived the challenge but with almost the same result as in 1953: 6,600 votes to Duff's 4,700. At the same time, Norman Porter lost his seat in Belfast leaving the leadership of ultra-Loyalism free for Paisley to grab. In his car on their way home from the count, Paisley, encouraged by the Protestant Unionist performance, suggested to Duff and Charlie McCullough that the time was opportune for UPA to take their electoral challenge to Belfast Corporation where elections were due to take place in May.

Duff and McCullough agreed. Duff had been an Official Unionist councillor in the late 1940s, but had resigned over a sexual scandal in the party. McCullough, a travelling salesman, wore a clean suit, was articulate and was thought a suitable choice to represent UPA in the City Hall, where the middle class Unionist establishment still reigned supreme. Duff chose the St George's ward in Sandy Row while McCullough stood in Woodvale in the upper Shankill.

They weren't the only Protestant Unionist candidates. John Wylie stood in Ballymoney where, a few weeks before the poll, a lurid series of anti-Catholic spectacles organised and stage-managed by Paisley had given him a platform.

In January 1958 Paisley brought over to Northern Ireland a converted Spanish priest, Juan Juarte Arrien and his wife, the daughter of an American Methodist minister, and toured them around 14 different locations to address crowds on the evils of Roman Catholicism - "The inside workings of Rome" or the more titillating "Life behind convent walls". His wife's subject was always "I married an RC priest", an unashamed appeal to the sexual curiosity of the strait-laced Northern fundamentalists. In early newspaper ads Arrien was described as "the priest who said 8,000 Masses and heard 50,000 confessions" although the latter were increased to one million by the end of his tour.

Arrien was a professional anti-Catholic, earning his living by taking his roadshow to any audience that would listen and afterwards contribute to his living and travelling expenses. Paisley had been told about Arrien by his NUP friend in England, Arnold Perkins, and realised that he would be a big draw.

Part of Arrien's attraction was that he was from Spain, where Protestants were still persecuted by Franco's fascist rule. His main drawing power, however, were the mock Masses that he staged, complete with Catholic vestments, a chalice and the communion wafer, which Catholics believe is miraculously transformed during the ceremony into the body and blood of Christ. Paisley had staged similar shows in the early 1950s throughout Northern Ireland, but to have a converted priest performing was, in the strange world of ultra-Protestantism, an enormous coup.

The Arriens' tour in January and February was, by all accounts, a big success, drawing large crowds everywhere. Paisley had to apologise to "the many hundreds of people" who couldn't get into the Ulster Hall for the tour's grand finale, but he announced that because of the response, he was bringing Arrien back in April for a repeat visit.

In mid-April, he duly returned and Paisley arranged an exhausting schedule for him. Arrien was to speak in Belfast, Coleraine, Derry, Lisburn, Rasharkin, Donaghadee, Newtownards, Downpatrick, Ballymoney and scattered Orange halls throughout County Down. Some of those towns had substantial Catholic communities and, deeply offended by Arrien's mock Masses, they strenuously objected.

Only in Ballymoney though, did anyone pay heed to their protests. There the local Catholic priest, supported by some Protestant ministers, wrote to the council objecting to the use of the town hall by Arrien and Paisley. The council listened sympathetically and cancelled Arrien's booking, as they had a similar anti-Catholic meeting by Paisley in 1954.

Paisley reacted immediately, turning the issue into a threat to Protestant and Unionist values by the Ballymoney councillors. *The Revivalist* thundered against the Catholic priest who had objected: "Priest Murphy speak for your own bloodthirsty, persecuting, intolerant, blaspheming, political-religious papacy but do not dare to pretend to be the spokesman of free Ulster men. You are not in the South of Ireland, Ballymoney is not

Fethard and the flag of this land is not the tricolour but the glorious red, white and blue of the Union Jack. Go back to your priestly intolerance, back to your blasphemous masses, back to your beads, holy water, holy smoke and stinks and remember we are the sons of the martyrs whom your church butchered and we know your church to be the mother of harlots and the abominations of the earth".

A bus load of UPA supporters was quickly organised to travel to the town two days after the council ban and, with Wylie and Arrien at his side, Paisley held a protest rally on the steps of the town hall. The councillors were denounced as "traitors" bent on stifling "the message of Protestantism" and there were scuffles between police and some in the UPA crowd.

Once more in imitation of a Reformation hero, Paisley nailed a protest to the door of the town hall, as Luther had his 39 Articles in Wittenberg four centuries before. Then he announced that John Wylie would take up the council's challenge at the polls and stand for a seat on the issue of the ban.

Wylie's election manifesto linked the council ban with the IRA's campaign - both were attempts to undermine and destroy Ulster's liberty and freedom to practise the Queen's religion. The voters of Ballymoney agreed. Wylie was elected with just over 600 votes while in Belfast, Duff and McCullough, who were both popular in their own right, topped the polls.

RIOT ON THE SHANKILL

Forcing confrontation was now an essential ingredient in Paisley's politics and in 1959 he helped to provoke one in Belfast which led to an outbreak of some of the worst anti-Catholic violence seen in the city for years. On the night of 17 June, Ulster Protestant Action called a rally at the corner of Percy Street in the lower Shankill Road and Paisley and McCullough addressed it. A large crowd of mostly young people had gathered, attracted by the music from an Orange band.

A witness recalled what was said at the rally: "Paisley was speaking and he said 'You people of the Shankill Road, what's wrong with you? Number 425 Shankill Road - do you know who lives there? Pope's men, that's who! Forte's ice-cream shop, Italian Papists on the Shankill Road! How about 56 Aden Street? For 97 years a Protestant lived in that house and now there's a

Papisher in it. Crimea Street, number 38! Twenty five years that house has been up, 24 years a Protestant lived there but there's a Papisher there now.'"

Incited by the rhetoric, and stirred up by the Orange music, the crowd marched up the Shankill Road and headed straight for suspected Catholic homes, breaking windows, throwing stones and daubing "Taigs out" with paint on the doors. Shops thought to be Catholic-owned were attacked and one, which had a display of crucifixes in the window, was looted. It was coming up to the "Twelfth", a traditional high point for Loyalist emotion, and tensions were already high following attacks on Protestant businessmen in the Shankill suspected of having Catholic partners. Two youths were arrested and later fined. The pair, Clifford McComish and David McConnell, share the distinction of being the first people in Northern Ireland to suffer in court the consequences of Paisley's invective.

Paisley himself was unapologetically pleased at the night's events, as a contemporary recalled: "Paisley rang me up to tell me about the great meeting. 'Did you read the paper this morning?', says he. Says I: 'You're responsible for that shop being broken into'. 'Not me', he said, 'I was in the car on the way home'." It wouldn't be the last time that Paisley would disclaim responsibility for sectarian violence caused by his anti-Catholic tirades.

A VICTORY AT DUNGIVEN

History was repeating itself in the late 1950s in more than one way; in 1959 another issue that had stirred up Loyalists in 1953 surfaced again for Paisley to exploit. Orangemen had forced Brookeborough's Government to concede their right to march over the Catholic Longstone Road in 1955, when Norman Porter and several hundred Orangemen had defied a Ministry of Home Affairs ban on their parade. The Government surrendered after that and in succeeding years, drafted in large numbers of RUC men to escort the Orangemen through.

In Dungiven, where in 1953 Catholics had forcibly stopped the Boveva flute band from parading through their streets, the Orangemen had made no further attempts to assert their supremacy. Content with having forced the Flags and Emblems Act out of the Government, the Orangemen had left the village in peace. In 1958, however, Orangemen marched through the town with a heavy escort of police, catching the local Catholics by surprise; the march had gone ahead thanks to a private agreement between the Orangemen and the Minister of Home Affairs, William Topping, and there had been no advance publicity.

There was little chance of Catholics being caught unawares again. When the Orangemen announced plans for a parade to be led by the Boveva flute band in June 1959 to mark the visit to Northern Ireland of Princess Margaret, the Government reckoned that Catholics would use violence to stop it and Topping stepped in to impose a ban. Three days later another planned march by the Boveva band was also banned. Behind the Unionist action was the fear, later admitted by Brookeborough, that sectarian violence could give Catholics a reason to support the IRA's flagging campaign.

Paisley immediately saw the hand of Unionist "appeasers" at work, capitulating to Rome and Irish Republicanism. On 10 July, two days before the Twelfth parades, he called a UPA rally and march in the Belfast shipyard to condemn the Government's action. Nearly 2,000 shipyard men, tough Loyalists, took part and the atmosphere in the yard, as the *Irish Times* reported, was tense: "More than one Roman Catholic avoided, as far as possible, speaking to Protestants - even Protestants they knew and liked. Some stayed away from work . . . for it was known that Ulster Protestant Action was holding a mass meeting."[2]

Paisley rounded fiercely on the government: "There are no Nationalist areas in Northern Ireland! Ulster is Ulster and the flag should be allowed to fly anywhere. Let us tell them that if necessary, the Protestants in the Queen's Island [part of the shipyard] will go to Dungiven and march behind the Union Jack", he roared. A vote of no confidence in Topping was passed as was a motion recognising "that Rome is the great enemy of Protestantism and Ulster".

At that time UPA was a small organisation - at most it could muster 2,000 members in the whole of Northern Ireland and had only three councillors in elected office. Despite this, Brookeborough's government felt that it couldn't ignore this pressure from an extremist fringe and Topping was authorised to issue a statement justifying the Dungiven ban. He did so almost apologetically, claiming that he had not banned the Boveva band parade, only rerouted it, and he maintained that he had Protestant support in Dungiven, even in the Orange Order, for his action.

Two days after the shipyard meeting, catcalls, boos and jeers greeted Topping from a crowd of 120 hecklers when he addressed Orangemen at the field at Finaghy, where the Belfast Orangemen assembled after their Twelfth parade through the city. Topping was prevented from speaking when the crowd struck up the Orange hymn, "The Sash" and UPA supporters mingled with the crowd distributing leaflets which read: "The plain truth is that the Minister capitulated to the threats of the rebels". At Coleraine there were similar disturbances.

Paisley's pressure had worked, as it would repeatedly with future Governments, and as similar pressure from other extreme Loyalists, like the Independent Unionists, had in the past. The Unionist Party's habit of answering its own extremists with appeasement was by then well established.

A few months later, Brookeborough gave them a sop and removed Topping from the Home Affairs Ministry - just as he had removed Maginess six years earlier. Shortly after that, Topping retired from politics to take up a judicial post in Belfast. Paisley could justifiably claim to have collected his first Unionist scalp; it certainly wasn't to be his last.

Topping's successor was Brian Faulkner, the young ambitious son of a shirt manufacturer. He had impressed Unionists with his anti-Nationalist rhetoric and had also established hard-line credentials when he joined Norman Porter in leading Orangemen over the Longstone Road in 1955 in defiance of the government ban. In July 1960, a year after Paisley had challenged the Government over the Dungiven ban, Faulkner took care not to repeat Topping's mistake and allowed the Orangemen to march through the village. The result was two nights of rioting between the RUC and local Catholics and a boycott of Protestant shops. Paisley's pressure had established the right of Loyalists to parade their triumphalism through Catholic districts - it was an important concession which Orangemen, often led by Paisley, have refused to surrender to this day.

The Dungiven saga had an interesting sequel. In July 1960 Nationalist MPs and Senators, despairing of getting satisfaction from the Unionists, asked for a meeting with a British Home

Office Minister to complain about the Orangemen's march. Mr Dennis Vosper, a Parliamentary Secretary in the Home Office, unexpectedly agreed, the first time a British Minister had ever listened to Nationalist complaints.

It was not, from the Nationalist viewpoint, a productive meeting - Vosper said he thought Brookeborough's Government made every effort to give the Catholic point of view a fair deal - but it marked a watershed in Nationalist tactics. From then on they would look increasingly to British politicians, not to Dublin, for a remedy to their grievances. Paisley's protest ironically began a process which would see the Nationalist case receive a growing sympathetic hearing in Britain.

MARTYRDOM DENIED

Within two weeks of the shipyard rally, Paisley was in the headlines again. This time, however, it was because of a religious protest, not politics, although the affair which brought him more notoriety, very soon took on a political colour.

Among the many British Protestant clerics who had attracted Paisley's ire over the years, it is probable that the Rev Dr Donald Soper, a former President of the Methodist Church in England and, at that time, a noted public speaker, was at the very top of the list. In theological matters Soper was a liberal; he did not believe that the Bible should be interpreted literally but rather as a collection of metaphorical tales which Christians should be free to explain rationally. This had led him to question and then to reject a central tenet in Free Presbyterian and general Protestant theology - the idea that Christ's mother, Mary, was a virgin when she conceived.

Soper was also, by the standards of the 1950s, a political radical. He was sympathetic to Communism and believed that the Russian leader, Nikita Kruschev should be the first president of a world government. He was also opposed to the nuclear arms race and was a strong British Labour party supporter. In addition he had supported the Northern Ireland Labour Party in the 1953 Stormont election and had spoken at campaign meetings in Belfast, an offence in Loyalist eyes graver than his rejection of the Virgin birth.

Paisley despised Soper for his politics and theology but he also had a more personal reason for disliking him. In 1954, on his own home base of Belfast, Soper had made a public fool of Paisley and he had neither forgotten nor forgiven him. In April that year Soper came to Belfast to hold a meeting at the blitz ground in High Street. In London, Soper regularly preached at Speakers' Corner in Hyde Park and had developed razor sharp reactions to hecklers. Despite warnings from friends that he could be mauled, Paisley decided to take Soper on.

Paisley brought supporters along carrying placards and as soon as the meeting began they heckled and interrupted him, but Soper very quickly had the upper hand. "Jeers of people supporting a questioner", reported the *News Letter,* "were drowned many times by the applause that greeted Dr Soper's withering replies. So effectively did he deal with the most persistent hecklers that at the end of half an hour he had succeeded in getting comparative quietness for his speech.

"His most persistent heckler was the Rev I. R. K. Paisley, Minister of Ravenhill Free Presbyterian Church and general secretary of the Free Presbyterian Church of Ulster. Mr Paisley stood beneath a banner proclaiming 'Dr Soper denies the Virgin birth of Christ' and he frequently interrupted to ask Dr Soper about his attitude to the Virgin birth. When Dr Paisley took off his hat halfway through the meeting Dr Soper commented 'Keep your hat on, the woodpeckers are about.'"[3] The crowd broke out in laughter. Paisley had been humiliated and the next day, all Belfast would read about it.

In July 1959 Soper paid a return visit to Northern Ireland for preaching engagements. On 1 August he was due to preach at Fair Hill, Ballymena, Paisley's home town. Paisley, Wylie and a recently converted Church of Ireland curate, Harold Magowan, travelled there, armed with placards and pamphlets, determined to silence him this time.

Soper never really had the chance to start his sermon. Paisley and his Free Presbyterians started heckling as soon as he stood up on the platform and kept it up for the best part of an hour. Each time Soper started to speak the Free Presbyterians shouted him down. Insults were traded; Paisley called Soper a Communist and Soper retorted that the Free Presbyterians were behaving like Fascists and intellectual rabbits. A Bible was thrown, apparently at Soper, by a Paisley supporter. The police moved in to keep order and eventually Soper was forced to leave the platform, which was immediately occupied by the victorious Free

Presbyterians who then held their own service. Soper later called the meeting "the most animal-like of any I have spoken at".

The following day Soper was pursued by Wylie and a group of UPA members to a Methodist church in Belfast where Wylie attempted to drape rosary beads over his neck. A large force of plain clothes police, alerted by the trouble in Ballymena, surrounded Wylie and escorted him away.

A week later Paisley, Wylie, Magowan and two other Free Presbyterian supporters were summonsed for disorderly behaviour and for the second time in as many years Paisley appeared in court.

The case came before Ballymena magistrates on 2 September with Paisley's friend, Boal appearing for him and the other accused. The case lasted five hours and at the end of it Paisley and his co-accused were found guilty and fined £5. Paisley immediately stood up and told the magistrate that he would not pay the fine and would go to jail for two months instead. Outside the court hundreds of people had gathered and they hoisted Paisley shoulder high, cheering him wildly.

Four days later Paisley held what he called a "farewell" service at his Ravenhill church and once again announced his determination to go to jail. So many people tried to jam into the church that 400 were left standing outside and Paisley himself had to use the side door to get in. Support for Paisley and his noisy protests was clearly growing.

The next day, only hours before the deadline for paying the fine expired, Paisley was suddenly deprived of his prison martyrdom. The British Prime Minister, Harold Macmillan, announced a general election to be held in October and the owner of a magazine called *The Unionist,* Mr George Allport, quickly moved to save Brookeborough's government the embarrassment of having three Protestant ministers in jail during the election campaign. He walked into the Crown offices in central Belfast and handed over £15 in the names of Paisley, Wylie and Magowan.

He later admitted that the imminent general election had caused him to act. The imprisonment of Protestant ministers, he explained, could cause repercussions far and wide, especially in marginal seats held by the Unionists. "We cannot have three Protestant ministers in prison in a Protestant state", he declared.

Paisley was angry at Allport's action and accused the Unionist government of putting him up to it. Then he announced that "certain influential people" had approached him to stand for the East Belfast seat but that he had not yet made a decision.

He withdrew that threat just before nomination day without explaining why, but at an Ulster Protestant Action Rally in the Ulster Hall a week before polling he gave a clue. UPA, he announced, had written to every Unionist candidate asking them two questions. Did they believe that the Union Jack should be flown without hindrance anywhere in Northern Ireland and, if elected, would they be prepared to sponsor legislation at Westminster proscribing Sinn Fein in Great Britain?

Only one candidate, the sitting member for East Belfast, Stanley McMaster, a barrister, had replied and had answered both questions in the affirmative. Paisley told the cheering crowd: "You may remember that many people in East Belfast have asked me to stand there. I am not going to do so, but I am glad to say that we have one man who is not ashamed to nail his colours to the mast. As an elector in East Belfast I will be proud to cast my vote on polling day for Mr McMaster. I trust you Protestants in East Belfast will take notice and support him".

East Belfast was normally a safe Unionist seat but in the previous 1955 Westminster election, the Northern Ireland Labour Party had done surprisingly well. By that stage the NILP had split over the Border with more Republican-minded members leaving to form the Irish Labour Party. The NILP loyalists stressed their allegiance to the Union in an effort to attract Protestant support. It paid off in the 1958 Stormont election when the party won four seats, and its support in Protestant working class areas like East Belfast was rising with unemployment.

A Paisley challenge in the constituency could have split the Unionist vote, conceivably giving Labour a chance of stealing it - but McMaster had, by his deal with Paisley, ensured his re-election. Twice, within the space of weeks, Paisley had shown that some Unionists were beginning to run scared of him - now it was clear that one Unionist MP owed him a favour.

"BROOKEBOROUGH OUT!"

Unionists had made the 1959 general election a plebiscite against Sinn Fein - that "snake which must never be allowed to crawl along the roads of Ulster", as Brookeborough put it - but some Nationalists were viewing it that way too. The IRA's campaign was getting nowhere, the jails were full of internees and the benefits of the Welfare State, particularly in education, were beginning to reconcile some more prosperous Nationalists to the idea of working within the State to reform it. Some Nationalist MPs openly urged Catholics not to vote for Sinn Fein, the first time this had ever happened.

Once again Sinn Fein were unopposed on the Nationalist side, but this time their vote dropped dramatically from the 152,000 votes won in 1955, to just over 63,000 votes. As the *News Letter* commented: "The bulk of those to whom they appealed have stood aloof and by so doing have shown convincingly that they do not want a campaign of violence waged on their behalf".[4]

Other Unionists agreed and interpreted the results even more positively. On 2 November, at a Young Unionist conference in Portstewart, County Derry, the chairman of the Unionist Council, Sir Clarence Graham, suggested the possibility of Catholics being allowed to join the Unionist party and even being selected as Parliamentary candidates. At the same meeting Brian Maginess made an appeal for an end to tribal politics. The Border was secure and accepted as a permanent fact, he declared, and now "greater toleration and co-operation between all sections of the community - whether of politics, class or creed - was desirable".

The rest of the Unionist party were aghast at their remarks and there was an immediate and violent reaction against them. They had dared to publicly question the central characteristic of the Unionist Party - its virtually exclusive Protestantism - and such was the controversy that there was talk of a split in party ranks if the matter wasn't settled.

On 7 November the Unionist executive moved to defuse the crisis. It issued a statement re-affirming the principles of Carson's and Craig's Unionism, which included the defence of "civil and religious liberty" - code language for Protestantism - and said that only those prepared to give unconditional support to those aims would be welcomed within the party. Faulkner went further, attacking the Catholic Church and declaring that talk of co-operation with Nationalists was "co-operation to achieve a united Ireland."

Three days later, the Orange Order came out in complete

opposition to Graham and Maginess. The Grand Master, Sir George Clark, declared that it was "difficult to see how a Roman Catholic, with the vast differences in our religious outlooks, could be either acceptable within the Unionist party as a member or, for that matter, bring himself unconditionally to support its ideals".

On 21 November, Brookeborough put the issue beyond doubt and dismissed Sinn Fein's poor performance as insignificant. "There is no use blinking the fact that political differences in Northern Ireland closely follow religious differences", he told Fermanagh Unionists. "If that is called intolerance I say at once it is not the fault of the Unionist party. If it is called inflexible then that shows that our principles are not elastic".

Two weeks later the Minister of Finance, a rising star in the Unionist party called Captain Terence O'Neill, appealed for party unity - in effect an end to the debate - by recalling Carson's warning that if divisions within Unionism "became wide and deep, Ulster would fall".

The Unionist Party, prisoners of their extreme past and their modern day extremists, had thrown away an opportunity to reconcile a significant number of Catholics to the Northern Ireland state. By their re-assertion of Protestant exclusivity and Catholic inferiority, they had once again sown the seeds of violent rebellion.

Although Brookeborough had rapped Maginess and Graham over the knuckles and killed off the debate before it had really started, Paisley and Ulster Protestant Action were furious with him. They demanded nothing less than the expulsion of the two men from the Unionist Party.

When that didn't happen, they organised a double-decker bus, filled it with placard - carrying UPA supporters and, led by Boal, drove up to Stormont Castle and held a protest meeting. One of Brookeborough's Cabinet ministers can recall the protesters standing in the cold outside the Cabinet offices, chanting "Brookeborough Out!" When Paisley was later to contrast the good old days of Unionism under Brookeborough with the treachery of his successor, O'Neill, this incident was always conveniently forgotten.

By this stage Boal was deeply involved with Ulster Protestant Action as its legal/political adviser and was developing political ambitions. In early 1960 he won the Unionist nomination for a by-election in the Shankill constituency - one Nationalist MP later alleged that UPA had infiltrated the Shankill Unionist Association to help him secure it - and in February 1960 he was returned to Stormont.

In an interview in the DUP newspaper, *The Voice of Ulster,* in December 1982, Paisley revealed that UPA had indeed been to the fore in securing Boal's nomination:

I remember the resignation of Harry Holmes and the vacancy in the Shankill seat. I took a leading hand in that movement, and, of course, it came to the contention for Shankill and a lot of the Protestant Action people were associated with Shankill and they suggested that Desmond Boal should go and run for the nomination which, of course, he did and got the nomination.

Then the Protestant Action decided that they would let the Unionist Party run their own campaign and we would run a parallel campaign backing Boal. So we had our own election machinery all running for him and we had our own election meetings as well. It was a most interesting election and Mr Boal had a tremendous victory.

Paisley and UPA were active throughout the campaign and Boal needed their help. That February was bitterly cold. Most of the Shankill area was covered in heavy snow and Boal succumbed to influenza and was out of action for most of the campaign. On the eve of polling, Paisley and UPA were out on the wintry streets urging Protestants to turn out for their campaign. "Some men suddenly become Protestants and Orangemen when they are looking for the nomination of a partiular party but Mr Boal has proved himself in the past to be 100 per cent Protestant", Paisley told them. With Boal's election, Paisley and UPA now had a friend and ally in the corridors of power.

By this stage, Paisley was dominating UPA's activities and was beginning to cause friction between himself and other equally tough-minded members. One UPA member can remember Paisley regularly over-riding Executive decisions to get his own way, much to the annoyance of other members. Some of his ideas were opposed by UPA's working class membership - like his opposition to Northern Ireland playing in the 1958 World Cup soccer finals in Sweden because they would have to play on Sundays; or the proposal to stand against a woman Unionist councillor in Belfast because it was rumoured that she was sexually involved with another councillor.

Things came to a head in the May 1961 elections for Belfast Corporation when UPA stood five candidates in Belfast, this time under the UPA, not Protestant Unionist label. In the meantime McCullough had left UPA to join the Official Unionists but Duff had stayed and once again stood in St George's ward, Sandy Row. Another UPA candidate in the ward was James McCarroll, one of Paisley's closest Free Presbyterian allies. McCarroll was a building contractor who was later to erect Paisley's huge Martyrs' Memorial church on the Ravenhill Road. In Woodvale, a shipyard worker called Jackie Bickerstaff stood for an alderman's seat and trying for council seats were Billy Elliot, another shipyard worker and a Shankill Road butcher, called William Spence, who was unrelated to the UPA chairman, Billy Spence. Another Free Presbyterian stood in Clifton in North Belfast.

Paisley threw his weight behind Duff and McCarroll and they were the only ones to win, but the method of their victory caused dissension in UPA ranks in Sandy Row and West Belfast. Their official Unionist opponents in St George's were Herbert Henry, whose family owned a glazier's shop in Sandy Row and John Armstrong and his wife Elsie, who ran a pub and bookmakers shop. Duff and McCarroll put a leaflet around the ward alleging that Henry and the Armstrongs employed Catholics and this at a time when "good Protestants" from Sandy Row were unemployed.

The tactic worked and only John Armstrong of the Official Unionists was elected. After the election Paisley and McCarroll were confronted by UPA supporters in Sandy Row, who were friends of the Henrys and Armstrongs. "They were criticised at a meeting for their smearing tactics, for it wasn't true, Henry and Armstrong didn't employ RCs", recalled an old Unionist party worker. "In fact it was found out that McCarroll himself employed five Catholics but he replied that he couldn't get Protestant bricklayers. Then he was challenged to sack them and the next day there would be five Protestants round to take their place but at that, McCarroll and Paisley just walked out".

Some of the UPA Executive wanted to take action against

Duff and McCarroll anyway, for it had also emerged that they had gone into the voting lobbies with Nationalist councillors in the City Hall. They were summonsed to an Executive meeting to explain themselves but never turned up and were expelled. Paisley's Premier branch objected and quit UPA. Paisley himself wrote a resignation letter to the Executive explaining that he wanted to leave politics to concentrate on his church building and religious work.

But there were also ideological differences behind the split. The core of UPA members on the Shankill Road and North Belfast had become disillusioned fighting the Unionist party from outside, and the growth in Labour party support had left them open to the charge that they were splitting the Unionist vote. They were getting nowhere and by 1961 they decided to infiltrate the Unionist party in an effort to make it more responsive to the demands of working class Loyalists from within.

In early 1962 the bulk of UPA's leadership on the Shankill - McQuade, Bickerstaff, Billy Spence and Billy Elliot - joined the Unionist party in Court ward, an area taking in the staunchly Loyalist lower Shankill and Crumlin Roads. They came with a recommendation from Boal. Millar later joined the Unionists in Dock to oppose a new threat, a Republican Labour councillor called Gerry Fitt, who was making his mark as an aggressive exponent of the Nationalist cause, while Ernie Lusty had joined the Unionist Labour Association, the Unionist Party's "working class" wing.

To Paisley, the separatist and bitter enemy of the Unionist establishment, this was anathema. Although he remained friendly with UPA, and continued to develop his relationship with Boal, he remained true to the promise in his resignation letter that he would stay out of politics. The promise, however, only lasted two years.

Ulster Protestant Action continued without Paisley until 1966, sometimes supporting him in protests, sometimes mounting their own efforts. During the O'Neill years its leadership drifted towards violence in response to his liberalising efforts and one member, the UPA chairman, Billy Spence, was responsible for the creation of the Ulster Volunteer Force, an organisation which was to become one of the most violent in Protestant history. Unlike UPA, the UVF carried out the threat to kill, and

UPA itself finally disintegrated in the bloody Summer of 1966 when it was blamed for the death of an elderly Protestant woman, burned to death in a petrol bomb attack meant for a Catholic pub.

The first three years of the 1960s were reasonably quiet for Unionism, settled by comparison with 1958 and 1959. In February 1962, the IRA formally abandoned its campaign and admitted that lack of Nationalist support had made it a failure. In June 1962, a Stormont general election saw no Loyalist challenge to the Unionist party, although the Labour party did increase its vote, a reflection of growing unemployment and some relaxation in community tensions, particularly in Belfast.

There was no sign, however, of any relaxation in the Unionist policies which had produced the 1955 Sinn Fein vote. Catholic grievances over discrimination, voting rights, housing and gerrymandering went unremedied and Faulkner allowed the Orangemen to parade their coat tails through Dungiven each year. There was no Catholic backlash however and, on the surface, it seemed that nearly everywhere Nationalists had accepted their lot.

The Brookeborough era finally came to an end in March 1963 and it was, ironically, Paisley's friend Desmond Boal who helped to instigate it and pave the way for the premiership of Terence O'Neill.

In February that year, he had collected the signatures of ten Unionist MPs calling for Brookeborough's resignation. Brookeborough was 75 and had been Prime Minister for 20 years - the natural desire for change was reinforced by discontent on the Unionist backbenches about rising unemployment. Boal had had the party whip removed when he voted along with the Labour party on a motion censuring the government over its economic policies, and other MPs were openly criticising the government on the same issue.

Brookeborough survived the challenge but in February, a scandal broke over a directorship in an insurance company held by Lord Glentoran, the leader of the Senate. Unionist MPs claimed there was a conflict of interest and the issue was turned against Brookeborough who immediately developed a "diplomatic" duodenal ulcer. On 25 March, after a decent interval, Brookeborough retired for health reasons.

There were two candidates for the succession; O'Neill -

Brookeborough's Finance Minister, a member of the Protestant landed gentry who could trace his aristocratic lineage back to the Plantation squires - and the hard-line Minister of Home Affairs, Brian Faulkner, a representative of Unionist commercial interests. Social class made O'Neill the favourite.

Unionist MPs had no choice in the matter, for in those days Unionist leaders, like British Tories, "emerged" after a mysterious round of consultations. Had they been given one, it is almost certain that they would have chosen Faulkner, for O'Neill was suspected of dangerous liberalism. Once he had been the victim of a "whispering" campaign in the Unionist Party alleging that he was encouraging Catholic recruitment to the civil service. O'Neill's Unionism, furthermore, was not rooted in anti-Catholic bigotry or hard-line Loyalism; he always stressed more the economic and social benefits which derived from the British link. Significantly, Brookeborough declined to make any recommendation when asked who he wanted as his successor.

At 6 p.m. on 25 March, over a whiskey and soda in the drawing room of Hillsborough Castle, the British monarch's representative in Northern Ireland, the Governor Lord Wakehurst, informed O'Neill that he was Northern Ireland's new Prime Minister, the successor to Craigavon and the inheritor of Carson's mantle.

Dublin politicians welcomed his appointment. The end of the Brookeborough era seemed to mark a watershed in Irish history. The new Unionist leader was a technocrat with little of the bitterness and overt bigotry of his predecessor. The Republic was furthermore entering a period of economic modernization and prosperity. Talks to negotiate a new trade treaty with Britain were under way and old Republican attitudes to the North were accordingly being questioned for the first time. The new man in the North symbolised the hope that all of Ireland might be modernizing and changing for the better.

Comparisons were immediately made with Sean Lemass, Taoiseach in the Republic since de Valera's retirement in 1959 and another technocratic politician. The *Belfast Telegraph's* Dublin correspondent, quoting political sources in Dublin, wrote:

He speaks like Lemass, only using Northern Ireland instead of Ireland and he makes the very same demands on his people — and with the same dynamic approach as the Dublin Prime Minister. Surely between these two there should be a common interest.

CHAPTER FOUR

The Traitor on the Bridge

*He [O'Neill] is a bridge builder he tells us. A traitor and a bridge are
very much alike for they both go over to the other side.*
Ian Paisley, January 1966.

If there was any reason for Dublin politicians to be optimistic
about the political climate when O'Neill took power at Stormont,
it was to be found primarily in the world of religion. By 1963,
international Protestant and Catholic church leaders had, for the
first time since the Reformation, started a constructive, healing
dialogue. In Ireland there was hope that this new spirit of
friendliness would spill over into political life and help reconcile
divisions within and between North and South.

After a faltering start, O'Neill did indeed start to talk to the
Republic in the mid-1960s and to make conciliatory gestures
towards Catholics inside Northern Ireland. They weren't
sufficient to satisfy most Nationalists but were enough to enrage
Paisley and other militant Loyalists. O'Neill's efforts at
reconciliation convinced Paisley that all the traditional values of
Unionism and Protestantism - summed up in those unyielding
Orange slogans, "No Surrender!" and "Not an inch!" - were
being sold out.

The principal accusation hurled at O'Neill by Paisley deeply
impressed many Protestants - the Prime Minister was "a
dictator" who was betraying Unionists behind their backs, a
modern Lundy scheming to open the castle gates to a hostile
Catholic army. Paisley played the role of the brave Apprentice
Boys and slammed it shut again.

He accelerated the noisy protests he had started against

Unionism in the 1950s and, in paramilitary-style organisations and on the streets, mobilised hundreds of Protestants behind his campaign to unseat O'Neill. He, himself, like Orange heroes of the past, was imprisoned for his defiance. It was an astonishingly successful campaign, tapping a nerve centre in Unionism, but it exposed Loyalism's deep insecurity and intransigence and brought to the surface violent and bloody opposition.

The first danger signals for Paisley had come with the emergence of the ecumenical movement in the late 1950s and 1960s, with its emphasis on conciliation between Catholicism and Protestantism.

This effectively began with the death in October 1958, of the arch-conservative Pope Pius XII, a pontiff notable for his hostility towards the Protestant faith. His successor, John XXIII, a much more liberal thinker, moved quickly to defrost relations between the Church of Rome and Canterbury. Five months after his accession he invited the British Queen Mother and Princess Margaret to Rome; in November 1960 the Archbishop of Canterbury, Dr Geoffrey Fisher travelled to the Vatican to heal a centuries-old hostility; the following May, Queen Elizabeth II, the head of the Church of England, cemented the new cordiality during a private audience in John XXIII's study.

Anglican leaders were not the only ones taking ecumenical initiatives. In 1962 the Moderator of the Presbyterian Church of Scotland, Dr Archibald Craig, travelled to Rome to meet the Pope and in Ireland the Presbyterian Moderator, Dr William Clark, publicly welcomed the new and growing dialogue. John XXIII also moved to improve relations with the World Council of Churches (WCC) and in 1961 the Catholic Church sent observers along to the WCC's New Delhi conference.

Within Northern Ireland, the Protestant churches moved more slowly. In a few places Methodists and the Church of Ireland shared church buildings, reflecting the moves in England towards theological unity between the Methodists and the Anglicans. And there were increasing contacts between individual Catholic and Protestant clerics in organisations like the Irish Association for Cultural, Economic and Social Relations.

Paisley and other fundamentalists in Northern Ireland viewed even these limited developments with alarm. Reconciliation with Rome, they believed, could only be achieved at the expense of

Protestant principles and, in Northern Ireland, that meant a dilution of Unionist principles as well. Inevitably, the logic of ecumenism pointed in the direction of Irish unity.

In the early 1960s, Paisley and his Free Presbyterians stepped up their protests against "compromising" Protestant religious leaders in response to this movement. The language of their protests became ever more vituperative. The Queen Mother was accused of condoning the murders of South American Protestants; Dr Craig, who had travelled to Rome, was "drunk with the wine of the Roman whore's fornication"; the WCC was so eager "to court the great whore" that at their New Delhi conference special privileges were to be given to "the black-coated agents of the Romish See"; Irish Presbyterians were "scarlet" partners in a Romish plot and Orange ministers had huge "yellow streaks" down their backs.

Every opportunity was seized to confront liberal Protestant clerics. Free Presbyterian pickets outside the annual meetings of the Presbyterian General Assembly grew in size, boisterousness and hostility and even the BBC began to take notice and feature Paisley protests in news programmes.

October 1960 saw Paisley and the then Presbyterian Moderator, Dr Austin Fulton trading public insults following a noisy Free Presbyterian protest during a lecture in Ballymoney by Dr George McCleod, a liberal former Scottish Moderator who had founded an inter-denominational community on the island of Iona.

Fulton, referring to Paisley, warned of the development of a "Fascist-type" movement in Northern Ireland led by "manipulators whose interest is power, and who are skilled in rousing passion and inculcating hatred in the name of religion". Paisley replied saying that there were three Fascist-type movements in Ulster and that Free Presbyterianism was not one of them; they were the Roman Catholic Church, the World Council of Churches and the IRA. He challenged Fulton to go to court to substantiate his allegations.

Paisley's was by no means a lone voice. To many ordinary Protestant churchgoers, reared on a diet of anti-Catholicism and anti-Nationalism, ecumenism was foreign and something to be viewed with deep suspicion.

This was reflected in Orangeism. In 1960, the Orange Order's Grand Lodge had set up a committee to investigate the implications of the Protestant churches remaining in the WCC. In the ministry of the Presbyterian Church as well, there were growing public signs of concern about this and the general spread of ecumenism.

In 1962, right-wing Presbyterians attempted to persuade the General Assembly to refer the issue of WCC membership to the more conservative, individual church Presbyteries, where it was likely to be strongly opposed, but the liberals won the day. Two years earlier, McCleod's visit had been opposed by many in the church and he was banned from speaking from pulpits in the Coleraine area. In 1964, sixty-nine Presbyterian ministers, three of whom became Moderators in the more conservative 1970s, issued a public statement expressing their concern at WCC membership.

Liberals still controlled the Presbyterian leadership, however, and the concerns of grass roots church members largely went unheeded. The ecumenical trend, like O'Neill's liberalism a few years later, was led by a small social elite who, to the fury of traditionalists, ignored the will of the grass roots. To Paisley and his supporters the "dictatorship" of Presbyterian liberalism was to be mirrored in the political world.

The inability of Protestant fundamentalists to reverse the liberal trend in their churches gave Paisley a perfect stick with which to beat those who believed in "fighting from within". His whole philosophy was separatist - "those within are easily shouted down, those without cannot be shouted down", became the recruiting slogan for Free Presbyterianism.

The louder he could shout, the more he earned a name among ordinary Protestants for forthright and unyielding opposition to the strange, unwelcome changes that were happening in their Churches and the quicker his own congregations grew. His appeal led him into bigger and more audacious protests.

One of John XXIII's first actions on becoming Pope was to summon a General Council of the Church's Bishops, called Vatican Two but popularly known as the Ecumenical Council, to review and modernise Catholic teaching. He hoped the Council would have relevance for Protestants and might accelerate ecumenical trends towards Christian unity. It was to be held in the Vatican in October 1962, and the WCC had accepted an invitation to send observers.

It was an ideal opportunity for Paisley to take his campaign right into the beast's lair. That August he was at the Amsterdam conference of the International Council of Christian Churches (ICCC), a deeply conservative amalgam of fundamentalists. There he met for the first time Bob Jones Junior, an American Southern Baptist who would become one of his closest friends and who shared his flair for gimmickry and marketing of religion.

Paisley was trying to join the ICCC at the time and, perhaps to impress them but also in the knowledge that he would reap enormous publicity for his cause, he announced on his return to Belfast that he and two other ministers, John Wylie and John Douglas, would be going to Rome to protest against the WCC's presence at the Vatican Council.

In the days before their departure, he orchestrated a series of publicity-grabbing stunts which kept his name in the headlines. Austin Fulton was picketed and interrupted in Coleraine during an address on the WCC. In a BBC interview Paisley called the Pope "the Roman Antichrist" and the Catholic Church "the harlot of Babylon"; the BBC was flooded with complaints and apologised. The next day he brought one hundred supporters to Broadcasting House and stuck posters on the walls calling the BBC "the voice of Popery". Then he announced that a group of Catholic priests had asked to meet him in Rome to discuss their leaving the Church - but they never materialised.

The three Free Presbyterians left for Rome on 8 October. Every twist and turn of their week-long trip was chronicled by the Belfast newspapers which received regular lengthy statements from Paisley. Even the Italian and British media, fascinated by this seventeenth century relic, showed interest.

They brought a home movie camera with them and produced a jerkily shot little film called "In the hands of the Pope's Gestapo" to show later to the faithful in halls around the country. The plot, reproduced in detail in *The Revivalist,* was full of Romish machinations and courageous Protestant defiance interspersed with examples of Catholic absurdities like the priest in one Rome church who granted confessions by tipping the heads of penitents "with a fishing rod".

According to *The Revivalist,* everywhere the three went in Rome, "eager hands" had stretched out to grasp their pamphlets but this was too much for the "Anti-Christ". First a Vatican official confronted them and tried to get them arrested, and then a policeman attempted to confiscate "the word of God", but they made their getaway distributing gospel tracts to nuns, priests and Bishops on the way to their *pensione*.

More harassment came on their second day. The police called at their hotel and they were taken, singing "I'm not ashamed to own my Lord", to the station. There "aggressive" *carabineri* refused them access to the British consul and threatened Douglas. Their passports were taken away and they were asked to sign a commitment that they would hold no more protests but "as Protestant ministers we absolutely refused to sign".

After three hours they were released but the Vatican was clearly alarmed at their presence for they were to be shadowed everywhere, even to the mouth of Vesuvius, by policemen. The Pope himself, claimed *The Revivalist*, was worried enough to order them barred from the Vatican. "Ever since we have been shadowed, police even sleeping in our hotel. All who visit us are requested to produce identity documents. Special doubling of the guard takes place when we approach the Vatican".

The Italian police denied all their allegations but that did not matter. Back in Belfast, where he called an Ulster Hall rally to recount the ordeal, they loved it and Paisley was a hero.

THE PROTESTANT ISCARIOTS

On the political front in those years there were also some signs of an easing of sectarian antagonisms. In 1962, for the first time ever, the Catholic Bishop of Down and Connor, Dr William Philbin, was a guest of the Unionist Lord Mayor of Belfast at the City Hall. During the same year the Orange Order had accepted an invitation from its Catholic counterpart, the Ancient Order of Hibernians, to start the so-called "Orange and Green" talks. The Nationalist leader, Eddie McAteer had addressed Young Unionists at Queens University, and after O'Neill's accession a party of Young Unionists had travelled to Dublin for talks with one of the branches of the main opposition party, Fine Gael.

So when on 3 June 1963, Pope John XXIII finally succumbed to cancer it was not surprising that Protestant leaders joined in the sympathy. The Presbyterian Moderator, whose General Assembly had just started when the news came through, paid tribute to him as did the Church of Ireland primate. The Governor of Northern Ireland, Lord Wakehurst, sent condolences to the Catholic Church and O'Neill, in his message to Cardinal Conway in Armagh said of the late Pontiff: "He had won widespread acclaim throughout the world because of his qualities of kindness and humanity".

The Lord Mayor of Belfast, William Jenkins, also sent a message to Bishop Philbin conveying his deepest sympathy "on the grievous loss of a good and saintly man who worked unceasingly for peace". The next day the Union Jack on the dome of the City Hall was lowered to half-mast, an unheard-of tribute from Unionism's capital city.

That night, outraged by all this, Paisley hurriedly called an Ulster Hall rally under the auspices of the old National Union of Protestants. For the best part of an hour he fulminated against "the Iscariots of Ulster" who had sent condolences to the Catholic church. "This Romish man of sin is now in hell", he roared to cries of "Hallelujah!" and "Amen" from the audience.

He then he led over 500 men, women and children on a two hundred yard march to the City Hall where an impromptu protest at the lowering of the Union Jack was held. It was an illegal march, for strictly speaking 48 hours notice should have been given but very few people imagined any action would be taken. After all, Paisley had staged impromptu marches and protests before and nothing had been done.

But then a week later something happened which seemed to indicate that the authorities were, at long last, ready to act against Paisley-style public rabble-rousing. In Smithfield, on the edge of Catholic West Belfast, a street preacher notorious for his bigotry was stopped by the police in the midst of haranguing the Unionists who had sent messages of sympathy to the Catholic Church - they, he said, were stooping "so low as to kiss the Pope's backside". When he resisted he was arrested and charged with disorderly behaviour. Nationalists welcomed the police action.

On 8 July Paisley and three others, including his Protestant Unionist colleague Councillor McCarroll, were summonsed for holding an illegal march (Paisley at first refused to accept his summons because it omitted his title of "Reverend"). In the meantime temperatures had been raised elsewhere by Wylie who went to the Catholic town of Dunloy in County Antrim to hold a religious service on the edges of a Gaelic football field where he proceeded to denounce Popery. The results were predictable - Wylie was attacked by a crowd wielding hurley sticks and they fractured his nose, destroyed his loudspeaker equipment and wrecked his car.

Paisley now had three parallel issues to exploit - his own impending prosecution, the police harassment of the Smithfield street preacher and "the Dunloy outrage". And they all pointed to the same thing - an accelerating betrayal of Protestant values by compromising Unionist and religious leaders. It would never have happened in Brookeborough or Craigavon's day.

The incidents had stirred up Loyalist militants. Boal raised the street preacher's arrest in Parliament, the letter columns of the Unionist dailies were full of letters denouncing the attack on Wylie, and there had been some public protests from Presbyterian ministers at their Moderator's show of sympathy with the Vatican. Paisley accelerated his protests. On 9 July he and 500 supporters staged another illegal march from his church to a city centre police station, demanding that others be prosecuted with him. Two weeks later, on the eve of the court case, he told a packed Ulster Hall that, once more, he would go to jail rather than pay a fine.

On the day of the hearing, 25 July, he marched several hundred supporters over from his church to the courthouse where so many tried to get in that the police had to close the doors of the building. Defending himself, Paisley accused the policeman who had arrested him, a Catholic, of bias, and tried to *subpoena* the Lord Mayor. He was fined £10 and given a week to pay or go to jail for two months; the other defendants were fined £5 or one month's jail.

The much hoped-for prison martyrdom loomed once more. He warned the large crowd outside the courthouse that anyone who paid the fine for him would be denounced as "a Lundy and a traitor" and he gave notice that the Lord Mayor would be challenged at the hustings over his treachery. From the courthouse he went to an Orange demonstration at Lisburn, attracting a crowd of 2,000. His prosecution, he told them, was part of the same Popish plot which had produced the World Council of Churches and the talks between Orangemen and Hibernians."The question was not Orange *and* Green but Orange *or* Green", he declared. Two years later the Orange-Green dialogue broke down when the Orange Order insisted that the Hibernians recognise Northern Ireland's constitution.

Paisley lodged an appeal against his conviction but abandoned it on 10 September. The next day someone paid his fine, denying him his prison wish for a second time, and he immediately accused the government. In a telegram to O'Neill he said: "Congratulations to you, the Minister of Home Affairs, the Crown solicitor, the police and the Unionist Lord Mayor on not permitting your law to take its course and on arranging for my fine to be paid. No Surrender!".

But he was wrong. Six years later an English businessman, Peter Courtney, then based in County Antrim, admitted that he was the anonymous donor. In a lengthy attack on Paisley written in September, 1969 he wrote: "You had filled me with your own hate which was destroying me too. Each time you were in the headlines I pondered coming over, buying a gun, and shooting you down at one of your meetings in the Ulster Hall."

A FORAY INTO DIVIS STREET

By the Autumn of 1964, O'Neill had been in office for eighteen months and while the glow which had greeted him was still warm, there was little concrete evidence to show that things were changing for Nationalists. The Irish Congress of Trade Unions, an all-Ireland body, had been given official recognition despite strong opposition from the likes of Faulkner, and a new economic strategy to attract modern industry had been adopted. There were plans for a new city to be called Craigavon, new motorways and a new University in Coleraine, but Catholic complaints went unanswered. O'Neill's technocratic modernisation was being implemented, but Northern Ireland's sectarian institutions went untouched.

In 1963 a Dungannon, County Tyrone Doctor and his wife, Con and Patricia McCloskey, decided that more direct action was needed. They organised Catholic women in Dungannon to protest outside the council offices against discrimination in housing allocation, and then they started to build up a dossier of other examples of Unionist bias in council employment, calling their project the Campaign for Social Justice. It was the start of what became the civil rights movement.

Interest in the Nationalist cause was also rising in Britain. A group of backbench Labour MPs formed themselves into the Campaign for Democracy in Ulster and called for an enquiry into Northern Ireland. The National Council of Civil Liberties was also pressing for a probe into the Special Powers Act which gave the Unionist government a free hand, without recourse to parliament, to flog, intern and to ban newspapers and meetings, among other powers.

In September 1964, the British Prime Minister, Sir Alec Douglas-Home, called a general election for the following month. His predecessor, Harold Macmillan, had been badly battered by a sex and espionage scandal involving his War Minister, John Profumo and there were signs that Britons were tired of thirteen years of uninterrupted Tory rule. The Labour Party, under Harold Wilson, looked set to win.

It was going to be a difficult election for the Unionists as well. Support for the Northern Ireland Labour Party (NILP) was growing and attracting Protestant votes. With only Republicans again standing in most Nationalist areas, and their vote unlikely to reach the heights of 1955, it was possible that enough Catholics and Protestants could desert their traditional camps to give Labour or other anti-Unionists a chance in some places.

Two seats were thought to be in danger: Mid-Ulster and the sectarian cockpit of West Belfast, where close contests were the norm. Harry Diamond of the Republican Labour Party was the favourite there. Opposing him for the Unionist Party was Jim Kilfedder, a barrister who had studied law with Boal at Trinity College, Dublin. Billy McMillen, later the Official IRA's Belfast commander, stood for the Republicans and Billy Boyd for the NILP. Unionists were worried that Billy Boyd could take enough Protestant votes to give the seat to Diamond.

The Unionists had good reasons not to want any anti-Unionists at Westminster. At the beginning of the campaign Harold Wilson had written to the NILP candidates promising "new economic vigour and social justice" in Northern Ireland if the Tories were defeated. He followed that up with a letter to the McCloskeys, which they published, promising that a Labour Government would outlaw religious discrimination and legislate against biased housing allocation.

Wilson's pledges cut right across the Government of Ireland Act which had reserved certain powers to Stormont and the Unionists, alarmed by this, moved to solidify their support. O'Neill made the "Republican anarchists" the main issue while Faulkner, speaking on Kilfedder's platform, said a vote for Boyd was a wasted vote: West Belfast was a straight fight between Unionism and Republicanism. They were tactics

Brookeborough would have been proud of.

To press home the message, the Unionist newspapers, quoting official sources, carried stories saying that the IRA was using the election to recruit members in preparation for a new campaign and were raising money for it in the United States. In part this was true. The Republicans *were* recruiting - one of the 1964 intake was a 16-year-old called Gerry Adams - but under the influence of a Marxist called Roy Johnston they were moving towards left-wing political agitation and away from military conspiracies.

1964 had up to then been a busy year for Ian Paisley. Two new churches had been built, his wife Eileen had stood unsuccessfully in the Corporation elections against the Lord Mayor on the issue of her husband's prosecution - Paisley was still unwilling to incur disapproval in the church by standing himself - and he announced plans for a "Protestant" weekly paper.

But in late September, just as the campaign intensified, Paisley abandoned his pledge given to the UPA leaders two years earlier and re-entered the worldly arena of politics in order to ensure a Unionist victory in West Belfast.

The issue which excited him and other Loyalists was, as it had been in 1954 and 1959, about a flag. At the start of the election campaign, the Republicans established their election headquarters in an abandoned shop at the bottom of Divis Street, where Catholic West Belfast meets the city centre. In the window they displayed a Starry Plough, the flag of James Connolly's Citizens' Army, and a small Irish Tricolour. The latter's display, though not illegal, could be banned under the Flags and Emblems Act. That gave the police power to remove a Tricolour if its display might cause a breach of the peace; in practice this meant if there were complaints from Unionists.

The flag, half-concealed behind a grimy window front, had been on show for some time but the local police, judging that discretion was the better part of valour, had decided to do nothing about it. By Sunday, 27 September, however, Paisley had heard about it and at an Ulster Hall rally he threatened to march his supporters to Divis Street to remove it if the authorities didn't act. It was a repeat of the threats made by the Independent Unionists in 1954 and by himself in 1959.

The previous day the *Belfast Telegraph,* quoting RUC sources, had reported that "anonymous telephone complaints" had been received about the flag and the next morning, Sunday, a conference was held in the RUC City Commissioner's office to decide what to do. There had also been threats that armed "B" Specials would take their own action and the Ministry of Home Affairs was consulted. Paisley's threat, later that day, to cause mayhem in West Belfast settled the matter. The police would act.

The question of how Paisley was alerted to the Tricolour has never been satisfactorily settled. At the time he said that he had heard about it from local Protestants and had complained personally to the RUC City Commissioner as early as the Friday before his Ulster Hall threat. Seven years later, during his testimony to the Scarman Tribunal of enquiry into the riots of 1969, he said the *Belfast Telegraph* had written about the flag "before I ever mentioned it". Senior RUC officers then based in West Belfast, when interviewed by the authors, agreed that the controversy only broke after the *Belfast Telegraph* article appeared. Their suspicion is that the Unionist Party manufactured the crisis for its own benefit.

Whatever the truth, the effect of Paisley's threat was instant. On Monday 28 September the RUC removed the Tricolour peacefully. Paisley called off his march and held a rally outside the City Hall instead. But Catholics gathered in Divis Street expecting him and there were clashes with the police.

There was more rioting the next night and buses were burned. By Thursday 1 October, the Tricolour was back in the Republican HQ window and this time the RUC, led by a Catholic Head Constable, Frank Lagan, smashed the window with pickaxes to remove it. More rioting broke out and the police brought in water cannons; petrol bombs were thrown by the rioters and the IRA sent out some of its men with handguns.

The riots, the worst Belfast had seen since the 1930s, had reverberations elsewhere. In Enniskillen, the RUC used their batons at a Republican election meeting when the Tricolour was flown; in Coleraine there were clashes between rival crowds when a policeman tried to remove a Tricolour, and in Dungannon a crowd of Loyalists disrupted a Republican rally with shouts of "We want Paisley".

The effect of it all was to solidify Unionist support in West Belfast and Kilfedder, who had joined in the demands for the flag's removal, easily won, pushing Billy Boyd into third place. During the campaign he had courted Paisley's support and at one rally in the lower Shankill, Paisley was pulled from the crowd to speak from his platform. On the night of the count Kilfedder publicly thanked Paisley for his victory - "without whom it would not have been possible" - and, as his jubilant supporters carried him off for a victory parade, they chanted "We want Paisley".

As the dust settled O'Neill, the liberal *Belfast Telegraph* and the Presbyterian Moderator combined to rebuke Paisley's "brainless" intervention but there was little doubt in NILP and Nationalist minds that he had done the Unionist Party a great service. The affair, though, had also enhanced his outspoken reputation among rank and file Loyalists. As one Nationalist Senator pointed out during a Stormont debate on the riots: "The Unionists thought that they had used the Reverend Ian Paisley but Mr Paisley in turn was convinced that he had trounced the Unionists".

For Paisley himself, the cheek of the Republicans in flying the Tricolour was a sign of much more trouble on the way. The real nature of Romanism had been revealed, he told a packed Ulster Hall, and the people who had kicked policemen in Divis Street would kick Protestants tomorrow. "Protestantism has faced many serious crises in its history. We are facing a crisis now and the province is heading for even greater crises". Thanks in no small part to himself, that was to be a prophetic statement.

A LUNDY IN STORMONT

The first of those "crises" began just after one o'clock on a cold January afternoon in 1965, four months after the Divis Street riots. A car carrying the Taoiseach of the Irish Republic, Sean Lemass, drew up to the entrance of Stormont House and Captain Terence O'Neill walked out to greet his visitor with four words: "Welcome to the North".

The historic act of inviting the Republic's Prime Minister for talks about economic co-operation was a calculated gamble by O'Neill. None of his predecessors had dared do it for fear of angering extremists and O'Neill admitted the dangers by keeping the visit a closely guarded secret from the Unionist party and the Orange Order. His Cabinet Ministers were not consulted. Only one, William Craig, was informed of the visit and then only the night before. A small group of civil servants - Cecil Bateman, the Cabinet Secretary; his assistant, a rising young technocrat called

Ken Bloomfield and O'Neill's private secretary, Jim Malley - had organised the whole thing out of sight of O'Neill's colleagues.

Despite the political risks, there were good reasons why, in 1965, the two Prime Ministers should meet. For both the North and the South, there could be considerable savings from increased trade between them and other forms of economic co-operation. Both had growing numbers of jobless and both were trying to attract foreign investment; the economies of scale made co-operation sensible.

But O'Neill had breached an important tenet of Unionist faith, one which every Prime Minister from Craigavon onwards had accepted: there could be no contact between Dublin and Belfast until the Republic recognised Northern Ireland's constitutional position within the United Kingdom. Nothing less than the Republic dropping its constitutional claim to the North would satisfy traditional Unionists.

Calls from Dublin for talks with the Belfast government had started as soon as Lemass took over from de Valera but each time, in 1959, 1961, 1962 and 1963, he got the same response from Brookeborough: "If he accepts Northern Ireland's constitution then I am quite prepared to meet him". Each time Lemass' reply was the same: the aspiration to Irish unity was inviolable. Unionist suspicions about the Republic's motives, furthermore, had been hardened by de Valera, who in 1957 had said that the best way to end partition was "to have as close relations as they could with those in the six counties and try to get them to combine on matters and interests common to them both".

O'Neill also had a few of his own hostages to fortune. A few days before he replaced Brookeborough he had publicly supported a Unionist backbench motion at Stormont which ruled out cross-Border contact until the Republic formally accepted the North's British link. A month later, as Premier, O'Neill declared: "I very much regret that the Government of the Republic has never seen its way to recognise the constitutional position of Northern Ireland. This attitude must continue to be regarded as an obstacle to meetings between the Heads of the two governments". On the "Twelfth" in 1964 he told Orangemen the same thing. Those statements would hang like an albatross around his neck for years to come.

Lemass made some efforts to overcome these obstacles but

without success. In July 1963, in a speech at Tralee in County Kerry, he came close to accepting the existence of Northern Ireland but followed that up with a diplomatic offensive against partition in Britain and the USA. Each time O'Neill counter-attacked. When the two men met on 14 January 1965 it came like a bolt out of the blue to most Unionists.

Paisley was the quickest to react. The following afternoon he and his two Protestant Unionist councillors, McCarroll and Duff, drove to the Stormont estate in a car trailing a huge Ulster flag. They staged a quick protest for the benefit of television cameras, showing placards which read: "No Mass, no Lemass", "Down with the Lundys" and "IRA murderer welcomed at Stormont".

Then they went into the lobby of Stormont Castle to deliver a protest letter to O'Neill. A civil servant accepted it on his behalf. The letter homed in on O'Neill's tactical errors: "By breaking your word and by acting without consulting the elected representatives of the Protestants of our country, you have adopted the tactics of a dictator and forfeited your right to be Prime Minister. We challenge you to go to the country on this issue. Surely the people have a right to a say in this grave departure from the stand of your predecessors in office".

Reaction elsewhere in Unionism was more muted. Only one Cabinet member, the right-wing Harry West, the Minister of Agriculture from the backwoods of Fermanagh, had protested by staying away from a tea and biscuits session with Lemass. On the backbenches only two MPs - Boal and the former Attorney-General, Edmund Warnock - had complained, the former with his usual dazzling rhetoric, about O'Neill's secrecy and his broken pledges.

Elsewhere, O'Neill's assurances that politics had not entered his talks, and that Lemass had, by coming to Belfast, given de facto recognition to Northern Ireland, appeared to have been accepted. The media on both sides of the Border had welcomed the new era of cordiality which was dawning. RUC chiefs, hopeful of better relations with Nationalists, had privately welcomed the meeting and even Brookeborough issued a supportive statement, albeit cautiously and carefully worded.

The Orange Order's Grand Master, Sir George Clark, had also praised the meeting, stressing the potential economic benefits, and saying that he was sure that the general feeling among Orangemen was that it would be regarded as a "non-political" issue.

Paisley knew otherwise. There was a gulf between the middle class leadership of the Order and its rural and urban rank and file. The leadership may have become more moderate over the years, but at grass roots level, the bulk of Orangemen were still deeply conservative and hostile to Catholicism. Many of them instinctively saw the O'Neill-Lemass meeting not only as "political", but as potentially dangerous to the Union as they saw it - a mechanism maintained only by perpetual domination of Catholics. Their resentment at the actions of their distant leadership could be easily roused, and Paisley was quick to realise that the ordinary Orangeman could be a ready convert to his cause.

Within a week of the meeting, he announced that signatures of Orangemen were being sought for a petition against O'Neill. At an enthusiastic Ulster Hall rally in front of 1,000 foot-stamping supporters, he once more denounced "the O'Neill-Lemass conspiracy" and announced that "Protestant" candidates would stand against every O'Neill supporter at the next election: "He is a bridge builder he tells us. A traitor and a bridge are very much alike for they both go over to the other side".

His increasingly useful aide, Noel Doherty, organised an "Orange Defence Committee" to garner Orange discontent - Paisley couldn't be a member as he had severed his links with the Orange Order three years before. Doherty distributed leaflets at Orange meetings pointing out that O'Neill had not consulted the Orange Order before meeting Lemass. "Are you going to sit by and allow this insult to be hurled at you?", the leaflet asked.

In February, when O'Neill paid a return visit to Lemass in Dublin, Doherty and McCarroll accused Sir George Clark of "treachery" to Orangeism and threatened to bring a complaint against both him and O'Neill to the Grand Lodge. When the Grand Lodge countered with a move to expel them, they accused the Unionist party of "manipulating the Grand Lodge in order to stifle the voice of Protestantism". The same sort of accusation had been made by the Independent Unionists a decade earlier.

Later that month O'Neill encountered the first of what were to be regular Paisleyite pickets, organised by John Wylie and some Free Presbyterians in Coleraine. Then on 25 February he

The Paisley family in the early 1940s. From left: Father, Kyle; Ian; brother, Harold; mother Isabella and sister, Margaret

At the opening of the Cabra church, 1952

Maura Lyons (*Belfast Telegraph*)

An early rival: Norman Porter
(*Belfast Telegraph*)

A Christmas pageant at the Ravenhill mission, 1953

Ian and Eileen on their wedding day, October 1956 (*Belfast Telegraph*)

The aftermath of Pope John 23rd's death: Paisley and John Wylie appear at Belfast magistrates' court on illegal assembly charges, July 1963 (*Stanley Matchett*)

Terence O'Neill and Sean Lemass on the steps of Stormont, January 1965 (*Pacemaker*)

The hero of the hour: Jim Kilfedder's West Belfast election victory in October 1964 brings congratulations from Loyalists (*Irish Times*)

Opening a Shankill Road Orange arch, 1966 (*Belfast Telegraph*)

With William McCrea and Billy Beattie on a Free Presbyterian picket, 1966 (*Belfast Telegraph*)

Leaving Crumlin Road Jail, October 1966 (*Irish Times*)

Leading a UCDC march through Ahoghill, Terence O'Neill's home village (*Irish Times*)

A Stormont protest against Jack Lynch's talks with O'Neill, 1967 (*Irish Times*)

narrowly escaped being besieged in the Unionist party headquarters in Belfast where he was a guest speaker. Only some alert police work saved him from being mauled by a mob of 2,000 marched over by Paisley behind Orange bands from Sandy Row, the Shankill and East Belfast.

Paisley told the crowd that O'Neill, aided by the *Belfast Telegraph,* had declared war on Loyalists. "They may control the police force, they may control the judiciary, they may control the powers that be, but we are determined to remain free. They can spill as much printers' ink as they like but we are prepared, if necessary, to spill our blood". As the crowd dispersed someone shouted: "Up the Falls and burn them out".

But O'Neill looked as if he was going to survive. The Grand Lodge gave him a vote of confidence as did the Ulster Unionist Council. Only two other MPs, Kilfedder and Sir Knox Cunningham who also sat at Westminster, had joined the ranks of the critics. In October, a Stormont general election saw no sign of the threatened "Protestant" candidates. Encouraged by a good result, O'Neill began to make overtures to Catholics, visiting their schools, drinking tea with nuns and priests and even entertaining Cardinal Conway.

It seemed as though O'Neill was going to get his own way, unchallenged within his own party. To unrepentant and now thoroughly alarmed Loyalists, it seemed, as 1965 turned into 1966, that the only voice of effective protest was coming from Ian Paisley.

After the Lemass-O'Neill meeting, Paisley, in a call for Protestant resistance, neatly summarised his political philosophy in an article in *The Revivalist:* "It is quite evident", he wrote, "that the Ecumenists, both political and ecclesiastical, are selling us. Every Ulster Protestant must unflinchingly resist these leaders and let it be known in no uncertain manner that they will not sit idly by as these modern Lundies pursue their policy of treachery. Ulster expects every Protestant in this hour of crisis to do his duty".

In 1966, the fiftieth anniversary of the Easter Rising in Dublin and of the slaughter of Carson's Ulster Volunteer Force on the battlefield of the Somme, some Loyalists were to answer that clarion call to action with devastating results for Northern Ireland.

It was, however, God's work which preoccupied Ian Paisley in the first weeks of 1966. In January it was announced that a Catholic priest would, for the first time, preach a sermon at Westminster Abbey, and Paisley, announcing plans for a protest in London, telegrammed the Queen to demand that the sermon be cancelled. On 21 January, accompanied by 30 of his ministers and lay church members and a delegation from the British section of the ICCC led by Pastor Jack Glass from Scotland and the Rev Brian Green from London, Paisley picketed Westminster Abbey. He attracted only bewildered stares from Londoners, the brief attention of a policeman but valuable headlines back home.

Back in Belfast, however, things were happening which were to show that he was nursing political ambitions as well. The O'Neill-Lemass meeting, O'Neill's overtures to Catholics and a growing pressure to admit Catholics to the Unionist party were combining to unsettle more and more Loyalists. Some were ready to move into more militant forms of political opposition. In the next three months, Paisley was to create vehicles which would both give them that opportunity and promote his own cause.

Their inspiration was the faithful printer, Noel Doherty who had followed Paisley from the inception of Ulster Protestant Action. Born and bred on the lower Newtownards Road in East Belfast, under the shadow of the shipyard cranes, Doherty's printing skills had already helped make *The Revivalist* a more professional product. In early 1966 he formed an idea which would allow Paisley to harness the political discontent that was all around him.

It was the coming Republican celebrations of the fiftieth anniversary of the 1916 Dublin Easter Rising that sparked Doherty's imagination. The air was already thick with stories of thousands of Southerners planning to pour across the Border to mark the anniversary and there was talk also that the IRA would use the event as a springboard for another campaign. Yet in Belfast, O'Neill's government was full of compromise and weakness; once more, as so often in Ulster Protestantism's history, Loyalists would have to look to themselves.

The result was the Ulster Constitution Defence Committee (UCDC), an idea which Paisley, seeing its potential, immediately endorsed. It was soon to be invested, at least in the eyes of its members, with Biblical meaning. At the head of the committee, Christ-like, was Paisley as chairman and underneath him were twelve committee members - "apostles" - called together by him, pledged as a body of "Protestant patriots" to defend the union, the Protestant monarchy and the Williamite Settlement. Its first meeting continued the Biblical parallels. Like the Last Supper it was held in a room above a restaurant. O'Neill was the "Judas" and Paisley would soon become the martyred saviour.

Doherty's idea caught on, and there was so much interest shown by Loyalists that the UCDC was snowed under with applications for membership. Paisley had the idea of forming the putative recruits into divisions of Ulster Protestant Volunteers (UPV), a name he thought up himself, as he later explained to the Scarman tribunal: "it had an historic connection with the formation of the state, with Carson's Ulster Volunteer Force and we were Protestants and Ulstermen". To underline the continuity the UPV adopted the old UVF's motto, "For God and Ulster".

Assisted by a Free Presbyterian Sunday school teacher called Billy Mitchell, who was later to gain notoriety as a modern UVF gunman, Doherty was made UCDC Secretary and given the task of touring Northern Ireland helping Loyalists to form UPV branches. His new responsibilities brought him into contact with people whose opposition to O'Neill did not stop at politics.

The UPV, who were at all times subservient to the UCDC, were organised in branches and divisions within counties, as was the Orange Order and other Loyalist institutions. Membership was open only to born Protestants - Catholics and RUC members were disqualified. Paisley always distrusted the police because they accepted Catholic recruits but members of the exclusively Protestant and often extremist "B" Specials were welcomed into the UPV. The UCDC was empowered by its constitution and rules to take "whatever steps it thinks fit" to expose unconstitutional acts by the government but there was a safeguard against accusations of lawlessness.

Rule 15 stated: "Any member associated with, or giving support to, any subversive or lawless activities whatsoever shall be expelled from the body". Paisley was given full authority to act in such cases. It would prove to be an extremely useful rule.

During the next few years the UPV acted primarily as a magnet for Orangemen and Unionist party members disillusioned with their leaderships - just as the Free Presbyterian Church attracted religious malcontents. Increasingly the UPV modelled themselves on the Orange Order. Some branches had chaplains and like Orange Lodges began their meetings with prayers or a reading from the Bible. A sash, white with red and blue fringes, was worn and UPV marchers lined up three abreast led by "Kick the Pope" bands. In later years the UPV proved to be invaluable in the development of Paisley's career. With 17 divisions throughout the North, and hundreds of members, it provided Paisley with a vote-collecting machine which he was able to transform into the Democratic Unionist Party.

"It was almost like a new Orange Order or Apprentice Boys", recalled an original member, "a body of like-minded people who felt that Ian Paisley was articulating on behalf of the Ulster people and for whom the Orange Order was too pro-establishment. It filled a gap".

Doherty also filled another gap, a communications gap. Aside from *The Revivalist,* which primarily serviced the Free Presbyterian Church, Paisley had no outlet for his political message. The local media were hostile to him and he had long lambasted them as his enemies. The BBC was "infested with Papists" and the *News Letter* was "cowardly"; but he reserved his strongest language for the "lying and treacherous" *Belfast Telegraph,* which under the ownership of the Thompson organisation and the editorship of Jack Sayers had enthusiastically supported O'Neill's liberal policies. In 1966 the *Telegraph* refused to carry adverts for Paisley's political or religious events and later when it sponsored a campaign to back O'Neill, Paisley began a Protestant boycott of the North's most popular daily.

Journalists too were his enemies. They were "the whirring multitudes of pestiferous scribbling rodents commonly known as Press reporters, newsmen and journalists . . . They usually sport thick-lensed glasses, wear six pairs of ropey sandals, are homosexuals, kiss holy medals or carry secret membership cards of the Communist Party. Most of them are communistoids without the guts of a red-blooded Communist, or Roman Catholics without the effrontery of a Pope Pius XII. Sometimes these anonymous editorial writers are a mixture of the two.

Spineless, brainless mongoloids. But, because of it, as maliciously perilous as vipers."

As he prospered later in political life Paisley soon learned that it was wiser to woo and charm the "pestiferous scribbling rodents" - something he now does with great aplomb - than to alienate them. His supporters however, as any Northern Ireland newsman can testify, still display the violent hostility to the media that they imbibed with Paisley's rhetoric.

Doherty's scheme, which he had been planning since 1964, was to start a "Protestant" publishing company to produce a regular paper, leaflets and pamphlets so as to by-pass the hostile media and get Paisley's thoughts directly to the Loyalist masses. Paisley was keen on the plan and not just because of its political potential - the more pious members of his church had been complaining for some time that there was too much politics in *The Revivalist*.

In 1965 Doherty acquired a large second hand typesetter and flat bed press and set up shop in a basement on the Ravenhill Road opposite Paisley's church, forming a company, "The Puritan Printing Company" with himself and Paisley as directors. In April 1966 the first issue of the *Protestant Telegraph,* with the slogan "The Truth shall set you Free" beneath its masthead, hit the streets of Belfast.

Its twelve broadsheet pages, at first produced fortnightly and then weekly, provided its Loyalist readership with a regular and often bizarre diet of anti-Catholicism - sometimes heavily laced with sexual innuendo. It became an outlet for bigotry, insecurity, ignorance, frustration and latent violence.

Typical of the paper's contents was the serialization of the works of Joseph Hocking, an American writer who specialised in lurid tales of Vatican plots - one epic, called "The Jesuit", told the story of a Protestant politician who rescues a young heiress from the clutches of priests just as they are about to steal her millions.

There were also articles on the "Hidden wealth of the Roman Catholic Church" and the scheming Pope Joan, "the female Pope who sat on the Throne of Peter". "The Love affairs of the Vatican", disappointingly short in detail, won a whole page in the paper to satisfy some inexpressible sexual yearning on the part of its readers. Homosexuality occasionally featured, like the story of two Dutch men who were married in a Catholic church. "Only in the Harlot Church of Rome would such a ceremony be conceived", thundered the paper.

Another series of articles dealt with one priest who had "destroyed or scandalised at least 1,000 married and unmarried females". Nuns, those female celibates whose mysterious convent life had excited Paisley's audiences in the days of the National Union of Protestants, featured too. "Any resident of or visitor to Belfast or Dublin may have noticed of late a rise in the number of nuns parading the streets. Their habit or costume is not the typical nun's garb. These modern nuns are novices, or in lay terms, apprentice nuns. One cannot help but admire their physical beauty, but their furtive smiles and glances show that they are not completely instituted nuns. It would appear that the statement made by some local wit is true: 'The older nuns are raving, while the younger ones are craving'."

The paper dwelt at length on Catholic plots like the formation of the ubiquitous "Catholic Action" in the RUC, in reality a harmless guild of Catholic policemen: "The cassock directs the constabulary", screamed the headline. "It could happen in Ulster!", warned one advertisement. "If the RC bigots have their way. The supression of civil liberties . . . the arrest of Protestant clergymen . . . the closing down and burning of Protestant churches . . . Roman Catholic padres as commanders of Protestant churches . . . long term imprisonment without trial . . . the execution of Protestant individuals and groups and more horrors! Impossible . . . Incredible . . . Unbelievable? Then my answer to the Roman Catholic extremists is . . . read *Catholic Terror Today* by Avro Manhattan. These things happened - not long ago - in a country with the same religious and political problems as Ulster. It is the most sensational, the most dramatic, the most revealing book ever!"

Together with these titillations, Paisley used the *Protestant Telegraph* to transmit his world view of the state of Northern Protestantism and Unionism to an audience far wider than the Ulster Hall or his rural gospel missions could ever reach.

One early *Protestant Telegraph* reprinted in full a sermon Paisley had given to mark the fiftieth anniversary in 1964 of the UVF gun-running expedition to Larne, County Antrim when Carson's volunteers were supplied with thousands of German rifles to resist Home Rule and if necessary the British parliament. It neatly encapsulated his philosophy and his view of himself.

His text was Daniel, Chapter 3, verse 18: "Be it known unto

thee, O King, that we will not serve thy gods" - or as Paisley translated it: "in the language of Ulster that means simply, 'No Surrender!'" The context was Biblical Babylon, a country subverted by an all-pervasive idolatry. Only three men could be found to resist it and there were, Paisley implied, parallels in Ulster in the growth of ecumenism and liberal Unionism - "surely this is the type of men which Ulster needs today, men who will really stand in this evil day", he thundered.

The modern Babylon, of course, was Roman Catholicism which all down the centuries had been the implacable foe of Ulster's Protestants. Quoting from Popes, priests and historians he gave examples. The massacre of Protestants in 1641 "when Rome sought to exterminate the Protestant planters of this Province"; the Williamite Revolution in 1690, when Protestantism successfully fought back and the 1798 rebellion, a clever plot by Rome because gullible Protestants were inveigled to join it.

The threat had returned in 1914, when a British government blackmailed by 80 Irish Nationalist MPs promised to give Ireland Home Rule but Carson and his UVF gunrunners, roared Paisley, knew who the real enemy was - Home Rule was Rome Rule. The proof was there, Paisley cried, pointing to an illuminated address fixed to the ceiling of the Ulster Hall which read: "Ulster would not only arm but if need be fight to the death against being robbed of her religious and civil liberties".

There were striking similarities between those early Unionist heroes and Paisley's campaigns against ecumenism and O'Neillism, the sermon implied. Like Paisley now, Colonel Crawford who had organised the gun-running faced danger, imprisonment, and the fatal weakness and cowardice of others. Paisley claimed that Crawford had recognised himself in the Free Presbyterian Moderator - he gave him a "treasured" copy of his account of the gun-running expedition.

The Orange Order and many in the Unionist party had opposed Crawford's plan out of fear, just as now they were too frigtened to resist O'Neill. But Crawford was inspired by God and Carson. God had actually whispered encouragement in Crawford's ear, just as he had told Paisley to work for a great revival in Ulster in 1949. Crawford had ignored the peril of prison and defied a British Government to save Ulster, as Paisley would do again. What Ulster needed now, Paisley shouted, was "a revival of the spirit of Carson" and the defiance of the three Babylonians who resisted the spread of idolatry. Paisley was clearly the man to provide it.

In one sermon Paisley linked his own campaign firmly into the traditional mainstream of Unionism and himself, inspired by God, risking imprisonment and surrounded by compromise, equally firmly into the tradition of Crawford and Carson. He was beginning to capture Unionism's talismen and, as he stepped up his campaign against O'Neill, his invocation of Unionism's past heroes would be a powerful weapon in his armoury.

A BRIDGE TOO FAR

His next battle against O'Neill over, of all things, a bridge, gave Paisley his first opportunity to demonstrate his continuity with Unionism's heroic and defiant past.

In mid-February 1966, Belfast Corporation met to decide the name of a new bridge across the River Lagan. The previous year the new city in County Armagh promised by O'Neill had been christened Craigavon in honour of Northern Ireland's first Prime Minister. The Unionists of Belfast now thought it appropriate to honour Carson, the other founder of the State, by naming the bridge after him.

The choice of Craigavon, coming after that of Protestant Coleraine instead of Catholic Derry as the site of the new University, had irritated Nationalists. This time the new Governor, Lord Erskine, anxious not to cause more annoyance, stepped into the bridge issue. Since Queen Elizabeth II was due to visit Northern Ireland in July he suggested naming it after her and she could open it. The Unionists on the Corporation reluctantly agreed.

Hard-line Unionists, however, were angry at this interference by Erskine, an ally of O'Neill's - Carson ranked much higher in the Loyalist pantheon than did the British monarch. Paisley's councillors together with Brookeborough, Kilfedder and Cunningham all objected. Then Carson's son, the Honourable Edward Carson, a rather dim former Tory MP turned law student, wrote to the Belfast papers objecting to this "slight" on his father's name.

It was Eileen Paisley who, on reading Carson's letter, had the idea of inviting him over to join her husband's protest rallies.

Paisley contacted Carson and he immediately agreed. Carson remembers them meeting in a pub in Ascot near his home to talk about the arrangements.

He duly arrived on 28 February and that night at a Paisley-organised rally in the Ulster Hall he called for Erskine's resignation and threatened "trouble" if the Corporation didn't reconsider its decision. Exultant at his new prize, living proof of the historic continuity and righteousness of his cause, Paisley challenged O'Neill to repudiate Ulster's hero: "Let the Prime Minister speak. Let him tell Ulster if he is for Carson or against Carson."

Paisley paraded Carson around in the following days. On 1 March, he and Carson reviewed the first rally of the Ulster Protestant Volunteers in Lisburn and Carson said that there was a "rot" in Unionism which began when O'Neill became Prime Minister.

That same day Harold Wilson called a general election in the hope of bolstering a slim Westminster majority and Paisley seized this opportunity. Four "Protestant" candidates would stand in the Belfast seats opposing O'Neillism, he announced, and one of them would be Carson's son.

The announcement was the signal for a bitter, back room struggle between Paisley and O'Neill. The public was told that Carson would probably stand in North Belfast, but in reality Paisley was trying to force the Unionist party to nominate him in West Belfast instead of Kilfedder.

Two emissaries, one of them a Baptist preacher friend of Paisley called Willie Mullan, met the Unionist party secretary, Jim Baillie, in an attempt to get agreement. Paisley meanwhile had learned that while at Trinity College Dublin, Kilfedder had attended meetings of the University's branch of the Fine Gael party. If Kilfedder didn't stand down, he threatened, the Shankill voters would be told of this Republican treachery.

But O'Neill outmanoeuvred Paisley. According to Carson, the Prime Minister had managed to lay his hands on a letter written by Carson some years before in which he had made a remark about widespread gerrymandering in Northern Ireland. The circulation of this letter would cause Carson and Paisley untold embarrassment and it led to Carson's last-minute withdrawal.

O'Neill and Paisley carried on their squabble for the allegiance of Carson during the rest of the year and O'Neill finally won.

When Carson's mother died some months later it was O'Neill who stood beside the grieving son at the funeral, not Paisley. Carson now says he bitterly regrets his brief liaison with Paisley: "I think you could accuse me of having preached a gospel of dissension instead of a gospel of reconciliation. That must have been the wrong thing to do and therefore I'm culpable".

Paisley carried through his threat against Kilfedder. During the campaign leaflets appeared on the Shankill naming him as a Fine Gael sympathiser. The NILP was responsible for circulating some but others came from Loyalist sources and Paisley was held responsible. Kilfedder lost the election by 2,000 votes to Gerry Fitt of the Republican Labour party who also represented Dock in the Stormont Parliament. Fitt was to use Westminster to gain considerable sympathy for Nationalists and, until he turned against Nationalism in the 1980s and was made a life peer, he was detested by Loyalists.

Thanks to a fall in the number of Protestant voters in West Belfast, Fitt would probably have won despite Paisley's assistance. But Shankill Loyalists, some of them former allies, believed Paisley had lost Kilfedder vital votes and they never forgave him. Their bitterness towards him would later that year provide Paisley with a perfect alibi.

However, by the next month, April, it was Paisley who had O'Neill on the retreat. The celebrations for the fiftieth anniversary of the Easter Rising had caused something near hysteria among Unionists. O'Neill and his Home Affairs Minister, Brian McConnell warned that the IRA could use them to foment trouble or even to re-start a military campaign. So 10,500 "B" Specials were mobilised for the Easter weekend, British army helicopters were sent to the Border and a special hot line was set up between the RUC and the Gardai in preparation for the dozens of parades and demonstrations to be held in Nationalist areas.

The largest Republican parade was to be held in Belfast the Sunday after the Easter weekend, on 17 April, when contingents from the Republic would join Northerners in a march from near the city centre to Andersonstown. Condemning the government for not banning it, Paisley announced a UCDC protest march to the Ulster Hall to take place at the same time and along a route which would pass the Republican assembly point.

Both parades were illegal, as the RUC had not been notified of them. Faced with the real possibility of ugly clashes, O'Neill's Cabinet had to choose which one to confront. Dealing with Paisley's parade would risk antagonising a wide band of Unionism and not just militants, for the Easter celebrations had alarmed even moderates. O'Neill chose to deal with the Republicans.

A special Cabinet meeting toyed with banning their march but that idea was dropped and instead stringent security measures aimed at curbing the Republicans were announced. All train services from Dublin on the day of the march were cancelled and extra police, armed with machine guns and given authority under the Special Powers Act to stop and question all traffic, were sent to the Border. It was the first example of Paisley's counter-march tactic, a tactic refined to an art two years later. It had its first outing that weekend and exposed, to the fury of Nationalists, the government's weakness in the face of extremist threats.

Six weeks later Paisley announced another march, this time to the Presbyterian General Assembly on 6 June to protest at the Church's "Romanising tendencies". This one would pass right by the Catholic Markets area near the city centre but the Home Affairs Minister, McConnell, who had recently shared an Orange platform with Paisley, did nothing to stop it - even though no Loyalist march had been allowed near the area since 1935 when Orangemen and Catholics had fought a fierce hand to hand battle there.

The consequences were utterly predictable, as Paisley and the authorities must have guessed. His parade, several hundred supporters with placards attacking the Catholic Church and singing "Onward Christian soldiers", marched from his Ravenhill church across the Albert Bridge to find 200 Markets' Catholics blocking the road at Cromac Square. The police moved in to force them off the road and a hail of bricks and broken guttering showered on to the Paisleyites; one youth, armed with an iron bar got within a few feet of Paisley before he was pinned to the ground.

After a few violent minutes, the Paisley parade was past Cromac Square and into the city centre but the fighting between Markets' Catholics and the police continued for several hours. There were repeated baton charges and an armoured car was brought in. By midnight eight people had been arrested and four policemen hospitalised. One of those arrested, and radicalised by the riot, was a 17-year-old seaman called Sean Flynn. Within a decade he was a leader of the Official IRA and when its more violent splinter, the Irish National Liberation Army was formed, he became a Belfast councillor representing its political wing. Paisley's protests recruited militants not just to Loyalism.

Unionists were less upset at the battle of Cromac Square - O'Neill firmly blamed the IRA for organising it and Faulkner laid the blame on a Catholic mob "lying in wait" - than they were at the scenes in Howard Street, outside the Presbyterian Assembly, which followed it. From Cromac Square, Paisley led his parade three times around the City Hall apparently waiting for Presbyterian dignitaries and their guests, including the Governor Lord Erskine and his wife, to file across Howard Street from the Assembly buildings for a reception in the Presbyterian hostel.

As they emerged from a side door a sea of angry faces and waving fists greeted them. The police hastily called in reinforcements to push the crowd back and with ropes they blocked off the road to make a passageway for them. As they walked across, insults, jeers and shouts of "Popehead", "Romanist" and "Lundy" were hurled. The new Moderator, Alfie Martin, a liberal cleric, was a favourite target but the crowd reserved its strongest abuse for Erskine because of his role in the Carson bridge affair. Lady Erskine was so upset that two days later she had to receive medical treatment for an aggravated heart complaint.

Grateful at the chance to strike back at this troublesome cleric for once, the Unionist establishment rounded on Paisley for insulting the Queen's representative and marring the Presbyterian Assembly. McConnell was sent to the Assembly to give a grovelling apology, the RUC collected evidence with a view to prosecuting Paisley and moderate Unionists vied to insult him with names like "the bloated bullfrog". But the condemnation was almost entirely reserved for the fracas at Howard Street - Catholics were blamed for the riot at Cromac Square.

In a Stormont debate, O'Neill compared Paisleyism to Fascism: "To those of us who remember the Thirties, the pattern is horribly familiar. The contempt for established authority; the crude and unthinking intolerance; the emphasis upon monster processions and rallies; the appeal to a perverted form of patriotism: each and every one of these things has its parallel in the rise of the Nazis to power".

O'Neill's verbal onslaught backfired. The comparisons with fascism made by him and others, notably Presbyterian leaders, only served to further strengthen Paisley's claim on traditional Unionism. All the famous Unionist leaders, from Craigavon through to Brookeborough, had been similarly condemned as Fascists by Republicans. By calling Paisley a Fascist, O'Neill placed himself in the Republican camp and Paisley among the Loyalist immortals.

A few weeks later, the Howard Street fracas finally gave Paisley the prison martyrdom he had been seeking since his days in the National Union of Protestants. But the strength of the Unionist reaction to it undoubtedly forced him to pull in his horns. When he later appealed to the wider Protestant electorate for votes, he realised that his violent picketing of General Assemblies could alienate Presbyterian voters - the largest section of the Protestant community - and he all but abandoned them. The political price of his pickets was further highlighted when he attempted to persuade right wing Presbyterian ministers to join his fledgling DUP in 1971. The memory of that aggressive demonstration was a large obstacle to their co-operation.

In other Unionist circles, however, the reason for Paisley's march on the General Assembly had struck a chord. For the best part of six years the Orange Order had been wrestling with the vexed question of Protestant membership of the World Council of Churches but had shelved it because of the controversy it would undoubtedly cause. But grass roots pressure was growing and in May 1966 the committee responsible for drawing up the resolutions to be passed at each Twelfth of July demonstration finally decided to face the issue.

The resolution which they formulated reflected widespread Orange unease at ecumenism, an unease which Paisley - still a regular and popular speaker at Orange demonstrations despite his break with the Order - had helped to foment. It condemned the visits to Rome by the Archbishop of Canterbury and the influence of the World Council of Churches on the trend towards "one united Church". It also called for a return to Protestantism based on sixteenth century Reformation principles.

By framing the resolution the Orange Order had given Paisley another victory. But some senior Orangemen also believe that it led directly to his aggressive march on the General Assembly. They suspect he got wind of it and decided to pre-empt the Orange demonstrations. Usually he mounted small pickets on the Presbyterian Assembly but that year, five weeks before the "Twelfth", he had organised a large and noisy march. Said one: "He had his spies who would tell him things like that and it was my view that he held his protest to get in before us and to show Orangemen that he was forcing the pace".

The resolution was introduced almost apologetically on the "Twelfth" by the Grand Master, Sir George Clark but he linked it with an appeal to Orangemen to bar Paisley from their platforms. The Order could be split, he warned, if brethren gave solace to a man who so viciously attacked a fellow Orangeman, Captain O'Neill. Paisley was now threatening the inner bastion of Unionism.

Six days before Sir George Clark's appeal was to fall on deaf ears, Paisley and six others, including two of his ministers, John Wylie and Ivan Foster, were charged with unlawful assembly in Howard Street. On 18 July, after another protest march from his church, they appeared in court, defending themselves and with Eileen Paisley taking copious notes.

An attempt by Paisley to call Lord and Lady Erskine, O'Neill, McConnell, Alfie Martin and the editor of the *Belfast Telegraph*, Jack Sayers - all his ecumenical enemies - as witnesses failed, and he abandoned the defence case. After a two-day hearing all seven were convicted and fined £30 and given 24 hours to enter into a bail bond of £30 to keep the peace for two years or go to jail for three months.

That day Paisley told an Ulster Hall rally that once again he, together with Wylie and Foster would choose jail before they would pay their fines or abide by the bail bond. And he went on to make a prediction: "With the help of God and the Protestants of Ulster, the day is coming when I will be in the House of Commons. The only way the Protestant people are going to be able to answer the ruling junta of Lundies in Stormont is to have someone there".

This time Paisley was going to go to jail. As in 1959 and 1963 someone eventually paid his fine but the anonymous donor couldn't sign his bail bond for him. On 20 July he was arrested at his Beersbridge Road home and taken off to Crumlin Road jail where, as Prisoner No 1271, he was joined the next day by

John Wylie and Ivan Foster.

The next day a thousand-strong crowd, chanting "We want Paisley", blocked the road outside Crumlin Road jail.The following night, a Saturday, a crowd of 2,000 gathered when the Shankill pubs emptied and was soon fighting the police. Catholic-owned pubs were looted and the police came under a hail of bottles. When baton charges failed to restore order, the police brought in water cannons to turn on the rioters. The Cabinet met in emergency session and in desperation announced a three month ban on all but traditional, i.e. Orange, parades and meetings in the city. An uneasy peace returned to Belfast.

Paisley had his martyrdom at last. Although he denied in the *Protestant Telegraph* that he had chosen prison for political advantage the truth was that, among his followers, it would elevate him to a hero of Biblical proportions. As for O'Neill, Paisley now had his "proof" that by imprisoning a Protestant minister in a Protestant state he was a traitor to all that Unionism had ever stood for. The Loyalist unrest would also be used by conspirators within O'Neill's own Cabinet against him.

BLOOD ON THE STREET

As much as Paisley savoured his martyr's cell, the experience must have been tempered by the knowledge that he had just escaped being charged with a much more serious offence: conspiracy to provide explosives for the purpose of endangering life or causing damage to property.

The complex web of events which were to lead to that had their origin in the bitter loss of the West Belfast seat to Gerry Fitt in March. With Fitt's victory coinciding with the emotive 1916 commemorations, enflamed Loyalists, blaming O'Neill's liberal policies, decided that extreme measures were needed to counter what they saw as a burgeoning Republican conspiracy.

Under the leadership of former Ulster Protestant Action chairman, Billy Spence, who had graduated inside the Unionist party to become Kilfedder's election agent, Loyalist militants, many of them old UPA hands, began meeting in a Shankill Road public house, the Standard Bar. They decided to form themselves into a Loyalist "army" to resist O'Neill and the IRA. With the 50th anniversary of the Somme looming in June, they decided to call their group the Ulster Volunteer Force in memory of Carson's men. Paisley's appeal for "a renewal of the spirit of Carson" had been answered.

The UPA had travelled the full Loyalist circuit. At first they had tried to change Unionism by agitation and electoral competition with the establishment party but that had failed. Then they decided to change Unionism from within and infiltrated the Unionist Party but that too came to nought. Now they looked to violence and conspiracy to achieve their goals.

The military commander of the UVF was Spence's brother Gusty, then a shipyard worker, but a man with some useful military experience - he had served with the British Army in Cyprus fighting against Colonel Grivas' pro-Greek guerrillas. He was the UVF's front man but there was little doubt in the minds of the RUC Special Branch that Billy Spence was the brains behind the organisation.

Three years later the Special Branch were to conclude that Billy Spence had formulated the UVF's strategy for 1966 - a clever plan which was designed to mislead the authorities into thinking that bombings and gun attacks carried out by the UVF were really the IRA's work. The idea was to halt O'Neill's "bridge building" policies and maybe even cause a reaction against him within the Unionist Party which would force his resignation.

For that, the Spences needed explosives and their search led them to the countryside, to the people who had access to dynamite - to quarrymen in County Armagh and particularly County Down where for decades Mourne granite had been cut out of hillsides to construct Belfast's solid buildings.

That brought the UVF into contact with rural Loyalists. Some were in the Free Presbyterian Church, such as Tommy McDowell, a Kilkeel, County Down quarryman who was to imitate Spence's 1966 plan of deception three years later with devastating results. The UVF soon began to construct small rural units and by the Summer of 1966 there were cells in South Antrim, Portadown, County Armagh, and Pomeroy, County Tyrone.

Some efforts to implement the plan of deception were made in Belfast. There was a bomb attack on the Unionist party headquarters and two shots were fired through the door of the Shankill home of Unionist MP, Johnny McQuade in April - that attack was carried out with his connivance for he had links with the Spences. They had been in Ulster Protestant Action together, had joined the Unionist party together and were members of the same Orange Lodge, "The Prince Albert Temperance".

The Belfast UVF, perhaps 15 to twenty strong, were tough characters, some with criminal records stretching back twenty years, and they were nearly all violently anti-Catholic. Almost inevitably they succumbed to old temptations and turned their guns on the traditional enemy: Catholics and Republicans. It was to be their undoing. The UVF's original plan of deception, as a senior RUC officer put it, "was destroyed by Belfast drunks".

On 7 May, a UVF member - an Ulster Protestant Action veteran who was subsequently jailed for arms offences - threw a petrol bomb at a Catholic-owned pub on the Shankill. It missed and crashed through the window of the house next door. An elderly Protestant woman, Martha Gould, was burned to death in the blaze. On 27 May, Spence and three other UVF members, George McCullough, William Millar and Hugh McClean, drove to the Falls Road with plans to shoot a prominent Republican called Leo Martin but when they couldn't find him they instead shot a Catholic drunk, John Scullion, who had the misfortune to cross their path singing Irish rebel songs. Two weeks later he died. At first the police thought he had been stabbed but his body was exhumed and a post-mortem discovered evidence of a bullet wound.

The climax to their campaign came at two o'clock in the morning on Sunday 26 June outside a pub called the Malvern Arms in Malvern Street, off the lower Shankill Road. Four young Catholic barmen who had stopped off at the bar for a late night drinking session stepped out on the street and into a fusillade of gunfire. Three were hit and one, Peter Ward, a barman in a city centre hotel, was shot through the heart and died instantly.

Rumours about the UVF's existence had been rife for weeks. In May it had threatened, in a statement phoned to the press, to declare war on the IRA, and at Stormont Nationalist and Labour MPs had asked questions about UVF recruitment of "B" Specials. The Home Affairs Minister, Brian McConnell, told them that there was no evidence that the UVF had anything but peaceful protest in mind.

The Malvern Street killing destroyed that complacency and

the Government had no option but to respond swiftly and strongly. Ironically. O'Neill had been in France at the time of the shooting, commemorating the part played in the battle of the Somme by Carson's UVF, and he hurriedly returned to Belfast to proscribe the organisation.

Within a matter of days Spence, McClean and another man, Bobby Williamson, were arrested and charged with the Ward murder. They had been drinking in the Malvern Arms earlier on the night of the killing and assuming the unfortunate Catholics were IRA members - the distinction is often a fine one in militant Loyalist eyes - had decided to shoot them. They were ultimately convicted and sentenced to minimum terms of twenty years.

Paisley was embroiled in the sordid affair when his name featured both at their trial and at two other related UVF trials. He knew two of the accused, Gusty Spence and Williamson, as he later told the Scarman tribunal. He had met Gusty through Billy Spence - in 1959 he and Boal had advised Gusty Spence during a protest he held at Belfast City Hall. The protest was against Gerry Fitt, who in a council debate had described Spence's regiment, the Royal Ulster Rifles, as the "murderers" of innocent Cypriot civilians.

A much more serious link with the killing came from the third accused, McClean. When charged with the Malvern Street murders, McClean told the police: "I am terribly sorry I ever heard of that man Paisley or decided to follow him. I am definitely ashamed of myself to be in such a position". Later, during the trial, it emerged that when detectives had asked him why he had joined the UVF, McClean had replied:"I was asked did I agree with Paisley and was I prepared to follow him. I said that I was".

During the trial a senior police witness gave evidence of more tangible links with Paisley. He had seen McClean carrying a placard on the Shankill Road in a Paisley-led march to the Ulster Hall on 16 June, a week after the Cromac Square riot and Howard Street fracas. At another UVF trial in 1966, that of three South Antrim men, Leslie Porter, George Bigger and William Blakely, on arms offences, evidence was given by police that McClean had accompanied the three, who were armed, all the way to the Ulster Hall where they went to have a drink in a city centre pub before rejoining the Paisley parade back to the Shankill.

Paisley and the UVF have always denied McClean's statements. Two days after the Malvern Street murder, Paisley, somewhat ambivalently, condemned the killing as a deplorable incident but "not as deplorable as those in which policemen like Norman Anderson (killed in 1961) were brutally butchered by the IRA". Of McClean he denied all knowledge : "I don't know Mr McClean. He is not a Free Presbyterian. Mr McClean was never a member of the UCDC, never was a member of the Ulster Protestant Volunteer Divisions and he has never been associated with me at all".

The UVF maintain that McClean was questioned about his statement by Spence in jail and gave an entirely different version. According to a senior UVF source: "He said that it was through Paisley's agitation that he had become interested and involved, the general Paisley agitation. There was never a hint of a link between Paisley and us". McClean, who died before finishing his sentence, attempted without success to have his statement rejected as inadmissable at his trial.

Paisley had much more compelling evidence to distance himself from the Malvern Street killers, however, evidence provided by some of those convicted of the crime. It came out of the bitter row between himself and Shankill Loyalists the previous March when he had undermined Kilfedder's election campaign in West Belfast with the story of Kilfedder's links with Fine Gael.

The person most angered by Paisley's behaviour was Billy Spence, Kilfedder's election agent. When Fitt won the West Belfast seat, he wrote an angry letter to Paisley on UPA notepaper accusing him of "treachery". Spence got thirteen signatures to the letter in imitation of the 13 young Derry apprentice boys who had slammed shut the gates of the city in the face of Catholic King James' army in 1689. Among those who signed it were his brother, Gusty and Hugh McClean, two of the Malvern Street killers.

When detectives came to question Paisley about the UVF, he handed over the letter to them as proof of his innocence. It cleared him but earned him even more animosity on the Shankill. All those who signed the letter were interrogated by the RUC and their homes searched for weapons.

Amid the tangled network of UVF plots and personnel uncovered by the RUC in the wake of Malvern Street there was, however, a much more direct link between Paisley's UCDC, the Ulster Protestant Volunteers and the UVF. The link was Noel Doherty, Paisley's closest lieutenant at the time.

Through his organising work for the UPV, Doherty had met Robert Murdock, a Free Presbyterian from Loughgall, near Portadown, County Armagh who had expressed interest in forming a local branch of the UPV. On 21 April, Paisley drove him and Billy Mitchell to Murdock's house from where Paisley went on to another meeting. At Murdock's house he met a quarryman called James Marshall and other men whose names, he later told police, he couldn't remember.

The conversation soon turned to violence. Doherty had been considering moving the UPV in a more "militant" direction and he had toyed with the idea of blowing up IRA monuments and, as his subsequent confession to the police recorded, his new friends were in a position to help him: "I learned that gelignite could be obtained through Marshall. It was also learned at the meeting that arms could be supplied. These men were of the opinion that IRA monuments [could be blown up] and IRA leaders could be shot".

According to Doherty's statement, Paisley arrived later that night at around 11 o'clock and after a cup of tea he drove Doherty and Mitchell back to Belfast. On 21 May, Doherty brought George Bigger of the Belfast UVF to Murdock's house, introduced him to Marshall and left some UCDC leaflets. A week later Bigger collected 27 sticks of gelignite, fuse wire and detonators from Marshall and hid them in a derelict house in the Northern suburbs of Belfast. Two days after that Doherty went to Bigger's home and was shown some of the gelignite and a revolver and the two men again talked of shooting IRA men and blowing up monuments.

On the strength of all this Doherty· was charged with conspiracy to provide explosives and was ultimately convicted along with Marshall and sentenced to two years.

When Doherty admitted his part in the conspiracy and told of the journey to Loughgall in Paisley's car, RUC detectives questioned Paisley. Afterwards they decided that he too could be charged with the same offence. However the office of the Attorney-General, Teddy Jones, advised against it - their view was that Paisley's connection with the enterprise was too tenuous to support a charge for any length of time. Possibly at the first bail application and certainly by the stage of a preliminary hearing, the charge would have to be dropped - all that could be gained was embarrassment for Paisley. That would leave the government open to the charge that it was persecuting a political opponent, a charge that might well redound to Paisley's advantage. Thus Paisley escaped facing one of the most serious charges in the criminal book.

Paisley has always denied knowing anything of Doherty's plans. In evidence to the Scarman Tribunal he maintained that on the way home from Murdock's home he never once asked Doherty or Mitchell what had been discussed: "I took it for granted that this was UPV business. I have so many commitments . . . that I cannot look into every detail". As soon as Doherty's involvement in explosives was known to him, he claimed, Doherty was expelled from the UCDC under rule 15. Other founder members of the UCDC have told us that another charge, perhaps more serious in Loyalist eyes, was levelled at Doherty as well: this was that pornographic books had been found in the Puritan Press printing works.

Doherty's confession revealed two things. Firstly, that the UCDC/UPV had helped to provide the UVF with explosives and secondly that through Doherty and Bigger, the link between the UCDC/UPV and the UVF stretched to McClean and Spence. The UVF deny any more substantial connection and the two UCDC members who were at that crucial meeting in Loughgall either will not or cannot add to the picture. Doherty now runs a successful publishing business in South Africa where he prefers to remain incommunicado, while Mitchell is serving a life sentence for a double murder in the H Blocks of the Maze prison, Long Kesh.

In all legal senses, Paisley had no connection with the UVF and the bloody events of the Summer of 1966, but in one important way his violent rhetoric and stormy Ulster Hall protests undoubtedly helped to create the atmosphere in which they thrived, as a former Free Presbyterian can attest: "Ian had that gift for inflaming people to boiling point. A man I knew, not a Christian - I needn't say that because Christians do get inflamed too listening to him - used to say that he would go to meetings Ian held in the Ulster Hall and that when he came out he could have killed the first Catholic he saw".

O'Neill attempted to blacken Paisley by listing the Ulster Hall speeches he had made before the Malvern Street killings in which he had thanked "the Ulster Volunteer Force" for their support. Paisley always insisted that he was referring only to Carson's force and O'Neill's efforts to link him in with Spence did him little damage. There was more evidence during the remaining months of 1966 that it was O'Neill who was under the greater pressure.

In August, apparently on Cabinet advice to make a conciliatory gesture, he met a Free Presbyterian delegation, led by Paisley's temporary replacement as Moderator, the Rev Bert Cooke, to discuss Paisley's imprisonment. The same month O'Neill sent a special message of reassurance to the Unionist party telling them that the Border and traditional Protestantism were safe under his government.

The message had been prompted, he said, by the worries of "one of those decent, sensible Orangemen who have long been the backbone of Ulster" who had said to him: "We had the Unionist party to defend the Constitution, and the Orange Order to defend our Protestant religion. Are these things still safe in Ulster to-day?". O'Neill assured Unionism that they were.

In September it became clear that not everyone in the Unionist party believed him. Boal circulated a petition critical of O'Neill's policies and for a few crucial days it looked as if O'Neill could be ousted. The real force behind the conspiracy was the ambitious Faulkner, but the attempted putsch - based partly on the discontent whipped up by Paisley, and partly on O'Neill's personal and political unpopularity - failed, thanks to a spy in the rebel camp who reported back to O'Neill after the rebels' clandestine meetings in Faulkner's home.

O'Neill was "quite hysterical", according to his Home Affairs Minister, Bill Craig. By the time Paisley was released from jail in October, he persuaded Craig to ban all the homecoming celebrations planned for him in Belfast.

O'Neill had good reason to be worried. The violence of 1966 was ugly and disturbing - three people had been killed and there had also been petrol bombings and intimidation aimed at Catholics throughout the year. That, and the political turmoil, had combined to cause the British to put their Irish neighbours under closer scrutiny.

A highly critical ITV documentary on Northern Ireland's sectarianism, the first ever made, had been shown in Britain - but banned in Northern Ireland - and the *Sunday Times* had published its seminal article "John Bull's political slum". Political pressure for change was also growing. Gerry Fitt and the Labour party's Campaign for Democracy in Ulster intensified their demands to discuss Northern Ireland affairs at Westminster - parliamentary convention forbade it - and Harold Wilson had summoned O'Neill to London to urge a speeding up of reforms. They were signs of things to come.

As for Paisley, the fruits of 1966 were at first in the Free Presbyterian Church. At the time of the Maura Lyons affair he had told his congregation that if he was ever jailed he would follow St Paul's example and write epistles from his cell to the faithful. In between his duties in the prison kitchen he fulfilled that promise, writing "an exposition" of St Paul's epistle to the Romans - once described as "the product of a powerful if confined intellect". His new friend, Bob Jones Jnr, awarded him an honorary doctorate from the Bob Jones University in Greenville, South Carolina in recognition of his prison martyrdom. It was Paisley's first legitimate academic award.

More importantly his imprisonment had won hundreds of new converts, attracted by his political message as much as by his fundamentalism. Over the next two years the number of Free Presbyterian churches virtually doubled, and in Belfast he made plans to build a huge new church further up the Ravenhill Road to accommodate the growing crowds.

Politically, though, he was still some way from the breakthrough. A week before his release, Eileen stood in a council by-election against an O'Neill supporter and was roundly beaten. It was a dirty campaign. Her opponent, Harold Smith, was Jewish and her election literature made an appeal to an older, more deep-seated bigotry: "The Unionist party are boasting that he is a Jew. As a Jew he rejects our Lord Jesus Christ, the New Testament, Protestant principles, the Glorious Reformation and the sanctity of the Lord's day. Mr Smith is not, and cannot be, a traditional Unionist. The Protestant Throne and Protestant Constitution are nothing to him".

Nevertheless, in July, in the midst of the UVF bloodshed and his own court appearance, there had been a sign that political approval could be on its way. An opinion poll conducted by Lancaster University revealed that one in five Protestants, some 200,000 people, were opposed to O'Neill's policies. Half were opposed to ecumenism and a quarter said they didn't approve of the O'Neill-Lemass meeting.

As Paisley addressed a large crowd of people who had gathered in Dundonald on the Eastern outskirts of Belfast to welcome him home from jail, he made a significant change in the slogan, coined that Easter, "O'Neill must go!". From then on Free Presbyterian placards would read: "O'Neill must go - O'Neill will go!".

CHAPTER FIVE

The Whirlwind

Captain O'Neill has sown the wind, now he is reaping the whirlwind.
Eileen Paisley, April 1969.

1967 was barely a month old when Paisley forced another retreat by O'Neill and demonstrated that the Prime Minister was fast losing any enthusiasm for confronting him and the Loyalist militants stirred up by his rhetoric.

The occasion was the proposed visit to Belfast by the Bishop of Ripon, Dr John Moorman, a controversial ecumenist who was the Church of England's observer to the Vatican Council and the leader of an Anglican delegation which was conducting unity talks with Catholic theologians in Italy. Moorman believed in one, united Christian church with the Pope, the leader of the largest constituent member, as head.

Concern in the Church of Ireland about his views on the Papacy had led to an invitation to come to Belfast in January to explain them. Such was the interest, that St Anne's Cathedral in the city centre had been booked and a large audience was expected.

His visit was like a red rag to a bull for Paisley who immediately announced plans for a "monster" march and rally outside the Cathedral. Once again he appealed directly to Orangemen to join him and thousands of leaflets were pushed through letterboxes in Protestant districts of the city calling for 100,000 Orangemen to join in protest "against the Romanising Bishop of Ripon".

The Orange Order, again under pressure from Paisley, joined the controversy. An extraordinary meeting of the Belfast Grand

Lodge was called to decide on protest action and officially the Order was said to feel "real concern" at the visit. Even the pro-O'Neill Grand Master, Sir George Clark was described as "perturbed".

The Church of Ireland authorities wanted the visit to go ahead. An important principle, their freedom of speech, was at stake. O'Neill, however, was worried at the prospect of ugly street scenes outside the Cathedral and intervened to prevent it. At a dinner party hosted by the Dean of the Cathedral, Dr Cuthbert Peacocke, he persuaded him to cancel Moorman's booking.

A guest at that dinner described what happened: "Peacocke wanted Moorman to come, saying that if someone didn't stand up to Paisley sometime, the thing would just keep on escalating but O'Neill, I think, was looking for the easy way out. Finally he managed to talk Peacocke into cancelling the visit, that there would be trouble if he didn't and that was that. But I've often wondered what would have happened had we taken a firmer line with Paisley earlier on".

If O'Neill felt under pressure the Orange Order was increasingly facing open defiance. After Paisley's imprisonment and before his own, Noel Doherty moved to capitalise on Orange discontent and set up a new organisation called "the Orange Voice of Freedom" to highlight the Order's "lack of leadership".

In August 1966, it announced plans for a march from the Shankill to the Ulster Hall, and in newspaper ads called on Orangemen joining the parade to wear their Orange collarettes. Both were challenges to authority - the government had banned all marches and meetings in the Belfast area and the Orange Order frowned on their members wearing regalia on any but officially sanctioned occasions.

Home Affairs Minister, Brian McConnell banned the march, once again using the Special Powers Act against Protestants, and earned himself heckles at the Black Preceptory's annual parade at the end of August. The Orange authorities threatened to take disciplinary action against the rebels but never followed through. During the rest of the year and in the early months of 1967, meanwhile, the number of individual Orange Lodges which passed motions deploring Paisley's imprisonment or attacking O'Neill's policies steadily grew.

Grass roots Orange disgruntlement finally came to the surface on the "Twelfth" in 1967 in one of the most violent and unruly commemorations of King William's Boyne victory ever seen in 20th century Orangeism.

In those days Orangemen who gathered at their "fields" throughout Northern Ireland each 12 July invariably passed three resolutions put to them by Unionist leaders before they lined up behind flute bands for the weary trek home. Traditionally, one re-affirmed loyalty to the Crown, one to the Protestant faith and the other paid a routine tribute to the Prime Minister and government of the day. The resolution honouring O'Neill in 1967 was, at many Orange venues, either openly scorned or ignored that Twelfth. At the County Tyrone gathering in Coagh, the bitterness towards O'Neill spilled into violence when the pro-O'Neill Westminster MP for Mid-Ulster, George Forrest was hauled down from the platform and kicked unconscious when he argued with a heckling crowd as the resolution backing O'Neill was being read out.

In Belfast, hundreds of people shouted down the platform speaker when the resolution was introduced and so confusing was the scene that nobody could be sure that it had been carried. In Tandragee, County Armagh the speaker could not be heard above the shouting and cries of "Up Paisley", "O'Neill must go" and "What about Lemass?". In Lisburn, County Antrim the hecklers used loudhailers and in Fintona, County Tyrone the resolution paid tribute to the government but deliberately omitted the name of the Prime Minister.

In Enniskillen, County Fermanagh there was a much more serious and deliberate snub to O'Neill from the Orange and Unionist establishment in the county. It was partly a reflection of unease with his policies but more a result of O'Neill's sacking of the Minister of Agriculture, Harry West, over a controversial land deal which O'Neill said conflicted with his Ministerial duties.

There, no resolutions were put to the Orangemen but O'Neill's predecessor, Lord Brookeborough referred in his speech to the first two while deliberately making no reference to the pro-O'Neill resolution. It was a calculated insult by the former premier. West also spoke and indirectly criticised O'Neill's liberalism. Echoing Paisley, he declared: "The type of Unionism being advocated today would not be acceptable to our forefathers". West's dismissal had created influential enemies for O'Neill.

During this period the Orange Order was also being pressurised over the question of Orangemen attending Roman Catholic religious ceremonies, a favourite complaint of Paisley's. Under the Order's rules this was an offence meriting expulsion but gradually, in the early 1960s, a blind eye had been turned to offenders.

In June 1967, thanks to the climate created by Paisley, the Order's attitude hardened. Two Unionist MPs, one of them Phelim O'Neill, a cousin of the Prime Minister's, were summoned to appear before their County Grand Lodges to explain their attendance at a Catholic service during a community week in Ballymena. Phelim O'Neill ignored the summons and was expelled a year later.

Elsewhere, the Worshipful Master of a Lodge in Larne was thrown out for attending a Catholic wedding and in Belfast, an Orangewoman who wanted to go to Rome to witness the ordination of a man whose father had saved her brother's life during the war was forced to cancel the trip. Soon other prominent Unionist liberals were under attack and there was talk of a split in the Order. The "Orange Voice of Freedom" meanwhile congratulated the Orange authorities on "the improvement" in their policies.

The strain was beginning to tell in the Order's higher echelons. In October, the Grand Master, Sir George Clark resigned. Officially the reason given was pressure of work on his County Down farm but the choice of his successor revealed otherwise. He was John Bryans, an elderly Orange veteran who unlike Clark had no overt connections with the leadership of the Unionist party. He was a non-controversial, little known figure and would not be an easy target for the Paisleyites. But his appointment was an admission that the Order could not control its extremists in the face of Paisleyite assaults.

Inside O'Neill's Cabinet meanwhile another contender for the throne was emerging. Following Faulkner's failed putsch in September 1966, the Home Affairs Minister, Bill Craig, previously an O'Neill ally, threw his hat into the ring in a bid to lead the dissident right wingers. One former civil servant recalled Craig telling James Chichester-Clark, then the Unionist Party Chief Whip, at the time "that he was going to outdo Faulkner and get to the right of him".

Craig signalled his rightward move in November 1966 when, in response to Nationalist complaints that Catholics were under-represented in top legal positions, he claimed that Catholics suffered from "educational and social deficiencies". The next month he dismissed a joint NILP - Trade Union delegation seeking the introduction of one man, one vote in local government with the remark that in this respect Britain was "out of step" with Northern Ireland.

In March 1967, to placate Loyalists, he prohibited celebrations to mark the centenary of the Fenian Rising and banned the Republican Clubs, a recently adopted guise for Sinn Fein which had been proscribed ten years earlier. The latter in particular was a clear concession to Loyalist extremists, for Craig had acted against RUC Special Branch advice - the police had accurate intelligence that the IRA's move towards left-wing politics, of which the formation of Republican Clubs was part, was causing dissension in the military-minded Northern units and a split was possible.

The ban once again gave Paisley an opportunity in the Autumn to demonstrate the effectiveness of his countermarch tactic. At Queens University, students had formed a Republican Club in October 1967, but the University authorities refused to recognise it and the RUC began an investigation. At meetings and debates the students condemned the ban and decided to organise a protest march in mid-November to Unionist party headquarters in the city centre.

Paisley immediately demanded that Craig ban the march and when he didn't, he called a rally to block the students' route. Five hundred Paisleyites waving Union Jacks gathered for the expected clash but at the last minute the RUC rerouted the students in the opposite direction. Carrying a coffin symbolising the "death of democracy", they marched to Craig's South Belfast home instead to hand in a protest note. Violence had been averted but Paisley had shown that he could almost dictate the authorities' response to his protests; it was a small but significant victory, a repeat of his success against the Republicans in Easter 1966.

1967 brought encouraging signs of growing political support for Paisley. In May, Eileen won a seat in the Belfast Corporation elections in a straight fight against O'Neill supporters while in Lisburn, County Antrim, two Protestant Unionists won seats.

An opinion poll in the *Belfast Telegraph* in December also

showed significant Protestant backing for his anti-O'Neill protests. 34 per cent of all Unionists said they agreed with what he said, while 44 per cent didn't think that he had tried to stir up bad feelings between Catholics and Protestants. A clear majority, 55 per cent, were opposed to the Unionist party curbing the influence of the Orange Order.

Paisley's largest following, according to the poll, was among middle-aged and older skilled and semi-skilled male Presbyterian workers in Belfast; those who felt most threatened by the changing climate around them and most nostalgic for the certitudes of traditional Unionism.

However, there was a far more alarming symptom of the gathering opposition to O'Neill. Earlier that year the RUC Special Branch had uncovered a plot to kill him. Loyalist extremists, probably in the UVF, had acquired a rifle with a telescopic sight and the RUC feared that they would try to carry out a Kennedy-style assassination. From then on a car carrying two armed policemen followed O'Neill wherever he went.

During 1967 and 1968 Paisley stepped up his anti-O'Neill protests to match the mood of growing Protestant anxiety. Whenever he or his supporters had advance knowledge of O'Neill's movements, a crowd carrying placards and jeering "O'Neill must go!" would be hastily assembled to meet him.

Some protests were comical, like the scenes at a troop review at Ballynahinch, County Down in May 1967 when O'Neill was followed by a placard-carrying Free Presbyterian who bobbed up and down in step with the Prime Minister behind lines of soldiers. Paisley won adulation from his supporters, and even the grudging grins of opponents, for the cheek of some of his protests like that in December 1967 when he, Eileen, Ivan Foster and a new ministerial recruit, William McCrea, threw snowballs at the car carrying Lemass' successor, Jack Lynch, as he left Stormont after a meeting with O'Neill, the first North-South contact since 1965.

Other protests were not so amusing, revealing instead the violence that always lurked not so far beneath the surface of Paisiey's protests. In May 1968, O'Neill was pelted with eggs and was hit beneath the eye with a coin as he left a Unionist party meeting in Woodvale in the Upper Shankill. Some 500 Loyalists had gathered when they heard he was there. Paisley addressed them on their right to protest and burned a photograph of O'Neill visiting a Catholic convent the week before. Once again, O'Neill only escaped the fury of the incited crowd thanks to nimble police work.

The Spring and Summer of 1968 saw a renewal of the frenetic campaign launched by his Free Presbyterian ministers during Paisley's imprisonment. Ulster Protestant Volunteer rallies were held, as one veteran remembers, "nearly every weekend", spreading the message and winning new converts. Between publicity grabbing anti-O'Neill stunts and a concerted campaign in Loyalist heart-lands Paisley was gradually organising and building up a loyal political constituency.

By February 1968 he felt confident enough about his growing support to announce that the UCDC would contest Westminster seats at the next election and that a Protestant Unionist candidate would oppose O'Neill in his Bannside seat: "Captain O'Neill wants to change the Unionist party into a party of half-breeds, half for Protestant Britain and half for the Roman Catholic Republic. Now is the time for the Loyalists of Ulster to stop the sellout and let the world know that this province is going to remain uncompromisingly loyal to the principles of the Glorious Reformation and Revolution".

At Easter, threats by the UPV to hold a countermarch in Armagh led to the government banning a Republican parade. Although the ban was defied, once again the countermarch threat had achieved its purpose, forcing the government into confrontation with Catholics and establishing a pattern which was to dominate the next twelve months.

Paisley aimed his protests not just at the figurehead but at his supporters as well. Many pro-O'Neill MPs found that by 1968 there were pockets of Paisleyites in every constituency, harassing and pursuing them while moderate, middle class Protestants opted out, as they had done even in Brookeborough's day.

As time went on this was to prove a crucial factor in the fall of O'Neill. One of his supporters at Stormont recalled the fearsome pressure he and other moderates were put under:

> The great thing about fanatics is that they don't go to the pub at night, they pack meetings instead. Every constituency meeting I had was a battle, a sheer struggle, the energy involved in trying to get decisions through and keep going was unbelievable.

They were there in the front rows at each meeting, they would be booing, stamping, and heckling abuse. If you were walking around the town they'd even be abusive to you, you'd get abusive phone calls in the middle of the night and at Glengall Street (Unionist headquarters) you'd have the police holding them back from spitting at you and trying to hit you. You're eventually broken because you think you're the only one who's saying anything because everyone else is against you. I think, looking back, that physically they completely undermined us and drove us out of politics by pure physical exhaustion.

The pressure told in some revealing ways. One MP can remember being taken to task by the Unionist Party Secretary, J. O. Baillie because he had declared his support for O'Neill at a constituency selection meeting early in 1968. "He told me: 'You shouldn't have made your stance quite so clear because you could have lost the nomination', but he himself was supposed to be an O'Neill supporter".

Inside the Unionist party, O'Neill's most effective critic was Paisley's friend, Desmond Boal whose verbal brilliance inspired the other dissidents. The two men had stood by each other during the turbulence of 1966. Boal defended Paisley's rowdy march to the Presbyterian General Assembly and was promptly sacked from the post of assistant to the Attorney-General, Teddy Jones. Paisley meanwhile stood by Boal when shortly afterwards he was named as co-respondent in a divorce case - "Dessie's reading the Gospel of St John", he would assure worried Free Presbyterians.

Boal's anti-O'Neillism was based, like the Independent Unionists of the early 1950s, on his working class antagonism towards the aristocratic and middle class Unionist leadership. Although not a religious fundamentalist, he, like Paisley, accused the Orange and Unionist hierarchy of "dictatorship" by ignoring the interests and wishes of the Protestant rank and file.

"He was anti-establishment and the word arrogance comes back to mind", recalled a Stormont colleague. "No one has been able to satisfactorily explain his motivation to me but I think he regarded O'Neill as the Big House still in charge and he resented that and O'Neill's arrogance bitterly. He resented any form of patronage or patronising by anyone, and to him the Unionist party was full of both. But without his ability to express and put into words others' feelings I don't think the campaign would have been nearly as successful". With Paisley on the streets and Boal in his party ranks, O'Neill faced a formidable double act.

Paisley had, by this stage, probably won the allegiance of most Protestant fundamentalists - a vociferous but limited section of Loyalist opinion - and had stirred up opposition to O'Neill throughout the Unionist Party. But he hadn't managed to persuade mainstream dissidents to join his separatist cause. The majority of them still believed that they could change the Unionist party from inside and they looked to alternative leaders within the party to oppose and ultimately replace O'Neill.

Faulkner, spurred on by his ambitious father, a textile millionaire who had long coveted the premiership for his son, had, at least for the time being, shot his bolt with the failed putsch of September 1966. Craig was only beginning to emerge as a rival candidate and had not yet gathered enough support to seriously undermine O'Neill, while Harry West was somewhat isolated in Fermanagh.

Other Cabinet ministers and MPs grumbled in the background, susceptible to Boal's rhetoric and constituency pressure, but not yet ready to rebel openly. O'Neill had put a brake on his dialogue with the Republic's government and although this didn't satisfy his opponents, it deprived them of an issue on which to challenge him.

That was all to change - for Paisley and the anti-O'Neill Unionists - when Nationalist frustration at the slow pace of promised reform spilled into civil rights street protest in the Summer and Autumn of 1968.

STRIKING THE FIRST BLOW

It had taken some time for it all to gestate. The Campaign for Social Justice, the Northern Ireland Labour Party and the British Campaign for Democracy in Ulster in alliance with Gerry Fitt had been patiently lobbying for change from 1963 onwards. These movements were a reflection of the new demands of an emerging Catholic middle class and of the impact of the British Welfare State on Northern Catholic attitudes. For the first time since the 1920s, they were aiming not to overthrow the State, but to reform it. It was proving to be a painfully slow process.

The transition from pressure to protest was inevitable and in

February 1967, the Northern Ireland Civil Rights Association was formed in Belfast. It was a coalition of Republicans, the Campaign for Social Justice, left-wing activists, the Communist Party and middle class Catholics. Initially, NICRA attempted to be broad based and moderate in its methods and demands. It even included a member of the Unionist Party on its executive.

But eventually, NICRA, which at first was uneasy about mounting street protests and worried about a Protestant backlash, succumbed to Catholic pressure for action. A strategy of non-violent protest marches around a series of political demands was formulated; one men, one vote in local government elections; an end to the gerrymandering of electoral districts; anti-discrimination machinery; fair allocation of housing; an end to the Special Powers Act and the disbandment of the "B" Special constabulary.

Although most in NICRA and other civil rights groups attempted to direct their protests in a non-sectarian fashion and made overtures to Protestants, especially in the working class, each of their demands was a threat to collective or sectional Unionist interests.

The demands for electoral reform and anti-discrimination measures particularly alarmed Unionists West of the River Bann, which divides Northern Ireland into the predominantly Protestant East and the Catholic West. Unionists kept power in local councils there only through rigging the electoral system and by the sectarian allocation of housing; NICRA's demand, if granted, would take away that power and hand it to their traditional enemies. Outlawing discrimination East of the Bann meant, in Northern Ireland's high unemployment economy, giving jobs to Catholics at the expense of Protestants, especially the Protestant working class.

In both areas, Unionists were either alarmed at the demand for the repeal of the Special Powers Act and the disbandment of the "B" men - their two major lines of defence against absorption into an all-Ireland Republic - or were instinctively disposed, with the encouragement of Stormont Ministers, the RUC and Paisley, to view Catholic street protest as another clever ploy by the IRA to foment a rebellion which force of arms had earlier failed to achieve.

No one was better able to articulate all of those threats to Protestantism than Ian Paisley. His warnings that the civil rights movement would be used by Republicans to stir up trouble would, as the trouble inevitably came, be seen even by non-fundamentalist Protestants as evidence of special prophetic powers. And his tactic of confronting the civil rights protests, while O'Neill and his ministers appeared to appease them, earned him new Loyalist converts. Thanks to all this, Paisley bridged the gulf between his limited fundamentalist religious support and the much larger Loyalist mainstream.

Inside the Unionist Party, the civil rights campaign gave the anti-O'Neillite Unionists the issue which they had previously lacked, as O'Neill desperately struggled to balance pressure from Catholics and the British government against immovable elements inside his own party.

This tension helped to create a coalition of differing interests inside the Unionist Party. Ambitious dissidents like Faulkner and Craig joined hands with the West of the Bann Unionists, the fundamentalist right wing and the Protestant working and lower middle classes, all of whom felt under political threat.

By the Summer of 1968 Catholic pressure on NICRA to raise the level of their campaign was intense. In Derry, for instance, a Housing Action Committee had been formed by left wing Republicans and Socialists and was holding protests against biased allocation of houses by the Unionist controlled Corporation. In Caledon in East Tyrone, the local Republican Club supported by the local Nationalist MP, Austin Currie, organised Catholics to squat in a house which the Unionist Council had given to the unmarried secretary of a Unionist parliamentary candidate.

When they were evicted by the RUC, the Campaign for Social Justice decided to hold a protest march from Coalisland to the centre of Dungannon on 24 August and NICRA agreed to support it. No Nationalist parade had ever been allowed into Dungannon's Market Square and the march was seen as Nationalist. The area was regarded by Loyalists as a Protestant redoubt and, when plans for the march were announced, they moved to stop it.

The initiative came not directly from Paisley but from two units of his rural Ulster Protestant Volunteers - in East Tyrone where the march was to be held, and its counterpart from South Derry, the first and largest of all the UPV branches. They met and decided to call a counter rally in Dungannon Market Square to coincide with the civil rights march in the hope of provoking a government ban. The government, for once, didn't rise to the bait. Undeterred, the UPV approached the local Unionist MP, John Taylor, and threatened trouble if the march was not diverted. Paisley later claimed that Taylor had also come to see him to ask him to call off the rally but he, Paisley, had refused.

The report of the Cameron commission, appointed by O'Neill in January 1969 to examine the violence that followed the civil rights campaign, recorded that Taylor brought this warning to the local RUC who immediately rerouted the march through the town's Catholic areas and away from the centre. Paisley had scored another victory.

Despite this the UPV followed through with its promised counter-rally. When the civil rights marchers arrived at Dungannon they found a cordon of police facing them blocking their original route. Behind them was a crowd of Loyalists, 500 strong, singing "God Save the Queen". The civil rights demonstrators, who included six Nationalist MPs, two Senators and the Sinn Fein leader, Tomás MacGiolla, replied with the Republican hymn "A Nation Once Again" and "We shall overcome" - borrowed from the American Black civil rights movement - and placards were tossed at the police.

Austin Currie compared the police cordon to the Berlin Wall and Gerry Fitt angrily shouted from the back of a lorry: "My blood is boiling - only that there is a danger to women and children I would lead the men past that barricade". A young girl speaker exhorted the crowd: "If you want to fight join the IRA!"

The *Protestant Telegraph,* never one for understatement, compared the march to the 1572 St Bartholomew's day massacre, whose anniversary fell on 24 August, when thousands of French Huguenots were butchered by Catholics: "This year it was celebrated in Dungannon by a Civil Rights march that almost ended in the rebel marchers attacking the police and the Protestants who had turned out to voice their disapproval". The RUC was praised and a warning issued to others who might emulate the civil rights marchers: "The policy of the UCDC, through the UPV, has been and will continue to be confront the enemy at every opportunity".

The Coalisland-Dungannon march set a pattern for all other civil rights marches. The protestors, despite their claims to be non-sectarian, would be seen by increasing numbers of

Protestants as a coalition of Nationalists and Republicans who, by flouting the law and attempting to "invade" Protestant territory under the cover of "civil rights", were in reality working to achieve the old goal of Irish unity and Catholic domination.

Paisleyite threats of counter-protests would invariably force the government to curb, reroute or ban civil rights demonstrations from areas regarded as traditionally Protestant. Nationalist anger at this would be compounded by the RUC's habit of treating them as the potential troublemakers at demonstrations; the police would invariably turn to face civil rights marchers and ignore the crowds of screaming Paisleyites behind them.

To Unionists the state itself was under threat from civil rights demands; to Nationalists the attempt to achieve equality of citizenship by peaceful, non-sectarian means was being resisted by the whole Unionist apparatus dancing to Paisley's tune.

After the Coalisland-Dungannon march Paisley intensified his protest activity. A fortnight later, he led the South Derry UPV through the town of Maghera to denounce the activities of Kevin Agnew, a local solicitor and leading Republican who had helped organise the Dungannon civil rights march.

To Paisley's fury, Craig rerouted the UPV parade away from the town's Catholic area to avoid confrontation. Craig had met Paisley to discuss the march and told him that local Unionists had objected on the grounds that there might be trouble. Paisley rounded on Craig challenging him to imprison Agnew, chairman of the local outlawed Republican Club: "I speak as one who was behind prison bars and as one O'Neill and his Lundies tried to silence, but so long as we have a breath we will not be silenced", he cried.

Craig needed no urging to do his Unionist duty when the civil rights protesters again took to the streets, for their target alarmed virtually every section of Unionism. It was the Maiden City of Derry, sacred ground to Protestants for nearly three centuries when it withstood King James' siege. Every 12 August, the Apprentice Boys commemorated the siege by parading to the ancient city's hallowed walls from where they could see stretched out below them, like King James' encamped army, the hostile slums of the Catholic Bogside.

In Nationalist eyes Derry - Protestants call it Londonderry to emphasise its Britishness - was "the capital city of discrimination" and a symbol of their second class citizenship. Although the city had a clear Catholic majority the electoral wards were gerrymandered to produce a Unionist majority on the Corporation. Housing conditions in Catholic areas had been deliberately neglected by successive Unionist administrations and Derry's unemployment rate for Catholics and Protestants alike was well above the Northern Ireland average.

In September, local Republicans and left wing activists announced plans for a civil rights march in the city to take place on 5 October and, reluctantly, NICRA agreed to support it. It was to be "non-sectarian" and to support this claim the march would start at Duke Street on the Protestant east bank of the River Foyle and end at the Diamond inside the city's sacred walls.

Paisley didn't need to announce a countermarch. Local Unionists called on Craig to ban the march while the Apprentice Boys announced plans for an initiation ceremony, which they claimed to be a traditional annual event, along the same route on the same day. No one had ever heard of it before but it gave Craig the perfect pretext to ban the civil rights march. He also claimed that IRA leaders were planning to join the civil rights demonstrators.

A large force of police was sent to Derry to enforce the ban. They blocked off Duke Street at both ends as several hundred civil rights protesters gathered. The marchers moved off but within two hundred yards they met a solid wall of police who first batoned the leaders, including Gerry Fitt, and then baton charged the crowd. Water cannons were used to hose the crowd, by now trapped between two lines of police.

The fighting spread to the Bogside and petrol bombs were thrown at the police. By the end of the day 77 civilians had been treated in hospital for injuries. The riots in Derry had reverberations much further afield than Northern Ireland. The police violence, condemned later by Cameron as "indiscriminate", had been captured by a cameraman from Irish television, RTE, and the pictures horrified audiences in Britain.

Paisley blamed O'Neill and "the folly of his appeasement policy" for the Derry riots. In the *Protestant Telegraph,* he thundered:

There is no doubt we have been betrayed by his policies. He

takes every opportunity to smear the Protestants and to eulogise and to condone the actions of the Roman Catholic Church and her puppet politicians and her puppet priests, cardinals, monseigneurs and canons.

Rome, when she is on the plane of equality, is like a fox. Rome has come to believe that she is on the plane of equality in Ulster, and this has been brought to pass by the encouragement of those hireling prophets occupying professed Protestant pulpits, the ecumenists - the World Council fifth column in our midst. These men have helped to swell the bloated head of the monster of Romanism. The bared teeth of the fox of Romanism have been seen at the weekend in the city of Londonderry, and remember this, that when Rome comes from a place of minority to equality and then to a place of majority, she is like a tiger ready to tear her prey to pieces.

The Roman tiger was on the loose and Paisley set out to cage it. His two latest lieutenants in this struggle were a bizarre former British Army officer and a more sinister figure from the darker side of Loyalism. Each in their own way were to leave an indelible mark on the career of Ian Paisley and on wider Loyalist politics.

The latter was John McKeague, a fierce anti-Catholic bigot from Bushmills, County Antrim who had been converted to Free Presbyterianism in 1966. A greying 38-year-old, McKeague moved with his mother to East Belfast in 1968 where he joined the Willowfield branch of the UPV and immersed himself in Paisleyite activity.

McKeague had a dark secret which was ultimately to prove embarrassing for Paisley. He was a paederast and before he had moved to Belfast, the RUC had questioned him about sexual assaults on two young boys; only the intervention of influential friends saved him from being charged. In the early 1970s he founded a Loyalist paramilitary group, the Red Hand Commandos, which consisted largely of young teenagers. McKeague himself was rarely seen in public without a youthful male escort.

McKeague was later to become a significant figure in Northern Ireland's Loyalist underworld. In 1969 he led the Shankill Defence Association, which was active in the sectarian riots of

August that year and was the precursor of the much larger and more violent Ulster Defence Association, of which McKeague was briefly chairman. He broke with the UDA in a dispute over money and in the resulting feud his home was petrol bombed by the UDA and his mother killed. The Red Hand Commandos which he then formed was responsible for one of the very first sectarian assassinations when a Catholic pedestrian was gunned down in North Belfast in 1971.

McKeague had the dubious distinction of becoming the only person ever prosecuted under the Incitement to Hatred Act. The charge arose from a Loyalist songook which he had published, one of whose ballads went: "You've never seen a better Taig than with a bullet in his back." He was acquitted.

The eccentric was Major Ronald Bunting, a 44-year-old mathematics teacher who had quit the British Army in 1950 after service in Korea and Malaya. He was also a member of Willowfield UPV, the same branch as McKeague. He'd had a strange political career before ending up in Paisley's arms. At one stage he had worked for the election of the Republican Labour MP, Gerry Fitt and then had moved on to the Clean Air society and the Ratepayers Association, on whose ticket he was elected a councillor in East Belfast.

He had also founded the Democratic Party, with himself as the only visible member, with the aim of creating "an all-Ireland union of minds" to stamp out prejudice. Bunting had joined in the chorus of condemnation when Paisley had staged his illegal march in 1963 to protest at the lowering of the Belfast City Hall's Union Jack when Pope John XXIII died.

By 1966 his political views had swung through an 180 degree arc. That Easter he went to St Patrick's cathedral in Dublin to lay a wreath in memory of British soldiers killed in the 1916 Rising. His action was a protest against Protestant churches joining the state sponsored 1916 commemorations. The protest brought him to Paisley's attention, the two men met and Bunting was "saved" for the cause.

By early 1970 Paisley had discarded both men, as he had close aides in the past who became either rivals or an embarrassment. Bunting was ditched when his views became more and more heretical - he eventually advocated unity centres where Protestants and Catholics could meet and talk and his son, Ronnie, had become embarrassingly prominent in the civil rights movement. (Later Bunting Jnr joined the Official IRA and helped to found the INLA. UDA gunmen shot him dead in 1980.) In a final bitter letter to Paisley, Major Bunting wrote: "Dear Ian, you are my spiritual father . . . but politically you stink".

McKeague was discarded in late 1969 at a time when rumours of his homosexuality had become rife in Loyalist areas - his boyfriend was arrested during the August riots and McKeague became so distraught it attracted comment. All that McKeague would ever say about his break with Paisley was that Paisley had summoned him to say that he had become "an embarrassment" and would have to leave the Free Presbyterian Church. Both men died in the 1980s - Bunting peacefully of a heart attack and McKeague violently at the hands of an INLA gunman.

McKeague's contribution to Paisley's campaign would come violently in early 1969 while Bunting's was more immediate. His principal "gift" was a wild imagination and a penchant for inventing fictional Protestant organisations like the "Knights of Tubal Cain", "Apprentices and Fellowcraft (Masters and Purplemen)" and the "Menatzchim" as covers for his anti-civil rights protests. Only one of his creations, the Loyal Citizens of Ulster, appeared to have any foothold in reality. It was a small group of UPV and UVF members whom he could call on for protests.

Their first foray came only four days after the Derry civil rights march when angry students at Queens University organised a protest march to Belfast City Hall. Paisley got to hear of it and blocked their way with 200 followers. The students were re-routed but near the City Hall their way was blocked again by six Paisleyite women. The RUC stopped the march and the students held a three hour sit-down protest on the street. They then marched back to the University where, after hours of emotional debate, they set up a civil rights group, calling it People's Democracy.

A month later Paisley and Bunting, with several thousand followers marched to the Diamond in the centre of Derry to lay a wreath of poppies at the war memorial. Paisley warned that the civil rights march four weeks earlier was "but the prelude to an IRA upsurge. The day when Ulster Protestants will have to face the worst IRA campaign in our history has been brought forward".

Events were now fast running out of the Unionists' control. The Nationalist party quit as the official Stormont opposition in protest at events in Derry and Jack Lynch flew to London to urge Harold Wilson to speed up reforms. The *Protestant Telegraph* warned: "Our fathers had to arm themselves in defence of previous traitors in Westminster and it seems as if history is going to repeat itself. Wilson and Lynch will not be dealing with weaklings like O'Neill when they come to deal with the hard core of Ulster Protestants".

On 3 November Wilson summoned O'Neill, Craig and Faulkner to Downing Street and pressed them to implement reforms. On their return to Belfast, the Cabinet wrangled over the package and it soon became evident that Craig was emerging as the hard man of the resistance to it. He had banned all civil rights marches from the walled centre of Derry after Paisley and Bunting's wreath laying ceremony, although it had been repeatedly defied by moderate Catholics in a Citizens' Action Committee led by a young schoolteacher called John Hume. A few weeks before, Craig had been a villain in Paisley's eyes but now he was becoming one of the last lines of resistance and he won plaudits in the *Protestant Telegraph*.

On 22 November O'Neill announced a limited package of reforms. There would be an Ombudsman, a points system for allocating council housing, the multiple business vote was abolished, Derry Corporation was to be replaced by a non-elected commission and the government would consider suspending parts of the Special Powers Act.

The package satisfied no-one. Hard-line Unionists saw it as the thin end of a large wedge while Nationalists complained that their central demand - one man, one vote - had not been conceded. Both sides resumed their contest on the streets. The UPV issued a virtual call to arms: "In face of these present awful and terrible events, when one by one the lights of freedom are going out, we, the members of the UPV, beseech you, our loyal brethren, for the sake of God, our country and our children, to forget all petty quarrels and jealousies and defend our constitution and liberty. He that would be free must strike the first blow".

NO SURRENDER!

The next NICRA march was scheduled for the centre of Armagh

on 30 November. Paisley had a personal interest in "striking a blow" to stop it. "He was furious when he heard about it", recalled a Free Presbyterian. "He was roaring 'No-one is going to march there. That's my city, that's where I was born. They're not going to desecrate my birthplace!'"

Paisley and a local Free Presbyterian, Douglas Hutchinson met the Armagh police on 19 November to tell them that the UCDC had made plans for "appropriate action" if the march was not banned. Their attitude, the RUC later told Cameron, was "aggressive and threatening".

A clue to what that "appropriate action" was likely to be came in the following days. A handbill warning people to "Board up your windows. Remove all women and children from the city on Saturday 30 November" was stuffed through letterboxes. Two days before the march, UCDC posters appeared in the town centre: "For God and Ulster. S.O.S. To all Protestant religions. Don't let the Republicans, IRA and CRA make Armagh another Londonderry. Assemble in Armagh on Saturday 30 November".

On the eve of the march Paisley asked for a meeting with O'Neill who turned him down but he secretly met Craig who assured him that his counter demonstration would be permitted. But the police made their own plans to stop Paisley mounting a protest. 350 policemen were to be drafted in by 9.30 am on the day of the march to seal off the route and there were to be roadblocks by 8.00 am on all roads leading into Armagh.

The RUC's plans were leaked to Hutchinson who immediately contacted Paisley. He was in the middle of a Church Presbytery meeting when Hutchinson's phone call came through. The meeting broke up with an excited Paisley issuing instructions to the church elders and ministers to round up their congregations and alert UPV divisions to make their way to the centre of Armagh before the police roadblocks went up.

Paisley arrived with Bunting and a convoy of 30 cars at about 1.00 am and they spent the night talking in small groups or sitting in their cars. Paisley told a police Inspector that he planned to hold a religious meeting and did not intend to interfere with anyone.

The RUC roadblocks were needed. As hundreds of Paisleyites converged on the city, searches of cars uncovered two revolvers and 220 other weapons including bill hooks, scythes and pipes hammered into sharp points. In the city centre meanwhile, the

Paisley crowd had swollen to several hundred and many were armed with sticks taken from a building site; Paisley himself was armed with a blackthorn stick and Bunting carried a large black walking stick. By midday the Paisleyite crowd had grown to 2,000; hundreds more had breached the police cordon around the city centre by knocking down a wall in an alleyway.

Paisley was told by the police that he was now holding an unlawful assembly - by no stretch of the imagination could his menacing gathering be described as a religious service - but he refused to disperse. The RUC had little option but to stop the 5,000 strong civil rights march before it collided with the Paisleyites with what could only be disastrous results.

Fortunately the marchers were well stewarded by Republicans and they agreed. Major violence was averted but there were one or two ugly scenes. An ITN cameraman was knocked unconscious by a Paisleyite wielding a lead-filled sock and an RUC man destroyed a BBC camera with his baton. As the crowds made their way home late that evening the streets in the city centre were littered with cudgels, bottles and rocks discarded by the Paisley mob.

To distinguish themselves from their civil rights foes in Armagh many of the Paisleyites had worn little blue badges on their lapels bearing the words "Save the *Clydevalley*". They were evidence of yet another effort by Paisley to link his own campaign to the Unionist heroes of old and to contrast the timeless values of traditional Unionism with the "appeasement" of O'Neillism.

The *Clydevalley* was the re-named *Mountjoy II,* a 470 ton steamboat which had smuggled 35,000 rifles and 3 million r ɔunds of ammunition from Germany to the County Antrim port of Larne in April 1914 to arm Carson's UVF for the expected fight against Home Rule. After that the old boat, one of the few iron-clad ships still afloat, had gone into trans-Atlantic commercial service. In 1966 she was discovered in Sydney, Nova Scotia and the South Antrim Westminster MP, Sir Knox Cunningham, a regular contributor to the columns of the *Protestant Telegraph,* appealed to Paisley for help in saving her from the scrapyard. He and the man who had discovered her, Sam Campbell, from Whitehead, County Antrim, set up a fundraising committee to cover the cost of making the *Clydevalley* seaworthy and bringing her back to Northern Ireland where she would be a floating Loyalist museum.

Paisley enthusiastically agreed. The *Protestant Telegraph* declared: "We must in these 'Ecumenical Days' remind our readers that but for the arming of the UVF the British Government of the day would have forced on us the tragic and unspeakable doom of a Dublin Home Rule parliament. Now we Ulstermen, whether at home or abroad feel that this tangible reminder of Northern Ireland's formation should be returned to her native land. The Southern Irish government bought out of public funds, for $30,000, the Irish Volunteer *Asgard* and have preserved her for their history. On the other hand our timid and unimaginative Ulster government, who, but for the *Clydevalley's* cargo wouldn't exist, are frightened to support this project. So finally it is left to us straightforward Ulster Protestants to ensure that our history is not forgotten".

The venture was a disaster. It was two years before enough money was raised to finance repairs and a crew. Finally on 5 October 1968, as the RUC and civil rights marchers were fighting it out in Derry, the *Clydevalley* set sail from Canada under Captain William Agnew, a retired master mariner from Kilkeel, County Down. Six days out of port the ship developed engine trouble and had to return for expensive repairs. Two weeks later the *Clydevalley* developed a list and more repairs were needed. Paisley's welcome home ceremony, complete with an honour guard of UVF veterans, Orange bands and an expected 25,000 crowd, had to be put off again and again. The cost was rising alarmingly. Between emergency repairs and the original refit the *Clydevalley* expedition ran up debts of £16,000.

Creaking and belching plumes of black smoke and with Paisley and some UCDC colleagues on board she finally limped into Larne on 14 December, nearly two months behind schedule. Only 4,000 turned up to welcome her and while Paisley put a brave face on it there was little doubt that the affair had been little short of a fiasco.

The *Clydevalley* never became a floating museum. She rusted away for years in Carrickfergus harbour while the local council and Sam Campbell's committee squabbled over who was responsible for her. Finally in August 1974 she was towed across the Irish Sea to a scrapyard in Lancaster to be broken up.

There were recriminations over the debts as well. Captain Agnew was left responsible for some of it and he died penniless, some say of a broken heart, not long after docking the ship in

Larne. Sam Campbell also died an early death. He had been left with all the *Clydevalley's* debts to clear and was, say those who knew him, a bitter man.

After his break with Paisley, John McKeague taunted him about the *Clydevalley's* debts in his newspaper *Loyalist News*. Money for the *Clydevalley* fund had been raised at UPV rallies but no-one had ever seen the accounts. When Paisley was elected to Stormont a year later, McKeague acidly commented: "If Mr Paisley upholds his promises to the people of Bannside as he has upheld his promises regarding the *Clydevalley,* we will have another O'Neill on our hands."

As the *Clydevalley* made her troubled journey across the Atlantic to commemorate Unionism's last rebellion against Westminster, history was repeating itself in a remarkable way in Northern Ireland. O'Neill, who had contemplated resignation after the Derry riots, was finding Craig increasingly rebellious and ready to exploit Unionist resentment at Harold Wilson's interference.

On 9 December, O'Neill decided to appeal over the heads of the civil rights movement and his own truculent colleagues in a television broadcast which became famous for the opening lines: "Ulster stands at the Crossroads". He appealed to the civil rights leaders to end their protests, promising that the reform package would be implemented but omitting any mention of one man, one vote.

He also took a swipe at Craig. "There are, I know, today some so-called Loyalists who talk of independence from Britain - who seem to want a kind of Protestant Sinn Fein . . . They are lunatics who would set a course along a road which could only lead at the end into an all-Ireland Republic. They are not Loyalists but dis-Loyalists; disloyal to Britain, disloyal to the Constitution, disloyal to the Crown, disloyal - if they are in public life - to the solemn oaths they have sworn to Her Majesty the Queen". Forty-eight hours later he sacked Craig when Craig insisted that Unionists did have the right "to resist" Westminster if it attempted to reduce Stormont's powers.

Craig was immediately transformed into a Paisleyite hero and at a rapturous Shankill Road rally hosted by Boal, he responded by declaring that there was room inside the Unionist party for Paisley's "vocal and virile movement".

For a few heady days though, it looked as if O'Neill had pulled it off. Moderate Protestants rallied to him and the *Belfast Telegraph* reprinted "I back O'Neill" coupons for thousands of their readers to fill in and post to him. Nationalist politicians welcomed his speech and NICRA and Hume's Citizens Action Committee in Derry called off all protests for a month. The peace was broken when the student People's Democracy movement announced plans for a march from Belfast to Derry to start on New Year's Day, 1969.

AN ABSENT HERO

Paisley and Bunting once again moved to stop the student march although there was one important difference in this effort to frustrate the civil rights movement. In all the previous protests, Paisley had played a prominent role. But in the days leading up to the infamous Burntollet ambush, it was Major Bunting who played the leading part. When the ambush took place - the most violent incident since 1966 - Paisley would be safely distant - politically as well as physically.

It was Bunting, not Paisley, who promised to "hinder and harass" the PD marchers with his "Loyal Citizens of Ulster" and it was Bunting, marshalling his taunting, Union Jack-waving followers, who was at Belfast City Hall when the small group of no more than 30 students set off on their 90 mile trek on New Year's morning. He was there at the fore again at Antrim town in the afternoon when he and other Loyalists persuaded the RUC to block the students by threatening violence and in some instances meting it out to the marchers.

The next morning, it was Bunting who mustered 400 Loyalists to block the bridge at Randalstown to the marchers and who led a cavalcade of cars in pursuit of the re-routed students to Toome. Again it was Bunting who met the students that afternoon outside Bellaghy in County Derry with another roadblock.

Paisley didn't properly enter the story until the third day when he and Bunting had what was officially described as "a courteous and congenial" afternoon meeting with the acting Home Affairs Minister, Captain William Long during which they asked him to ban the remainder of the PD march.

That night when Paisley and Bunting addressed a Loyalist rally in Derry's Guildhall, it was Bunting's call to Loyalists "who wish to play a manly role" to "arm themselves with whatever protective measures they feel to be suitable", which really laid the basis for the next day's horrifying violence, not Paisley's invective about the IRA and Civil Rights. It was also Bunting who, with military precision, later that night organised the next day's violence from an Orange Hall at Killaloo on the eastern outskirts of Derry.

And when the students walked into the well-organised ambush at Burntollet bridge, some ten miles from Derry, the following morning to be showered with boulders, rocks, bottles and bits of iron and to be beaten with batons, spiked clubs and cudgels by 400 Loyalists, it was Bunting who the ambushers looked to for leadership. Of Paisley there was no sign at all.

An Orange ballad published in John McKeague's *Loyalist News* two years later celebrated the real hero of Burntollet:

On the 4 January in the year '69,
The rebels left St Patrick's Hall thinking all was fine,
To get to Londonderry was all they had to do,
They little knew what was in store for them at Killaloo.

At a place that's called Burntollet, Major Bunting took his stand,
And said "Men, do your utmost to smash this rebel band
They're coming down in hundreds and you are 72",
They answered "No Surrender! We're from Killaloo".

Burntollet has gone down in extreme Loyalist mythology as a famous victory over Catholic rebels, but very few who celebrate it as such ponder the unusually forbearing role of the man they would unhesitatingly view as Ulster's most forthright Protestant leader. Few have ever been tempted to ask what would have happened had there been deaths at Burntollet, as there might well have been, or serious injury. Who would have taken most responsibility and perhaps even the legal consequences - Paisley or Bunting?

The PD march and the Burntollet ambush had a devastating impact on Nationalist attitudes to O'Neill and the RUC. The day after Burntollet, O'Neill issued a statement, 90 per cent of which was taken up with an attack on the "foolhardy, irresponsible and hooligan" civil rights marchers. Bunting's ambushers, on the other hand, had, he said, merely played "into the hands of those who are encouraging the current agitation".

O'Neill's mild rebuke to the Loyalists coupled with his strongly worded criticism of the students lost him virtually all of the Catholic sympathy generated by his television broadcast in December. To make matters worse, his cousin, James Chichester-Clark, the Minister of Agriculture, had consorted with Bunting's men in Maghera during the march and had interceded on their behalf in an effort to get the march banned. It was further evidence to many Nationalists of respectable Unionism and extreme Loyalism acting in cahoots.

O'Neill had also threatened to mobilise more "B" Specials if the civil rights marches and Loyalist counter-protests continued and this outraged Catholics - many of those who had ambushed the students at Burntollet were "B" men. One well researched estimate put their number at nearly 100, a quarter of Bunting's entire force. Putting more "B" men on the streets was a threat to Catholics and was precisely what the Loyalists wanted.

The greatest damage, though, was done to RUC-Catholic relations. During the march the police had re-routed the students several times and on two occasions the new routes led directly into Bunting's path. Suspicions that the RUC were on the Loyalist side were fuelled by the sight of them mingling amicably with Bunting's men at roadblocks and occasionally joining in the Loyalist taunts.

The Burntollet ambush led to allegations of active collusion between the police and the Loyalists. Afterwards they were accused of knowingly leading the marchers into the attack and of doing little to stop it when it started. Some police were even accused of joining in the attack on the marchers with Bunting's force.

In Derry city antagonism between the police and Bogside Catholics reached new heights. On the night that Paisley and Bunting had addressed Loyalists in the Guildhall, sectarian fighting had been followed by repeated RUC baton charges into the Bogside. The next night, after the stragglers from Burntollet had made it into the city, policemen, many of them apparently drunk, went on the rampage in the Bogside breaking windows and doors and beating up people. The Bogsiders hastily constructed barricades to keep the police out and "Free Derry" was born.

Although the Cameron report exonerated the RUC of most of

the marchers' accusations of bias, it had harsh words to say about the force's behaviour in Derry: "A number of policemen were guilty of misconduct which involved assault and battery, malicious damage to property . . . and the use of provocative, sectarian and political slogans". Burntollet and its aftermath created a level of Catholic hostility to the police from which, arguably, the RUC has never fully recovered.

The student march also polarized opinion, squeezing out moderate voices on both sides of the community. Along the route Catholic-Protestant hostility sharpened to a dangerous degree leading, for instance, to rioting not just in Derry but also in Maghera where hundreds of Loyalists had gone on the rampage against Catholic property. The stage for the slide into a bloody Summer had been set.

It was Paisley who chose the next battlefield for a confrontation and it was a more safely familiar one than the fields of County Derry. After his Armagh demonstration he and Bunting had been charged with taking part in an unlawful assembly. They spurned the chance to postpone their trial for five months, an offer made to all alleged miscreants by the Attorney-General, Basil Kelly, in the wake of O'Neill's "Crossroads" broadcast, and elected for an early hearing.

On 27 January their case came before magistrates in Armagh and Paisley soon had the courtroom in turmoil. He accused the magistrates of having already made their minds up and refused to apologise for contempt of court. When Bunting tried to make a speech he was ordered out of the court. Paisley together with his followers tried to follow but were stopped by the police. Amid scuffling and cheering, Paisley could be heard bellowing from the back of the courtroom: "If I was a Roman Catholic I would be allowed to leave".

Eventually he and Bunting were allowed to leave and the case went on in their absence. As they were each found guilty and sentenced to three months imprisonment Paisley addressed a crowd outside the courthouse. To shouts of "No Surrender" and "No Popery" he claimed he had been bullied, insulted and kicked inside the court. He was once more the peaceful but defiantly resolute Protestant leader persecuted by brutal police and victimized by O'Neill's "appeasing" government.

The next day brought an opportunity to polish the martyr's image. When the police called at his Beersbridge Road home to arrest him, Paisley was in conference with John McKeague. There was an argument at the door, a glass panel was smashed and Paisley cut his little finger - later he claimed that a policeman had put a foot through the door and that his finger had been almost severed. The police allowed him to have medical treatment but the next morning as he was leaving hospital they arrested him and took him off to jail. Newspaper photographs showed a heavily bandaged and righteously indignant Paisley between two police officers loudly protesting that the police had broken their word.

He served less than 24 hours in jail. The ruling Presbytery of the Free Presbyterian Church had urged him to lodge an appeal - "they said he was much too important to the Church and must never go to jail again", recalled one Free Presbyterian. He signed a bail bond and was released, abandoning Bunting to serve out his sentence alone.

A CALL FROM THE PROTESTANT PEOPLE

In the next week, however, a political crisis inside the Unionist party gave him the first real opportunity to demonstrate his growing political support. The crisis had been precipitated by the Burntollet ambush after which, in response to British pressure, O'Neill set up the Cameron commission, headed by a Scottish judge, to enquire into the causes of the violence since 5 October 1968.

Three days later, on 23 January, Brian Faulkner resigned from the government in protest at what he called "the political manoeuvre" of appointing Cameron. The next day his ally, the Minister of Health, Billy Morgan, also quit and a week later 12 dissident MPs led by Boal, Craig and West publicly called for O'Neill's resignation and demanded a party meeting to decide the issue. Significantly their complaints about O'Neill echoed Paisley's - the rot, said Craig, had set in when O'Neill had invited Lemass to Belfast without consulting the Unionist party. "Some people would put it this way", he went on. "We have moved too far towards a form of presidential government and not Cabinet government".

When the rebels congregated in a hotel in Portadown on 3 February, a meeting which became known as "the Portadown Parliament", O'Neill decided to appeal above the heads of his party's extremists to the electorate and called a general election for 24 February.

No-one was to know that it would be the last general election ever to a Stormont parliament. Perhaps appropriately, it was also the most confused election in the history of Northern Ireland. Pro-O'Neill official Unionist MPs were opposed by hard-line unofficial Unionists while anti-O'Neill MPs faced unofficial pro-O'Neill Unionists.

Altogether some 60 Unionist candidates stood, each laying claim to reflect the legitimate voice of Unionism. It was the beginning of the break up of Unionism, the rending of the umbrella under which in the past so many different social, economic and political interests had sheltered. Things were no less complex on the Nationalist side, where the old Nationalist party found itself opposed by civil rights leaders and left wingers from the Peoples' Democracy.

Sensing the coming election, or perhaps armed with advance knowledge of the impending meeting of the "Portadown Parliament", Paisley had earlier set about organising his biggest ever march and rally in Belfast. He staged it on 1 February and let it be known that he was going to make an important announcement.

The march's starting point was the Shankill Road and there, for an hour before moving off, the streets were black with thousands of people and traffic was brought to a standstill. Mothers had dressed their babies in red, white and blue, the Shankill was in a Twelfth-like festive mood and the hero of the day was Paisley - six hundred "I'm backing Paisley" badges were sold out within half an hour.

When it did move off, led by three Lambeg drummers, the "Young Conquerors" flute band and a sea of Union Jacks and Ulster flags, women pushed forward in an attempt to touch Paisley. In Royal Avenue, as the chant "O'Neill must go!" developed into a massive roar, Paisley was hoisted shoulder-high and, grinning broadly, was carried into the Ulster Hall.

Inside, the scene was like an American political convention. The back of the hall was draped in a huge Orange banner and Union Jacks hung down from the balconies. On the platform more Union Jacks and Ulster flags were waved in tune to the crowd's chant of "O'Neill out!" So excited and aroused were the crowd that Paisley had to appeal three times for calm.

He brought them cheering to their feet with his first words, an appeal to back the 12 rebel MPs. There was uproar when he declared that Ulster Protestants would "fight and die" if necessary, to defend the Union and pandemonium when he made his "important announcement": he would fight O'Neill in Bannside at the next election.

Despite the excitement, Paisley had in fact chosen his words carefully, mindful of his past pledges to stay out of politics. He would enter the political arena, he said, only "if a crisis arose and he was needed to support the Protestant people". The crisis had now arrived. The crisis, of course, has lasted from then to now and its endurance has been used by Paisley again and again to justify remaining in the political arena.

Five other Paisleyite candidates were chosen to contest seats when O'Neill announced the poll. The Prime Minister, using words he later regretted bitterly, welcomed their entry: "It could be a healthy thing to have the real strength or weakness of this movement tested at the polls", he said.

Two of the candidates were Free Presbyterian ministers and two others were members of the church. The fifth, Bunting, had stayed loyal to Methodism. The ministers, John Wylie and Billy Beattie, stood in North and South Antrim respectively; Charlie Poots chose Iveagh and William Spence fought in Bloomfield in East Belfast. Bunting stood for the Victoria seat, also in in East Belfast.

The Protestant Unionist label which Paisley had first used back in 1958 against Brian Maginess was resurrected but this time there was an enlarged Free Presbyterian church and the UPV divisions to help gather in the votes. Its manifesto was also redolent of those far off days and of the Independent Unionists before them.

It was a mixture of uncompromising, traditional Unionism and social and economic populism. A call for strong law and order and the mobilisation of the "B" Specials to deal with civil rights protests was coupled with demands for halving of the unemployment rate, a crash housing programme and a rise in household incomes "by 25 per cent".

In Bannside, Paisley didn't confine his attacks on O'Neill to his bridge-building policies. He borrowed an issue from Michael Farrell, the Peoples Democracy candidate, and complained bitterly about the plethora in Ahoghill of dry closets - outside lavatories which cannot be flushed - as an example of O'Neill's neglect of his home town.

His electioneering style was also traditional, awakening memories among older voters of the uncompromising campaigns of Craigavon and Brookeborough. He would parade - a towering figure, sporting a UPV sash, a white raincoat and a Russian cossack hat - through villages and towns behind a forest of Union Jacks.

Following him would be dozens of his supporters in the UPV's red, white and blue regalia. Accompanying them would be Orange bands beating out familiar and rousing Loyalist ballads - "The Sash", "Dollies Brae" and "The Green, Grassy Slopes of the Boyne" - or Lambeg drummers clattering out incessant war-like rhythms. It was colourful, exciting stuff, luring young and old alike to hear Paisley speak. With minor variations it has been his successful formula ever since.

The world's media was drawn to Northern Ireland by the Bannside contest and it was Paisley's campaign which gave them the exciting pictures and stories. O'Neill's campaign, by contrast, was dull and creaking - Bannside had not been contested since the formation of the State and O'Neill had difficulty getting a machine together.

The two men never met during the contest, neither on nomination day nor at the count - drawing the telling barb from Paisley that O'Neill was "a superior creature". O'Neill contented himself with long distance attacks on Paisley. Paisleyites, he declared, were dinosaurs suitable for relegation to "the natural history museum of politics". The Paisleyite riposte was inevitable: if they were dinosaurs then so too were Carson, Craigavon and Brookeborough.

The result shouldn't have surprised anyone but it did. O'Neill won the seat with 7,745 votes but it was a pyrrhic victory. For hard on his heels, only 1,414 votes behind, came Paisley; in third place was the PD leader, Michael Farrell, whose 2,300 votes were evidence that substantial numbers of Catholics still distrusted O'Neill.

The other Protestant Unionists polled a total of 19,000 votes, a creditable performance but completely overshadowed by their leader's humiliation of the Prime Minister. From then on Unionist politicians who had dismissed Paisley as a noisy and troublesome nuisance began to see him as a real political force.

No-one could see O'Neill surviving another challenge.

When the Unionist party reassembled at Stormont, O'Neill found most of his opponents back on the benches. The election had solved nothing while in the constituencies, party organisations had been divided and embittered.

The greatest change, though, had taken place within Nationalism where the Nationalist party leader, Eddie McAteer was beaten by John Hume in Derry and other civil rights leaders like Ivan Cooper, Paddy O'Hanlon and Paddy Devlin defeated traditional Nationalist opponents. People's Democracy candidates had also done well - in April one of their leaders, Bernadette Devlin, was elected to Westminster to represent the former Republican stronghold of Mid-Ulster. A sea-change in Nationalist thinking was taking place.

In alliance with Gerry Fitt and Austin Currie the new Stormont MPs combined to form an articulate and initially a moderate opposition. In August 1970 the coalition was formalised when they formed the Social Democratic and Labour Party; within another year however, under pressure of violent events, they were to abandon Stormont as a forum for reform.

Paisley's supporters meanwhile were jubilant and saw the hand of the Almighty at work in Bannside. A crude ballad celebrating his achievement was quickly penned:

> God has raised a leader
> To fight for Protestant truth
> His name is Ian Paisley
> You've heard of him I'm sure
> He's slandered by the pressmen
> By adults and by youths
> But God is with our leader
> To help to fight for truth.
>
> Following Jesus, that's what Paisley does
> Nothing will harm him, no matter where he goes.
> Pray for him dear people, pray with all your might
> That God will over rule in Ulster here tonight.

It was the civil rights movement, more than any religious or political protest campaign he himself had created, which gave Paisley legitimacy among Protestants. The civil rights movement made demands for reform which, even without Paisley, Unionism would have been hard pressed to grant, but with Paisley crying "Lundy!" at every sign of moderation it was impossible. But to traditional Unionists, he was their saviour - more and more of them saw him as the only obstacle in the way of victory for the civil rights movement and by extension, their own defeat.

One of those who became a Paisley follower during those days was Wallace Thompson, then a teenager in Ballymoney, County Antrim. He joined the UPV and later, after graduating from Queens University, Belfast, became a senior official in the DUP.

I had been brought up to believe that Northern Ireland was a Protestant, British state. I had loved the trappings of Orangeism and very many of my reactions were a basic gut feeling that we had this portion of land and we had to guard it; it was my homeland and any giving in at all to the forces of Nationalism was a disaster.

I can recall going through a fleeting pro-O'Neill phase, a belief that his attempts at reconciliation were reasonable. But as events developed and the CRA took off my first reaction was like a red rag to a bull - here we have the old Nationalism rearing its ugly head and I rejoiced at the hammering the Nationalists received in Londonderry on October 5th, 1968. This was the stuff they deserved.

So Paisley seemed to articulate basically the way I felt. I can recall discussing things with friends at school and them agreeing with me. Here was a man who was speaking out, who was seen to be doing something in the middle of all this changing situation.

Paisley's name for "speaking out" - saying publicly and loudly what many Protestants thought privately was, and still is, one of the key reasons for his political success.

THE FALL OF O'NEILL

O'Neill's days were now numbered. His opponents mobilised the larger Unionist bodies against him - the 400 strong Standing Committee and the 900 strong Unionist Council - in an effort to get the grass roots to eject him. But other forces conspired to bring him down as well.

On 25 March, Paisley and Bunting were returned to Crumlin Road jail after they dropped their appeals against their conviction for the illegal Armagh demonstration. Five days later at 3.55 in the morning a large explosion wrecked an electricity sub-station at Castlereagh, six miles from the centre of Belfast. Everyone, the RUC included, assumed the bomb was the work of the IRA.

During April there were four more explosions. On the 20th a bomb damaged an electricity pylon at Kilmore, County Armagh and at the Silent Valley reservoir in the Mourne mountains in County Down a large bomb fractured pipes feeding supplies to Belfast and North Down. Four days later another device fractured a water pipe at Templepatrick, County Antrim which fed supplies from Lough Neagh to Belfast. Between them the two bombs cut off three-quarters of Belfast's water supplies and for the next ten days there was water rationing in the city. The last bomb damaged another pipeline near Annalong, some four miles from Silent Valley.

O'Neill announced the mobilisation of 1,000 "B" Specials and the formation of a special Cabinet security committee while the RUC ordered all officers, bar those on traffic duty, to carry guns. British Army helicopters were used to keep a watch on electricity and water pipe lines and eventually troops supplemented "B" Specials guarding power installations.

If they were intended as gestures to appease his right wing, they failed. The bombings, widely thought to be the IRA's work, had hardened Unionist opinion and there were signs that three or four of his erstwhile supporters were about to join the dissidents. To forestall a humiliating rejection, O'Neill resigned on 28 April, three days after the last explosion.

O'Neill left Northern Ireland two years later, selling up his house in Ahoghill to settle in England. In the New Year's honours list in 1969 he was made a life peer and chose the title, Lord O'Neill of the Maine. In Britain and abroad he was lauded as a brave statesman overwhelmed by irrational bigotry.

To Paisleyites, O'Neill was a Lundy; to many civil rights leaders he was a phoney liberal. The most trenchant assessments of his premiership come, however, from his former political allies in Northern Ireland.

One recalled:

Terence was a decent man but very difficult to work for. First of all we regarded him as an Englishman, not an Ulsterman. He didn't understand the Catholics and he certainly didn't understand Paisley - both were foreign to him in every way.

He was also "Big House", with servants and all that goes with it. That put him out of touch with ordinary people. I remember talking to a journalist who went to Ahoghill to see what people there thought of him. The local grocer told him that the nearest sight he ever had of O'Neill was of his wife riding down the main street on her horse. It didn't help that he was a lofty person and a bit haughty. He was also shy and awkward and not very good with people and that cost him. While Faulkner was busy chatting people up, O'Neill was nowhere to be seen and I can remember Jim Malley (his private secretary) forcing him to go down to the members' room to have a few drinks with his backbenchers.

His worst mistake was failing to sell his policies to the party and to root out the extremists. The best example of that was the Lemass meeting. Paisley and Boal jumped on that as an example of his dictatorship but even after that he should have been out pumping hands and twisting arms, the sort of thing any political leader should do. But I don't think he had the strength of will.

Was he a liberal? I suppose everyone remembers that awful patronising comment of his about how frightfully hard it was to explain to Protestants that Catholics could live like decent Prods if they had a good job and a television set. I don't think he was ever conscious of what he was - he was more a symbol created by people around him like Bloomfield, who wrote his speeches, Sayers, Malley and Harold Black, the Cabinet Secretary. They injected him with liberalism.

During April, Eileen Paisley had taken over the reins from her husband and led protest rallies demanding his release in Cookstown, County Tyrone, in Armagh and elsewhere which attracted thousands of suporters. Her husband's imprisonment had affected her deeply. "Before she was never interested in politics but when Ian went to jail that time she became hard and bitter", recalled a church member.

When the bombs started to explode it seemed all her husband's terrible prophesies had come true - "Captain O'Neill has sown the wind, now he is reaping the whirlwind", she said. When O'Neill resigned she thanked God for his intervention. Free Presbyterians everywhere were euphoric. Their leader had said "O'Neill must go!", then "O'Neill will go!" and now he had gone. An ex-Free Presbyterian remembered how Paisley's flock reacted: "The disappearance of O'Neill was God's work and now all their problems were going to be solved". On the Shankill, meanwhile, less pious Loyalists lit bonfires and danced in the street.

Paisley himself didn't have long to wait to join in his flock's celebrations. O'Neill's successor, James Chichester-Clark, declared an amnesty on 6 May, five days after he narrowly defeated Faulkner for the Unionist leadership, and Paisley was freed from jail. At a victory rally on the Shankill Road, Paisley pledged his support for the new Prime Minister provided he did not stray from traditional Unionism. "We don't think he will", he added.

CHAPTER SIX

A Cat on a Hot Brick

I wanted to know if Dr Paisley knew who was doing these jobs and asked Mallon. He said, "Certainly he does, You have to tell him, and you haven't to tell him. He knows and he doesn't know".
Statement of convicted bomber, Sammy Stevenson, 12 November 1969.

Terence O'Neill left the premiership blaming the explosions of March and April 1969 for forcing him out of Unionist politics - "they literally blew me out of office", he wrote later - and for some time the authorities encouraged the idea that the IRA or some other extreme Republican group was responsible.

After the Silent Valley explosion, for example, the RUC claimed that the bombings were following an IRA "blueprint". The purpose of the Silent Valley explosion, a police spokesman said, was to cause a diversion of police resources to enable civil rights supporters in Derry to occupy a local police station. Allegations like this helped enormously to substantiate in Protestant minds, the central theme of Paisley's campaign - that the civil rights movement and the IRA were indistinguishable.

Claims by Nationalist MPs that Loyalist extremists were responsible brought official denials and on one occasion a hint from the Minister of Home Affairs, Robert Porter, that if the IRA was not involved then it was almost certainly the work of one of the IRA's splinter groups. That was the nearest the Government came to publicly admitting that their original suspicions were wide of the mark.

The truth did not emerge until 19 October that year, five months after the last explosion, when the charred but still living body of a man was found inside the perimeter of a power station at Ballyshannon in County Donegal in the Irish Republic. Scattered around him were 180 sticks of gelignite, wiring and fuses; in the lining of the man's coat were inscribed the initials "UVF". He was rushed to hospital but died within 24 hours.

The dead man was Tommy McDowell, a quarry foreman from near Kilkeel, County Down. He was also a Free Presbyterian who had helped to build the Kilkeel church in 1967; a fierce Loyalist, he played the drum in an Orange band and was a member of the South Down UPV with a long association with violent Loyalism. The RUC eventually discovered that he was part of the network which had helped supply Gusty Spence's UVF with explosives back in 1966 - in 1972 Spence paid tribute to his "hallowed" memory.

McDowell was a principal figure in all of the 1969 bombings. He had supplied the explosives from quarries he worked in, he had planted three of the bombs himself and had given others tuition for the remaining explosions. He had escaped the net when the RUC rounded up the UVF in 1966 and it had taken his death to alert the RUC to his activities. The explosions were the culmination of Billy Spence's strategy of deception which he had devised back in 1966 and three years later it worked with devastating effect, earning the 1969 bombs an interesting footnote in Northern Ireland's recent violent history as the only known example of a paramilitary group fooling the authorities into believing that its violence was the work of an opposing group.

The police enquiry that followed his death not only established that McDowell had helped to organise and carry out the Spring bombing campaign but also led directly to senior members of Paisley's Ulster Constitution Defence Committee and the UPV. Once again Paisley was to be plunged into association with violence and conspiracy.

It had taken the RUC some time to conclude that Loyalists were really responsible and much longer to admit it, even amongst the force's higher echelons. The prevailing ethos in the RUC at the time mirrored that of the Unionist Government. Republicans and Nationalists were seen as the only threat to the State, and despite the killings carried out by Gusty Spence and the UVF in 1966, the idea that Protestants could use violence against institutions in Northern Ireland was plainly unacceptable. One senior officer told the authors what the reaction of his colleagues was when, after the first bomb, he raised the possibility of Loyalist involvement at a conference of high ranking detectives: "They looked at me in amazement and some even laughed".

Terence O'Neill got a similar response when he suggested the same thing. Just before his resignation he and his principal aide, Jim Malley, had come to the conclusion that the bombs were the work of extreme Protestants and O'Neill, as he recorded in his autobiography, raised this with the then head of CID, Bill Meharg: "He looked aghast and his reply was to the effect that Loyalists would never destroy their own country". Inside the force Special Branch surveillance of Loyalist extremists was, with the exception of the Shankill Road, virtually non-existent - all their energies were spent pursuing the IRA.

The RUC did have some important clues indicating that responsibility for the bombs might not be as clearcut as their public statements suggested. Earlier in 1969 militant Protestants had demonstrated that they had both the wherewithal and the will to bomb; in January a Republican monument had been blown up in Toome, County Derry and in March and April bombs had been left outside Catholic churches in County Down and County Antrim. In May the Nationalist MP, Austin Currie, handed over to the Minister of Home Affairs the names of two men he alleged had been involved in the anti-O'Neill bombs - one of them was subsequently charged - but Currie's information was not pursued at the time. "We thought he had a political axe to grind", recalled a senior Special Branch man.

McDowell ought also to have come under police attention at an early stage - he was well known to the police and Mourne Catholics as an extremist who didn't bother to hide his support for Paisley's anti-O'Neill campaign. He was a regular visitor to the UCDC headquarters in Belfast, which was under Special Brance surveillance after the riots of August 1969, and inside the Free Presbyterian Church, according to one former member, suspicions that he was involved in the bombings was a topic of speculative comment.

Forensic tests at the scene of each explosion had established that quarry dynamite had been used and that the devices were crude affairs which were possibly the work of someone with experience of quarry work. McDowell not only had access to explosives and the necessary skills but he lived only 800 yards from the scene of the Silent Valley explosion and near the site of another bombing which had clearly been caried out by Loyalists in February.

That was at the Longstone Road, the scene of bitter disputes in the 1950s over Orange parades, when the "Long Stone", a huge phallic-shaped boulder which Catholics painted green, white and gold to mark the edge of their territory, was blown up. Unused sticks of quarry dynamite were found at the scene afterwards. Local Catholics clearly suspected McDowell's hand in this and the other bombings; in May the Nationalist MP for Mourne, James O'Reilly, came close to naming him during a Stormont debate as the man who blew O'Neill out of politics. Despite all this, McDowell was never once questioned by the RUC.

The RUC also had another important clue which was never disclosed. According to a high-level Government source, a member of the Free Presbyterian church contacted a senior CID officer two weeks after the first explosion in March and told him that unnamed members of Paisley's UPV were responsible. The Cabinet was informed and told that the police now had a definite line of enquiry to follow.

Although the RUC were by this stage virtually convinced that supporters of Paisley had carried out the bombings they lacked evidence. The story of how they came by that evidence can now be pieced together from RUC and former UCDC/UPV sources.

The story started at Sunday morning service in Kilkeel Free Presbyterian church on 19 October, a service attended by McDowell, a female relative and two other men who were to be his accomplices on a bombing mission to the Irish Republic. After the service, which ironically included a sermon on the evils of violence, McDowell and the other three packed a van with sticks of gelignite and pretending to be tourists on a Sunday outing set out for County Donegal. As night fell they made their way to the power station outside the town. Their plan was to blow the station up and cut off electricity supplies to most of the county; it was to be the Loyalist reply to what they saw as the growing interference in Northern Ireland's affairs by the Fianna Fail government of Jack Lynch.

The plan badly misfired. McDowell climbed over the perimeter fence and his accomplices started passing the bomb-making material through to him. But it was a tight squeeze and McDowell had to lean over; as he did so he touched a live connector, there was a blinding blue flash and McDowell screamed and fell to the ground, unconscious and badly burned. The others panicked and fled believing him to be dead.

McDowell was found by Gardai within the hour and taken to hospital in Ballyshannon. Before he died he was visited by a senior Free Presbyterian Minister, a close confidante of Paisley's, but he apparently never regained consciousness. The story was circulated that McDowell had been kidnapped by Republicans, taken over the Border and killed and then his body planted inside the power station to convince the authorities that Loyalists had attempted to blow it up. It was Billy Spence's deception plan in reverse and it was Paisley's explanation when questioned about McDowell's death at the Scarman Tribunal.

McDowell was buried in his native Kilkeel. The local minister conducted the service and Free Presbyterians from far and wide turned up. McDowell was a widely known and popular figure but one prominent Free Presbyterian, Ian Paisley, was absent. McDowell's colleagues in the UPV and senior figures from the UCDC did turn up, though, and were photographed by Special Branch detectives hidden in the hills above the graveyard. When some of them were arrested the first sight that greeted them in the RUC's interrogation rooms were blown up photographs of themselves standing at McDowell's graveside.

Within a week the RUC had arrested one of those UPV colleagues, a man called Sammy Stevenson, a 46-year-old former "B" Special who lived off Donegall Pass in central Belfast. A full time worker in the UCDC's HQ in nearby Shaftesbury Square and a member of the UPV's Cromac branch, he had been on the RUC's list of suspects for the bombings for around three months and had been questioned about them a number of times. In early October, he had helped McDowell to "scout" the Ballyshannon power station and had been in on the planning of the attack.

In August he had been badly wounded during sectarian rioting on the Shankill and Falls Roads and earlier in the year he had been arrested a number of times and questioned about rioting offences - he played such a prominent role at Paisleyite protests that he was known to the police as "the man in the white raincoat". On one occasion the police had searched his home and discovered a revolver holster but couldn't find the accompanying gun and he was released. A Sergeant in the Special Branch from Donegall Pass RUC station had been detailed to keep an eye on him and had befriended him in a casual sort of way, visiting him for chats in the UCDC HQ.

To the surprise of detectives Stevenson talked freely about his and McDowell's role in the bombings and, impressively, he placed himself in a central role, thus convincing the police of the truth of his confession. The shock of McDowell's death had loosened his tongue.

In a series of statements made from October through to December, Stevenson confessed to his own part in the explosions and his links with the UVF - of which he claimed to be "Chief of Staff" - and named ten other men, all members of the UCDC and the UPV, who he alleged had also been involved.

Stevenson himself was convicted on 5 December and sentenced to twelve years imprisonment. His links with the UPV were detailed in court and the prosecuting counsel commented that Stevenson "was prepared to create disorder with the object of bringing about the release of the Rev Ian Paisley, who was at that time in prison, and of bringing the downfall of the then Prime Minister".

Stevenson offered to turn Queens Evidence against the men he had named in his statements - he was Northern Ireland's first ever "supergrass" - and in February 1970 the first of three trials began, each with Stevenson, by now confined to a secure area of Crumlin Road jail, as the Crown's major witness.

Those accused of conspiracy to carry out the various bombings were: John McKeague; William Owens, a Ballymoney, County Antrim teenager who was staying with McKeague in Belfast; Frank Mallon, the UCDC's treasurer, whose brother Hercules had taken over as UCDC secretary from Noel Doherty; Derek Elwood, a "B" Special and Belfast UPV member; Trevor Gracey, circulation manager of the *Protestant Telegraph;* William Gracey and three UPV members from County Armagh - John Love, a Sergeant in the "B" Specials, David McNally and Robert Murdock, who had been acquitted of explosives charges in 1966 when Doherty was convicted. The tenth man was Robert Campbell from Kilkeel.

They were variously charged with conspiracy to carry out all the bombings except Silent Valley - the RUC had concluded that that was a solo effort by McDowell. All bar McKeague, who had parted with Paisley by this stage, had registered as Free Presbyterians when they were remanded to prison. During their confinement they were regularly visited by Free Presbyterian Ministers.

Stevenson alleged that Mallon had played a central role in the bombings, initiating them and providing him with UCDC money to pay McDowell for explosives and for the hire of cars used to transport the bombing teams. The others, he claimed, had played various supporting roles in planting the bombs. In the event he proved to be unimpressive in the witness box and was easily discredited by the defending barristers - he had been in jail twice for larceny and was portrayed as an unreliable witness with a score to settle with Mallon over the alleged theft of money from UCDC headquarters.

The Crown furthermore had no corroborating evidence to support Stevenson's word, and nearly all the defendants had remained silent during police questioning. Someone, though, was clearly worried that the jury might nevertheless believe Stevenson. During the first trial a small bomb exploded in the hallway of the Crown Court building - it had been planted by a Shankill Road UPV member to intimidate the jury. Whether that clinched it or not remained a jury room secret. Either way the jury decided to acquit all ten defendants - they were hoisted shoulder high and carried out of the Crown Court building by jubilant Loyalists.

A second trial of Mallon and two of the other defendants came to the same conclusion and the third and final trial wound up in early March with the acquittal of Mallon, who had been re-arrested and charged with another conspiracy charge. Stevenson was transferred within a year to Wakefield prison in England, safely out of the reach of vengeful Loyalists, to serve out the remainder of his sentence. He later complained that the police had welched on an agreement on an early release in return for his testimony.

One of those acquitted was certainly guilty and that was John McKeague. Years later, long after his break with Paisley, he would, according to colleagues in his Red Hand Commando organisation, boast that he was the one who really masterminded the bombings, not Stevenson.

The first trial had caused a sensation in Northern Ireland. Stevenson's statement to the police had dragged Paisley's name into the sordid conspiracy and what he had to say about Paisley was made public in the courtroom. Although there was never a question of Paisley being charged with involvement in the bombings, the whole affair was acutely embarrassing, coming at a time when the church's expansion and the prospect of election to Stormont had emphasised his need for respectability.

During the trial Stevenson described an incident he alleged had happened inside Donegall Pass police station the previous August when he was being questioned about the explosions. It brought Paisley uncomfortably close to events.

During a break in police questioning, he was visited in his cell, he said, by Paisley and Mallon. Paisley asked a District Inspector if Stevenson would be subjected to any more questioning that day and the officer assured him that he wouldn't be. The District Inspector started to leave the room and was followed by Mallon and another policeman. Stevenson went on: "I was last. The Rev Paisley went to go out the room and then stopped, came back and bent down and whispered in my ear: 'Did you talk?'"

At that time Stevenson had been a close aide of Paisley's for some six months. Their association dated back to O'Neill's "Crossroads" election in February 1969 when Stevenson had volunteered to work in Major Bunting's election campaign. Stevenson was interviewed by the authors in 1980 and according to his account Paisley asked him after the election campaign to take on the full-time job of looking after the UCDC offices, dealing with housing and welfare queries from the public.

In that capacity Stevenson occasionally acted as Paisley's bodyguard, travelling with him to meetings in the country; he accompanied Paisley to Armagh in March for Paisley's appeal against his prison sentence. He was also asked to organise the guarding of Paisley's new church, the Martyrs Memorial on the Ravenhill Road, then in the process of being built. Stevenson marshalled a squad of about 30 Free Presbyterians, some of them "B" Specials armed with .303 rifles, to stand watch over the church in rotation 24 hours a day.

Stevenson also had another role in the UCDC HQ which Paisley apparently did not concern himself with. He was the UCDC's "security officer" and as such, organised guards on the building in case of Republican attack. For that eventuality the UCDC had a modest stock of shotguns and handguns, the former legally held, the latter of more dubious status.

Occasionally there would be as many as six or seven guns on the premises, according to Stevenson. His claim has been independently supported by four people who were either UCDC/UPV members or Free Presbyterians at the time. Two revolvers were normally kept in the main office, another was held by a guard on the first floor, two were held by guards at the door and there were a number of shotguns on the top floor. There, one guard would keep an eye on adjoining rooftops from the skylight in the attic. The Northern Ireland Office, according to a reliable British government source, has a photograph of this armed guard taken by the Special Branch.

Other parts of Stevenson's statements, just as embarrassing as the alleged incident in Donegall Pass RUC station, were not disclosed at any of the trials but some time later, protected by privilege, they were revealed at the Scarman Tribunal.

One of these described an alleged meeting which Stevenson said he had with Paisley at the home of a man called Hubert Nesbitt in Belfast on the night Paisley was released from jail in May: "Mrs Nesbitt brought me into the living room where I saw Dr Paisley, Mrs Paisley and Hubert Nesbitt. The Doctor came across to me, put his arms around my shoulder and said "You're a boy and a half; well done, but you will have to lie low now for a while".

Questioned at the Scarman hearings, Paisley strongly denied that this conversation had taken place, as he also denied any knowledge of the explosions before or after they happened. He had met Stevenson once in Nesbitt's home, he admitted, but that was to talk to him "about his wife and spiritual problems". This was, however, the first time that Paisley's relationship with the Nesbitts, a couple who had had considerable influence on his career, had ever been publicly aired.

Hubert Nesbitt was a well known lay Baptist preacher in Belfast and a senior foreman in Mackies engineering factory. He was a good friend of Paisley's father and had known Ian Paisley since he was a baby - "I used to sit him on my knee", he told the authors in 1980. He had preached in Belfast in the 1940s with the original Bob Jones, the founder of the now large evangelical empire, and claimed that he had paved the way for Paisley in the United States by introducing him to Bob Jones Junior and other influential and wealthy American fundamentalists.

Nesbitt married late in life to Elizabeth McRoberts, a former matron of the Samaritan and City hospitals in Belfast. She had become a fan of Paisley's as early as 1947, just after Paisley received his "call" to the Ravenhill Evangelical Mission, and was a regular attender at his services from then on. Nicknamed "the Duchess", she doted on Paisley and during the early, often impecunious days of his ministry had lavished her generosity on him. The smart suits he always wore when preaching were often bought by her.

When the couple married, Hubert Nesbitt retired from Mackies to help his wife run a private nursing home on the Ravenhill Road. In 1966 when Paisley was looking for a site on which to build the Martyrs Memorial church, Mrs Nesbitt sold him the nursing home and the couple moved to nearby Hampton Park and opened a second home. It was here, according to Stevenson's allegation, that Paisley and he met.

In a remarkably frank interview with the authors, Nesbitt boasted of the important contacts he had made for Paisley over the years, particularly in the Police. Every Sunday night without fail he and his wife would host a dinner party after Paisley's church service for twenty or thirty guests, Unionist politicians and evangelical lawyers and policemen, with Paisley in the seat of honour. The guests would sit down under the gaze of a large oil painting of Paisley.

He counted, he claimed, senior English and Scottish evangelical policemen among his friends and in the RUC he was on very good terms with high ranking Christian CID officers. On one occasion, in 1975, he had arranged a secret meeting at his home between Paisley and a very senior RUC officer who had come to Nesbitt saying that he had important information to pass on to the DUP leader. At that time ceasefire talks had started between the British government and the Provisional IRA and the British had agreed to set up incident centres which would be manned by Sinn Fein members to monitor the truce while talks between the IRA and the Northern Ireland Office went on. The exercise was code-named "Operation Rampart" after the tower at Stormont Castle which housed the civil servants who liaised with the Provisionals.

The Northern Ireland Office wanted those manning the Sinn Fein incident centres to be issued with legal handguns - this was partly for protection and partly as a gesture of good faith. The RUC had strongly objected, Nesbitt said, and there was a row between the NIO and police chiefs. The policeman who contacted him wanted to tell Paisley in case the NIO got away with their plan and in due course the meeting took place.

Another Stevenson statement read out at the Scarman hearings included this damaging allegation: "During my meetings with Mallon at my home and in his car outside my home Mallon was always telling me to be very careful, that nothing must leak out that Dr Paisley had anything to do with any of the explosions or had any previous knowledge of them. I wanted to know if Dr Paisley knew who was doing these jobs and asked Mallon. He said 'Certainly he does. You have to tell him and you haven't to tell him. He knows and he doesn't know'."

That statement was made to the police on 12 November, about three weeks after his arrest but a month later on 11 December, after his own trial and his agreement to turn Queens Evidence, Stevenson hardened up this allegation considerably and, in a significant fashion, apparently altered its context.

The new allegation was made in a deposition by Stevenson at a hearing at Newtownards Magistrates court in front of all ten accused. A transcript of the proceedings reads: "McDowell was killed blowing up the Ballyshannon power station. His death had a very great effect on me. I realised that it was time to call a halt to these things in view of the danger to life. I approached Mallon on the subject of the explosions, the reason being to find out if Dr Paisley was aware of these things. He said he was fully aware of them and the persons who were responsible for doing them".

In the intervening month Stevenson had seemingly switched the conversation with Mallon from after McDowell's death to the middle of the first bombings. More importantly Paisley's alleged knowledge was promoted from "he knows and he doesn't know" to being "fully aware" of both the explosions and those responsible.

At the time that Stevenson's allegations first became public knowledge, in December 1969, Paisley claimed that the government was conspiring to "tie him in" with the bombings and that at one stage the police had even set out to arrest him. He coupled this with an allegation that the government was trying to get him certified as mentally ill.

It looked as if Stevenson's embellishment of his first statement was indeed an effort to "tie" Paisley closer to the conspiracy but not, apparently, by the authorities. The police never officially questioned Paisley about the bombs. He had, as he pointed out in the *Protestant Telegraph*, the "perfect alibi" - he was in jail when they exploded.

The full story of the 1969 bombings, as related by some of those involved, cannot, for legal reasons, be told nor can the part played by those who suggested the targets and the timing. At least a dozen people know the entire story - most of them escaped the RUC's attention at the time - and some of them fear swift retribution if it were ever told.

Although Paisley was never shown to be culpable, a long thread, stretching back nearly fifteen years, associated him and his campaigns with the climate within which Loyalist violence flourished.

Out of Ulster Protestant Action, which he had helped to found, sprang Gusty Spence's UVF. Through the UVF came the ties with other Paisley creations and followers - the UCDC, the UPV, Noel Doherty, Tommy McDowell and Sammy Stevenson. From them came intrigue, murder, violence and finally a conspiracy that successfully subverted a government and destroyed Terence O'Neill, the Prime Minister Paisley had demanded "Must Go!". No evidence was ever produced to associate Paisley with any of those violent events but all of those who carried them out were, in one way or another, inspired by him.

"I remember the night the first trial ended", recalled a veteran Free Presbyterian. "There was a Sunday school party going on in the church and we were all expecting the jury's verdict to be announced at any minute. We were very busy but there was somebody up the road who had a television set and Ian, who was like a cat on a hot brick, had us up and down the road to that TV all night. He was worried that night I can tell you".

CHAPTER SEVEN

The Bog of Bitterness

This victory is a victory of true evangelical Protestantism against the apostasy of ecumenism . . . I believe we have come to the kingdom for such a time as this.
Ian Paisley addressing the session and Presbytery of the Free
Presbyterian Church after his election victory in North Antrim, June 1970.

After O'Neill's resignation in April 1969, and Paisley's release from jail, Northern Ireland quickly and inexorably slipped towards disaster. While the civil rights movement intensified the demands for reforms from the new administration, Chichester-Clark, who was much more a prisoner of his right-wing than was O'Neill, vacillated and pleased no-one.

And in the background there were increasingly ominous signs of the violence to come. Just before O'Neill quit, Derry had seen its worst violence to date when Paisleyites and Bogsiders battled it out in the city centre after the government banned Nationalists from holding the commemoration march from Burntollet bridge. During the riot a 56-year-old man, Samuel Devenney, was badly beaten by police in his home and died three months later.

In mid-May there was more evidence of the growing hostility between the RUC and Nationalists when the police clashed with Catholics in the Ardoyne district of North Belfast and petrol bombs were thrown. A month later the Shankill Defence Association (SDA) emerged onto the streets for the first time under the leadership of John McKeague, and forced the government to ban a Republican march to the City Hall. The SDA had been founded by UVF leader Billy Spence in May, ostensibly to agitate against housing redevelopment in the area but Spence had turned the organisation over to McKeague and two leading Free Presbyterians, the Rev William McCrea, Paisley's assistant minister and a Protestant Unionist called Alan Campbell.

In early July there was sectarian rioting in Armagh and in Lurgan and on the "Twelfth" in Dungiven, County Derry a march by the Boveva flute band, whose activities had so stirred Paisley and the Independent Unionists in the 1950s, led to fighting between Catholics and the police. Later that month there was more rioting in the town and a Catholic man was killed and the Orange Hall badly burned. In Belfast there was trouble at the bottom of the Shankill Road when Orangemen passed the grossly mis-named Unity Flats, a Catholic ghetto.

Paisley meanwhile began to show signs of turning against Chichester-Clark. At a UPV rally in Bessbrook, called to protest against a civil rights march in nearby Newry, he warned Chichester-Clark that he would have to get rid of O'Neillites in his party: "It was a long hard struggle to get rid of O'Neill. If necessary there will be another long hard struggle to get rid of O'Neillism and the Lundies in the Unionist party at Stormont". Other more mainstream Unionists echoed Paisley: Harry West accused Chichester-Clark of being panicked into promising civil rights reforms.

On 2 August there was more trouble at Unity Flats after rumours spread on the Shankill that junior Orangemen had been attacked by Catholics. McKeague's SDA attempted to invade the flats but were repulsed. Three days of rioting followed between Catholics and police on one hand, and Protestants and the police on the other. The Shankill was looted by frustrated Loyalists, a Catholic was killed when he was hit on the head with a police baton and trouble spread again to Ardoyne where the SDA and Catholic vigilantes intimidated each other's co-religionists out of their homes.

Despite Nationalist warnings of major violence, Chichester-Clark refused to ban the upcoming Apprentice Boys parade in Derry on 12 August, an event which nearly everyone thought would end in disaster. Banning it would undoubtedly anger Unionist extremists and, as he had shown during the Burntollet march, Chichester-Clark was not the man to defy the extremists in his party.

The predictions all came true. In the afternoon the Bogsiders and the Apprentice Boys clashed, and within minutes barricades had been erected and petrol bombs were raining down on the police as they tried to demolish them. By nightfall the police were firing cartridges of CS gas into the Bogside and Catholic Derry and the Northern Ireland State were at war.

The next day, as the Bogside rioting continued, civil rights supporters staged demonstrations elsewhere in Northern Ireland to draw off police manpower from Derry. Trouble spread to Coalisland, Strabane, Newry, Dungannon, Lurgan and West Belfast where police stations were attacked and barricades erected. That night the Prime Minister of the Republic, Jack Lynch, intervened: in a TV broadcast he said that the Stormont government had lost control and he called for a United Nations peace-keeping force to be sent in. The Republic, he said, would not "stand idly by" while innocent people were injured and he announced that Irish Army field hospitals would be dispatched to the Border.

An angry Chichester-Clark replied the next day with a verbal rebuke and the announcement that 8,000 "B" Specials were to be mobilised to help the police. But it was no use. The RUC were undermanned and exhausted and the British Prime Minister, Harold Wilson, alarmed at what might follow the mobilisation of the "B" men, authorised his Home Secretary James Callaghan to deploy British troops in Derry. That evening a company of the Prince of Wales Regiment marched into the centre of Derry, set up barbed wire barricades and the RUC withdrew. Peace returned to the Bogside where jubilant Catholics celebrated what they saw as a victory. For the first time in Irish history Catholics had welcomed the sight of British soldiers marching into their streets.

In Belfast, though, the violence intensified. That night there were sectarian clashes in four areas of the city - at interfaces between the Shankill and Falls and between the Shankill and Ardoyne. In a confused situation Catholic homes were burned out by McKeague's SDA men, the RUC fired Browning machine guns in the lower Falls and there was sniping across sectarian boundaries.

By the end of the night, five people had been killed, four Catholics and a Protestant, dozens of houses had been firebombed and in Armagh a Catholic man was shot dead by a party of "B" Specials. On the next afternoon, 15 August, 600 British troops were sent into Belfast, establishing "peace lines" between the Shankill and the Falls and, the next day, in Ardoyne. They arrived too late to stop a row of Catholic homes in Bombay Street, off the Falls Road, from being gutted.

Britain was now directly involved and at Downing Street meetings later in the month Chichester-Clark was forced by Wilson's *diktat* to accept measures which would ultimately strip his government of the "B" Specials, control of the RUC and many local government powers.

The agitation which Paisley had orchestrated against O'Neill's mild attempts at change, the civil rights protests generated by O'Neill's subsequent caution and the aggressive and violent counter-demonstrations organised by Paisley had led Northern Ireland to its gravest crisis. Only three years later the last vestiges of Unionism's once unchallenged authority would be confiscated by Westminster when Stormont was suspended and Direct Rule from London imposed. Paisley's campaign to re-establish "traditional Unionism" would result instead in its final dissolution.

The Cameron report, although confined to events before the dreadful summer of 1969, laid considerable blame at Paisley's door for the violence which preceded it. Its comments on both Paisley and Bunting's performance at Armagh and Burntollet, could, some would think, equally apply to July and August 1969: "Both these gentlemen", intoned Cameron, "and the organisations with which they are so closely and authoritatively concerned must, in our opinion, bear a heavy share of direct responsibility for the disorders."

As at Burntollet, Paisley kept a low profile during the August riots. Another disciple, John McKeague, played the part of Major Bunting, marshalling the troops of the Shankill Defence Association in petrol bomb attacks and intimidation. On 2 August Paisley made a brief appearance on the Shankill to appeal for peace - at the Scarman Tribunal he claimed he had led a crowd in the singing of the 23rd Psalm in an unsuccessful attempt to cool them off - but during the height of the rioting he was rarely seen.

His next appearance was on 15 August on the upper Shankill "to do welfare work and to see parishioners of mine that live up in that area", he told Scarman, while Protestants and Catholics fought fierce battles in streets only yards away. He presented himself at the Scarman hearings as a public spirited cleric trying to stop disorder and violence, while at the same time bravely catering to the spiritual and physical needs of his parishioners.

Paisley's fleeting appearances on the Shankill during the August riots were to do him a lot of damage among Loyalists who expected more from a leader who claimed to embody a renewal of the spirit of Carson. His disowning of Gusty Spence had already done him considerable harm three years earlier - especially as Spence developed into a living Loyalist legend - but, as one Loyalist paramilitant remembers, his forbearance during the violent days of August 1969 did him more.

> On the Friday night that the troops came in I saw Paisley at the top of Percy Street. There was still fighting going on at the bottom of it around Andrews flour mill. There was a bus across the street and people were ferrying in petrol bombs from both sides and flat topped lorries were moving families out. Suddenly there was a flare up and people surged towards it. Paisley appeared standing at the corner of Northumberland Street and was surrounded by five or six old women who were holding on to him. "I have to get down there to help my people" he was saying but the women were holding on to him: "You can't go down there Dr Paisley, it's dangerous". There he was a big hulk of a man being held back by these old women; if he'd wanted to he could have got free of them. It would have been like bursting out of a paper bag.

He was active in other less direct ways, however. On 13 August, the night after the Bogside riot started, Paisley and a group of other Loyalists, some of them UCDC members, some of them Unionist party members, met Chichester-Clark to demand the immediate mobilisation of the "B" Specials. The Prime Minister told them that that might lead to British soldiers being sent in. Once that happened Westminster would have control and the result might even be the suspension of Stormont.

The "B" Specials occupied a special place in Paisley's view of Unionism. They were the descendants of Carson's UVF, an entirely Protestant force well represented in the UPV and a body of men Paisley could trust unlike other agencies of law and order. Like other Loyalists, Paisley also claimed that the "B" men's local knowledge had been a vital factor in defeating the IRA in the past. "The 'B' Specials were always Ian's favourite. He felt they were the only people who could be trusted. The RUC were a mixture, they had Catholic members, and there were always questions in his mind about their loyalty but the 'B' Specials could always be relied upon to do what was necessary for the defence of the Protestant heritage", recalled a Free Presbyterian colleague.

Paisley then had an idea which he suggested to Chichester-Clark. He could raise a "People's Militia", a force of thousands of dedicated Loyalists which he would put at the government's disposal to defend Northern Ireland alongside the RUC against the IRA conspiracy then unfolding in the Bogside. The Prime Minister gave an encouraging answer: "It might come to that," he said. Enthused, Paisley set about recruiting his Loyalist force. The idea of a "Third Force" - loyal, Protestant, determined and, most importantly, officially sanctioned - was born. The idea was to recur time and again in his later political life - Paisley once more imitating Carson.

An ad was placed in the *News Letter* two days after the meeting with Chichester-Clark calling on Protestants to enroll, and a special recruiting form was printed. The recruiting effort lasted for weeks: "Ian quite often interviewed volunteers himself. They signed on at the Martyrs Memorial and then they enlisted at Shaftesbury Square (UCDC HQ). People came from all over, hundreds of them. They were asked questions, valid questions like could they handle firearms. I remember Ian saying to one man 'Can you get some of the hard stuff if you need it?' and I don't think he meant whiskey. Ian liked to use that sort of language, it sounded funny sometimes to hear him using gangster-like language". The scheme was finally abandoned in November when Stevenson confessed to the Spring bombings. The police raided Frank Mallon's office in Shaftesbury Square and took away hundreds of completed forms, containing the names and addresses of a potential private army.

During the August riots, and indeed for nearly two years afterwards, many militant Loyalists looked to the UCDC headquarters for material assistance in their fight against the Catholic/Republican menace. Many of those who subsequently rose to prominence in the UDA and UVF got their first taste of action with UPV men from Shaftesbury Square. They include this present day leader who remembers well the UCDC's influence: "In those days if we wanted help we went to the

UCDC. They were the first to help us out when Glencairn Protestants were intimidated out by the Ballymurphy Catholics in 1970 and it was a place where weapons, men and transport were always available".

The first clumsy Loyalist attempts to smuggle guns into Northern Ireland from Scotland and England were mounted by men who frequented the UCDC headquarters. One notable gunrunner, whose experience was subsequently utilised by the UDA, was later jailed for life for murder. Another, Raymond Pavis, a UPV man who once swore "to kill every Catholic on the Falls" if Paisley was ever harmed, met a more tragic end. He was shot dead by the UDA on the doorstep of his Castlereagh home in 1972, when it was discovered that he was selling guns to Republicans as well. The UPV and the UCDC had, at least in Belfast, a seminal influence on the development of Loyalist paramilitarism.

Although not noticeably active on the streets himself during the violent events of August 1969, Paisley kept his East Belfast congregation up to date with events with lurid versions of what was happening in West Belfast. At the Ulster Hall on the Sunday after the first killings and burnings he told his flock that he had evidence that the Falls Road Catholics had set fire to their own homes. The story that Protestants had been responsible was a lie - all the Catholic homes were stocked with petrol bombs so when one was set on fire by Catholics, they all went up in flames. Furthermore he had evidence that a Catholic church in Ardoyne had been used as an arsenal and that its priests had been handing out sub-machine guns for use against Protestants. Later he said he had first hand information that IRA units had taken part in the shootings: on the Falls Road "men were sitting on sandbags with machine guns in their laps" while the police did nothing.

His own Beersbridge Road house, he claimed, had been "sprayed with automatic fire" by the IRA and the RUC had fired after their fleeing car; it later transpired that a car had backfired in the street.

He also had versions of Protestant casualties suitably embroidered to highlight Catholic barbarity. Like the fate of James Todd, a Protestant vigilante shot dead some days after the August riots:

The young man and two of his friends were doing Peace Corps

duty, trying to keep the peace and help the situation - a hopeless situation - in this district; and the Roman Catholics said "Come down and talk to us. We want to make a treaty of peace with you so that we can control our districts and there will be no trouble." These three Protestants went down into the Roman Catholic district to talk with the Roman Catholics; and as they turned their backs to return to the Protestant area, young Todd was shot dead.

In the United States which he visited in early September to counter a fund-raising tour by Bernadette Devlin, he tailored his message to suit the political prejudices of his audience. At Bob Jones University in deeply conservative, anti-Communist South Carolina he told a gathering of fundamentalist students, in an address called "Northern Ireland - What is the real situation?": "Listen, my friends. What is happening in Ulster today will happen in America tomorrow. Make no mistake about it. O may God open our eyes to see the conspiracy, the international conspiracy, that is amongst us! May He help us to see that there is a deliberate association of attacks against law and order and for revolution and anarchy and Marxism in the land!"

The British were now seen by Loyalists to be on the Catholics' side. By intervening to help the Catholics the British Army had not only done the unthinkable but had made the problem worse. Quite a few Loyalists believed that, left alone, they would have solved the problem of civil rights agitation: "If only the bloody British Army hadn't come in", the *Sunday Times* reported an unnamed Unionist Senator as saying, "we'd have shot ten thousand of them by dawn".

The presence of barricades in West Belfast and Derry, built to repulse Loyalist attacks, became the immediate focus of Loyalist agitation. The RUC had, in many areas, effectively been expelled while the Army stood by and apparently co-operated. Behind the barricades, Loyalists liked to imagine, were hordes of IRA men arming themselves and planning attacks on Protestant areas while the British Army did nothing.

Delicate negotiations to restore normality by dismantling the Belfast barricades were in fact going on between the British Army and the Central Citizens Defence Committee, a group encompassing church leaders, Catholic businessmen and IRA leaders but Loyalists were impatient. There were clashes on the

Shankill with the Army and Chichester-Clark, as sensitive as ever to right wing pressure, publicly demanded that the barricades come down. His intervention nearly scuttled the British Army's delicate talks.

Political events were also unsettling Loyalists. In September the Cameron Report was published and, as expected, slated the Unionist Government for lack of leadership and vindicated Nationalist complaints of sectarian discrimination in jobs, housing and electoral arrangements. Cameron's lavish praise for the moderation of John Hume infuriated Paisley, who had been harshly admonished in the report. "I remember the way he used to snarl about 'Saint Hume'", recalled a former Free Presbyterian.

The British, who exercised influence if not entire control in Northern Ireland through the Home Secretary, James Callaghan, had furthermore insisted that Chichester-Clark undertake a series of reforms. Housing provision was to be taken away from local councils and given to a central body; local government was to be reorganised and stripped of many of its functions; the ombudsman promised by O'Neill was to be appointed and measures to outlaw job discrimination in the public sector and to curb sectarian incitement were announced. On a wider, and much more disturbing front, Callaghan announced a government enquiry into the RUC and the "B" Specials to be led by Lord Hunt, the conqueror of Everest and reputedly a descendant of one of the 13 Apprentice Boys of Derry.

On Friday 10 October 1969 the Hunt report was published. Although Loyalists had anticipated its recommendations, seeing them in black and white was a nasty shock - the RUC was to be disarmed, the hallowed "B" Specials were to be scrapped and replaced by a new part-time "non-sectarian" force, which would attempt to recruit Catholics, and the British Army General Officer Commanding, Lt-Gen Sir Ian Freeland, was placed in charge of all security operations.

Although Chichester-Clark and the Minister of Home Affairs were to be included in a new security committee, to hard-line Loyalists this was a thin film of sugar coating on a bitter pill. To add to their discomfort the RUC was to be led by an Englishman, Sir Arthur Young who replaced the pro-Unionist, Anthony Peacocke as RUC Inspector-General. Chichester-Clark accepted the report. To outraged Loyalists it seemed that he was meekly acquiescing in the removal of all the safeguards which had kept Northern Ireland out of an all-Ireland Republic.

During that weekend of 10 October the Shankill erupted. Fierce rioting broke out and soon deteriorated into a shooting war between Loyalist gunmen and British troops - the first serious gunbattle of the "Troubles". By 2 a.m. on Sunday, two Protestants had been killed by the Army and a policeman shot dead by Loyalists, the first civilian fatalities caused by the British Army since the Aden campaign and the first RUC fatality since the IRA's 1956-62 campaign. Ironically the policeman was shot dead by people protesting against his disarming. Sixty-six other people were injured, 37 of them by gunshot. Paisley accused the Army of showing "SS-style brutality".

GOD RAISES A LEADER

During these turbulent weeks Paisley turned against Chichester-Clark's "pussy footing, fence straddling" government with increasing venom and made the restoration of law and order - a demand which other Loyalists understood to mean the subjection of Catholics - the main issue in Unionist politics.

At the end of August, at a press conference in UCDC headquarters which was guarded by young men carrying clubs, he declared war on the Irish Republic and called for a boycott of Irish trade and currency. In September he threatened to call a general strike if the government did not restore law and order by sending the police back into the Falls Road. He warned Chichester-Clark that if the government continued "its policy of selling out Protestants, there would be an affair in Ulster that all the restraining voice I might raise will no longer be heeded".

He predicted that the government in the Republic would stage an incident on the Border and use it as a pretext to get the United Nations involved - "if that happens it will be the end of our province" - and he organised a 100,000 strong petition to oppose the disarming of the "B" Specials.

He told Callaghan during a brief interview that as far as Catholic complaints and the British reforms were concerned "the incidence of unemployment and the shortage of houses can be attributed exclusively to the Papist population. These people breed like rabbits and multiply like vermin".

Paisley's increasingly violent invective was being echoed elsewhere in more mainstream Loyalism. The principal voice - and Paisley's major competitor for hard-line Unionist support - was that of Bill Craig, the aggressive former Home Affairs Minister sacked by O'Neill. To the dismay of many right wingers Craig had not been included in Chichester-Clark's Cabinet. In September, in an effort to mobilise non-Paisleyite Loyalism, he re-launched the Ulster Loyalist Association (ULA), an umbrella for right wing official Unionists, which had been started back in 1962 by former members of Ulster Protestant Action to protect Protestant jobs from Catholic encroachment. Paisley was not invited to join - much to the disappointment of many at its first rally - but his old rival from NUP days, Norman Porter, was.

Like Paisley, Craig's language became increasingly violent as Loyalists got more agitated over the reform programme and the RUC's expulsion from areas like the Falls Road. Craig attacked Chichester-Clark's administration, calling it a "rubber stamp" government. He warned, not for the last time, that Northern Ireland was on the brink of civil war. He also took a leaf from Paisley's book and urged Loyalists to raise a force like Carson's UVF. In October he told a ULA rally that he wouldn't rule out the use of arms if Westminster suspended Stormont. Craig was to be a formidable rival to Paisley for years to come.

As 1969 turned into 1970 the Loyalist backlash began to take on a more violent shape when the UVF - by now a mixture of hardline UPV men, the remnants of Spence's UVF and other Loyalists grouped around a well-known criminal family on the Shankill - started a bombing campaign aimed at Catholic targets and moderate Unionists and Protestants. The moderate New Ulster Movement, a ginger group of liberal Protestants who later formed the Alliance Party, was a particular target.

The traumatic and turbulent events of August 1969 had, at the same time, thrown militant Republicanism into turmoil. In December 1969 the IRA split into two factions when hard-liners in Belfast and Dublin broke off to form a rival organisation committed to the use of the gun. They had long been opposed to the left-wing policies of the Republican leadership - despite the success achieved by the part they played in the civil rights movement - but it was the leadership's growing interest in electoral politics which caused the final break. That, they felt, would lead to the ultimate Republican heresy: the formal recognition of the two parliaments in Ireland and thus the recognition of partition itself. The lack of IRA weaponry to protect Catholic areas in Belfast during August was the final straw.

The new group took on the name Provisional IRA, after the 1916 declaration of a provisional Irish Republican government, while those who remained loyal to the political faction were renamed the Official IRA. At first it was the Officials who outnumbered and outgunned the Provisionals - but all that was to change when the Loyalist backlash intensified with the election to Stormont in April 1970 of Ian Paisley.

There were two by-elections held that month, both on the 16 April. O'Neill's departure to the House of Lords made the Bannside seat vacant and Paisley immediately announced he was standing. In South Antrim, meanwhile, an O'Neill supporter, barrister Richard Ferguson, had resigned after a series of violent threats against him by Paisley supporters had made life intolerable for his family.

Paisley's minister in Dunmurry, William Beattie, was put forward without much hope of doing well, for he faced a strong opponent, Billy Morgan, an anti-O'Neillite former Health Minister and evangelical lay preacher who had resigned from O'Neill's Cabinet in sympathy with Faulkner. In Bannside, on the other hand, a Paisley victory, despite Captain O'Neill's 1,400 vote majority, seemed a distinct possibility.

Paisley had made the restoration of law and order, the disarming of the RUC and the disbandment of the "B" Specials the main planks of his campaign: "I want to see the gun back on the belts of Ulster policemen and I want the Specials back on our streets. No more Republican enclaves! No more Republican pockets through the country! We're going to hold this province for our children and the Union Jack is going to fly through every part of it!", he roared.

Chichester-Clark was soon alarmed by Paisley's campaign. Reports came back from the constituency that the official Unionist, Bolton Minford, was getting crowds of less than 100 at his meetings - and many of them were there to heckle - while at his colourful rallies and marches Paisley was attracting up to 5,000.

He decided to try to turn the prospect of a Paisley victory to the Unionists' advantage by stressing the horrors that might follow it. Virtually the whole Cabinet was mobilised to work for Minford. Finance Minister, Herbie Kirk, spoke for them all when he predicted that a Protestant Unionist government would cause Westminster to impose direct rule or to abandon Northern Ireland altogether to a future of poverty and interminable dole queues, and others soon joined in.

Other levers of traditional Unionism were pulled. Minford's cousin, Nat, the leader of the Stormont Commons, declared that Unionism still stood for "a Protestant parliament for a Protestant people", an effort to out-Paisley Paisley which probably lost the party any hope of attracting Catholic support.

The ageing 82-year-old former Premier, Brookeborough, whose golden era was constantly invoked by Paisley as the benchmark against which modern Unionist treachery should be measured, was brought up from his Fermanagh farm to help out: "I speak to you as a man who came through some of Ulster's most trying days, who was proud to fight for my flag and country and who was privileged to lead this province for two decades. Do you think I would mislead you now?". The reports from Bannside showed no sign of optimism, though - Paisley was still getting the crowds while Minford was getting a touch time on doorsteps.

In a last desperate effort to stave off defeat, the Orange card was played. The Imperial Grand Master of the Orange Order - the world leader of Orangeism - Captain Laurence Orr, who was also a Unionist MP at Westminster, appealed to Orangemen to vote for Minford "both for the protection of the Union and for the furtherance of the just society".

Chichester-Clark issued his own eve of poll message spelling out the stark alternatives: "The results of these by-elections will be taken by the world at large as an indication of the road which Ulster now chooses to follow. I have explained the choice as I see it - to go forward on honest, progressive and acceptable democratic principles or to stagnate in a sterile and ultimately destructive bog of bitterness."

The voters of Bannside preferred the bog of bitterness. Paisley romped home with 7,980 votes, 1,200 ahead of Minford. "This is the dawn of a new day for Ulster. Good night Chichester-Clark", quipped Paisley to his delirious followers at the count in Ballymena Town Hall. On a more serious note Paisley paid tribute to the real architect of his victory - "God has done a great thing for us, whereof we are glad", he prayed.

If the government was shocked by the Bannside vote, it was stunned by the result in South Antrim. Confounding all the predictions, Beattie came nearly a thousand votes ahead of Morgan to win the seat. It was a humiliating double blow for Chichester-Clark.

The government's post-mortem was an uncomfortable affair and the lessons were clear. The whole weight of the Cabinet had been thrown behind the Bannside campaign but to no avail. In the face of Paisley's powerful appeal to Protestant fears the Orange ace had been turned into a deuce and Brookeborough was just ignored. Unionist voters clearly regarded Chichester-Clark's government as weak on law and order and too responsive to Westminster pressure for reform.

The first to publicly spell it out was Craig. "What has happened in Bannside and South Antrim could happen in many other constituencies", he warned. "Traditional Unionist supporters throughout the length and breadth of the country are disturbed about the policies the government has committed itself to without the support of the party".

Paisley, sponsored by Craig and Boal, made his victorious entry into Stormont a few days later to deliver his maiden speech - an attack on Faulkner's successor in the Ministry of Commerce, a liberal former television producer called Roy Bradford. The speech was widely regarded as a flop but Paisley could nevertheless find considerable cause for comfort - the worm was turning inside the Unionist party and soon its gyrations would be visible to all.

Only a week after Bannside and South Antrim, Chichester-Clark came under siege at the Unionist party's annual conference. His local government reforms were rejected and he only narrowly survived a motion criticising his "weakness" in the face of Westminster pressure. He was attacked for "betraying the 'B' Specials and the RUC", and his own speech was interrupted by cries of "No Popery!" and "Keep Ulster Protestant!".

In the midst of this gathering backlash Harold Wilson called a Westminster general election for 18 June. Paisley, who had said after Bannside that he already had his eye on better representation of Northern Ireland at Westminster, immediately announced that Protestant Unionists would stand in eleven of the twelve constituencies.

The threat set alarm bells ringing in the Unionist Party, for three normally safe Unionist seats were in danger of being lost to Nationalists if Paisley's Protestant Unionists managed to repeat their Bannside and South Antrim performances. They were South Down, held by Captain Orr; Armagh, held since 1959 by Jack Maginnis and Londonderry held by the Prime Minister's brother, Robin Chichester-Clark, ostensibly a liberal Unionist, who had been parliamentary private secretary to the Conservative Prime Minister, Sir Alec Douglas-Home. All had substantial Nationalist populations and a Protestant Unionist vote of around 5,000 could be sufficient to split the vote and hand them to the traditional enemy.

The Unionists quickly acted to save their seats and evidence of deals with Paisley soon emerged. Politicians, who only two months before were fiercely denouncing Paisleyism, now energetically courted it. In South Down, Orr boasted unashamedly: "I am a Protestant Unionist. But I am official Unionist. Here in South Down I am glad to say we are united and my nomination papers have been signed by members of Paisley's Free Presbyterian Church and by Unionists".

In Armagh, Maginnis humbly thanked Paisley for not standing a candidate. "I wish to acknowledge my appreciation of the decision of the Protestant Unionist Party not to oppose me. I fully realise they had and still have valid reasons for doing so and it is only their extreme loyalty and patriotic love for our province that has stayed their hand at this particular time when the common enemy is uniting behind a Unity candidate. I pledge myself, if elected, to defend the Constitution and the good name of this province and County Armagh in particular with much greater zeal than ever before".

In Derry, the local Protestant Unionist Association claimed that they had struck a deal with the Prime Minister's brother and a detailed account of private meetings between officers of Robin Chichester-Clark's constituency party and their officers was made public. Harold Wilson seized on this and challenged the Conservative leader, Edward Heath, to say whether Chichester-Clark would get the Tory whip. At the British Liberal party conference, the Unionists were accused of "surrendering to Paisleyism in the biggest display of collective funk in British politics since Munich".

Paisley proudly boasted about the deal, saying that talks had taken place "at the highest level" and that the Prime Minister had been fully aware of them. That drew a denial from Chichester-Clark which did little to convince anyone. He, himself, had not been party to any deal, he said, although there had, he admitted, been a meeting between Paisley and the Unionist Party Secretary, J. O. Baillie. This, he went on to claim, had only been to impress on the Protestant Unionist leader the risks of splitting the vote.

There had never been a suggestion that the government "would be willing to compromise their policies if Protestant Unionists were not to stand" he maintained. Few Nationalists and only the most credulous Unionist Party supporters believed him. But the toadying to Paisley worked. Only two Protestant Unionists stood - Paisley in North Antrim and Beattie in North Belfast - and the threatened Unionist seats were saved.

Against this background Paisley easily won the North Antrim seat, some 2,700 votes ahead of the sitting member, Henry Clark. "This victory", he declared, "is a victory of true evangelical Protestantism against the apostasy of ecumenism . . . I believe we have come to the kingdom for such a time as this". Whatever role God had played, the truth was that in the space of two months the Protestant backlash, partly led and mostly directed by him, had propelled Paisley first into Stormont and now into the Mother of Parliaments.

THE BIRTH OF THE PROVOS

The backlash soon evidenced itself in another more violent way and with disastrous results. The summer's Orange marching season was getting into full swing during the election campaign and Chichester-Clark was in danger of losing the Orange Order's backing. The Order had already published its resolutions for the Twelfth and had deliberately omitted the routine pledge of loyalty to the government. Instead it called for strong law and order.

Although the previous Orange marching season had propelled Chichester-Clark into the crisis he now faced, the Unionist backlash, dramatically given a new form by the three Paisleyite election victories, meant that there was little chance that he would take a firm line with Orangemen in 1970, whatever the cost.

One Orange march had already provided evidence that

relations between Catholics and the British Army were under strain and that the reform programme, whatever its merits, was having little impact in the ghettoes. In early April an Orange march in the upper Springfield Road sparked off a night of clashes between Ballymurphy Catholics and British troops. When the Unionist newspapers complained the next day that there hadn't been enough soldiers to quell the trouble, 600 soldiers were sent in and there was a full scale riot complete with petrol bombs and CS gas - an indiscriminate weapon which alienated entire streets at a time.

In early June another Orange march paraded up the Crumlin Road towards Ardoyne and a horrified local Army commander tried to re-route it at the last moment. Two nights of Protestant rioting, complete with sniper attacks, followed. Any attempt to interfere with the hallowed right of Orangemen to march where they pleased was, it was evident, going to run into fierce opposition.

During the build up towards the climax of the Orange marches, Britain was preoccupied with the general election and the changeover to Heath's Conservative government which followed it. So when Orangemen proposed another march on 27 June past Ardoyne and also through West Belfast past the scenes of the previous August's fighting, there was little to motivate British intervention and even less inside Chichester-Clark's Cabinet.

The RUC Chief Constable, Sir Arthur Young, and the Foreign Office's representative in Belfast, Ronald Burroughs, saw the danger and urged that the marches be banned. Their advice was ignored. "Chichester-Clark maintained, exactly as he had the previous year, that his followers would destroy him if the marches were banned", reported the *Sunday Times*. He was even opposed to rerouting the marches. The right wing backlash had paralysed the Cabinet.

Chichester-Clark had first-hand experience of troublesome extremists and had learned that the easiest way to deal with them was to give in. At the time of O'Neill's "Crossroads" election he had found to his horror that his South Derry nomination, regarded almost as a family heirloom, was being challenged by a right winger. The rival was William Douglas, the Boveva bandmaster whose Dungiven parades in 1959 had given Paisley his first victory over a Unionist Government. Chichester-Clark only narrowly survived this challenge and from then on went out of his way to appease extremists.

When he succeeded O'Neill as premier one of his first acts was to draft a letter to the Free Presbyterian Church giving them "unqualified" assurances that "traditional" Unionist attitudes on the Border would be upheld and that no North-South dialogue would take place without full Cabinet permission. The unmistakable message was that he was no O'Neillite; his obeisance to Paisleyism was almost total.

The June 1970 Orange marches, as everyone feared, brought Northern Ireland closer to the abyss. The first trouble broke out in West Belfast between Catholics and Protestants but this soon developed into a pitched battle between British soldiers and Ballymurphy Catholics.

Rioting spread to other sensitive areas but that evening it got much worse. In Ardoyne there was a confrontation between Orangemen and Catholics and stones, bottles and petrol bombs were thrown across the Crumlin Road by rival crowds. A gunbattle followed which left three Protestants dead.

In East Belfast, there had been tension all day after an Orange parade passed the small Short Strand area, an enclave of some 5,000 Catholics surrounded on three sides by Protestants and penned in by the River Lagan. That night Loyalists made an attempt to petrol bomb the area's Catholic church, St Matthew's, but a small group of Provisional IRA gunmen, led by the Belfast commander Billy McKee, opened fire on them from inside the church grounds. The Loyalists returned fire but the night ended with two Protestants killed and two fatally wounded.

The British Army, too overstretched elsewhere in the city to intervene in the Short Strand gunbattle, had sealed off the bridges over the Lagan to stop West Belfast Loyalists from joining the fray - but in Catholic minds it looked as if they had opted out in order to give the Loyalists a free hand.

That weekend saw the real birth of the Provisional IRA and laid the basis for its growth. Provisional leaders could now argue in Catholic areas that they, not the British Army, were the only people who could be trusted to defend their areas from Loyalist attack. That was reinforced by messages from other sources that weekend. The indulgence shown to the Orangemen was, in Catholic eyes, evidence that Unionist bigotry prevailed even over the impartial British while the defeat of the Labour

Government promised worse to come. That weekend the Catholics began to turn against the British.

The third achievement came in the long term. Small, isolated Catholic areas like Short Strand had in the past been regarded as hostages for the good behaviour of other Catholic districts of Belfast - the fear that Loyalists might wreak revenge on such areas had, for instance, been one of the factors which persuaded the IRA to confine its 1956-62 campaign to rural areas. Having, in 1970, proved its capacity to defend areas like the Short Strand, the Provisional IRA's hand was freed to intensify its assault on the Northern Ireland State - one result of that was the fierce bombing campaign launched in Belfast some six months later.

If the Orange marches marked the beginning of the end of the honeymoon between Catholics and the British, the Falls Road curfew a week later sealed it. On the urging of Chichester-Clark, the British Army was ordered by Heath's government to take a firm hand with the next outbreak of trouble. An arms search in the lower Falls Road on 3 July provided that opportunity.

The confrontation that followed developed into a riot and gunbattles, and the area was saturated with CS gas. By nightfall the British GOC, Freeland, had ordered a curfew of the entire area which lasted for thirty-five hours, during which there were wholesale searches of homes, beatings and some looting by troops. By the end of it four people had been shot dead and an entire community embittered. In the next six months the Provisional IRA grew from a few dozen activists to over 800.

From there Northern Ireland sank deeper into the abyss. The Provisionals stepped up their bombings and shootings and, as Loyalists bayed for tougher and tougher security measures, Chichester-Clark was forced to resign in March 1971. The new hostility between the British Army and Catholics, fuelled by tough anti-riot tactics and a policy of wholesale arrests, wrecked attempts by his successor, Brian Faulkner, to woo the SDLP with political concessions - following the deaths of two Catholics in Derry the SDLP walked out of Stormont.

In August 1971 Faulkner tried the Unionists' ultimate weapon, the internment of Republicans in an attempt to crush the IRA. Inevitably it made a bad situation worse. IRA recruitment and violence increased in pace with Catholic resentment and anger and the death toll leaped into the hundreds. Just as ominously, Loyalist paramilitaries emerged and multiplied - the largest of them, the Ulster Defence Association, was to account for most of the 600 assassinations of Catholics in the next five years. The violence that followed made other conflicts in Irish history appear tame.

Finally, in January 1972, the killing of 13 Catholics in Derry by British paratroopers on what quickly became known as "Bloody Sunday", exposed the bankruptcy of Faulkner's security policy and an indifferent British government was forced to act. Stormont was suspended by Heath and Direct Rule imposed.

The train of events which led to the prorogation of Stormont had started with Paisley's election victories in Bannside and North Antrim. They gave an aggressive and, to establishment Unionists, a frightening shape to the Loyalist backlash. Faced with it, Chichester-Clark quailed from interfering with the 1970 Orange marches and from the violence which followed them, the Provisional IRA gained credibility and support.

Throughout the history of Northern Ireland, the response of most Unionists at all levels of government to Loyalist extremist pressure was invariably to placate them with concessions that drove Catholics further and further away from any accommodation. During his own political career Paisley had amply demonstrated the vulnerability of Unionist governments to such pressure. From the Orange marches in Dungiven in 1959 through to the fall of O'Neill and the violent response he orchestrated to the civil rights movement, Paisley had virtually made Unionism his prisoner.

Following his two election victories Paisley received a congratulatory letter from Willie John McCracken, the Independent Unionist whose 1953 election campaign against the liberal Brian Maginess marked the beginning of a campaign against liberal Unionism.

Paisley replied saying that "the battle is only beginning", and asking for McCracken's prayers for divine wisdom and guidance "in the new and heavy responsibility which is now resting upon us". A handwritten note at the end of the letter urged McCracken to pick up his Bible and turn to St Paul's Epistle to the Ephesians, Chapter six, verses 19 and 20: "And for me, that utterance may be given unto me, that I may open my mouth boldly, to make known the mystery of the gospel. For which I am an ambassador in bonds: that therein I may speak boldly, as I ought to speak".

By "speaking boldly", Paisley had helped to destroy the slim chances of reconciliation between Northern Ireland's bitterly divided communities and had set it on a violent and bloody course. "Speaking boldly" would help to ensure that the battle, which Paisley prophesied in 1970 was only beginning, would, sixteen years later, show no sign of ending.

Part 2

Free Presbyterian Churches in Northern Ireland and The Republic

BELFAST
✝ Martyrs Memorial
✝ Mount Merrion
✝ Sandown Road
✝ John Knox Memorial

Rathlin Island

DONEGAL

ANTRIM
Coleraine ✝
✝ Limavady
Garvagh ✝
✝ Ballymoney
✝ Rasharkin
✝ Cloughmills
✝ Larne
✝ Ballymena
✝ Randalstown
✝ Carrickfergus
✝ Antrim
Newtownabbey
✝ Bangor
✝ Newtownards
✝ Ballygowan
✝ Portavogie
BELFAST
Dunmurry
✝ Lisburn
✝ Hillsborough
✝ Ballynahinch
✝ Crossgar

DERRY
✝ Derry
Portglenone ✝
Magherafelt ✝
✝ Mulvin

TYRONE
Castlederg ✝
Omagh ✝
Sixmilecross ✝
Cookstown ✝
Dungannon ✝
✝ Clogher Valley
Aughnacloy ✝

ARMAGH
✝ Lurgan
Portadown ✝
Armagh ✝
Tandragee ✝
Markethill ✝
✝ Dromore
✝ Banbridge
✝ Moneyslane
Mullaglass (Newry) ✝

DOWN
Lough Neagh
✝ Kilkeel

FERMANAGH
Kilskeery ✝
Lough Erne
Enniskillen ✝

MONAGHAN
✝ Drum
Tullyvallen ✝

CHAPTER EIGHT

The Fearful Fundamentalists

*The only effective answer to encroaching Romanism
is a revived and revitalised Protestantism, believing the Bible,
proclaiming the Bible and practising the Bible.*
Ian Paisley in his book *The Fifty Nine Revival.*

The Free Presbyterian Church of Ulster, founded, led and totally dominated by its perpetual moderator, Rev Dr Ian Paisley, is a very small church indeed. According to the 1981 census it had under ten thousand followers in Northern Ireland. This made it smaller than the Plymouth Brethren, a puritan sect most of whose members don't even believe in voting in elections, preferring to let God make the political decisions. The Baptists had 40 per cent more followers, the Methodists were six times bigger and the Presbyterians, with nearly 340,000 adherents, were more than 35 times larger.

Despite this, Paisley's church is a remarkable success story. Formed only 35 years ago, it is now a well established feature of the Northern religious landscape: it has 59 congregations, 49 of them in Northern Ireland, the other ten in the Republic of Ireland, England, North America and Australia. Most of them meet in splendid new churches: between 1970 and 1983 a spectacular building programme, financed almost totally from church collections and covenants, saw 28 new churches built at a cost of nearly two and a half million pounds.

The church has a theological college in County Down; a radio station in County Antrim; a publishing company in Belfast; and its own schools in Kilskeery, Co Tyrone, Ballymoney, Newtownabbey and Bangor. Its Martyrs Memorial church in East Belfast is one of the largest Protestant churches in Europe. Its services are broadcast on the BBC. 80 per cent of the politicians of the North's second largest political party belong to it.

Why has such a small and young church had such a phenomenal impact in Northern Ireland? Part of the answer is that its leader is the most powerful and charismatic politico-religious figure the North has seen this century. In a period of crisis thousands of fundamentalist Protestants have turned to him religiously as hundreds of thousands of less fundamentalist Protestants have done so politically.

Many who declare themselves as Presbyterians, Baptists or even just Protestants on census forms go to their own churches in the morning and to the local Free Presbyterian church in the evening. At times of political crisis the evening congregations at Paisley's own Martyrs Memorial church in East Belfast expand dramatically. It only needs the occasional slaughter of innocent Protestants - the latest example was the 1983 attack on the Darkley Pentecostal hall in South Armagh by the previously unheard-of Catholic Reaction Force - to make Paisley's analysis of the "Troubles" as a plot by the Church of Rome to eradicate Ulster Protestantism, seem very credible indeed.

That fear is the real key to the church's success. Paisley's religious appeal, like his political appeal, is to the traditional obsession of Northern Protestants: their history of being an embattled religious minority in Ireland. All its elements are rooted in that history: it takes its puritanism from the rigid beliefs of the 17th century Scottish planters; its separatism and elitism from their feeling that they were a small band of civilised Christians surrounded by barbarian hordes; its hatred of Catholicism from fears going back to the 1641 massacre of the Protestant settlers by the Catholic Irish they had dispossessed; its religious enthusiasm from the "Great Revival" of 1859.

It is this last surprisingly little-known episode that provides Paisley with his ultimate solution to all Northern Ireland's problems: its need for another "heaven-sent, sky-blue, Holy Ghost revival" of evangelical religion. His earliest book was about the extraordinary outpouring of religious enthusiasm of that year, which started in the village of Kells near his home

Sammy Stevenson, wearing a trilby, accompanies Ian and Eileen to Armagh courthouse, March 1969. Behind him is John McKeague, his co-conspirator in the bombings which ousted O'Neill (*Pacemaker*)

Brookeborough meets a friend on his way to a meeting proposing a no-confidence vote in O'Neill (*Pacemaker*)

His master's voice: Major Bunting at an anti-civil rights protest (*Pacemaker*)

Desmond Boal (*Belfast Telegraph*)

Bob Jones Junior at the opening of the Martyrs Memorial, October 1969 (*Belfast Telegraph*)

In victorious mood after the Bannside and South Antrim by-elections, 1970 (*Belfast Telegraph*)

Supporters carry John McKeague out of Crumlin Road courthouse after his acquittal of the 1969 bombings (*Belfast Telegraph*)

Paisley outside the UDA headquarters in East Belfast in 1977 (*Crispin Rodwell*)

Major Chichester-Clark (*Irish Times*)

Kincora boys' home housefather, William McGrath (*Allan McCullough*)

Paisley with Northern Ireland junior minister Don Concannon on Rathlin Island (*Belfast Telegraph*)

Paisley, William Craig and Clifford Symth (*Belfast Telegraph*)

Paisley with Loyalist paramilitaries in Larne during the UWC strike in May 1974 (*Associate Newspapers*)

Paisley at home in his study (*Pacemaker*)

Peter Robinson posing with automatic rifle during a visit to Israel (*Pacemaker*)

Rev William McCrea (*Pacemaker*)

town of Ballymena.[1]

It was a bizarre phenomenon, especially since its greatest impact appeared in the North's most strait-laced communities: church after church, the majority of them Presbyterian, witnessed scenes of uncontrollable religious hysteria. Whole congregations fell prostrate on the ground moaning, weeping and beseeching God for forgiveness and salvation. People went into trances, had kicking and screaming fits, or dropped to their knees sobbing and crying aloud in prayer in the middle of crowded streets.

Ordinary farmers and labourers, claiming to have the power to impart the Holy Spirit to converted sinners, harangued huge crowds on village squares and city streets. By the end of 1859 it was claimed that 100,000 people throughout Protestant Ulster had been converted to "born again" Christianity.

In his 1958 commemorative account of the 1859 Revival Paisley wrote that it had "strengthened Ulster in her stand against Roman Catholic agitation and without doubt laid the foundation which enabled Ulster under the leadership of Lord Carson to preserve her Protestant position". The lessons for contemporary Northern Ireland were grim and clear, he warned:

Only a revival on a parallel scale can save Ulster from the engulfing tides of evil with which she is encompassed. The dark sinister shadow of our neighbouring Roman Catholic state, where religious liberty is slowly but surely being taken away, lies across our province . . . Not only have we this enemy without but we have a strong fifth column of sympathisers and compromisers within. The only effective answer to encroaching Romanism is a revived and revitalised Protestantism, believing the Bible, proclaiming the Bible and practising the Bible.

The people he was addressing that warning to were above all the members of the North's largest Protestant denomination, the Presbyterian Church in Ireland. Many ordinary Presbyterians were "evangelicals". They held to the simple unchanging Protestant doctrines taught by Calvin and the Scottish puritan John Knox: that the only way to salvation and heaven was through faith in Jesus Christ alone and through unquestioning belief in an infallible Bible.

217

They harked back to the kind of Presbyterian orthodoxy which became dominant in the Irish church after 1830. In that year Henry Cooke, conservative in religion and Tory in politics, had triumphed against a liberal and anti-establishment faction which was refusing to subscribe to the church's 17th century Westminster Confession of Faith. This Calvinist declaration, drawn up in the middle of the English Civil War, stated that the Bible was the sole doctrinal authority and designated the Pope - "that man of sin and son of perdition" - as the "antichrist". To many Northern Irish Presbyterians in the late 20th century it is an anti-Catholic document that still strikes a deep and powerful chord.

The Westminster Confession of Faith was a weapon that Paisley would use again and again against a Presbyterian leadership trying to play down its anti-Catholic antecedents. Not that there was any real possibility of Northern Ireland's largest Protestant church ever discarding it completely: as recently as June 1986 the General Assembly in Belfast voted against following the example of its Scottish counterpart and scrapping its offensive description of the Pope.

However, there was a 20th century Presbyterian skeleton that Paisley was able to wield with even more effect: the trial in 1927 of Irish Presbyterianism's most influential thinker, Professor Ernest Davey, as a heretic. Davey was a liberal, a sympathetic student of radical new ideas, and a re-interpreter of Presbyterian theology: a "modernist" in the language of his conservative opponents. As such he was blamed by those opponents for most of the the church's ills, particularly its lack of old-time revival enthusiasm and its moves towards ecumenism. To such people Davey was the leader of what Paisley called the "fifth column" of Catholic sympathisers and theological compromisers inside the church.

Many of these people, while retaining nominal membership of the church of their forefathers, started to look elsewhere for the old doctrines they felt were missing from Presbyterian pulpits. They found them in the sermons of itinerant evangelists who preached total separation from sinful pleasures such as drinking, smoking, dancing and company-keeping with the opposite sex, and devotion to a life spent in the glorification of God.

Or they went to hear the hellfire sermons of preachers from

the Christian Workers Union, founded by the fiercest Presbyterian evangelist of the 1920s, W.P. Nicholson, whose earthy language, aggressive pulpit style and denunciations of loose morals had brought revivalism to thousands of working class Belfast Protestants. This was the face of Ulster Presbyterianism which came closest to the stereotyped image of American-style fundamentalism: close-minded, belligerent and separatistic.

This was also the Presbyterian constituency Paisley was aiming at when he set up the Free Presbyterian Church of Ulster on 17 March 1951. The new denomination was fundamentalist, believing in the absolute authority and literal truth of every word in the Bible. It was unashamedly anti-Roman Catholic, swearing every minister and elder to uphold the Westminster Confession's doctrine of the Pope as the antichrist.

It was "separatist", pledged to keep itself apart from and undefiled by the slightest contact with any church which had World Council of Churches connections or other ecumenical tendencies; and it was "evangelistic", a "soul winning" church that believed in the need for a repeat of the 1859 Revival as the only answer to Northern Ireland's baneful brew of religious and political problems.

This combination produced a xenophobic brand of Protestantism that was singularly suited to Northern Ireland. It appealed to just the kind of people who had been converted to "born again" Christianity by 1859-style revivalism and Nicholson's crusades. In the country they were the hard-working puritan farmers, shopkeepers and self-employed tradesmen and their wives who had attended his father's church in Ballymena and followed him in Crossgar in 1951. In Belfast they were tradesmen again, and the odd small businessman, and loyalist shipyard and factory workers who had been reared on a diet of street and mission hall preachers like Paisley, spouting salvation and damnation on every corner.

In short, they were bigots. They believed they were inherently superior to their Roman Catholic neighbours because of their religion. They were "born again" Christians, living in the "light" of true Protestantism, free men who communed with God without the interference of priests or man-made rituals. Catholics, on the other hand, were benighted and ignorant souls who were enslaved by the "darkness" of Roman superstition, the idolatry of the Mass, and the rule of the papal antichrist.

Such a view tallied perfectly with the superiority they felt anyway as the descendants of the people who had "civilised" Ulster. And if the Catholics were poor, that was precisely because they were priest-ridden; were told by their church to breed large families; defiled the Sabbath; were not imbued with the Protestant work ethic; drank and gambled. Thus the underprivileged position of Northern Catholics was nothing to do with injustice: quite the opposite - it was living proof of God's justice in rewarding those who followed the true religion.

VOMIT-EATING DOGS AND SLIMY TOADS

Paisley made it clear from the beginning that the first target of his new denomination would be the Irish Presbyterian Church that had unwittingly spawned it. More specifically he chose as its first hate figure the principal of its Assembly's Theological College, Ernest Davey.

To Paisley, Davey was a "vomit-eating dog" who had "poisoned Assembly's College"[2] with teachings that were "the mere vapourising of carnal conceited intellect, totally unable to meet man's deepest need".[3] He was the leader of the school of "God dishonouring, Christ blaspheming, Bible defaming, soul damning modernism".[4]

If Davey was the most identifiable prophet of "modernism" the Irish Presbyterian Church as a whole was guilty of the related and equally heinous sin of compromise with Roman Catholicism. Thus a proposed invitation to a Catholic priest to speak at an East Belfast Presbyterian church prompted Paisley to pillory its clergy as "a lot of milk-and-water, spineless, soft-tongued, velvet-gloved pussyfoots . . . They may make suitable presidents for evangelical societies and vice-presidents for pink lemonade societies, but on the battlefield of Protestantism they are stamped as sulking cowards whose peace-at-any-price policy nauseates both God and man".[5]

When Paisley paused from his weekly tirades against the

Presbyterians, he turned to attacks on every other conceivable Protestant denomination. It did not seem to matter whether they were ecumenical Methodists and Anglicans or fiercely evangelical Pentecostalists and fundamentalist Baptists: the message was the same. Everywhere there was error and enmity to the true path of Free Presbyterianism, Paisley was warning his little flock, and they must be ever-vigilant in their determination to remain separate from such faith-weakening "apostasies".[6]

But the real enemy, uniting all the modernists, heretics and "apostates", was the ecumenical World Council of Churches (WCC). Formed in 1948, this brought together nearly 150 Protestant churches from 44 countries, among them the Irish Presbyterian Church, to explore the causes of disunity in world Christianity and to clear the way towards closer co-operation and ultimate reunion. The Roman Catholic Church declined an invitation to its founding conference in Amsterdam in 1948, but by the late sixties was starting to send observers to its meetings.

To Free Presbyterians, the new body marked a huge step towards reversing the Reformation by moving towards unity with Rome. Paisley denounced the Archbishop of Canterbury of being ready "to barter our British heritage to the Blaspheming Bachelor of the Tiber".[7] He accused the Irish Presbyterian Church of wanting "to play their full part in the marriage of an emasculated Protestantism to the scarlet-robed hag of the seven hills."[8]

A secondary line of attack, attuned to the Cold War hysteria of the fifties, was against the WCC's attempts, eventually successful, to persuade the Orthodox churches of Eastern Europe to join - this was portrayed by Paisley as an unholy alliance between ecumenism and Communism.

Surprisingly little attention was paid in the first decade of the new church to attacking Catholicism itself: the principal protagonist was seen instead as the "enemy within", those Protestant churches and clergy prepared to compromise on their historic stand against "popery" for the sake of social and spiritual harmony in Northern Ireland.

However, sermons on the excesses of the Roman church - if possible spiced with sarcasm and sexual innuendo - were still the favourite fare of most Free Presbyterian congregations.

Paisley was particularly skilful at portraying Protestant horror at the priest, a mere man, hearing confessions:

I would go into the dark and damnable confessional, where my poor Roman Catholic countrymen entrust their wives and daughters to him, and while the tyrant was pressing his odious and obscene investigation, putting the poor creatures on a moral rack till they sink with shame at his feet, I would drag the victims forth from his grasp and ring in the monster's ear - No Popery![9]

The language of his first lieutenant, John Wylie, a former electrician from Dundonald on the outskirts of East Belfast, often verged on the pornographic: he once described a Church of Scotland moderator who had the audacity to visit Pope John as "this slimy toad, with his sewer-like mind, 'sniffing around' for an opportunity to feed his lustful appetite on the impurities of popish paganism."[10] In a 1961 article Wylie claimed that Pius XII was behind Nazism, that all Popes were "sensual, unholy, unclean and as bloodthirsty as a bloodhound", and that "the extermination of six million Jews is a mere drip in the bucket when compared to the wholesale murder of both Jews and Gentiles by the murderous popes in the Vatican".

One of the church's early problems following its formation in 1951 was that apart from Paisley and Wylie they had no preachers of any real calibre. In order to fill his early pulpits Paisley was forced to take on men who had little to offer except an ill-defined identification with his sect's theological position.

The ministers at the denomination's founding church in Crossgar were a case in point. The first incumbent, George Stears, was a returned missionary from South America who only took on the job, after pressure from Paisley, because he was in poor health and had nothing better to do. He lasted three months.

His successor, Sidney Lince, was an English butcher from a Plymouth Brethren background. He lasted longer than Stears and even served a term as the church's moderator - the only Free Presbyterian minister other than Paisley to have done so - before stepping down in the face of the big Ravenhill man's continued domination of every meeting from the floor. But he left in the late fifties, sick of living in a damp, rat-infested farm outhouse, and tired out by groundless allegations of immoral conduct and rows over theology which at times even spilled onto the street outside the little church - to the great amusement of passing members of the Lissara Presbyterian Church it had broken away from.

The third minister, who remains there to this day, was a quiet-spoken and retiring County Antrim man from a Church of Ireland background, Cecil Menary, who ran the Crossgar church with little reference to the evangelistic barnstorming and political controversies taking place elsewhere.

Paisley fully intended, of course, that a new breed of minister, tutored in his own particular brand of fundamentalism, should come through the ranks of the church itself. But first, conscious of his extremely limited resources, he approached the Free Church of Scotland - evangelical Presbyterians nicknamed the "Wee Frees" - to see if they would train his ministers. They consulted with a leading Irish Presbyterian theologian in Belfast and declined.

So in October 1952 he opened his own "theological hall" in a back room in the Ravenhill church. There he moulded the three men who would be his faithful understudies for the next 35 years: John Wylie, John Douglas and Bert Cooke. Both Douglas and Cooke were from the working class streets off the Lower Ravenhill Road: Douglas had been Paisley's first convert the Sunday after his arrival at the church in 1946, and Cooke was the son of a plumber who had been one of the original breakaways from Ravenhill Presbyterian Church. A few years later a strict young man called Alan Cairns joined the class - he would later become the denomination's hard-line theologian.

The theological hall had its teething problems. Its first two "professors" were a wandering Scotsman who had seen service in three churches and held an unrecognised American doctorate, and a less than competent Ballymena-born Texas-based fundamentalist.

Bad experiences with such men of letters apparently did not deter the ambitious young moderator, only too aware of his own lack of formal education, from acquiring a few equally dubious credentials. From the early fifties, following the custom of other evangelical preachers, Paisley started to add letters to his name. Firstly he joined learned societies open to the public, and the initials FRGS (Fellow of the Royal Geographical Society),

FRPhS (Fellow of the Royal Philosophical Society) and MRSL (Member of the Royal Society of Literature) appeared after his title.

In 1954 he moved into more questionable territory. He received a bachelor of divinity degree from the Pioneer Theological Seminary in Rockford, Illinois, and seven months later an honorary doctorate in divinity from the same institution.[11]

Six years later, following the death of its founder, Rev Robert Hansen, the Pioneer seminary, run as a correspondence college from his former home and offering degrees for as little as 25 dollars, was charged by the US Federal Trade Commission with misrepresenting Bible theology and philosophy home study courses. Before his death Hansen had himself pleaded not guilty to a federal charge of sending obscene literature and photographs through the mail.

By that time Paisley had sent off for another American degree, this time an MA awarded on submission of a thesis from the Burton College and Seminary in Manitou Springs in Colorado. The *Revivalist* claimed he was working on a PhD thesis for the same college on the subject of the 1859 Revival.

Unfortunately Burton, like Pioneer, was listed by the US Department of Education as a "degree mill', defined by that authority as an organisation, often without even a campus or a teaching staff, which awards degrees, usually by mail, without requiring students to meet the standards "established and traditionally followed by reputable educational institutions". In other words, both Paisley's degrees had come from bogus and disreputable correspondence colleges.[12]

The lack of trained Free Presbyterian ministers continued to be a problem into the 1960s, despite a trickle of faithful graduates from the theological hall. David Leathem, the minister involved in the Maura Lyons case, had to be disposed of because he had espoused the heretical doctrine that some Christians could reach a state of "sinless perfection".

In 1959 Paisley appeared to have carried off a spectacular coup when a Church of Ireland curate in Antrim, Harold MaGowan, resigned to become a Free Presbyterian minister - the first and only recruit from the ranks of the Church of Ireland or Presbyterian clergy. MaGowan had fallen out with his local rector over a wide range of issues. These included MaGowan's insistence on preaching the imminent "Second Coming" of Christ to earth, and his objections to the use of the parochial hall for mixed Protestant-Catholic dances.

However, the new recruit turned out to have an independent turn of mind: he criticised the annual charade of electing Paisley moderator without opposition; he wanted to install a "high church" style communion rail in his church; and he complained about his paltry minister's salary, eventually breaking the church's rules by taking a supplementary job in a Belfast insurance office. In 1963 he resigned, together with his family and a couple of friends he had brought with him from the Church of Ireland, and formed a short-lived "Independent Free Presbyterian Church" of his own.

At Whiteabbey, north of Belfast, a whole string of prospective pastors tried without success to get a congregation which had been formed as long ago as 1953 off the ground. Among them were Crossgar founder member Cecil Harvey, later to become a maverick politician who, unusually for a Free Presbyterian, spent most of his career in Unionist parties other than Paisley's DUP; and Ivan Foster, who was at Whiteabbey as a student minister before earning his spurs by being jailed with Paisley in 1966.

The Sunday school superintendent at Whiteabbey, Billy Mitchell, was to go to jail in a different cause. In the seventies he became a leading member of the violent and illegal UVF, and was imprisoned for life for the murder of two UDA men. Mitchell believed that once "saved" nothing he did could lose him his place in heaven, and was still writing articles from jail on Calvinism for the UVF paper *Combat* into the 1980s.

Finance was less of a problem for the denomination than personnel. From the beginning a number of better-off members contracted or "tithed" a proportion of their income to the church in line with the biblical exhortation to Christians to give 10 per cent of their wealth to God's work. At Crossgar and Ballymoney a few farmers went further, selling land, machinery and livestock to help it get started. At Ravenhill Paisley could rely on the advice of a number of men who were successful small businessmen.

One of these, an office-bearer in the church in the fifties and early sixties, used considerable amounts of his own money to help purchase the churches at Antrim, Whiteabbey and

Dunmurry. He was also able to act as a front man when someone selling property to the church did not want to be seen letting it go to the Free Presbyterians for fear of losing business from customers belonging to other churches.

This manner of buying up property persisted well into the 1970s. In 1972 the Presbyterian Church itself sold an empty church in the Cliftonville area of North Belfast to a well-known evangelical property developer, Ted Burns. Burns, unknown to them, was an ardent Paisleyite who was later to become a DUP Assembly and Convention member. Several months later it reopened as the John Knox Free Presbyterian Church.

Inevitably money matters led to feuds, which were only exacerbated by Paisley's bellicose temperament. The same man who had contributed so much to purchasing buildings for churches left in 1963, after a bitter row over money allegedly not paid back, and the admittance of a divorced man to the congregation. The quarrel had started over the will of an elderly woman member who had left Paisley £800, a sizeable sum in those days, for his own use - money which the businessman claimed should have gone to the church.

It smouldered for several years but eventually flared into an ugly war of words. Despite the wall of secrecy erected around the affair by Paisley and his elders, several Sunday school teachers took the businessman's part when he accused Paisley, in the biblical language so favoured by Free Presbyterians, of being "earthly, sensual and devilish". He and around 30 other members resigned shortly afterwards.

There was a nasty little epilogue. Shortly after his resignation, the businessman opened his door one evening to two young men who started to threaten and abuse him. He swung at them with a golf club and slammed the door. Several years later he ran into one of them again. This time the young man was in a mood to talk, and told the businessman that after he had left the Church Paisley had complained so bitterly about him that he and a friend had decided to teach him a lesson. "We'll do it for the Doc," they told each other.

One thing the Ravenhill church did not lack in the early sixties was people in its pews. While other Free Presbyterian churches remained small, and the denomination as a whole had barely a thousand followers by 1961, Paisley was building a personal reputation as the most explosive anti-Catholic preacher since

Thomas Drew and "Roaring" Hugh Hanna a century before. He was also developing his famous "altar call" technique, borrowed from turn of the century American evangelists, in which he appealed for people to come forward and be "born again" into Christianity.

Over the years he has refined this to a fine art of psychological manipulation. An American researcher, David Taylor, who spent over two years as a regular attender at Paisley's church, has recorded how this works.

Paisley often ends his sermon by warning the congregation in the most graphic and apocalyptic language that they are just "a gasp of breath" away from eternal damnation. Having delivered himself of this dire message, he then asks them to stay behind for a short meeting after the service in order to find out how they can avoid such a fate.

Those who do will hear Paisley at his most powerful and persuasive, as he delivers an impassioned plea for "sinners to come to Christ". The congregation sing the haunting refrain of a familiar hymn: "Just as I am, without one plea. But that Thy Blood was shed for me. And that Thou bids me come to thee. Oh Lamb of God, I come".

Paisley steps down from the pulpit and paces up and down in front of the congregation, urging the unsaved few to put up their hands and come forward: "That's right, just lift your hand, anywhere in the meeting. Just lift your hand and say 'Yes preacher. Here is my hand. I'm going to come'".

Suddenly the temperature is turned up. He tells those who are already converted to rise to their feet, leaving only a few lonely "sinners" still sitting. Again and again he urges those who want to "close with Christ" to stand and come forward. He searches the pews in front of him for the handful of people still in their seats. Stewards pace the aisles ready to escort anyone ripe for conversion down to where Paisley is standing in the altar area. The pressure is tremendous. One former steward recalls one man sitting frozen in his seat and muttering desperately to him - "Get me out of this place".

But it works. In the sixties and seventies, hundreds, even thousands of people were "saved" through such high-pressure appeals, although in later years, because there were fewer newcomers at his services and he tended to talk more about politics, the numbers declined. Most of his followers agree with his manipulative methods: "Some of those people are under the heavy burden of sin. They need to be prodded to get them to come in," one Martyrs Memorial member told Taylor. However it is an aspect of Paisley's ministry that some ministers and elders have criticised him for, to the extent that he was forced for a period to drop its most high-pressure element - the isolation of the sitting sinners.[13]

THE YEAR OF THE GREAT PUSH

"The walls of Zion are breached and its doors are burned with fire. The enemy has most certainly come in with overwhelming power". That was Paisley's message in the first issue of *The Revivalist* in 1966. "We believe that God has called the Free Presbyterian Church of Ulster to the Kingdom for such a time as this". With the shrewdness of the supreme opportunist, portrayed as the foresight of the prophet, he saw that the heightened sectarian atmosphere of that year could be turned to the advantage of his militant little sect.

Paisley's imprisonment that summer following the Free Presbyterians' protest outside the Presbyterian General Assembly could have robbed it of that advantage. In the event his temporary removal forced his younger ministers, as yet relatively untouched by political controversy, into taking up the torch. And the Stormont government's ban on all open-air rallies within 15 miles of Belfast compelled them to campaign in areas as yet uncanvassed by the church.

The young East Belfast triumvirate of Bert Cooke, John Douglas and Alan Cairns found it easy enough to adapt the anti-ecumenical rhetoric they had learned at their master's knee in the back room at Ravenhill to tirades against ecumenism's political face, Terence O'Neill.

They discovered little groups of sleeping Paisley supporters, many of them still church-going Presbyterians, who had heard his powerful preaching on the gospel hall circuit over the previous 15 years. One of these was Richard Reid, later to become a DUP Convention member and Free Presbyterian elder, who until then had no Free Presbyterian congregation near his home at Pomeroy in South Tyrone.

He, in common with many rural evangelicals, believed Paisley when he said he was being persecuted for his Protestantism, because he had seen him being treated as a leper by the Presbyterian establishment as long ago as 1951. Reid travelled all over Northern Ireland attending protest rallies in 1966 while Paisley, Wylie and Foster were in prison.

"The best thing that ever happened for the Free Presbyterian Church was the day that we were put in prison," declared Paisley at the Ulster Hall on his release from Crumlin Road jail. "For God has let these things happen unto us for the furtherance of the Gospel". For him it was the fulfilment of a 20 year-old ambition.

His jail term made him famous. Both disgruntled evangelicals and people of gut Loyalist sympathies but no particular church affiliation flooded to Free Presbyterian services, recalls one trainee minister in Armagh. It had taken the best part of 15 years to form the dozen churches that were in existence at the beginning of 1966. Now 12 new churches were started in barely two years: two in South Down, three in North Armagh, two in the Lagan Valley, and one each in Ballymena (with the affiliation of his father's church), Tyrone, Fermanagh, South Derry and Derry city.

This big push set the pattern for new churches in the future. The usual procedure was that a small group of people who already attended a Free Presbyterian church in a neighbouring town would ask that church to organise a mission, usually lasting five weeks, in their own vicinity.

Advertisements would be placed in the paper read by local Protestants for an "Old Time Gospel Campaign" to be led by Ian Paisley ("Come and Hear this Mighty Man of God preach the grand old Gospel with Power") and exhorting people not to miss the services "or you may miss Christ forever". This combination of the North's most controversial evangelist and the age-old appeal to the Protestant psyche guaranteed a big turn-out. The services would take place in a local hall, often an Orange hall, a tent pitched on ground provided by a local sympathiser or occasionally even in the open air.

Thus the tent mission at Dungannon in August and September 1967 was organised by the Armagh church and its new minister, Bert Cooke. Paisley preached on Sunday evenings to congregations of a thousand people and more than 90 people were "saved" during the five week campaign.

William McCrea, then a diffident 19 year-old only a few months out of school, made a big impact when he led the hymn singing. McCrea came from Stewartstown, north of Dungannon, and had joined the Armagh congregation after hearing Mrs Paisley address a protest rally in the town during her husband's imprisonment the previous year.

On the Friday night before the mission ended Paisley asked those who wanted a Free Presbyterian Church in Dungannon to raise their hands. The following Sunday the first meeting of the 21st congregation of the Free Presbyterian Church of Ulster took place in the mission tent, and local leaders claimed 150 applications for membership were requested. Shortly afterwards a portable hall was erected near the site where the mission had taken place. Five years later Paisley returned to Dungannon to open a new 300-seat church, built and furnished in just over a year, largely by voluntary labour.

Now he planned a big new church in a more middle-class area further up the Ravenhill Road, in the grounds of a nursing home he had bought from a well-heeled Baptist couple, the Nesbitts. On 4 October 1969, as Protestant mobs gathered in the Shankill Road and East Belfast to attack the Catholic enclaves of Unity Flats and Short Strand, the American fundamentalist Bob Jones Jnr opened Paisley's new Martyrs Memorial Church opposite the Ormeau golf course.

Paisley claimed it was the largest Protestant church, apart from cathedrals, built in the United Kingdom since the Second World War. It had pews for 1,450 people, but was capable of seating 2,300 if extra chairs were brought in. It had cost over £170,000 , £120,000 of which had already been raised: £20,000 from two American fund-raising trips by Paisley and the rest by collections and individual donations from church members.

Six thousand people attended the opening. It was the most triumphant moment of Paisley's clerical career. He taunted his opponents in the established churches with the splendour of his new shrine, and "the prosperity of God's people" in comparison with their falling memberships and paltry fund-raising efforts: "They have to have daffodil teas and pea-soup suppers and jumble sales and domino dinners and pyjama picnics. It's the way they raise their money, the poor old ministers pleading - 'If you've any dirty old coats and any torn pants you don't want, God'll take them from you'".

The 1971 census showed that the membership of the Free Presbyterian Church had risen more than sevenfold since 1961, to over 7,300. The vast majority had joined it in the previous five years. In 1970 Paisley was claiming congregations at Martyrs Memorial of 1,400 every Sunday morning and nearly 3,000 in the evening.

In the summer of 1971, as Northern Ireland was plunged into a re-run of its violent origins, with the start of the Provisional IRA's bombing campaign and the clamp-down of internment, Free Presbyterians were celebrating the opening of their 32nd congregation. Like some poisonous growth on a sickly plant, their bright new temples to separatism and sectarianism were among the very few beneficiaries of the collapse of Terence O'Neill's timid attempt at reform. In the midst of carnage and chaos, Paisley's church had finally arrived.

UNDER ONE MAN'S HAT - HOW NOT TO RUN A CHURCH

Presbyterianism can claim with some justice to be the most democratically-run denomination in Western Christianity. In Ireland, its bottom rung is the "kirk session", made up of the minister and elected laymen, the elders, in each church. Ministers and elders take the same ordination vows. Above them is the church's basic decision-making body, the "presbytery", bringing together the ministers and elders from all the churches in one area. Its decisions can only be overturned by the church's annual General Assembly, consisting of a minister and representative elder from each of Ireland's 560-odd churches. Presbyterians claim this system is derived from those laid down both by Old Testament prophets like Moses and the early Christian Church under Peter and Paul.

This is the system of government that Paisley and the Crossgar breakaways objected to in 1951, claiming that "the ecclesiastical hierarchy of Church House (the church's headquarters in Belfast) is as unbending as the Vatican, and ministers and elders fear the denominational biggies in the same cowardly manner in which the priests fear their superiors".[14] The ultimate irony is that the alternative system Paisley has instituted over the past 35 years, while continuing to lay claim to the democratic traditions of Presbyterian government, has in practice perverted it into a ruthlessly hierarchical, secretive and arbitrary despotism. The despot, of course, is Paisley himself.

Two characteristics of Free Presbyterianism immediately

undermine any claim to democratic church government. Firstly, apart from a few months in the early 1950s, Paisley has been the church's permanent moderator, in sharp contrast to the Presbyterian rule that this leading post should be rotated annually among ministers.

Secondly, the church has no constitution: when challenged on this in the church's ruling presbytery - Free Presbyterianism has only one presbytery for the whole denomination - Paisley has been known to wave the minute book angrily at the questioner and claim that *it* is the church's constitution. On other occasions, particularly when a cabal of senior ministers meets secretly to discuss controversial issues, such as the treatment of troublemakers, no minutes are kept.

The story is told of an English Baptist visiting Paisley in the early 1950s and asking him where the presbytery meetings of his church took place. "Under this hat", replied Paisley, smiling and pointing to his head.

The exercise of power may have widened slightly since those days, as the church has grown and Paisley has taken on an increasingly onerous political workload. But it still rests with the moderator and his cabal of trusted senior confidants: John Douglas, clerk of presbytery and thus the church's effective administrator since 1970; deputy moderator Bert Cooke; Alan Cairns (now in the US); Ivan Foster, now the head of the church's education board; and Jim Beggs, the minister at Ballymena and Paisley's brother-in-law and election agent.

Paisley and Beggs are not the only members of the church's leadership who are related. Douglas, Foster and Paisley's former political lieutenant, the Dunmurry minister William Beattie, are also linked by marriage. The only member of the new generation of ministers to break into this core group has been David McIlveen, the hard-working young East Belfast minister who stands in for Paisley at Martyrs Memorial when he is away on political business.

These are the men who deal with any serious problems that arise in the church, such as potentially disruptive disagreements over theology. An infallible Bible and an awe-inspiring charismatic leader do not encourage dissent at the best of times. But the atmosphere of fear and total obedience these men enforce often appears to have more in common with the medieval Papacy than the "protesting" tradition of Martin

Luther. The traditionally Protestant concepts of freedom of expression and the primacy of the individual conscience have been turned on their heads in Free Presbyterianism. Paisley's church is no place for the Protestant dissenter.

George Hutton of Larne was one of those dissenters. He was the son of one of the original Crossgar breakaways, who had let his 90 acre farm in the rich East Down agricultural belt and sold his cattle and machinery in order to raise money to help the struggling new denomination. His father worked for four years as a full-time pastor in the church before his health gave way and he had to return to the farm.

Hutton remembers RUC men lurking outside the family home during the disappearance of Maura Lyons, and being told not to take lifts from strangers for fear that Free Presbyterian children would be kidnapped in retaliation. His father was one of the most respected members of the church's ruling presbytery, and his son grew up in an atmosphere of puritan "good living", deep devotion to the Free Presbyterian Church and affection for its moderator.

However, when Hutton wanted to study to become a minister in the church, his father recalled that money lent by him to build it up in the early years had never been repaid, and cautioned him against it. Hutton failed to heed his father's advice and went on to study for the ministry at the church's theological hall in the early 1970s.

He was a good student, although in his latter years there he was starting to gain something of a reputation for being a stickler for the Calvinist doctrine of predestination - the belief that sinful mankind needs God's grace in order to achieve salvation, and this grace is given only to an "elect" predestined by Him, and not to those who are "saved" by their own decision. It is an élitist doctrine to which Paisley also subscribes, although his efforts from the pulpit to convert every Tom, Dick and Mary who came into his Martyrs Memorial Church often appeared to indicate otherwise.

The reasons for Hutton's expulsion from the church combined a peculiarly Northern Irish mixture of disputes over theology and Sunday observance, tension between religion and politics, and personality clashes in his Larne congregation. Hutton believes that it was his determination to preach the doctrines of Calvinism, plus his opposition to Paisley's high-pressure

American techniques of persuading people to become "born again" Christians, that decided the church's leadership to get rid of him.

The first he knew that he was in any real trouble was in September 1977 after he and his elders - the Larne church's governing "session" - barred a fellow-elder, a leading DUP activist in the town, from the communion table. The man was censured for opposing Hutton's theology and trying to divide the congregation against him, while members of his family were accused of working on Sundays, a serious charge in a sabbatarian church like Paisley's.

Hutton had already made himself unpopular with the local DUP earlier in the year when he had preached a strong sermon against Freemasonry and criticised the Orange Order for using masonic rituals. This, not surprisingly, led to allegations that some of the town's leading DUP-supporting Masons had had second thoughts about casting their votes for the party in that year's crucial local elections.

On this occasion the suspended DUP man complained to Paisley, and at the next monthly presbytery meeting the Free Presbyterian moderator overruled the Larne session's decision. Hutton angrily contested his ruling, alleging that there were too many people in the church who treated Paisley like "some kind of Pope".

This comment, he believes, sealed his fate. The Free Presbyterian Church's special court of inquisition was activated and a commission consisting of Paisley's most trusted lieutenants, led by John Douglas, Bert Cooke and Ivan Foster, descended on Larne to investigate the dispute. Before they questioned him, Douglas took Hutton into a back room and counselled him to admit that a mistake had been made, and the disciplinary action should be dropped against the DUP man. When Hutton refused, Douglas warned him that if he was not careful he would be finished in the church.

When it came to the actual investigation, the commission seemed interested principally in pressing on him an allegation that he intended to split the Larne congregation and start his own church, a charge strongly denied by both Hutton and his elders. Despite this, their interrogation went on for a gruelling eight hours, until 4.30 in the morning. Cooke and Foster went straight from Larne to Paisley's home, where he was waiting up to receive their report.

The following week Hutton was summoned to see Paisley at the Martyrs Memorial church and told by him that he should take a few weeks rest, a suggestion he agreed to. That night, however, friends told him if he did not appear in his Larne pulpit the following Sunday Paisley would make sure he never preached in it again. He took their advice and told his elders he would take the morning service in Larne as usual.

When Paisley heard of this he was furious. The next presbytery meeting was at Limavady later that week and at it he accused Hutton of lying to him by promising not to take any more services during his leave of absence. Hutton was sent into a side room while his case was discussed.

Through the wall he heard various members of the church's ruling body echoing and embellishing Paisley's remarks about him being a liar, a fanatic, a "hyper-Calvinist'. "They verbally mutilated me, tore me to pieces", he recalled. Shattered, he told them that after more than a quarter of a century of being reared, worshipping and ministering in the church he had no option but to resign from it.

At that point, on the edge of despair, and doubting even the existence of the Christian faith that had been his whole life, he says he even contemplated suicide, an act normally as unthinkable for a Calvinist as for any Catholic:

> The shock to the system was so devastating that I really thought of drowning myself. It wasn't as though the thing had gone on for a long time, fighting a case through a procedure. I'd been in good standing in the church, then all of a sudden I'm rejected. My session were supporting me one day; suddenly without me knowing why, 24 hours later, they had turned against me. The papers were running around having got word of it through one of the DUP men - they were coming looking for me. My wife used to go out to the shops and come back in tears because of the attitudes and treatment of the Free Presbyterians she'd meet. I was despised in the church I had loved and been reared in. I was suddenly the off-scouring, the scum of society.

He heard nothing more for two months, and in that time a small group from his Larne congregation, unhappy about staying on after his departure, asked him to hold Bible and prayer meetings with them. Eventually he received a letter from John Douglas telling him that he could not resign from the church's ministry while under its discipline. Instead a notice was published in *The Revivalist* explaining that "the presbytery had no other option but to reject Mr Hutton's resignation and to dismiss him from the ministry of the church and excommunicate him from membership".

For a minister to be excommunicated from a church calling itself Presbyterian is as rare and terrible a punishment as it is in the Roman Catholic Church. It leaves a moral and spiritual stigma in the North's tightly-knit Protestant community far beyond the bounds of Free Presbyterianism. What John Douglas called Hutton's "mismanagement" of the Larne church was apparently so subversive of the denomination that his punishment had to be the most cruel and draconian available to the Free Presbyterian leadership.

There was no redress, no appeal, no Christian compassion - but eight years on Hutton is remarkably free from bitterness. "God put the fight back into me and I am still going stronger than ever in His ministry", he says. He has now his own small independent evangelical church in Larne. The only clue to its traumatic origin is the clause in its constitution which denounces the Free Presbyterian Church for "the despotic rule of a hierarchy, displayed in unprincipled inquisitorial power and clandestine meetings".

George Hutton's principal sin was that his little rebellion came at exactly the wrong time for that hierarchy and its high priest. Political miscalculations had led Paisley into the debacle of the May 1977 workers stoppage, forcing him into a promise, quickly broken, that he would quit politics and devote himself full-time to the church.

But for the first time since the great breakthrough of 1966 there were problems in the church too. For the first time it was becoming too big to be personally controlled by one overworked preacher-politician and a couple of obedient lieutenants. There were signs of dissent among recent intakes of students to the theological hall. Despite a rigid discipline which discouraged the questioning of lecturers and imposed "lines" for misdemeanours, some students had dared to query both Paisley's theology and his practice, particularly his methods of pressurising people into becoming "saved".

Towards the end of 1976 the students were called one by one before a panel of ministers chaired by Paisley to be interrogated on their beliefs - "it was a form of inquisition", said one of those questioned. Two students were judged to have particularly subversive views. One of them, a Scotsman who had already spent several years as a missionary in Peru, was told when he started work as a student minister that he would have to submit his sermons for vetting by a neighbouring minister. Both men left the church in early 1977.

Later that year there were more rumblings. One young minister had collected quotes from Bob Jones and other American fundamentalist associates of Paisley's denouncing extreme Calvinism. He had drawn up a petition to demand that Paisley stop attending conferences where such denunciations were made. Another minister was writing a paper criticising Paisley's perpetual moderatorship and theological somersaults over the years.

At the presbytery meeting in the autumn of 1977 at which he was due for re-election as moderator, Paisley referred to rumours of dissatisfaction with his leadership. This prompted a chorus of denials, declarations of loyalty and admiration, and eventually an unopposed motion that he should continue in office. It was the classic ploy of the uneasy autocrat intent on reaffirming his authority.

Hutton's excommunication was effectively the end of any incipient rebellion. The next three years saw the departure of two of his closest associates: Norman Green, the English minister of the Omagh church, and George Wylie, John Wylie's eldest son, a schoolteacher who had trained for the ministry in Scotland and was once considered to be one of the denomination's best theological minds.

The former resigned over the involvement of the church in DUP politics. The latter was first blocked by the leadership from becoming an elder, and then was excommunicated in as ruthless a fashion as Hutton. When one elder suggested that young Wylie should have the right to appeal to presbytery, Paisley said he had been put out of the church on his instructions and out he would stay.

Fear of what might happen to them kept three or four more potential rebels in the fold, voicing their doubts only to their closest friends. "There's not one minister in this presbytery secure," muttered one young minister to an elder at a meeting shortly after Hutton's expulsion.

THE MINISTRY OF FEAR

Fear is what keeps most Free Presbyterian dissidents in line. Paisley has successfully convinced the majority of his church's members, as well as many people outside it, that he is God's chosen man and there will be divine retribution on anyone who goes against him.

He never tires of repeating the text from Isaiah his mother gave him on his entry to the ministry: "No weapon that is formed against thee shall prosper; and every tongue that shall rise against thee in judgement thou shalt condemn. This is the heritage of the servants of the Lord".

He has pointed to the untimely deaths of several of his adversaries as evidence of God's vengeful hand behind him: men like former Northern Ireland Prime Minister Brian Faulkner, killed when he fell off a horse; Judge Rory Conaghan, who sent him to jail in 1969, killed by the IRA; and J. L. Sayers, the editor of the *Belfast Telegraph* who led the attacks against him in the sixties, and who later died from a heart attack.

One young man expelled from the church confided to friends that he had been afraid to drive his car immediately afterwards. According to another former member who knew Paisley at Ravenhill and Martyrs Memorial for over 20 years:

He has built up a kind of aura around himself that he is something very special - he is the Lord's anointed. He says "the Lord spoke to me, the Lord has shown me" - he particularly uses phrases like that when someone leaves the church. He almost always preaches on the text 'Touch not mine anointed - Do my prophets no harm' - the suggestion being, of course, that he is the Lord's anointed and therefore you touch him at your peril. He honestly expects God to do it: to deal with his enemies, to deal with the people who leave the church and turn against him. There is a deep-seated ruthlessness about Ian. With his overwhelming personality, he uses everything - his height, his voice, the threat that he is God's servant. He wields that, holding it over people, generating fear - he loves to make people afraid - so that even people who know he's done wrong are afraid to say anything about him. He has built a kind of almost Messiah-like image of himself.

Theological deviations were not the church's only headache. In the late 1960s one of its most dynamic young ministers became involved with a homosexual group around the chairman of the Shankill Defence Association, John McKeague. When Paisley broke with McKeague in the autumn of 1969, this young man was quietly moved out of Belfast to a rural backwater. A few years later, when he started his own congregation, a decision was taken that it would be treated separately from the denomination's other churches, and would be kept at arm's length with no representation on the ruling presbytery in case of scandal.

In 1973, largely to prevent the same man from standing for the DUP in elections to the Northern Ireland Assembly, a rule was passed by the presbytery barring all Free Presbyterian ministers, apart from Paisley and William Beattie (who were already members of the prorogued Stormont parliament), from running for political office. This rule was relaxed in the 1980s to allow a number of ministers - notably Ivan Foster and William McCrea - to run for the Northern Ireland Assembly and the House of Commons.

Such pragmatic moves, usually determined by political considerations, were the cause of what little dissent remained in the church. In the late 70s Paisley faced some angry opposition, notably from John Wylie, by then in poor health and close to retirement, when he opportunistically changed his line on two church-related issues. He decided to run for the European Parliament, thus going against two decades of Free Presbyterian denunciation of the EEC as a Roman Catholic conspiracy. And he wanted to allow Freemasons to be church members, despite centuries of evangelical Protestant denunciation of all such oath-bound secret and secular socities.

In the 50s, like most devout evangelicals, Paisley had been virulently opposed to the Masons: one acquaintance from those days remembers him saying they got their strength from "the excreta that runs from the sewer-pipes of hell". As late as the early 1970s Bert Cooke was teaching student ministers that a Mason could not be a Free Presbyterian.

Now suddenly Freemasons were to be allowed in, although not as office-holders. Wylie lost his temper and stormed out of the presbytery meeting. Ivan Foster too was deeply upset. But inevitably the sheer weight of Paisley's authority swung the meeting behind him.

Some elders put the startling change of policy down to the masonic help Paisley had been reported as receiving both to finance the DUP and to build new churches in America: one remembered a Free Presbyterian function in the USA attended by a number of men prominently displaying their masonic rings. Paisley's argument on this potentially divisive issue was a shamelessly opportunistic one: that the church would only stunt its growth and alienate potential recruits if it banned or took a hard line against the Masons.

This politician's logic had increasingly become a feature of Paisley's thinking as he strove to build up first his personal political reputation and later the Democratic Unionist Party. It was reflected in a lessening of the stream of abuse against other Protestant churches and, more specifically, the disappearance of Paisleyite pickets on the Presbyterian General Assembly in the early 70s. "He realised that too much opposition to the church that a man believes in probably loses his vote at the end of the day," says former church elder and DUP Convention member, Richard Reid.

By the 1980s Paisley had little cause to fear any rebellion among his ministers. He was happy to leave the day-to-day running of the church in the hands of John Douglas, a highly efficient administrator who is quite prepared to be ruthless in defence of the interests of Free Presbyterianism if required.

The majority of the younger ministers are men who have spent a lifetime in the church, and have usually been "saved" through the ministry of Paisley or one of his senior lieutenants. Few of them have any formal higher education outside the church's own theological hall. Thus they have studied in an atmosphere totally insulated from the heretical outside world, and guaranteed to mould them in the Ulster fundamentalist mould Paisley demands - "indoctrinated and stamped out as Ian's wee tin soldiers," is how one former minister puts it.

Those who are unhappy with the overlap of the church into politics cope by not concerning themselves with matters beyond their own congregations. Paisley himself is only too conscious of these tensions. Whatever he is doing, he tries to attend the annual get-together of ministers and students every January at Kilkeel, a South Down fishing village, in order to check up on morale, loyalty and theological orthodoxy among his subordinates.

THE STRANGE WORLD OF MARTYRS MEMORIAL

The mid-1970s marked a watershed for the Free Presbyterian Church. In February 1975 *The Revivalist* boasted that Paisley's church was "fast outstripping the Methodist Church, one of the four main churches in Ireland, in size and income". The building programme was particularly impressive that year: an £80,000 church in Armagh on a hilltop site rivalling those of the Catholic and Church of Ireland cathedrals, and new churches costing £68,000, £70,000 and £150,000 under construction at Omagh, Portadown and Magherafelt respectively. At Ballymena plans were under way for the most splendid showpiece of them all: a £300,000 replacement for Kyle Paisley's modest tabernacle which would rival even his son's own huge church in East Belfast.

Every weekend a veritable army of Free Presbyterian voluntary labour criss-crossed Northern Ireland to work on these sites for the glory of God and Ian Paisley: foundation-diggers, bricklayers, joiners, plasterers, plumbers, electricians, glaziers, painters, gardeners, upholsterers, cleaners, plus hundreds of lady helpers who brought flowers and sandwiches and cups of tea.

In May 1975 Paisley opened his first and only church in the Republic at Coragarry, beside the uniquely all-Protestant Monaghan village of Drum. Perhaps crossing the Border was a symbolic mistake: for once the seed did not take, and in its first 10 years the new congregation rarely rose above 20 souls.

The truth was that although the press continued to call it "the fastest-growing church in Ireland", the decade-long forward rush of Free Presbyterianism was starting to lose momentum, even to grind to a halt. All but two of its 49 Northern Irish churches were in place by the end of the 1970s.

One important area of zero-growth was among the working class people of Belfast's sprawling Protestant housing estates. Although they might pay lip service to their religious heritage by sending their children to the nearest Protestant church's Sunday school, and would turn out in their thousands to vote for Paisley at election time, they seemed indifferent to his church.

This was particularly so in the most famously Protestant area of them all, the Shankill Road. Here a tradition of independent street-corner gospel halls, plus memories of his political unreliability in the 1960s, combined to make the area stony ground for his evangelists. It appeared to make no difference that some of the city's best-known Loyalist paramilitary leaders - men with a large following on the Shankill - were regular worshippers at Martyrs Memorial.

There was something grimly appropriate in the attraction of the "hard men" of Loyalism to the fiercest preacher of political Protestantism, who himself had been a leader of paramilitary groups in the 50s and 60s. Among them were Shankill Defence Association leader John McKeague before he and Paisley fell out in late 1969; Davy Payne, who would become one of the UDA's most feared operators in North Belfast; and Ken Gibson, the East Belfast UVF leader, who was a member of the Sunday afternoon men's bible class. Tommy Herron, the UDA leader killed in an internal feud in 1973, was another occasionally seen at Paisley's church.

A more regular attender was William McGrath, the leader of the strangest of all the paramilitary groupings, Tara. McGrath was a homosexual who believed that Northern Ireland's Protestants were the lost tribe of Israel. Among the more bizarre demands in his group's political programme were the closure of all Catholic schools and colleges, and the banning of the Catholic Church as an illegal organisation. He had been involved in political agitations with Paisley as far back as the Divis Street riots in 1964.

Another leading lay member with paramilitary connections was Trevor Gracey, who ran the Martyrs Memorial Male Witness, a group of men who held services in the Aughrim Street mission hall in Loyalist Sandy Row and open air services elsewhere in the Belfast area. It was the successor to the Sovereign Grace Protestant Crusade, a group of lay evangelists at the old Ravenhill church who had shamelessly mixed religion with politics, and worked with Ulster Protestant Action running an anti-Catholic bookstall in Belfast's Royal Avenue. One of their most popular themes was the paranoid claim that Catholics were moving to live in key areas in order to block off the main access roads into the city.

Gracey had been a defendant along with McKeague in one of the 1969 bombing trials. But his real claim to notoriety came later when, after being appointed by Paisley as the first director of the church's Ebenezer Home for alcoholics, he ran away with the home's cash and his teenage secretary, abandoning his wife and children.[15]

Objections to the way Paisley and his small cabal of ageing elders ran the church were rare. Fear of Paisley's ferocious temper kept all but the bravest quiet. The secretary of the church's missionary council, a strong-minded woman from North Belfast called Valerie Shaw, was one person who did object and suffered for it. In the 18 months before she left the church in 1975, she tried unsuccessfully to get Paisley to investigate allegations against William McGrath, then a housefather at the Kincora boys' home in East Belfast, that he had sexually abused young men in the past. Paisley, who a couple of years later would launch a "Save Ulster from Sodomy" campaign against homosexual law reform, did not want to know.

When she approached two other senior ministers, Ivan Foster and Alan Cairns, their response was to warn her that if she continued to press the matter she would divide the church and Paisley would "destroy" her. Six years later, following revelations in a Dublin newspaper, McGrath and two other men were jailed for buggery and other sexual offences against the Kincora boys.

After Valerie Shaw left, the church's ruling presbytery passed a ruling that no woman could ever again hold office in the church. If anything, Paisley until then had been less restrictive about women in the pulpit than other ultra-conservative evangelicals, although they were never allowed to lead prayers or services. Their principal role, as in churches the world over, was as cooks and skivvies.

"We made the tea and buttered the bread," is how one former member remembers it. She recalls the women at Martyrs Memorial catering for 6,000 people over three days of services and meetings during the annual Easter weekend Bible Convention. Some years earlier, at Paisley's bidding, they slaved through the night to provide hot sit-down meals for 5,000 people at the Ulster Hall.

Another area of concern, even among the ageing "yes men"

who made up the Martyrs Memorial "session", was the increasing politicisation of Paisley's sermons. "He used to go on about the latest crisis for an hour and then tack an appeal for souls on at the end, or in the last two minutes mention the Bible," says one former member.

A related headache was the wild fluctuations in attendances. At time of crisis people flocked in their thousands to the more political evening services. But the core of people who took part regularly in the church's activities was relatively small. Towards the end of 1976, when times were fairly quiet, attendances fell off, people were not coming to prayer meetings, the amounts in the collection plates were down, and Paisley felt it was time to re-inject some fervour into the congregation by a strong dose of "revival" enthusiasm.

Over a period of a month on either side of Christmas he raised the tempo of his sermons and of his exhortations at prayer meetings. In response there was a rise in the number of conversions, complete with the occasional dash of drama, such as the old Presbyterian pulpit-builder who died 22 hours after being "saved".

The prayers were led by senior men like the Tipperary-born elder Bob Newman, later to become deputy mayor of Belfast. Paisley's children, Rhonda, Cherith and the twins Ian and Kyle, all prayed. Ten year-old Kyle counted 31 people praying out loud at one meeting. It was a marvellous way to restore the church's morale.

Revival campaigns had always been a regular feature at Free Presbyterian churches. The previous year over 340 people had been converted during a five week campaign in Ballymena, still the most fertile ground of all for the evangelism of its favourite son.

However, even the most spectacular crusade could not alter the fact that in most of Northern Ireland the church appeared to be exhausting its natural constituency: evangelicals unhappy with the ecumenical stand of the larger Protestant churches, who either identified with, or were not overly worried about, the political involvement of Free Presbyterianism. The more Paisley turned to politics, the less that constituency was likely to expand.

At the same time, the Irish Presbyterian Church, from which the denomination had recruited many of its early members, was clearly moving to the right. The late 60s and early 70s had seen the emergence within it of a new generation of evangelical ministers whose theology was little different to Paisley's, and who ·were eventually to vote their church out of the World Council of Churches (WCC).

It was no coincidence that the campaign inside the Presbyterian Church to pull out of the WCC coincided with the "Troubles", and the pretext was the WCC's decision to grant humanitarian aid to liberation movements fighting against apartheid and white minority rule in Southern Africa. Many conservative Presbyterians saw the Provisional IRA and the African guerilla groups as part of the same worldwide terrorist network. They were encouraged in this belief by Paisley's anti-WCC tirades: he hammered home the message that support for terrorism was the inevitable result of the WCC's "blasphemies" against Christ and the Bible, which had led it to seek closer association with the Church of Rome.

In a parallel effort inside the church, the ultra-conservative Tyrone minister, Robert Dickinson, a senior Orangeman and formerly a prominent member of both the Unionist and Vanguard parties, led an anti-WCC ginger group calling itself the Campaign for Complete Withdrawal (CCW).

In 1976 a motion in the General Assembly to disaffiliate from the WCC was lost by 481 votes to 381. Outside, Paisley and his supporters had mounted their first picket on the assembly since the late 60s. Some observers believed it was the bullying presence of the picketers which had swung the vote against leaving, and some of the more astute Paisleyites thought that was precisely the purpose of the exercise: to keep the Presbyterians in the World Council so Paisley would still have that stick to beat them with. "We don't want them out, because even if they come out they are still the same rotten old church anyway," one former Free Presbyterian remembers a plain-spoken Martyrs Memorial man saying at the time.

Two years later Dickinson's group succeeded in reversing the 1976 vote and getting a specially convened assembly to suspend the church's WCC membership. This became outright withdrawal in 1980. In 1985 Presbyterianism's rightward movement culminated in the election of Dickinson to the moderator's chair.

It was ironic, then, that as Ulster Presbyterians turned inwards and away from international church movements, Paisley's church started to investigate the possibilities of expanding into new fields of potential growth abroad: in North America, Australia and continental Europe.

The first opening came in Canada in 1976, when the minister of a 35-member fundamentalist Presbyterian church in Toronto retired. The elders wrote to the Free Presbyterian minister at Tandragee, County Armagh, a former aircraft designer called Frank McClelland, who had once lived in Toronto and worshipped at the church, to ask him to take over. After consulting with Paisley McClelland said he would, on the condition that the congregation joined the Free Presbyterian Church.

When it became clear that Paisley would himself inaugurate the new constituent church, the Attorney-General of Ontario tried to get him banned from Canada as a "racist demagogue". Despite this, and despite a decision by a Toronto education board to bring forward the date for demolishing the building in which the new church planned to meet following protests by local residents, the ceremony went ahead as planned in September.

Paisley, of course, was no stranger to Toronto. His father had been a friend of the old Baptist fundamentalist pastor of its big Jarvis Street church, Dr T. T. Shields, since the 1930s, and Paisley had himself preached there on a number of occasions. His brother Harold, a Brethren evangelist, had also lived in the city since the mid-1960s, although relations between the two men had been strained for many years because of the theological differences between them, and Harold's unhappiness about Ian's involvement in politics.

The next move was into the Southern hemisphere. Three preaching tours of evangelical churches in Australia by John Douglas and a young Banbridge minister, Fred Buick, led to a tiny congregation at Port Lincoln in South Australia asking for affiliation. Buick, a particular favourite of Paisley's, was sent out. But the congregation remained small, and in 1984 he moved to Perth, the boom town of Western Australia, to start a congregation in an Orange Order-owned church among new immigrants, many of them from Northern Ireland.

BOB JONES AND THE BIBLE BELT CONNECTION

However, the real breakthrough for the Free Presbyterian

Church abroad came in 1977, with the opening of Paisley's first church in the United States, on the doorstep of Bob Jones University in Greenville, South Carolina, the so-called "Buckle of the Bible Belt".

Paisley had first come in contact with the Bob Jones family at an anti-World Council of Churches conference in Amsterdam in 1962. Paisley and Bob Jones Jnr, the son of the founder of the university, immediately recognised each other as kindred spirits: militant fundamentalists, not afraid of incurring the odium of ecumenists and liberals by their ferocious attacks on the Roman Catholic Church, and their insistence on "separation" from all Protestants who had any contact with it.

The two men, both from Baptist backgrounds, also share a profound hostility, bordering on paranoia, towards any religious group, however evangelical, which has any time for ideas deemed by them not to be based on the infallible Bible. Even in American fundamentalist terms, Jones is an ultra-fundamentalist. From him Paisley learned about the extraordinary variety of deviations from true American Protestantism: dubious Southern Baptists, neo-evangelicals like Billy Graham (already a favourite Paisley target) , followers of "neo-orthodoxy", "pseudo-fundamentalists", false revivalists, and the "new pentecostalists" of the charismatic movement - a particular anathema to Jones.

Roman Catholicism and deviations from fundamentalism were not the only subjects Jones had strong and unfashionable views on: he was also an apologist for slavery, arguing that the average black worker on a plantation in the Deep South before the American Civil War was better off than the average black unemployed man in America's urban slums in the late 20th century.[16] And, not surprisingly, he was a ferocious anti-Communist, seeing the face-off between Taiwan and Communist China as a confrontation between Christ and the antichrist.

Such views had made him a friend and supporter of some of America's foremost racist and far-right politicians: Governor George Wallace of Alabama, Governor Lester Maddox of Georgia - whose speeches were occasionally reprinted in the *Protestant Telegraph* - and Senator Strom Thurmond of South Carolina. All three were honorary degree-holders of Bob Jones University.

In 1964 Paisley paid his first visit to Bob Jones University, the self-styled "world's most unusual university". It is run as an unashamedly fundamentalist institution, dedicated to the "training of young people in the clear principles set forth in the Scriptures", and to "combating all atheistic, agnostic, pagan and so-called scientific adulterations of the Gospel".

Despite this, it is not a bible college but a fully-fledged university campus of 5000 students from almost every state in the Union and around 30 foreign countries. For years it fought a series of costly court actions against the US government in a rearguard attempt to keep out black students: its founder, Bob Jones Snr, believed that the separation of the races had been ordained by the Bible.[17]

On the campus there is no smoking, drinking, swearing, rock music or unchaperoned dating. The authorities have the right to expel any student who "in the opinion of the University, does not fit into the spirit of the institution" regardless of whether he or she obeys its rules.[18] Security is tight - the campus guards carry guns, and some years ago applied unsuccessfully for permits to carry automatic rifles and machine-guns.

Paisley's rumbustious personality and aggressive preaching style made him an immediate hit - Jones believes he is one of the world's greatest contemporary preachers. In 1966 Jones travelled to Belfast to confer on him an honorary doctorate of divinity on his release from prison. He was later co-opted to serve on the university's board of trustees. He has visited the Greenville campus on over fifty occasions, and every Spring he is the star turn at its bible conference, where he preaches to up to 7000 people in a colossal new auditorium which he himself opened and dedicated.

Over the years Jones has become Paisley's closest friend and confidant. He is a sophisticated and worldly man for a fundamentalist; well-travelled, a lover of theatre and literature, a collector of sacred paintings. He is particularly proud of his reputation in the US as a Shakespearean actor, and has used his theatrical training to help Paisley take the rough edge off his Ballymena accent and adapt his style and presentation to a broader audience. The effect of this can even be seen occasionally in Paisley's Belfast pulpit, as he lapses into the folksy Southern drawl of an American "Bible Belt" evangelist.

Paisley also learned from Jones the techniques of marketing his message for a wider public by buying time on commercial radio stations, and recording his sermons so that he could sell them as tapes afterwards. By the late 1970s he was selling over 50,000 tapes of his sermons every year, and by the mid-1980s his voice could be heard regularly on religious radio shows in the Isle of Man, South Carolina, Philadelphia, Toronto, Vancouver, Sydney (Australia), West and South Africa, Zimbabwe, India and Sri Lanka.

So it came as no surprise in 1977 when a congregation of conservative Presbyterians in Greenville, who had been without a minister for some time, heard Paisley preach at Bob Jones University and asked Jones to approach him to see if he could provide them with a pastor. They were unlikely to find one from the ranks of American Presbyterianism, which was largely liberal and ecumenist in theology.

The church was situated on a valuable site with ample room for expansion, and Paisley jumped at the chance of a bridgehead into the USA. In the summer of 1977 his trusted lieutenant, David McIlveen, was sent to open up this new endeavour. In the event McIlveen, a typically home-loving Belfast man, decided not to take up the offer of the permanent minister's job, and it went instead to one of the church's senior men, the hard-line custodian of its theological line, Alan Cairns.

Greenville and Toronto were to act as a springboard for the formation of five more North American churches and the beginning of several more embryonic congregations by the mid-1980s. Cairns, true to his calling as a theology teacher, started an extension of the church's theological hall at Greenville. By 1986 its first half-dozen students, all Americans, were working to build churches in Florida and New Hampshire and to start up congregations in Georgia, Arizona and California.

New churches have also been started in Philadelphia, Calgary and Vancouver, all of them with a strong Northern Irish exile flavour. In September 1985 Paisley was picketed and heckled as he preached in a tent in Londonderry, New Hampshire - the site of an early 18th century Ulster Presbyterian settlement - to the first all-American congregation of the Free Presbyterian Church. It had been started earlier that year by a converted Catholic businessman and is now led by the church's first American probationary minister, a Bob Jones University graduate trained at Greenville by Cairns.

As yet all the American Free Presbyterian congregations are

very small - apart from Greenville and Toronto, attendances at services are rarely of more than 40 people, and the Philadelphia church barely keeps going. However, at the very least, a Paisleyite seed has been sown in American fundamentalist soil.

FROM CATHOLIC SPAIN TO PROTESTANT CAMEROON

A less fertile field for proselytism has been Spain. The Free Presbyterian Church's mission board, set up in the mid-1970s, decided to send its first missionary to Spain, traditionally a source of dreadful fascination for Ulster Protestants. The persecution of Protestants by Spanish Catholicism reaches back to the Inquisition, and forward to the middle of the 20th century, with the Franco dictatorship's discrimination against and non-recognition of the country's tiny Protestant minority.

As far back as 1962 Paisley and Wylie had driven across France for an exploratory look at "papal, fascist, priest-ridden Spain". One disastrous attempt had already been made to send a totally unprepared young couple to Spain before John Hanna and his wife from Ballymoney travelled to Madrid in 1978. They attached themselves to a little evangelical Presbyterian church in a suburb of the Spanish capital called Alcocorn.

Paisley visited them later that year and immediately caused a split in the tiny world of Spanish Presbyterianism. In the wake of his visit, the Alcocorn congregation, until then one of the four constituent churches of the Reformed Presbyterian Church of Spain, broke away. The presbytery of the Spanish denomination, on the advice of an American Presbyterian missionary who had been working with them, had declined a suggestion by Paisley of association with his church. However, the pastor at Alcocorn put the offer to his congregation and the majority, perhaps swayed by Paisley's promise of financial help, voted to secede and link up with Free Presbyterianism.

In September 1986 two more Paisleyite missionaries were due to join the Hannas in Madrid. However, although the post-Franco atmosphere of unbridled freedom of religion and expression has been very conducive to the growth of Protestant sects, the hard-line separatist message of Free Presbyterianism has so far won few converts.

Outside Spain the number of Free Presbyterian missionaries working abroad has declined sharply in recent years. In the late

1970s there were around 20 church members working for a variety of interdenominational missions in places as far apart as West Africa, India, Papua-New Guinea, the Canary Islands, Brazil and Eastern Europe.

However, Paisley was not happy with this. He denounced a whole range of extremely conservative evangelical missions, a number of which had regularly taken on Free Presbyterians, for sending out people who had "sold out to the ecumenical movement and the charismatic movement".

It appeared that even at the furthest and loneliest ends of the earth he wanted Free Presbyterians to "separate" themselves from fellow-missionaries with dangerous ecumenical or charismatic tendencies. Accordingly in 1981 the church's mission board, in order to preserve its "separatist doctrinal position", decided to concentrate on sending out its own missionaries in the future.

The few long-term Free Presbyterian missionaries tend to ignore such advice. One of the more remarkable of these is Bill Woods, who has been in Brazil for more than a quarter of a century and has obtained a medical degree from a Brazilian university, plus qualifications in dermatology and eye treatment, so that he can work with leprosy sufferers in the Amazonian jungle.

Woods is now one of only six Free Presbyterians working for interdenominational missions. The church's other missionaries - four in Spain plus a young woman in Kenya working with an anti-ecumenical local minister - now come directly under its mission board. The board's next project is to send a young woman to work with Indian tribes in Bolivia in 1987.

The mission board is not the church's first international initiative to have faced constraints because of Paisley's ultra-separatist position. In 1963 the church joined the anti-WCC International Council of Christian Churches (ICCC), led by the maverick American Presbyterian Rev Carl McIntire. This body, which claimed the adherence of 111 churches in 51 countries by the mid-1960s, was totally dominated by the towering physical presence of its founder.

McIntire had been expelled in 1936 from his church in the quiet middle-class town of Collingswood, New Jersey, by the liberal United Presbyterian Church, but had taken most of his congregation with him to form his own fundamentalist Bible

Presbyterian Church. In 1941 he had set up the American Council of Churches to combat the "apostasy" of the ecumenical US National Council of Churches, and seven years later started the ICCC in competition with the World Council of Churches.

However, the most powerful medium for his ferociously anti-ecumenical, anti-Catholic and anti-Communist views over the past 25 years has been his "20th Century Reformation Hour" radio shows, which have reached an estimated American audience of up to 20 million people.

In them he has accused everyone from Billy Graham to the Archbishop of Canterbury of being involved in a huge conspiracy to turn the Western world towards atheism, ecumenism and Communism. He has said that "progressive and liberal are Satan's pet words". Even in the Cold War atmosphere of the 1950s his loony anti-Communism sometimes went beyond acceptable limits: in 1953 he clashed with the US State Department over an ICCC scheme to float bibles attached to balloons across the "Iron Curtain".

McIntire might appear to have been tailor-made to be Paisley's natural ally. But they were both quarrelsome and bellicose, with an enormous sense of their own importance, and an unwillingness to play second fiddle to anyone - Paisley had made this clear from the beginning, when he had refused to sit on the ICCC executive with his old adversary, Norman Porter. This similarity in temperament, when coupled with their overwhelming physical size - both men are six feet three inches tall - led to growing friction as Paisley, the younger man, gained in confidence and reputation.

When McIntire and the Bob Jones family fell out following yet another breakaway by McIntire, this time from the American Council of Churches he himself had founded, Paisley told him that he stood "with the Bob Joneses on all these matters because they stand with the Word of God".[19]

By the mid-1970s the Free Presbyterian Church was out of the ICCC, citing as the reason for leaving the insufficiently separatist stance of several of its member churches. Paisley was also unhappy at McIntire's growing tendency to identify the principal enemy as Communism rather than Catholicism, and to welcome right-wing Catholics on his demonstrations.

The result was the formation by Paisley and Jones of a new, mainly American grouping called the World Council of

Fundamentalists, which held its first gathering in Edinburgh in 1976. McIntire angrily declined an invitation, calling the Congress "a motley crowd".

The previous year McIntire had been deported from Kenya, where he was holding a counter-conference to the World Council of Churches, after the ICCC's press office had ignored a government instruction to avoid political issues by publishing a statement comparing Rhodesia with Northern Ireland, and praising Rhodesian Prime Minister Ian Smith for upholding Christian civilisation in Africa. Now in his eighties, McIntire, although as irascible and fractious as ever, and retaining much of his huge radio audience, is close to being a spent force in the world of right-wing fundamentalism.

Paisley, on the other hand, largely through his relationship with Bob Jones, is now a respected figure in American and international fundamentalist circles. He is part of a team of prominent preachers who travel to bible conferences and preaching conventions all over America. He has even opened his own stop on the tour with the Lough Erne Fundamentalist Convention, held every summer in Enniskillen. In the Southern "Bible Belt" he is a celebrity, billed by Jones as "the founder and pastor of the greatest church in all of Europe". Here he easily swaps his anti-Catholicism for the anti-Communism demanded by his ultra-conservative American audiences.

He has also accompanied Jones on tours of the Far East, attending fundamentalist conferences and visiting ministers and bible colleges in Japan, South Korea, Hong Kong, the Philippines, Singapore and India. In Singapore in 1977 he prayed with the deputy prime minister, an evangelical Protestant with a fierce reputation for cracking down on Communists. While in Manila for the 1980 World Congress of Fundamentalists he, along with Bob Jones and his son, Bob Jones III, spent nearly an hour with the then president, Ferdinand Marcos, who confided to them his worry that the Pope was coming to the Philippines the following year to make trouble and stir up the uneducated masses.

Contacts made through the ICCC and Bob Jones have also taken him to South America and Africa. In the Cameroon Republic in equatorial West Africa, he has taken under his church's wing the anti-ecumenical Orthodox Presbyterian Church of the Cameroon, whose General Assembly he addressed in 1985.

Nearer home the Free Presbyterians have also gained a foothold in England. In April 1982, on the eve of the visit to Britain of Pope John Paul II, the little Protestant Reformers Memorial Church, in a rundown part of central Liverpool, requested affiliation. It provided a link, through its former pastor, H. D. Longbottom, the last member of the Liverpool Protestant Party to be mayor of the city in the 1940s, to a strain of sectarianism which had long ceased to exist in England.

Three years later, a similarly tiny evangelical congregation at Oulton Broad in Suffolk, in the parliamentary constituency of the then Northern Ireland secretary, Jim Prior, became Paisley's second church in England.

Paisley's closest friend and associate in England is Rev Brian Green, a financial consultant and fundamentalist Baptist minister who runs his own church at Hounslow in West London. Paisley usually stays with Green when attending the House of Commons; their families occasionally take holidays together; and Green's wife works as parliamentary private secretary to Paisley and his fellow Democratic Unionist MPs, Peter Robinson and William McCrea.

Paisley and Green sit together on the British Council of Protestant Christian Churches, a normally dormant grouping of small ultra-conservative churches which was reactivated to organise opposition to the Pope's visit. In the past Green has worn other more sinister hats. He is well-known as a National Front sympathiser, stood in Islington in the 1970 general election as an independent with National Front backing, and has often led that party's unofficial Remembrance Day service for Rhodesia's white dead.

South of the Border there has been no advance on Coragarry. Paisley made one trip to Dublin to preach in the Mansion House and was pelted with tomatoes. Two young men sent to Dublin as missionaries have pulled out, leaving as the only Free Presbyterian presence south of Monaghan a young woman evangelist who has the unenviable task of putting across the gospel according to Ian Paisley in Cork.

All this foreign and missionary activity had repercussions on the church back in Northern Ireland. The principal consequence was the foundation in 1979 of the Whitefield College of the Bible, named after the great English 18th century Calvinist preacher, as a combined theological hall and missionary college. In 1981 it moved to magnificent new premises, valued at £200,000, in a large country house on 30 acres on the banks of the river Bann near Banbridge in County Down.

Until its foundation most Free Presbyterian missionaries had been trained at evangelical bible colleges in Britain. But true to form, Paisley became increasingly worried that they were being exposed there to dangerous heretical teachings. It was clear that he was anxious to mould a new generation of church leaders and missionaries, who would be as firmly imbued with militant separatism and fundamentalism as the ministers he had taught in the back room at the old Ravenhill church.

Paisley's first recruit from that era, John Douglas, became principal of the new college. Its student body is now around 25 strong, of whom just over half are studying for the ministry. They act as a kind of elite corps in their smart blue uniforms, with kepi-style caps for the women, at missions and open-air meetings around Northern Ireland.

They venture across the Border on occasions for door-to-door tract distribution: the Republic is still seen by most Free Presbyterians as the next best thing to darkest Africa when it comes to putting Christian courage to the test in the face of unbelief, superstition and idolatry. They also participate in political protests. Not surprisingly, they leave off their uniforms for both these endeavours.

The underlying emphasis to much of what they are taught is the importance of preaching. Paisley has been known to tell them that if they are not preachers, there is no place for them in his church. Following in the master's footsteps, they are taught to plan their sermons with the aim of "winning souls".

The Portadown minister, Ken Elliott, who is highly regarded by Paisley, teaches a course called "personal evangelism", in which he explains techniques of attracting people to church or gospel mission services and persuading them to come forward and be "saved" once they are there. According to former students, he stresses that during such services the preacher should not give advance warning that he is about to make an "appeal for souls" in case "Satan comes in and closes people's ears", but should try to catch the congregation unawares.

The Jesuits have nothing to teach the Paisleyites about ruthlessness and deviousness in Christ's cause. Their fanatical zeal for winning souls is just one more example of how their church has become a mirror image of the Roman Catholicism they so abhor. Their leader's mastery of the jesuitical half-truth, his papal-style domination of the church's government, and the inversion of the Protestant emphasis on the primacy of the individual conscience and the right of dissent are others.

This mirror image of conservative Catholicism appears again in their shared belief in the sanctity of the family, their hostility to and censorship of liberal social and sexual ideas, and their insistence on majority rights at the expense of religious minorities. They are both absolutist: "The Free Presbyterian believes that if his church is the true church, then everything else is false - it's absolutely black or white, there are no shades of grey," says one former student minister. As absolutists, they echo each other's claim to an all-exclusive relationship with God: to conservative Catholics, Protestantism is heresy; to Free Presbyterians, Roman Catholicism is anti-Christian.

DR PAISLEY'S FIVE DISCIPLES

In yet another parallel with the Catholic Church, the control of education is increasingly seen by Free Presbyterian leaders as the key to the perpetuation of the Paisleyite message into another generation. Thus it is no coincidence that the five ministers in charge of this vital area are also Paisley's most important assistants.

John Douglas is the shrewd and, if necessary, ruthless apparatchik and manipulator. He is the right-hand man who is strong enough, because of his efficient running of the denomination and his greater theological knowledge, to be the only church leader ever to dare to rebuke Paisley in other people's hearing.

David McIlveen, the college registrar and convenor of the mission board, is Paisley's right-hand man in another, more personal, sense: he runs his errands and stands in for him at Martyrs Memorial. McIlveen usually leads the church's pickets on sex shops, "anti-Scriptural" films and plays like *Jesus Christ Superstar,* "satanic" rock singers like Ozzy Osborne, and other manifestations of indecency and blasphemy which Free Presbyterians find offensive. His modesty and sincerity appeal strongly to the more pietistic, less political members of the congregation. McIlveen is sometimes spoken of as a potential successor to Paisley at the big East Belfast church.

Deputy moderator Bert Cooke is not as strong a character as Douglas. He was particularly uneasy at having to lead the Loyalist rabble in political protests during Paisley's imprisonment in 1966. But he is the church's most respected preacher after Paisley, and is a recognised expert on the biblical prophecies about the end of the world that many Free Presbyterians set so much store by.

Alan Cairns was acknowledged, until his departure to America in the late 70s, as the church's best theologian. He was known as a hard-line Calvinist - "Double Dogmatic Dick" was one of his nicknames - who believed that Calvinism was too difficult a doctrine to pass on to congregations.

Although not at all a political animal, Cairns' ideas on that subject were similarly extreme: he has been heard to say that Catholics should not be allowed to vote because of their disloyalty to the Northern Ireland state, a view which is held privately by a considerable number of Free Presbyterians.

The last of the church's five "educationalists" is also the most political, Ivan Foster. Foster, convenor of the education board which oversees the church's four schools, is considered inside the church to be one of Paisley's blue-eyed boys. A former trainee film editor with Ulster Television, he is as happy as his leader to be involved in controversy and confrontation.

He has no great intellectual gifts - his wife, the principal of the first Free Presbyterian school, at Kilskeery in South Tyrone, provides those. But he is in great demand around the churches for the aggressiveness of his preaching. The same aggressiveness led him to become the self-styled commander of the Paisleyite "Third Force" in Fermanagh in 1981, the only minister apart from Paisley and William McCrea to take a leading part in that Loyalist mobilisation.

The church's other two "political" ministers rate much lower down its hierarchy. William Beattie's heyday was the period up to 1970, when his pioneering efforts led to the setting up of several new congregations, and he made headlines by winning the South Antrim seat at Stormont. But his abrupt manner, the smallness of his congregation at Dunmurry, and his effective removal from the DUP leadership in the late 70s have done nothing to improve his status inside Free Presbyterianism.

William McCrea is enormously popular with ordinary church members for the fieriness of his preaching and the power of his singing - many younger Free Presbyterian women respond to him with the kind of sexual excitement their less religious contemporaries reserve for pop singers. He is now a gospel singer with an international reputation and a series of records, over half of them recorded in Nashville, which have sold several hundred thousand copies on both sides of the Atlantic.

Even Free Presbyterians see McCrea as a hard-liner. He officiated at the funeral of one of the UVF men killed blowing up the Miami Showband in 1975 when other DUP politicians were told to stay away. He refuses to share a platform or a recording studio with any singer or musician who is not a "born again" Christian. He is shamelessly sectarian: at the 1986 DUP conference he objected when a speaker compared a young Protestant killed by a plastic bullet to an earlier Catholic victim. But his early connections with dubious paramilitary figures have kept him out of the core group which controls the denomination.

These men have all been trained in Paisley's image. In their sermons McCrea, Foster and dozens of lesser-known ministers use the same biblical language, the same imagery of Protestant martyrdom and militancy, the same mixture of messianic religion and doomsday politics - even the same dramatic bellowing and whispering delivery.

They have also been taught to put over two central themes which mark them out from their counterparts in all other evangelical churches. The first is their passionate optimism that a spiritual revival will ultimately save Northern Ireland from the encroachments of Catholicism. And the second is the fierce and unashamed aggressiveness of their antagonism to that Catholicism.

This is the secret of the success of the Free Presbyterian Church of Ulster. In a period of deep crisis, the Free Presbyterian message is full of zeal and optimism. At the same time it makes explicit what for many evangelical Protestants is unspoken and even, in this democratic day and age, a little shameful: their continuing belief that, because of their religion, they are superior to Irish Catholics.

Embarrassing and extreme it may appear, but the Free Presbyterian analysis of the conflict of the last 20 years is shared by tens of thousands of more timid souls in other denominations, the kind of people who would occasionally go to a Paisley service in order to keep up their morale.

It is no coincidence that the growth of Paisley's church happened during those years of battle. Extreme Protestants, unhappy about having to live on equal terms with their Catholic fellow-citizens, and later feeling under increasing threat from the violence of the IRA, have turned to Paisley's preachers for reassurance. From them they have heard the comforting fable that they are a much-maligned "people of God", bound for a heaven reserved only for the chosen few who have faithfully followed the true faith. The parallel with conservative Roman Catholicism is unmistakable.

Paisley is happy enough to portray himself as a kind of modern Moses leading his people, like the persecuted Old Testament nation of Israel, to some unspecified promised land. Thus in a sermon in 1981 to mark the anniversary of the church's founding, he pledged:

> The next 30 years will be the greatest 30 years that we have ever seen in Northern Ireland because God has given us a firm base from which to work. The Free Presbyterian Church is more capable now to fight Popery and the Ecumenical Movement than ever she has been before. And God is saying to this church on its 30th anniversary - "Fear not, little flock, it is the Father's good pleasure to give you the kingdom".

However, he finished that sermon with a hint that, like Moses, he might not be there to finish the job. He said that SDLP leader John Hume had told him that when he died the Free Presbyterian Church would die with him. "I replied - You are a fool. When I die, God will send some young Joshua to lead us into the promised land".

As Paisley passes his 60th year there is no sign of any young Joshua. His personal paranoia about rivals and the church's oppressive structures have not encouraged the rise of any strong-minded young alternative leader. Most of the younger generation of ministers are cowed by him. They busy themselves with running their own congregations and pay scant heed to the burning political or ecumenical controversies of the day. They are pale shadows of the fanatical anti-Catholic controversialists of the 1960s.

Paisley has a few years in him yet, and he will certainly stay on as head of the church even if he leaves politics. But its future after him is also bound up with those politics: because if the Northern Ireland conflict ever comes to an end, the Free Presbyterian Church will have nothing to offer that is not already provided by a rightward-moving mainstream Presbyterian church and half a dozen apolitical evangelical sects with older and deeper roots in Ulster's Protestant soil. In contrast Paisley's church, like the man himself, is a creature of the "Troubles". There is no reason to believe that it will outlive either of them.

CHAPTER NINE

For God and Ulster

I believe that Ian Paisley was raised for this day.
DUP deputy leader Peter Robinson addressing DUP annual conference,
April 1986.

We in Ulster and we in the DUP are privileged that in this, Ulster's hour of need,
God has raised up a man to stand in the gap for God.
DUP Chairman James McClure introducing Ian Paisley
to DUP annual conference, April 1986.

Every year, generally on a Saturday around mid-April, one of the most unusual political gatherings to be seen in these islands takes place, normally, these days, in a hotel on the eastern outskirts of Belfast. From Belfast itself and from every town and county in Northern Ireland, members of Ian Paisley's Democratic Unionist Party congregate for the annual conference of Northern Ireland's second largest political party.

Year in, year out DUP conferences follow the same pattern, a pattern unlike any other party conference in the rest of Ireland or in Britain. At first glance it looks normal - delegates have a list of motions to debate, standing orders are adopted and there are the set piece occasions without which any party conference would be incomplete: the chairman's address, the party leader's speech and so on.

But there are features to a DUP conference which make it

unique in Western Europe. The first difference comes home very early on, at the opening of proceedings. A Free Presbyterian minister, usually the ever popular Rev William McCrea MP, is invited up to the platform to say a few words. His "few words" last for the best part of five minutes. First he takes the delegates through a reading from the Bible and then he prays - in passionately archaic language - for Ulster, for Protestantism and for the Democratic Unionist Party.

> O God our father, we pray that even today that thou wilt come and visit our beloved province. We pray, our God, that thou wilt come and visit us and that thou wilt breathe upon this province and so work in Ulster that thou wilt, out God, destroy the works of the devil. O God bless this party. O God our help in ages past, our hope for years to come, our shelter from the stormy blast and our eternal home.

The second major difference becomes quickly apparent when the debates start. The delegates show their insecurity, their barely concealed violence, in speeches and motions demanding the hanging of IRA men, the sealing of the Border, search and destroy missions launched in Catholic areas and the bombing of Dublin by the RAF; their fear, an ancient one, but fuelled by sixteen years of IRA violence, is of political and clerical Catholicism whether in the South or the North, of conspiracies to destroy their way of life, to suck them into the unimaginable tyranny of Popery. The motions and speeches reflect it all.

Each motion is duly proposed and seconded, as at any normal political conference, but all those who make their way up to the rostrum beneath the platform to speak, do so with the same uncritical, favourable voice. Most motions are passed unanimously with no votes or speakers against. The odd dissenting voice has been known to make itself heard. But these are rare occasions, so rare that they have entered DUP mythology to be remembered and talked of almost in awe.

Another difference, the most striking of all, is evident throughout the day. It is the deference, the adulation shown to the party leader, Ian Paisley - "the Doc" or "the Big Man" as he is affectionately called by the faithful. Still a physically overpowering figure, perhaps heavier these days than good health should permit and with a full head of almost white hair testifying to the gathering years, he sits up with the platform party, among his inner circle of acolytes, beaming down on the delegates like a happy grandfather at a Christmas family dinner. Occasionally he interjects with a loud "Amen" or "Hear, Hear" to signal his approval of a point made by a speaker.

It is, in fact, more like a family gathering than a party conference. A happy family, united, as the best Christian families are, under the benevolent and all-wise leadership of its paterfamilias. There is, as Paisley's second in command, Peter Robinson puts it, "a oneness" about the DUP which marks it out.

The climax of the day comes after a lunch of plain but plentiful food - soup, meat and three veg followed by a generous pudding and all washed down with gallons of orange juice or coca-cola. Food is the one approved vice in the DUP, shared by nearly all and especially by its leader whose gargantuan appetite is legendary. The well-fed delegates settle down in their seats, eyes glowing and a little, almost visible, ripple of anticipation stirring among them, as their leader is introduced. It is what most of them have come for - Ian Paisley, the boldest Protestant leader since Edward Carson, in full flight.

For the next hour he takes them through a litany of their fears and hates - Margaret Thatcher, Garret FitzGerald, Peter Barry, Charlie Haughey, Gerry Adams, Danny Morrison, John Hume, the Anglo-Irish Agreement, the Irish Republic, the Roman Catholic Church, the Northern Ireland Office, the media, the IRA, the SDLP and the Alliance party. Their enemies are legion. Once upon a time he would have included a list of Protestant enemies as well, Unionist politicians, past and present, whose weakness and compromise threatened to undermine and destroy Protestant Ulster - but not since the Hillsborough agreement was signed. Now past foes have become necessary allies in the common fight.

His voice rising or falling to punctuate or emphasise, he constructs little word cartoons to make his points or with jokes and barbs drives them home. The delegates, like an orchestra, respond to the conductor's baton, laughing at his jokes, hissing and growling at his enemies, cheering and applauding his defiance and loud assurances of resistance. He has them spellbound for the entire speech. At the end they rise to a man and woman and roar out chorus after chorus of "Paisley is our leader, we shall not be moved".

The party which Paisley bestrides like a colossus is now the unchallenged rival for Protestant support in Northern Ireland. It started from humble origins, though, with the tiny Ulster Protestant Action and the roadside election campaign of Albert Duff in 1958, but gradually it grew with Paisley's protests against the modernisation of Unionism. First there were the Ulster Protestant Volunteers, then the Protestant Unionists - all the time Paisley tapped a growing Protestant following until his own election to Stormont and Westminster brought the impulse to broaden into the DUP.

The transition from Duff's 4,700 votes to the staggering 230,000 votes won by Paisley in the 1984 European election took 26 years. In between, Paisley collected a belt-full of Unionist scalps, of enemies or Loyalist rivals. Some fell directly to him, others due largely to his efforts - O'Neill, Chichester-Clark, Faulkner, West, Craig and Ernest Baird. Slowly but surely he undermined the Unionist establishment and removed competitors, one by one, from the scene. With each departure his party grew, absorbing other politicians' lost support like a sponge. Now there are only two Unionist parties - his and the Official Unionists - when once there was five.

At virtually every election from 1973 onwards the DUP increased its share of the total Northern Ireland vote and with it the claim to speak for more and more Protestants. It particularly prospered under the proportional representation system of voting, which allowed Protestants to vote for the DUP without splitting the overall Unionist vote, but faltered at first past the post Westminster elections when the fear of vote splitting weakened it.

To begin with the party contested only a few constituencies - the original UPV and Protestant Unionist heartlands in the main - but gradually its horizons expanded. That expansion brought the DUP into more and more contests with other Unionist parties and each time the DUP grew at the expense of their Protestant competitors. An examination of the DUP's record which is confined to those contests reveals it steadily eating into the total vote, and by implication the Protestant vote. 11.6 per cent of the total vote for the 1973 Assembly; 14.7 per cent for the 1975 Convention; 18.7 per cent in the 1977 council elections; 27.3 per cent in the 1979 Westminster election and then a peak of 29.8 per cent with Paisley's European victory in the same year. In that election, Paisley outpolled all the other Unionist candidates put together.

In local council elections the story was the same. Between 1973 and 1981 the DUP's vote trebled while that of its Official Unionist rivals shrank by a third. In Belfast, controlled by the Official Unionists for 60 years, the DUP's growth underlined its working class appeal. In 1973 it had two seats on Belfast council and 6,000 votes. By 1981 it had won 16 seats and 33,000 votes while in the same period the Official Unionist vote slumped from 83,000 to 30,000. The DUP had succeeded in winning over large chunks of the Protestant working class while the Official Unionists became increasingly a middle class party.

The DUP thrived during crises like the 1981 Republican hunger strike when at council elections it matched the Official Unionists for the first time ever. When Protestant anxieties calmed, its support declined, as during 1982 and 1983 when Mrs Thatcher reigned supreme, her "Fortress Falklands" mirroring Unionism's new found confidence. When uncertainty then rose with London-Dublin talks and the rise of Sinn Fein so did the vote for Paisley and the DUP. The DUP vote has become a barometer of Protestant angst.

It was clear from the very foundation of the DUP that Paisley harboured the ambition of turning it into a major, if not the major, voice of Unionism. He had many hurdles to overcome - not least among them his earlier reputation for splitting Unionist organisations and for turning Protestant against Protestant in churches and Orange lodges. Added to that was the reluctance of many respectable Protestants to support a man who was a troublemaker and an infamous street rabble rouser.

There was little he could do to rectify those mistakes but there was one obstacle he could do something about - his party's image as the political wing of the Free Presbyterian church. With the help of Desmond Boal, his old friend from the days of Ulster Protestant Action, he moved quickly to remove it. The background to that and the formation of the DUP reveals a deep pragmatic streak in Paisley's nature and strong evidence that, for him, political ambition often comes before religious principle.

The roots of the DUP lie in the introduction of internment without trial in August 1971, a measure demanded by Unionist right wingers and regarded by Faulkner as the panacea for the IRA's accelerating campaign. Internment was an abject failure, alienating almost the entire Catholic population including its moderate middle class. It was a failure too in security terms - in the four months before August four British soldiers and four civilians had been killed but in the four subsequent months thirty soldiers, eleven policemen and seventy-three civilians died violently. The ranks of the Provisional IRA meanwhile were swelled almost to bursting point.

Internment also exacerbated sectarian tensions especially in Belfast to a feverish pitch. Rioting, burnings and intimidation, aimed mostly at Catholics, reached unprecedented levels and hard-line Loyalists demanded tougher and tougher action against the IRA. Paisley was again to the fore demanding the re-formation of the "B" Specials and the creation of a "Third Force" of Protestants to assist the British Army and RUC. He linked up with Craig and the pair addressed a huge rally in East Belfast demanding stiffer security measures.

The failure of internment, however, quickly brought pressure on the British government for a new political initiative - from their opposition parties and from Jack Lynch's government in Dublin. Before internment the SDLP had walked out of Stormont and they had pledged never to return to normal politics until internment was ended. Someone needed to throw them a lifeline.

Recognising, almost too late, how desperate the situation was the British Prime Minister, Edward Heath, invited Faulkner and Lynch to tripartite talks at Chequers, his country home, in September 1971. It was the start of a process that would ultimately produce proposals for a power sharing Assembly at Stormont and a Council of Ireland. Loyalists were immediately alarmed, despite Faulkner's assurances that no constitutional matter was on the agenda, and they sensed another O'Neill-type betrayal. Boal and Johnny McQuade, another veteran of Ulster Protestant Action, immediately resigned from the Unionist party and were soon joined by others.

No one can now remember quite who, but someone proposed that the various dissident right wing Loyalist elements, both inside and outside the Unionist party, should get together to discuss ways of frustrating Faulkner. Those involved were Paisley, Craig, Boal, the Rev Martin Smyth, then head of the Belfast Orange Order and another right wing Presbyterian, the Rev Bertie Dickinson from County Derry who was to go on to become Presbyterian Moderator in the 1980s. A couple of dozen other less well known Unionists joined and they met regularly from mid-September onwards in a hotel in central Belfast. They called their group the Unionist Alliance.

Inevitably the idea of forming a new right wing Unionist party combining all the anti-Faulkner elements was floated. There is now intense disagreement among those involved about what was agreed. Some say there was never any real discussion of a new party; others say that agreement in principle to form it had been reached. It scarcely matters who is telling the truth, for Paisley pre-empted the matter.

On the night of 29 September a bomb planted by the Ardoyne unit of the Provisional IRA exploded in a Shankill Road pub called the Four Step Inn killing two people and injuring 20, several of whom had to have limbs amputated. It was a frightening escalation of the sectarian warfare that had followed internment.

As news of the bombing came in, a Unionist Alliance meeting in the Grand Central hotel in Royal Avenue was just breaking-up. Paisley and Boal rushed straight to the scene and, as the bodies were being carried out and angry Loyalists began gathering on the streets, Paisley announced that they would soon have a channel for their anger - he was forming a new party to be called the Democratic Unionist Party.

That effectively killed off any chance that people like Craig and Smyth would join. To do so would look as if they were following Paisley's initiative and would give him the first claim to leadership. Smyth had another reason - his Presbyterian colleagues had never forgiven Paisley for the decades of insults meted out by the Free Presbyterian church.

In the next few weeks a smattering of Official Unionists left to join the new party but the parliamentary leadership was confined to a small and familiar core - Paisley, Beattie, Boal, McQuade and Charlie McCullough, a Unionist Senator. All but Beattie had been together in the days of Ulster Protestant Action.

The name of the new party was redolent of the years before UPA when the Independent Unionists had attempted to start a party called the Ulster Loyalist and Democratic Unionist Association. But it was Boal who thought up the name and persuaded Paisley to abandon the Protestant Unionist tag.

His reasoning was simple. The Protestant Unionists were the

Free Presbyterians under a flag of political convenience. As such, other Loyalists would be deterred from joining because of its religious exclusivity or would be reluctant because its leader and members had such a bitter history of attacking their religious denominations.

The choice was straightforward. Either the Protestant Unionists could stay as they were, the political wing of Free Presbyterianism - with little prospect of growing beyond the narrow confines of a fundamentalist, evangelical constituency - or the party could broaden its base and appeal to the wider Loyalist community.

Paisley chose the latter course and assiduously excised many of the old Protestant Unionist characterists. When the party's draft constitution was drawn up, for instance, it included as one of the party's aims the maintenance "of a Protestant monarch under the terms of the [Williamite] Revolution Settlement [of 1688]". This smacked of Protestant Unionism and Paisley rejected it. Others disagreed, notably John Wylie who felt that the new party should be open only to "saved" Protestants. When Paisley launched the DUP Wylie kept his Protestant Unionist branch in Armagh going but it soon folded up - even the most zealous Free Presbyterians preferred to be in the Loyalist mainstream.

Boal, who became the DUP's first chairman, also wanted the party to be socially radical and to have no links with the Orange Order. Boal felt that Orangeism should be a purely Protestant religious organisation free from the control of any party, especially the Official Unionists. Like other Loyalists he believed that the Official Unionists' control of the Order had weakened and compromised its Protestant principles. These were Boal's own political roots in the Protestant working class asserting themselves.

He had also become convinced during the O'Neill period that the Official Unionist party was undemocratic in its structures and unresponsive to the demands of rank and file Unionists. The important decision-making bodies in the Unionist party, like the Unionist Council and the Standing Committee, were full of the leadership's nominees - even MPs' wives were empowered to vote at meetings. His main charge against O'Neill, echoing Paisley's cry of "dictator!", was that O'Neill was snobbishly autocratic.

Wallace Thompson, a founder member of the DUP, can

remember Boal touring the country like an evangelist, explaining his hopes and ambitions for the DUP: "He explained that it would be a party which would continue to be right-wing on law and order but that there was a need in Northern Ireland for a party with radical social and economic policies which could embrace all people, whether they were RC or Protestant. I think the man did genuinely believe that this was an opportunity to broaden it out to produce a sort of radical alternative to the official Unionist party which was seen by Boal as the pro-establishment conservative party which was right-wing on all things and ironically soft on violence and terrorism. In some ways he was reviving the old Independent Unionist tradition and trying to secularise it as much as he could".

Of those lofty aims only one survived - the social and economic populism which already had its place in the Protestant Unionist make up. The DUP soon established a loose Orange link - not with the official Order but with the small Independent Orange Order which had broken off in 1903 over a row caused when a Loyalist shipyard worker defeated an Official Unionist candidate in an election. Its roots in Loyalist populism were the same as the Independent Unionists and ultimately Paisleyism. Paisley, although never a member of the Independent Orange Order, addresses their "Twelfth" gathering in County Antrim each year.

Boal's hope that Catholics might be attracted to the DUP was hopelessly naive, and there is no evidence that any conscious effort was made by him or anyone else to foster it. Within a few short years the DUP had re-asserted its old Protestant Unionist/Free Presbyterian identity. The aspiration to "democracy" in the DUP also died a quick death - after Boal's eventual departure the DUP became more monolithic under Paisley's control than any other party in the history of Unionism

Boal was partly to blame. He was reluctant to take time off from his increasingly busy life at the Bar to devote the energy needed to build the DUP and to attract non-Free Presbyterians. He was also intolerant of grass roots Loyalists who had problems digesting his idealistic message, as Wallace Thompson recalled: "I can remember Boal trying to explain to a stubborn wee woman what the DUP was all about but he lost his temper and walked out in disgust. 'I don't have the time to explain to people who don't have the brains to understand', he said". Boal increasingly opted out of the DUP's affairs until 1973 when he resigned. Despite his proposal, made in

1974, of a radical federal Ireland solution to the Northern Ireland problem he and Paisley have remained close friends.

The real difficulty, though, was that the Protestant Unionists, in reality Paisley's Ulster Protestant Volunteer divisions, had only changed their name, nothing else. They dominated the new party at the party's inaugural meeting in the Ulster Hall on 30 October 1971, the DUP adopted the same county-wide organisational structure as the UPV. UPV veterans and Protestant Unionists were elected to thirteen of the fifteen positions on the DUP organising committee. One founder member estimated that 70 per cent of the audience were UPV/Protestant Unionist members.

Most of them, of course, were also Free Presbyterians and it wasn't long before it became apparent that Free Presbyterianism was to dominate the DUP. From the very start DUP meetings opened with a Bible reading and a prayer while early executive meetings were held in a gospel hall in Aughrim Street in Sandy Row - the hall had been Albert Duff's and after his death it had been absorbed into the Free Presbyterian church. Not unnaturally, no clergymen from other Protestant denominations have ever joined the DUP, such is the overwhelming Free Presbyterian aura in the party.

The Free Presbyterian influence was symbolished by Paisley himself who, despite his early history of critical attacks on politically active evangelists, refused to resign his church positions. The perpetual moderator of the Free Presbyterian church now became the unchallenged leader of the DUP.

At grass roots level the overwhelming majority of DUP members were, from the very beginning, Free Presbyterians. The rise of Craig's Vanguard in protest at the suspension of Stormont coincided with Paisley's conversion to integrationism, a strange and unpopular cause for Loyalists. Militant non-Free Presbyterian Loyalists preferred the familiarity of Craig's campaign and flocked to him, not to the DUP.

The dominance of the Free Presbyterians soon became apparent and still is - when the DUP began returning elected representatives. In the 1973 power-sharing Assembly and the 1975 Constitutional Convention all but one of the party's team was in the church. Of the 74 councillors elected in 1977, eighty-five per cent of those whose religions were ascertainable were, according to one reliable study Free Presbyterians. In 1981 this rose to 89 per cent. In the 1982-8 Assembly, 18 of the 21 DUP Assembly members were Free

Presbyterians and four of them were ministers.

The Free Presbyterian influence in the DUP underlines a major difference between its brand of Unionism and others, a difference that has its roots in the plantation of Ireland by seventeenth century evangelical Protestants surrounded by displaced and hostile Catholic natives. It also helps to explain why so many church members get so fanatically involved in DUP politics.

While a significant number of Official Unionists, especially in the middle class, regard the Union with Britain as intrinsically worthwhile for social and economic reasons and identify with Britain in cultural ways, the DUP view of the Union is much more fundamental. They regard it principally as a mechanism through which they can best avoid absorption into a Roman Catholic Irish Republic with the resulting destruction of the Bible Protestantism that they hold so dear.

It leads them to a siege mentality; to the belief, savagely held, that Catholics must always be repressed, for the slightest relaxation could lead to disaster - Croppies must always be made to lie down and Loyalists must be ever alert to the danger that they might not. This explains their anti-Catholic bigotry and their violent opposition to O'Neill's mild reforms or indeed any change. It produces a view of their relationship with Britain which is akin to a legal contract - "We will remain loyal to Britain as long as Britain remains loyal to us". Their loyalty is to the British Crown - as long as it remains Protestant - and to Westminster, as long as it protects traditional Protestantism in Northern Ireland.

The readiness of Protestants to rebel against Westminster as well as the occasional manifestations of an independent Ulster sentiment, has its roots here. It is a deep strain in Northern Ireland Protestantism and Paisley has successfully tapped it. His followers' first allegiance is to Protestantism, not to the Union. Their official slogan is: "For God and Ulster". As Paisley has often told his supporters: "The Alliance party is the political wing of ecumenism but the DUP is the political wing of evangelical Protestantism".

Inside the DUP this leads Free Presbyterians to see their political work in an entirely different light than activists in any other political party. Their political activity becomes an extension of their religious convictions - they are in fact "doing God's work" in the DUP, or as one former DUP member put it, "working out their own salvation" inside the party.

This can be seen and heard from Free Presbyterian pulpits where DUP events and political affairs feature regularly in sermons and announcements. It can be seen in the select DUP caucuses that exist in many churches where small after-Sunday service meetings are held to decide issues before the local party branch meets. It can be seen in the pressure on people to join both church and party and to leave one if they break with the other.

Most dramatically, it can be seen at election times when virtually the entire energies and membership of the church are thrown behind the DUP, a feature of the party which took other rival Unionist parties entirely by surprise at the start.

"The church is really the machine which achieves things in elections", recalled a former party member, himself never a Free Presbyterian. "The minister will be one of the chief organisers for election campaigns and there's a total dedication by virtually every member of the congregation. The whole church turns out for canvassing, for poster plastering, for fund raising, for providing the mechanisms on polling day, transport etc. The active membership of my branch was small to judge from those who attended meetings but at election time we'd have more people than we could cope with".

A former church member explained their motivation: "They bring an evangelical fervour to electioneering because electioneering is part of the crusade, because it's spiritual warfare, part of their spiritual work. Some more pious church members do object saying it's all unspiritual and worldly, but at election time their objections count for nothing and the whole church becomes centred round it. It's the same battle for God and Ulster, that's the key". The DUP sets out to win votes with the same energy as the Free Presbyterian church uses to win souls.

This dependence on Free Presbyterianism has its drawbacks, most notably in finance. The obvious wealth of the church, the history of Paisley's famous "plastic bucket" collections, makes many assume that through subsidies from the church the party is also rich. There is a consequent apathy about fund raising. As a result the DUP has had continual financial problems, which membership subscriptions were inadequate to solve. Often it has had to be rescued by generous interest-free loans from sympathetic businessmen or affluent members. The party treasurer, David Herron, is one who has dipped into his own pocket a number of times.

There are also church-imposed restrictions on types of fund raising which add to the DUP's difficulties. Any method of raising money which smacks of gambling or games of chance is, for instance, automatically ruled out. Raffles and ballots, the basis for many another political party's finance, are forbidden as are, needless to say, social evenings where alcohol may be consumed.

By 1975 the DUP's financial problems were becoming acute. The party was beginning to expand, new branches were established and a full-time headquarters staff was hired with the aim of fighting elections more professionally. But all this needed more and more money. Paisley was persuaded that a new and professional approach to party finance was needed and so Wallace Thompson, who had joined the UPV as a teenager and was now a graduate from Queens University, was hired as the DUP's full-time finance officer with the task of solving the DUP's financial crisis.

He was, as he says, "continually walking a tightrope" between what was and was not a scripturally acceptable way of raising money. Eventually he hit upon an idea which seemed perfect - gospel concert evenings featuring evangelical, country and western-style groups playing music and songs which would not only raise money but would bring young people into contact with the DUP. But he soon ran into trouble.

There were problems because anything that was slightly rock and roll was considered "of the Devil". If a group came along, and one member was in a church which was a member of the World Council of Churches there was a problem because he was apostate and Free Presbyterians weren't allowed to mix with people like that.

My aim was to bring in young people and therefore I wanted the music to appeal to them but some ministers opposed us. For example I advertised a concert with the Rev William McCrea which used the phrase "In Concert" and I was condemned as that was an expression used by the worldly entertainment scene, pop groups, the Beatles or whatever. "In Concert" was regarded as taking away from what it really was, which was an evening of praise for the Lord.

If the Church of England could once be described as the Tory party at prayer then the DUP is the Free Presbyterian Church at the hustings. And if the Free Presbyterians dominate the DUP, then the Moderator of the Free Presbyterian church completely dominates both. Just as Ian Paisley created and built a Church in his own image, so he has created and built a political party.

GOD'S MAN FOR THE HOUR

Inside his church Paisley is the unquestioned leader who gets his way in virtually every major decision about its theology, policy and direction. But in the church there have been examples of dissent from the odd minister or theological student who has challenged him, albeit unsuccessfully, over his permanent moderatorship or his straying from Calvinist orthodoxy.

In the DUP, however, the monolith is complete. Paisley's authority is total, his word is final and his freedom of action in policy formation, selection of election candidates and treatment of dissent is unique among Western political leaders. Only totalitarian regimes or military dictatorships have produced similar sorts of leaders.

His dominance of the central executive, the DUP's governing body which decides day-to-day party policy and which determines election manifestos and the agenda for party conferences, illustrates the degree to which his authority is absolute.

"From my experience", recalled Wallace Thompson, "Paisley's word was the last word and when Paisley spoke, it was regarded as being the ultimate. I know that in executive meetings when Ian wasn't there, we would take decisions by ourselves. But if he came in late or turned up to the next meeting and disagreed with what had been decided, even over minor things like party functions, there would never be any attempt to contradict him. You got much more freedom of debate when he wasn't there but even so it was very often a case of 'Wait till we see what the Doc says'."

Another former executive member, who preferred to remain anonymous, agreed: "I can remember one particular night when Paisley wasn't there we decided to include integrated education in the party election manifesto because it had been passed at conference and Paisley had spoken in favour of it. But then he turned up towards the end and was furious with what we had done because he felt it would lose us votes. 'I won't have this!', he shouted. 'I'm not standing for it, I will not have this!'. He kept going on until they had to vote on it again and threw it out. People are very loath to say that they won't do what Paisley wants because a lot of them believe that it's basically his party".

That accords with the experience of another former executive member, Clifford Smyth: "Policy making in my day was very difficult because the executive would arrive at a policy and then Paisley would jet in from Westminster and say 'Listen Brother, you can't do that because I've just been to Westminster and if you knew what I knew you'd do it differently'. And the policy would be all changed. They were totally dependent on this man and things always went to him for final approval."

Paisley's authority is so absolute because his followers believe he is God's agent or "man for the hour" sent by divine intervention to protect what both they and he believe is the last bastion of Bible Protestantism in Europe. Like Old Testament prophets, Paisley defied authority and was persecuted. Accordingly he has, in the eyes of his flock, special God-given powers which set him above all other party members.

"In the Old Testament, God sent prophets at times of spiritual and political decline in Israel's history and Ian Paisley is seen as one such man sent from the Kingdom to lead Ulster in her own troubles", observed Thompson. "He's referred to as God's man, a prophet among us who therefore speaks with extra authority".

It is Paisley's power of political prophecy which, for his supporters, validates this claim and gives him semi-Biblical status, a status which Paisley does little to contest and which also reaches out into the wider Protestant community outside the DUP/Free Presbyterian fold. From his early church building days, when he castigated the newly emerging religious ecumenism, right through to the Anglo-Irish agreement, the fact that Paisley warned of dangers, quickly identified them as threats to Protestantism or Unionism and was proved correct, are seen as evidence of his God-given powers.

Typical of those who hold this view of Paisley is Fred Proctor, a Shankill Road businessman who was one of the first Protestant Unionist councillors in Belfast: "I certainly believe he's been chosen for something because he just came at the right time, chosen by God.

"He has never led the people into a blind alley yet and he's certainly a modern prophet as far as I would be concerned. He can forecast very accurately the way things are going and most of his predictions have come into being. You ask any member of the Unionist community and they'll tell you that if Paisley says something is going to happen, it happens sooner or later.

"He prophesied the birth of the IRA, he said that they would come into being. During the civil rights movement he said that eventually the country would be in chaos. He said that there were people involved in those days who were Communists who would be thrown aside when the time came and would be overtaken by Republicans, which eventually did happen. He prophesied Direct Rule in 1971 and a few months later that happened as well. To me he's never been proved wrong in any of the predictions he has made - they have always come into being".

The fact that sometimes the prophecies fail to materialise is also taken as proof of another of Paisley's special qualities - his early warnings work. "He predicted that Captain O'Neill was leading the country towards a United Ireland with a view to him being the first President of a United Ireland", continued Proctor. "I know that didn't come true but that's precisely what O'Neill was trying to do. He didn't succeed at the finish because people like Ian Paisley saw through him and saw what he was doing and stopped him". Whichever way the prophecies turn out, Paisley wins.

The idea that some of Paisley's prophecies, such as the birth of the IRA, may be self-fulfilling never occurs to his most devoted supporters. "His ability to prophesy always impressed a lot of people and even now they will say that Ian is always right, that he always knows what is going to happen but they never seem to notice that some of the events he prophesied, he actually engineered", commented one disillusioned, former Free Presbyterian.

His impressive physical strength and his ability to work sixteen hour days for weeks on end are seen as further proof of his almost divine status. Many of the Old Testament prophets were endowed with similar physical powers and many of them, like Paisley, could also call upon God to strike down their enemies. "I've heard him so many times saying that God had taken his judgement on people like Faulkner, that people who spoke against him came to a sorry end. He would see that as being

God's judgement on them, that anyone who speaks out against the Big Man will not have a happy end", said a former senior party member.

To supplement all these qualities Paisley has other more conventional attributes. His towering six foot, three inch bulk is an asset in itself, sufficiently intimidating to win most arguments and to quell dissidence. But allied to that is a quick and endearing sense of humour and an amazing ability to remember even the minutest detail about party members. They combine to produce a very special affection for him by his followers.

"I've seen us going to some remote farmhouse and Paisley will walk in and not only will he remember the names of everyone in the house but also that last Easter wee Billy had an operation for an appendix and that the daughter got engaged six months ago. He'll greet them all as long standing friends, ask after wee Billy and the daughter, discuss problems with the cattle over tea and scones and then pray with them. By the time we'd leave you could see the effect he'd had upon them. There's no other Unionist politician ever had that touch and I don't think there ever will be", recalled a close colleague.

Because Paisley has this Old Testament prophet status his followers rarely question his actions and forgive him for all transgressions. Thus the mother of a man imprisoned for serious offences committed in the furtherance of Paisley's cause could invoke the Bible to forgive Paisley for his part in her son's downfall. "Well maybe he did wrong", she told the authors. "But then King David did bad things as well and was responsible for a man's death but God had chosen him too."

Paisley's embroilment in the Kincora scandal was another example. The allegation that he failed to act when warned about the homosexuality of the home's housefather cut little ice with the vast majority of DUP members. "A few asked themselves questions but most accepted his explanation and dismissed the allegations as another perfidious plot against him. There's always hostility towards people who doubt Paisley", recalled a party member.

Equally, few inside the DUP ever ask what happens to the vast sums of money collected in large plastic buckets at Paisley's protests: "God's man for the hour is accountable only to God", is the acid comment of one former DUP apparatchik.

The real key to Paisley's power, however, is that he mirrors the insecurity that lurks deep within all Northern Ireland Unionists, the belief that everywhere there are enemies conspiring against them. Paisely feeds that paranoia with one hand but with the other calms it with his own certainty.

For those inside Paisley's fold there is a comforting certitude, but at a price - in return his followers surrender their trust and their freedom of action and unquestioningly accept his leadership and interpretation of events. As one ex-party member put it: "Paisley could ask ten party members to knock down a wall and it would be knocked down faster and more efficiently than anyone else could do it but not once would any of those ten stop and say, 'Hang on, why are we knocking this wall down?'".

Unquestioning obedience to ·Paisley can lead to the most astonishing political gymnastics by DUP members but it never seems to disconcert them. "I remember a party meeting back in 1979 before Mrs Thatcher was elected and Sammy Wilson, who has a name for being a bit of a radical, was speaking", recalled Thompson, who described the scene:

Paisley was due to speak but he was late, so Sammy went ahead without him. He warned the audience of the dangers of a Conservative government coming in and praised the Labour government's policy in Northern Ireland in terms of economic growth. He felt that a Conservative government would lead to widespread unemployment and would adopt measures which would cause social deprivation. The audience cheered wildly at this and obviously agreed with him wholeheartedly.

Then Ian came along and in Ian's speech he said that he trusted that God would deliver Ulster from the curse of Socialism which was against the scriptural teachings and he prayed that soon in Britain we might see the return of a Conservative government. Again the audience cheered wildly. They had forgotten entirely what Sammy had said; it's whatever Ian would say that would carry them. I'll never forget the look of disbelief on Sammy's face.

The cult of Paisley worship inside the DUP is such that most politically active rank and file members regard themselves as mere Paisley surrogates. At election time, candidates tour housing estates in vans plastered with pictures of Paisley and with recordings of Paisley's speeches blaring from loudspeakers.

"He's really the one who's standing for election, they all see themselves as standing in for him", recalled a former DUP councillor. "And then when the results are being given out the councillors, one by one, would stand up and say 'I wish to thank Dr Paisley for getting me elected' or 'I want to thank Dr Paisley and the voters for voting for Dr Paisley'. And these are all grown men, mind you."

As Wallace Thompson soon discovered in his work raising money for the DUP, none of his schemes could match Paisley's own personal appeal. "I don't know whether they fell under the awe of having Ian Paisley at their home or what but whenever I would arrive with him they just wrote the cheques out. I would have tried and tried by myself but it never worked, but with Paisley it worked straight away. He'd just say 'Brother we're in severe difficulties' and they would say 'Yes, Yes, Yes', as they were reaching for their cheque books".

Paisley's semi-divine authority in the DUP gives him a unique freedom to decide which party members should be permitted to stand for election. This in turn allows him to weed out potential dissidents or pretenders to the crown long before they have time to develop a following inside the DUP.

"In all my experience in the DUP", commented an old DUP hand, "Paisley would never allow anyone he felt held conflicting views to himself to get selected. It just never happened and it didn't matter that the local branch wanted that person. If 'the Doc' said no, that was it."

One person with personal experience of this is Clifford Smyth, a former DUP Assembly and Convention member: "Paisley was free to go into a constituency and say this brother or another should stand. I remember he came to me in the vestry in the Martyrs Memorial and said 'Would you stand in North Antrim?'. There was no question of the party in North Antrim having a say. They didn't even know me. It was self-selecting - I simply went there and they accepted his decision and endorsed me."

Paisley enjoys another special freedom which flows from his authority within the DUP. While other Unionist political leaders have to consult their parties to arrive at a general agreement on policies, Paisley suffers from no such constraints. He can instantly define and articulate the DUP viewpoint on any major issue confident that no-one in the party would dare challenge his right to do so.

In a party with such monolithic pattern of behaviour, dissent from or rivalry to Paisley is rare. When it does occur, God and Paisley together take care of the dissenter. "He just freezes it out. He won't accept it and tells people 'I won't have it!'", observed one DUP member who was once on the receiving end.

> . . . If the trouble persists the person is made to feel less than loyal because they've spoken against an authority which derives its power from the idea that he's "God's man for the hour". Most people think they're doing wrong if they speak against him. They think they're challenging the will of God. So if you speak out against Ian Paisley you're made to feel that you're going against God. You know that old joke about Paisley being the Protestant Pope? Well, it's not a joke. His authority *is* semi-Papal.

Clifford Smyth was also disciplined by Paisley but his experience was far more brutal than most: "Paisley's position wasn't just tolerated, it was accepted in some way as the natural order of things. It wasn't tolerated like Stalin's was, because the alternative was the Gulag archipelago, but because they accept his world fundamentalist view that God is in his heaven and Ian Paisley is his man in Ulster".

There is, however, fear in the DUP, the same fear which has made past Unionist governments and present Unionist rivals his virtual prisoners. It is the fear of being denounced as a "Lundy", an execrable traitor to the Loyalist cause. Paisley is able to do this because he has made all the values of traditional Unionism his and his alone. Thus all other Unionists are judged by his definitions and standards of Loyalism. It applies outside the DUP and it certainly applies inside the DUP.

Dissidents have little if any opportunity to argue their case within the party or to seek by persuasion - as in other normal political parties - to win converts over to their argument. If at the end of the day they refuse to accept unquestioningly Paisley's authority or the authority of those few who exercise it with his approval and on his behalf then they have little option but to leave.

Roy Beggs, the former DUP Mayor of Larne, County Antrim was one. In 1980 he accepted an invitation from Dun Laoghaire council in County Dublin, to lead a delegation of Larne councillors on a visit to celebrate Dun Laoghaire's golden jubilee. He saw the visit as part of his wider duties as a Mayor representing all sections of Larne society and as part of an effort to encourage cross-Border tourism. But he had breached the party's manifesto pledge to disdain all contact with the Republic and with the minimum of discussion beforehand he was suspended from the DUP. He eventually resigned to join the rival Official Unionists.

Another to quit in similar circumstances was the DUP deputy Mayor of Belfast in 1983, Ted Ashby, whose offence was to attend an ecumenical church service honouring the RUC. He resigned complaining of "character assassination by supposed party colleagues". Billy Belshaw, the Mayor of Lisburn, resigned in the same year after an internal row followed his attendance at an EEC dinner at which the Taoiseach of the Irish Republic, Garret FitzGerald, was the guest of honour.

Like Beggs and Ashby, Belshaw had sought to represent all his constituents, not just those who supported the DUP. But even limited freedom of action is frowned upon in the DUP and no mechanism exists to accommodate any deviation from the party line or to reconcile dissidents with the leadership. In the words of one bruised former dissident: "If you stray from the path, you're out".

Occasionally more ruthless methods are employed to stamp out dissension. In 1976, for example, the Newtownabbey, County Antrim branch of the DUP was purged by the Rev William Beattie when it suggested that at its next conference the party should debate a motion welcoming Catholic members, provided that they were prepared to accept the party's Loyalist principles. Beattie, who objected to the very idea of sharing the DUP with any Catholic, seized control of the party meeting which discussed this proposal and ruled it out of order. Most members followed what was obviously the church's line and acquiesced while those who objected, remnants of Boal's supporters, had little option but to resign.

Paisley himself rarely takes a direct hand in meting out discipline and generally leaves these matters in the hands of people like Beattie or more often his deputy, Peter Robinson. In disputes between party branches he adopts a strategy which he employs also in the church, as one former member of both observed: "He steers clear generally but privately plays up to both sides. If it persists he tries to stamp it out by taking the most pragmatic decision, i.e. by taking the side of the majority. There's never an attempt to sort out the facts or to reconcile differences, it's all determined by what's in the DUP's best interests. There's no structure for that. If you fall victim, you're out".

KANGAROO COURTS

Another tactic employed in the church has been used in the DUP as well but much more sparingly - the "kangaroo court". Clifford Smyth was the victim of such an inquisition and the experience has clearly left scars. His story also reveals one of the DUP's darker sides, an aspect of the party's links with the freakish side of Northern Protestantism which is kept well hidden from public view.

Smyth was a member of Tara, a strange Loyalist paramilitary group founded in 1966 by William McGrath, a well known evangelical preacher in Belfast who had been associated with Paisley's religious protests back in the 1950s and early 1960s. McGrath was also a British-Israelite. He subscribed to the bizarre idea that the Protestants of Northern Ireland were the lost tribe of Israel. British-Israelites also hold that the British monarchy is directly descended from the Old Testament King David through a Jewish princess who had made her way to Carrickfergus, County Antrim. McGrath also believed that in the far off mists of antiquity, Ireland had been a Protestant nation which had been captured by Catholicism.

His mission, he believed, was to reconvert Ireland to Biblical Protestantism - Tara's slogan was: "We hold Ulster that Ireland might be saved and Britain be re-born". Tara's proclamation demanded the outlawing of the Catholic Church. According to one former member, Roy Garland, who described his experiences in the organisation in a series of *Irish Times* articles, Tara would, once it achieved power, burn Catholic churches and destroy Catholic images. Catholic education would also be banned and only evangelical Protestants would be allowed to teach.

McGrath also claimed the Irish Gaelic culture and language for Protestantism. The name Tara is itself derived from the seat of the ancient Irish Kings in County Meath. He also formed an

Orange Lodge called "Ireland's Heritage" whose banner was inscribed in Gaelic. Elements in the Irish government got excited at this, seeing in it evidence of a re-awakening of the spirit of Wolfe Tone among Northern Protestants: the current President of Ireland, Patrick Hillery, who was then Foreign Minister corresponded with the Lodge and a picture of its banner was featured on the cover of the Department of Foreign Affairs' bulletin.

McGrath's strangeness wasn't confined to his political and religious beliefs. He was one of a significant number of sexual deviants who have, over the years, been attracted to Paisley's violent gospel. Others have included a senior party figure who was reputedly a transvestite, another senior figure who beats up his wife and at least three paedophiles, including the notorious John McKeague.

McGrath was also a paedophile whose conviction in 1981 for serious sexual offences committed against young boys in care at the Kincora home in East Belfast, dating back to 1971, caused Paisley, a strong opponent of the liberalisation of homosexuality laws, severe embarrassment.

Like Paisley, McGrath was an apocalyptic prophet who from the mid-1960s onwards was predicting an imminent Catholic/Republican rebellion in Northern Ireland and ultimately war between the Republic and the North. He formed Tara - which described itself as "the hard core of Protestant resistance" - to prepare for the expected "doomsday" and by 1969 had formed it into platoons of ten men, armed and organised under his leadership.

In August 1969 he went with Paisley to see Chichester-Clark to offer to form a "People's Militia" and was active with Paisley recruiting members afterwards. At this time most of Tara's members were "B" Specials or small businessmen and farmers, but the riots of 1969 attracted a tougher element from the Loyalist working class areas of Belfast, who were eager for a confrontation with Catholics.

Tara was however, a "doomsday" organisation only, which would use its guns only when the Loyalist Armageddon had arrived and Irish unity was threatened. As far as the hard element was concerned the "doomsday" had arrived in August 1969 and impatient for action they left, reputedly with most of Tara's guns, to join the UVF. The remnants of Tara were young, well-educated, lower middle class Protestants with a zealous faith in McGrath's gospel.

They rarely if ever got involved in violence and most of their energies were spent attacking other paramilitary groups like the UDA and UVF for "gangsterism". In this they often employed the techniques of black propaganda. Although small in number, Tara's members were enormously influential through their overlapping membership of Unionist political parties, churches and the Orange Order.

On McGrath's urging some had joined the youth branch of the Official Unionists while others joined the DUP. Smyth was one of the latter but he wasn't the only one - David Brown, the deputy editor of the *Protestant Telegraph* was another as was at least one other DUP convention member. Tara was also represented in the Free Presbyterian Church where the idea that Ulster Protestants were God's élite, descended from the chosen people of Israel, struck a chord. Church members included a senior administrative figure and one minister.

Paisley tolerated dual DUP/Tara membership until September, 1976 when a mysterious and embarrassing document began circulating among extreme Loyalists. Known only as the "Folio" document, from its title "Folio 4782/9/76 LB", it was marked "classified and confidential" and purported to be an official British intelligence report describing plans for a coup d'état in Northern Ireland which was being planned by senior DUP figures.

According to "Folio" the mastermind behind the coup d'état was John McKeague, now Paisley's bitter enemy, who, via two allies - a homosexual DUP member and a UVF man who had become a Free Presbyterian lay preacher - had gained control of one of Paisley's closest political aides. The latter two "had something" on this man, "Folio" explained, "the nature of which was not known" except that in recent months Free Presbyterians had become aware that the DUP aide had "personal problems which have caused him to be extremely depressed . . . and which have caused his wife to have a nervous breakdown".

Using this hold on Paisley's aide, according to "Folio", McKeague was planning a coup d'état. At McKeague's direction, Paisley's aide secretly recruited Loyalists to a new DUP-sponsored paramilitary force which would lead the revolt. In the Summer of 1976 he hosted recruiting meetings of former

"B" Specials in Counties Armagh and Tyrone and told them that "something big . . . militarily" was on the way and that arms buying expeditions to the United States were being organised by senior DUP personnel. They were told they were joining the DUP's paramilitary outfit but in fact the ex-"B" men were tricked into joining McKeague's own organisation which would be the real spearhead of the coup d'état, when they signed false oaths. Legally their allegiance would be to McKeague not the DUP.

"Folio" went on to claim that the DUP aide had held secret meetings with the UDA in East Belfast and their agreement to join in the planned coup d'état as the Belfast company of the DUP's paramilitary group was negotiated. According to "Folio" that was followed by agreement in principle to stage the takeover: "In early September, a meeting of the DUP executive was told . . . that nothing remained for the party [but] to engineer a coup d'état".

"Folio" had more strange tales to tell. Unknown to the DUP the UDA had secretly tape-recorded the meeting and planned to use the tape "to ensure there is no jumping on and off the bandwagon" by the DUP. Paisley's party, in other words, had been tricked into planning and organising the coup d'état and would be blackmailed into remaining a party to it. It was an extraordinary story of a labyrinthine plot.

Copies of the "Folio" document were sent by its anonymous author to Paisley's political rivals in the Official Unionist party and to the Northern Ireland Office. Paisley, according to DUP sources, received a copy from an NIO official.

It was all very embarrassing because at that time Paisley and the DUP were actually working along with other Loyalists in a "United Action Council" on plans to stage a Northern Ireland-wide strike in the Summer of 1977. The appearance of "Folio" indicated that someone was aware of the plans and was determined to destroy them by smearing tactics.

The hand of Tara and William McGrath was immediately suspected. "Folio" smacked of Tara's black propaganda and McGrath himself had long been suspected by other Loyalists of links with British intelligence. This suspicion was apparently well founded; during investigations into an alleged cover up of the Kincora assaults, RUC detectives discovered that McGrath had worked for MI6 in the 1950s when he was associated with an evangelical group which smuggled Bibles across the "Iron Curtain".

Under McGrath's direction, Tara had also adopted an integrationist policy, advocating the full constitutional union of Northern Ireland and Britain devoid of any regional parliament. Tara saw Paisley's strike plans as leading logically to an independent Ulster and would automatically have opposed them.

As a leading Tara figure, Clifford Smyth was also suspected of either writing the document or supplying McGrath with information to write it. One night, shortly after "Folio'"s appearance, he received a phone call asking him to come to Paisley's house. When he arrived he found that he was to be the sole defendant in a trial conducted by a DUP "kangaroo court".

> I was just summoned early in the evening to Martinez Avenue [Paisley's home]. I squeezed out of them the information that there would be others there and when I got there, there were five of them - the senior party officers - and they all sat around me in a sort of semi-circle and threw these questions at me. I sat in an armchair with Paisley on my left and the others on my right.
>
> The questioning went on for well over an hour and was very intense, like an interrogation. It was one of the most intense meetings I've ever been at in terms of emotional atmosphere. The questions were put to me time and again, and I was put under a lot of pressure. I was asked about various people and I just couldn't answer because it wasn't in my power or knowledge.
>
> Eventually I said "Well look, the only way out of this is for me to resign from the party". It was only after that and I saw their reaction that I realised that the whole evening had been calculated to reach that objective.

Smyth afterwards attempted to appeal to Paisley directly in writing but in the end Paisley abruptly closed the correspondence. Smyth had not been expelled from the party but forced out - that meant he had no right of appeal through DUP structures. He also found that among former DUP and Free Presbyterian friends he was suddenly persona non grata.

Elsewhere in the DUP, Smyth's sudden departure was accepted without a murmur, even though he was at the time one of the DUP's most able and influential members. A former party member remembered how others reacted: "He had transgressed in some way by crossing Paisley and that was enough. No explanation was given and no-one made any attempt to tease out the facts from headquarters".

Drastic action like that to stamp out dissidence is rare enough because in the last analysis Paisley's special Biblical claims for himself are sufficient to ensure blind allegiance on the part of the DUP grass roots.

Like the Free Presbyterian Church, the DUP is a Paisley monolith and as such it shares with his Church one major irony. Paisley offered the DUP to Loyalists as an ostensibly "democratic" alternative to the Official Unionist party in the same way as his Church offered Protestants a "democratic" alternative to Presbyterianism. In practice, though, both the Free Presbyterian Church and the DUP have turned out to be the antitheses of democracy - institutions whose common characteristic is worship of and obedience to one man. Despite a natural pride in their tradition of rugged independence this has failed to deter Protestants from flocking to both.

Notwithstanding his theological hold on the DUP membership, Paisley is on constant guard against potential rivals who may emerge from the lower ranks. He exercises vigilance through his chairmanship or membership of every important DUP organ from the central executive down to the Westminster constituency party. In this way he has his finger on the pulse of every influential section of party sentiment and is able to quickly spot any challenge to his authority.

One significant alteration in the DUP's rules and constitution, introduced by Paisley, reveals the depth to which his fear of rivalry runs. It followed the local council elections of May 1981 when the number of DUP councillors doubled from 74 to 142.

At a stroke the number of potential rivals had also doubled and Paisley acted to curb them. Prior to 1981, the DUP constitution allowed the councillors' body, the Local Government Association, to operate fairly autonomously, free from Paisley's direct interference. It was the only major body in the party in which ambitious politicians could carve out a following and a claim to higher elected office free from constant deference to Paisley. Politicians like Peter Robinson, Rev William Beattie, Rev Ivan Foster and Rev William McCrea had come to prominence during the 1970s by this route.

Following the 1981 election, however, Paisley suddenly created a new local government party organ, a Councillors' Association, and appointed officers to it who were all renowned for their personal loyalty to him. They would act as his watchdogs. The irony of course is that as a modern prophet whose followers idolise him, Paisley has no need to keep such a tight rein on the DUP machine. The fact that he feels that he has to reveals much about his fear of rivalry and competition.

THE RISE OF THE "DUPPIES"

Paisley's vigilance has seen off a number of putative rivals in the various organisations he has been associated with over the years. Some like Noel Doherty went to jail and then disappeared into obscurity; others like Bunting and McKeague were ditched when they became embarrassments; others like Norman Porter he broke with, while some like William Beattie, a victim of his own political miscalculations, he broke.

One man has survived longer than any and is now seen not just as the heir apparent, but as an aggressive rival plotting to over throw Paisley as the DUP leader. He is Peter Robinson, the 38-year-old MP for East Belfast and DUP deputy leader since 1980.

Born and raised in the Castlereagh hills on the eastern outskirts of Belfast, Robinson became an avid Paisleyite when he was a 17-year-old grammar school boy preparing to sit his "O" level exams. During the turbulent and violent year of 1966 he attended Paisley's meetings in the Ulster Hall and was converted to the cause. Those who remember him from those days recall a crude anti-Catholicism: "I remember him on his holidays in Portrush with a mate following two nuns down the street yelling 'Popehead! Popehead!'", said a schoolmate.

When Paisley started the Ulster Protestant Volunteers, Robinson immediately enrolled and became chairman of the Lagan Valley branch. When Paisley formed the DUP, Robinson joined as a founder member. On leaving school Robinson worked for a spell in an estate agent's office but his devotion to Paisleyite politics was to make that a short stay.

In 1968 he wrote a pamphlet called "The North answers back" giving the Paisleyite answer to the civil rights campaign. That brought him to Paisley's attention. Paisley recognised an articulate talent in Robinson, and when he was elected to Westminster in 1970 he made Robinson his secretary. Under Paisley's patronage he forged through DUP ranks to a position of unprecedented influence. Paisley's promotion of Robinson was the first sign that he was prepared to make room for ability - previous lieutenants were notable for their intellectual poverty as well as their unquestioning awe of Paisley.

Robinson made his name among the rank and file as a forceful advocate of tough measures against the IRA, always a popular issue in the DUP. Aside from the hardy annuals - the re-introduction of hanging, long minimum prison sentences for terrorists and search and seizure operations in Catholic areas - Robinson travelled to Israel four years ago to make a detailed study of anti-Palestinian security tactics. Among the Israeli ideas he urged should be adopted was the electrification and mining of a fence around the Border. He also won favour with the DUP's Free Presbyterian element when he organised the "Save Ulster from Sodomy" campaign in 1976 against the liberalisation of anti-homosexuality laws. None of these, however, are sufficient to explain his rise.

The key to Robinson's success does not lie either in his natural political ambition or his frequent declarations of undying loyalty to his leader - although these have become more muted in recent months - but in administrative skills which have made him indispensable to Paisley, particularly as Paisley's political and religious workloads in Britain, Europe, and the United States have grown.

Robinson's organisational skills, augmented by an obsession with modern office technology and gadgets, were responsible as much as any other factor for transforming the DUP into a coherent, well organised political party with a ruthless commitment to winning votes.

For the first two years of its life the DUP was, in the words of a founder member, "chaotic and directionless". Boal was then chairman and his view was that the DUP would, because of its democratic appeal, virtually rise up from the Loyalist grass roots by its own momentum. That of course didn't happen. Party meetings were infrequent and growth was negligible. By 1973 the DUP had the same number of branches as when it started and all of those were inherited from the UPV/Protestant Unionists.

In that year Boal left and Robinson became party secretary

and then two years later full-time general secretary. During those two years he helped to transform the party. Straightaway the DUP moved out of the old Shaftesbury Square UCDC headquarters - "an awful place, full of bird droppings from the holes in the roof", recalled one old hand - into new party headquarters in South Belfast. A full-time secretary/typist was also hired.

Ensconced in his new office, Robinson set about regularising and centralising the DUP's affairs. Party branches were for the first time levied on a regular basis and revenue started to flow in. Communication with the branches was improved, and a set of rules for their meetings and procedures for selecting candidates was issued. Branches also started to receive well-written briefs on election techniques, and meetings of important party bodies like the Executive and the Delegates Assembly - an internal sounding board - were held on a more regular basis.

More importantly, a party constitution creating new party structures which would help to co-ordinate the DUP's membership and election efforts was drafted and got Paisley's imprimatur. Party branches, previously based on the North's six counties, were also re-organised to parallel the twelve Westminster constituencies, the basis for elections both to a Stormont Assembly and the House of Commons.

This re-organisation was in place for the election to the 1975 Constitutional Convention, the successor to the ill-fated power sharing Assembly set up in 1973. It was also in place in 1976 to take full advantage of the splintering of Bill Craig's Vanguard party, the DUP's main Loyalist rival, over Craig's stubborn backing for an emergency coalition government with the SDLP, a suggestion that appalled hard-line Loyalists.

From there on the DUP expanded in virtually every important Protestant area of Northern Ireland, creating new branches and expanding others as Vanguard's support was soaked up. The credit was virtually all Robinson's, as the rank and file recognised: "Whatever else he is, Ian is not a great man for the details of organisation. It was Peter who was really responsible for making the DUP into what it is now. He was very dedicated and effective, working all the hours of the day".

Robinson's work had also placed him in a perfect place to launch his own political career, something which he proceeded to do with the determination he had shown in building up the DUP.

His power base was to be East Belfast, and not long after he adopted a full-time political life he set about learning the tricks of the constituency. In 1974, when the DUP, Vanguard and the Official Unionists were in the anti-Sunningdale alliance, the United Ulster Unionist Coalition, he acted as Craig's very efficient election agent and Craig won easily.

The following year Robinson stood unsuccessfully in the Convention elections for East Belfast but two years later he was elected to Castlereagh council and there discovered the route that would take him to Westminster and to the DUP succession.

It was a traditional route for any ambitious politician - hard work, endless meetings with government bureaucrats and patient lobbying for his constituents. "Peter always used to tell us that the only way to get the support of the people was to go out and work for them", recalled an East Belfast contemporary. In 1978, Robinson persuaded Paisley to move DUP headquarters from South Belfast to the Albertbridge Road in East Belfast, a move which more than one party member suspected was engineered to benefit his political ambitions. "Break-ins were given as the reason", recalled one, "but it was as bad on the Albertbridge Road. It was really to get him a base to fight for the Westminster seat, all geared to building up his own empire".

To win the seat Robinson would have to beat Craig and he set about it with his customary single-mindedness. "Peter had this idea when Craig fell over Voluntary Coalition", recalled a former senior party member. "He got someone to dig out an old photograph of Craig standing with O'Neill when they met Jack Lynch back in 1967. Harry West was in the same photograph but he was still in favour so he was neatly sliced off the photograph. Then they made it up into a leaflet to hand out round East Belfast with the slogan 'Craig - once with Lynch, now with Cosgrave' [Irish Taoiseach at the time]".

In early 1978, with a Westminster general election looming on the horizon, Robinson set up a small committee of trusted allies to plan the coming campaign. "They were tireless in their work and dedication to the battle against Craig", remembered one who saw them in action. "They researched Craig completely, digging up all sorts of stuff against him and even made up little jingles. But there was an atmosphere of dirtiness about it all that I didn't like, such as misrepresenting what Craig had said and done. Some of it was clever admittedly, like their election slogan 'Craig can't win'. The vote was going to be split three ways and that persuaded some people that they could only vote for Robinson. But I didn't like it".

Robinson also had help in the election campaign from the largest Loyalist paramilitary organisation, the UDA. He has always had more freedom to consort with shadier elements of Northern Protestantism than Paisley who finds himself constrained by his more pious Church members. The UDA liked Robinson - and still do - thinking him tougher than Paisley as well as sympathetic to their ideal of an Independent Ulster. During the campaign their members canvassed for him, their Newtownards Road headquarters was plastered with his posters and they provided cars and workers on election day. Robinson has returned the favour in various ways, most notably by backing the UDA's campaign to achieve segregation from Republicans in the North's jails. He is one of the few Unionist politicians willing to be publicly associated with the "hard men".

Some of his supporters employed even stranger election practices, much to the horror of rural DUP members. A few months after Robinson's own election campaign, volunteers from East Belfast went to Ballymena to help out in a council by-election and their methods astounded the local activists, most of them Free Presbyterian. "The East Belfast lot came complete with their various costumes for personation and the Ballymena people were amazed and disgusted. It showed up the gap between them", remembered a DUP man.

Robinson's careful planning worked a treat. In the May 1979 general election he defeated Craig - who was admittedly an ill and tired man by this stage - by 64 votes, overturning a huge 17,000 majority. At the same election Paisley's old ally from UPA days, Johnny McQuade, won the North Belfast seat for the DUP. With North Antrim once again safely Paisley's, it was a remarkable triple triumph for the DUP.

Since then Robinson has successfully defended the seat twice and short of political suicide or a sudden conversion to moderation by Protestant voters, the seat looks safe for his lifetime.

Those results have probably made Robinson invulnerable to Paisley's axe and have spared him the ignominious fate suffered by so many of his predecessors. Alone of all of Paisley's previous lieutenants, Robinson has secured electoral and political independence free of Paisley's whim and patronage.

He has done this in two ways. Firstly, by a clever use of the Proportional Representation system of voting and secondly, by building a base and following independent of the Free Presbyterian Church.

The former was dramatically illustrated at the 1981 local council elections when in Castlereagh Robinson won over 3,500 votes while his two running mates had brought in between them a mere 73. Robinson exceeded the quota needed for election by over three times and when his surplus vote was distributed his two running mates were swept in. At a stroke Robinson had publicly demonstrated his personal hegemony in Castlereagh, achieved considerable prominence throughout Northern Ireland and had subordinates in the local DUP organisation whose allegiance would be to him, not Paisley.

The latter has been a more gradual process and one that has been dictated largely by the characteristics of his East Belfast constituency, an area which has a very large working class population based in the Harland and Wolff shipyard, the Shorts aircraft factory and other engineering plants.

Working class Protestants by and large find the dogmatism of Free Presbyterianism less acceptable than do the lower middle classes or rural Protestants who populate its pews. They like to drink and gamble and have a more relaxed attitude to sexual morality. And although their Loyalism is often as intense, it has little of the confining puritanical fervour found in Free Presbyterianism.

Robinson has succeeded in separating the DUP from the Free Presbyterian Church in East Belfast by secularising the party there in a fashion which Desmond Boal would have approved.

"When he looked at East Belfast and the votes he needed to win and sized up the hard core DUP in it - which basically boiled down to the Free Presbyterian Church - he hadn't a hope of winning it. So he had to broaden the base to bring in people whose loyalty was to the party not the Church and to give him credit he worked incredibly hard to do it", recalled a colleague.

Robinson loosened the ties between Church and party firstly by physically separating them - by holding party meetings in non-Church property so as not to alienate non-Free Presbyterian Loyalists. He then made a concerted drive to recruit non-Free Presbyterians by stressing the DUP's Loyalist and populist social and economic credentials.

He himself stopped attending the Free Presbyterian Church - he's now a member of another evangelical sect called the Elim Pentecostal Church - and this was symbolically important. Free Presbyterians are virtually alone among Northern fundamentalists in their belief that they have the right to impose their theology on the rest of society. Other evangelicals tend more to internalise their beliefs - they believe their theology is right for themselves but shirk foisting it on the world at large. Many of those around Robinson now are members of similar sects.

There is one area where this is important for working class Protestant politics. That is the question of Sunday observance. Strict Free Presbyterians believe that Sunday, as the Lord's Day, should not be desecrated by leisure pursuits which would detract from its sanctity. In Ballymena and other rural DUP strongholds where Free Presbyterianism is strong, councils controlled by the DUP have closed swimming pools, parks and leisure centres on Sundays, much to the annoyance of Catholics.

A similar policy in Belfast would undoubtedly lose the DUP working class Protestant support - indeed the DUP in North Belfast split in 1983 over this issue - and Robinson has been to the fore in urging flexibility. In Castlereagh the DUP is "local optionist", that is, it leaves it to local communities to decide whether Sundays should be sacrosanct. That view is shared by most of the DUP in Belfast.

There is evidence also that he has persuaded Paisley to follow him some of the way. Paisley's attitude towards Sunday observance is now more flexible and pragmatic than ever and approximates to Robinson's - in early 1986, for example, he told a delegation from the Reformed Presbyterian Church, whose theological college was his alma mater, that only the democratic vote of the people could impose Sunday observance, not the theology of one particular Church. One of the results of this flexibility is that the DUP has been able to exploit a lucrative class division within Protestantism at the expense of the Official Unionists, gaining working class voters, who might otherwise have been discouraged, through its economic populism and strong Loyalism. Free Presbyterianism, once the cornerstone of the DUP, is no longer a selling point.

In another important sphere Robinson's secularising influence has had a wider impact on the DUP. In 1982 he finally persuaded Paisley to kill off the *Protestant Telegraph* and replaced it with a much more temporal paper called *The Voice Of Ulster*. Out went the Popish plots and in came a well written political paper, geared to the rational dissemination of DUP views on a wide range of constitutional, security, economic and social issues. It even included a page of cookery tips for busy DUP wives - another area where the differences are apparent.

"The difference between Robinson's brand of DUP and the Free Presbyterian brand", commented a former East Belfast member, "can be seen in their wives. Look at Robinson's wife, Iris; she's glamorous, attractive, cuts her hair fashionably, she wears trouser suits and fashionable clothes, she's in keeping with this secular, working class image. Compare her with Ann McCrea or Eileen Paisley - sensible hair styles, no make up, plain, matronly and very good cooks and housewives. The very models of Free Presbyterian womanhood."

Robinson's rise in the DUP coincided with an influx of young graduates into the party. Able, articulate and ambitious, these "duppies" suddenly came to the surface at the 1982 Assembly elections, taking the media by surprise. Robinson is their de facto leader and spokesman and their emergence has produced two distinct strands in the DUP.

The contrast with the older, traditional DUP member was striking. Most of the old guard had only the most basic education, a simple unquestioning faith in fundamental Protestantism and an equal faith in the infallibility of Ian Paisley. Invariably their route into the DUP was via the Free Presbyterian Church.

The new breed were different. Some were Free Presbyterians but many were not. They had been attracted to the DUP principally because it was so much more attractive than the rival Official Unionists. The DUP's Loyalism was more strident and its image much less stuffy and middle class. It could provide an outlet for youthful radical social and economic views, which the conservative Official Unionists couldn't, and more importantly a route for political ambition. The Official Unionists are a party of middle aged people; political apprenticeships are long and elected office the preserve of the older generation.

The new DUP breed were also bright and rose through the ranks quickly, providing Paisley with a cadre of skilled advisers, hard workers and a dedicated middle management. Most of them have found elected office in local government but a few have risen to higher standing.

Prominent among them is Jim Allister, a close ally of Robinson's who comes from Ballymena, County Antrim. He is a barrister who graduated from Queens University Belfast in 1976. In 1980 Paisley made him his personal assistant in the European Parliament and two years later, at the age of 29, Allister was elected to the Stormont Assembly. He and Robinson play a crucial role in developing party policy and election tactics and sort out disciplinary problems on Paisley's behalf.

Another is Alan Kane from Cookstown, County Tyrone, also a barrister who graduated in 1981 and who at 24 was elected to the Assembly. Jim Wells, a graduate in geography and town planning from Moira, County Down, was, at 25, also elected to the Assembly and is the DUP's full-time Finance Officer. Nigel Dodds, 27, is another barrister from Enniskillen, County Fermanagh who graduated with a first class law degree from Cambridge in 1980. Paisley has appointed him his assistant in Europe to replace Allister.

Thirty-three-year-old Sammy Wilson, one of the older "duppies", is an economics graduate from East Belfast and was a teacher before Robinson gave him a full-time job in the Assembly as the DUP's press officer. This in itself was an astute move by Robinson as Wilson's pleasant personality and noticeable lack of bigotry went down well with the media and gave the DUP a human face. Known as "Red Sammy" because of his advanced social views, Wilson was elected Lord Mayor of Belfast in 1986.

What most of these people and the other less prominent "duppies" have in common is that they were all produced by the Queens University branch of the DUP started by Clifford Smyth in 1971. As the IRA's campaign intensified in subsequent years and support for it was reflected among Catholic students at the university, the DUP branch became a magnet for young, hard-line Loyalists.

It was never a large branch, perhaps 30 at most, but under Jim Allister, who was the first chairman, it became the most effective and aggressive block of Unionists at Queens. Its favourite tactic was to confront Republican students who were organised in IRA support groups, such as anti-H Blocks committees, and to challenge the dominance of student politics which Catholics had enjoyed since the civil rights movement of the late 1960s.

Allister formed and led a coalition of DUP members and right wing members of the Official Unionist branch and planned election campaigns based on an anti-Republican, anti-Communist broad front in order to increase Unionist representation on the Students' Representative Council. At one stage they managed to win nearly half the seats and put a brake on Students' Union subsidies of left-wing and Republican causes. Allister himself ran for President of the Students' Union in 1975 and came a good second.

Although fiercely anti-left wing, the branch promoted social and economic populism in its news sheet. It was responsible also for the DUP's adoption of integrated education - Paisley surprisingly spoke in favour at the party conference and swung the vote but he refused to include it in election manifestos. The DUP students also caused controversy at the party's conference in 1976 when they spoke against a favourite Free Presbyterian hobby horse - the religious censoring of books.

Some of the membership were fiercely Free Presbyterian, some members of other fundamentalist sects, like Elim and the Baptists, but a surprising number had no fixed religious views. These latter did not survive the transition from Queens to the wider DUP and even the Free Presbyterians met great resentment from the old guard.

"We were regarded by the rest of the party as suspect", recalled Wallace Thompson. "There was a feeling in the DUP that anything intellectual was not good, that we couldn't be trusted completely. Their attitude was 'We'll have to watch these fellows in case their education goes to their head and they become compromising or soft'. It was part of the anti-intellectualism that's within fundamentalism and Ulster Protestantism in general."

Paisley, perhaps feeling his own lack of formal education, encouraged the Queens' members for sound pragmatic reasons. "Paisley wanted to and needed to broaden the base of the party otherwise it would have become stagnant, and he wasn't capable of holding it all together. He also felt embarrassed by some of his older people who didn't have the brains to scratch themselves with. He was afraid they'd destroy the party", commented another member of the branch.

It was Robinson, though, the party's General Secretary at this time, who had the freedom and time to cultivate the Queens branch and it was Robinson who became their leader, as one contemporary recalled:

> Robinson gained all of the Queens branch because they couldn't go through university politics on a fundamentalist evangelical platform. You've got to rationalise, consider you argument, be articulate and think. Don't forget we weren't insulated like the rest of the DUP, we had to argue with SDLP and Alliance party students. Those who do that will obviously end up in the same wing of the party as Peter Robinson, because that's what he does.
>
> Anyone who goes through Queens gets his mind broadened from the religious and academic point of view, not broadened in that you change your views, but you learn to articulate them. You're always looking for answers, reasoning out and which is the basis for Paisley's power with the rest of the DUP. The transition from Queens to Peter Robinson was automatic.

Robinson thus has a power base in the DUP and an increasingly influential one at that. This, together with a more aggressive role than Paisley in opposing the Anglo-Irish agreement, has, not unnaturally, fuelled speculation that he is working to unseat his mentor from the party leadership.

Robinson has a unique advantage in this task. Unlike any of his previous lieutenants, Paisley is deeply indebted to Robinson. The spectacular growth of the DUP and with it Paisley's own impressive electoral achievements were the work of Robinson and his small band of like-minded disciples.

He has also directed most of the DUP's election campaigns, producing the ideas and issues which have eaten into support for their principal rivals in the Official Unionist Party. And on at least one occasion, during the debacle of the 1977 Loyalist strike, Robinson's strong nerves and firm advice rescued a hapless Paisley from political disaster.

Together with his own strong and independent electoral base in East Belfast, this has given Robinson a status that no other Paisley aide has come near to achieving - a position close to equality.

This is particularly true in the wider world of Northern Loyalism, outside the rigid confines of the DUP, and especially among the new generation of Loyalists who are too young to remember the vigorous, defiant Paisley of the 1960s, the Paisley who led and directed the Protestant revolt against O'Neillism and who went to prison for his Loyalist principles.

The Paisley they know is a more cautious, pragmatic politician who has steered clear of direct confrontation with the authorities during the 1986 campaign against the Anglo-Irish agreement, signalling in unmistakable terms that he would much prefer dialogue and negotiation. He is to them, "a man of straw", as one cynical Unionist put it, who one day threatens civil war and the next day quickly retracts it, a leader whose circumspection matches his advancing years and declining physical powers.

The Clontibret incident in August 1986 said it all. While Peter Robinson led Loyalist mobs across the County Monaghan border where they attacked the village's police station and beat up members of the Garda Siochana, Paisley was, at this hour of crisis, 3,000 miles away in the United States on a preaching tour.

Robinson's arrest and prosecution by the Southern authorities immediately elevated him into a new Loyalist hero, his defiant martyrdom matching that won by Paisley in the 1960s. As he languished in a Monaghan police cell awaiting his fate, Robinson extended the parallels with that more youthful Paisley - he asked for a Bible to read, sang Orange ballads throughout the night and on the eve of his court appearance in Dundalk, County Louth a week later, he invoked God as his protector, echoing Paisley's claim of a special relationship with the Almighty. Amid growing media speculation, Paisley was forced to make a hasty return to Belfast to deny reports of a leadership crisis in the DUP and to re-assert his own authority.

The odds, though, are stacked against Robinson should he try to depose Paisley from the DUP leadership. Whatever qualities he has that are popular with hard-line Loyalists - his willingness to consort with paramilitaries and his apparent greater readiness to lead the Loyalist troops "over the top", among them - Robinson lacks the special prophetic charisma which forty years of religious and political protest have given Paisley. That remains Paisley's strongest defence against usurpers in the DUP where in terms of finance, personnel and political commitment, the Free Presbyterian Church forms the backbone of the party and will remain so as long as Paisley is its unchallenged Moderator.

Although Robinson has, through the influx of "duppies", built up an influential and forceful following in the DUP, they are still a small minority compared to the Free Presbyterians.His policy of deliberately distancing himself from the Free Presbyterian Church, however, may also give him an added appeal to a Protestant constituency whose memories of Paisley the bitter schismatic, and foe of the Protestant establishment, always limited Paisley's own popularity.

While all that may give Robinson a strong claim to Paisley's political inheritance and even the putative leadership of a wider alliance of Loyalists, it is still Paisley who commands the unchallenged allegiance and reverence of the DUP rank and file. To the bulk of them, Paisley is both their spiritual inspiration and the personification of all the religious and political values of the traditional, uncompromising Unionism that they hold so dear. Ultimately, they believe the DUP belongs to Paisley and that God has given him the DUP to work out the divine salvation of Ulster Protestantism. Peter Robinson cannot compete with both the Almighty and Edward Carson.

CHAPTER TEN

At the Grass Roots

Oliver Cromwell was God's man. And I feel that's what we need today:
men of God who are dictators of nations, men to direct them in the right way . . .
I believe that Ian Paisley too is a man raised up by God,
like Moses, Elijah and King David.
Allister Lucas, Free Presbyterian elder, Antrim.

Eight miles west of Belfast, on rising ground which gives a view of
the Belfast hills in one direction and Lough Neagh in the other,
stands the neat, brightly painted farmhouse home of the Lucas
family. Allister and Jean Lucas are both in their early thirties: he,
a small dark-haired man with a merry laugh and an articulate
flow of talk; she, slim, pretty and eager to express her own ideas.

Allister keeps cattle, many of them high-quality Friesians, on
180 acres of good pastureland, just over half of it rented. Jean,
when she is not looking after their four young children, works as
a nurse to people needing constant care in their homes.

They are leading members of Antrim Free Presbyterian
Church: both teach in its Sunday school, Jean plays the organ,
while Allister is the church secretary, an elder and a lay preacher.
He is also secretary of the South Antrim Imperial Association of
the Democratic Unionist Party and was a DUP member of
Antrim District Council for four years up to 1981. In religion and
politics they are passionate supporters of Rev Ian Paisley.

But the real passion governing their lives is their "born again"
faith in evangelical Christianity. Allister was brought up as a
Presbyterian farmer's son in the South Tyrone border country
where neighbours were cousins of Ian Paisley's father. He still
has a crystal-clear memory of the August day he was "saved" as
an eight-year-old boy at a children's meeting organised by

itinerant mission preachers near his home:

> I heard the simple gospel message that I was born in sin, Satan
> and iniquity; that mankind are sinners - by nature they don't
> walk after God, they go away from God and do evil . . . I
> realised then that I couldn't get into heaven with this sin and it
> had to be dealt with. And there's only one way to have your sin
> dealt with - the Lord Jesus Christ, the perfect God-man, he
> took my place, my punishment, because my sin had to be
> punished - I couldn't appear before a righteous God with sin.
> Christ bore my punishment for me on the Cross - therefore
> when I trusted him, I depended upon him alone and nothing
> else. It was a work of the spirit of God on my life. I could say as
> a boy of eight that I knew that a change had taken place . . .
> There had been a definite change. I knew Christ personally
> then and I still know that I'm indwelt by the power of God, the
> Holy Spirit.

For Jean Lucas "salvation" came later and more traumatically: at
the age of 14 in the aftermath of her mother's death. She grew up
in a strongly Presbyterian family near Bangor in North Down,
where her grandfather's house, with its biblical message painted
prominently along one gable wall, is still an eye-catching
landmark on the road to Belfast.

Her parents laid down a strict puritan discipline for their
children - no dances, no make-up, no going to the cinema. Jean,
although unhappy that she was not allowed to enjoy the same
pleasures as her schoolfriends, also agonised about not having
been converted to "born again" Christianity.

In 1969 her mother was taken ill during a Christmas shopping
trip to Belfast, and died soon afterwards. In answer to her
mother's deathbed prayer, Jean felt a change in her - what
evangelical Protestants call a "conversion experience" - and
decided that "the things of God were the most important things
to me".

Before her death her mother had started attending Ian
Paisley's Martyrs Memorial church in East Belfast and had tried
unsuccessfully to get Jean to join her. Even after her conversion
Jean, like many people from a respectable Presbyterian
background, was still extremely suspicious of Paisley. She
thought him "very loud - he was always fighting with people, and

didn't like Roman Catholics - the usual things that people think about him".

When she was eventually persuaded to go to Paisley's church by her brother she was impressed both by its size, and more importantly, by the power and clarity of his preaching. She had come from a background which placed a high value on preaching: she had heard many of the leading evangelical preachers of the day, often with her father at meetings of the W.P. Nicholson-founded Christian Workers Union. But she had never heard anything like the Free Presbyterian moderator's impassioned delivery of the evangelical message. Later, as she became a regular attender at Martyrs Memorial she found his exposition of the Bible an enormous help in her new faith.

Allister's path to Free Presbyterianism had started when he first heard Paisley preach in a gospel hall outside Dungannon as a boy of nine. He heard him again as a 15-year-old at a tent mission in Dungannon in 1967, when he remembers several thousand people flocking to one of his Sunday afternoon services.

While a student at Greenmount Agricultural College in County Antrim, Allister and two friends underwent the ceremony of "total immersion" baptism in a local Pentecostal church.[1] Shortly after leaving college he bought his present farm in South Antrim, and, as Ulster Protestants moving to a new area tend to do, started to shop around for a new church.

At home in Tyrone he had been very active in the local Presbyterian church, where the minister was an evangelical - "preaching salvation through Christ alone". However, at his new Presbyterian church he found a minister who preached a very different - and in Allister's eyes unbiblical - message: the liberal, "modernist" doctrine that everyone had "the light of Christianity" within them.

So he travelled the ten and a half miles over the hills and across the city of Belfast to hear Ian Paisley preach. The Free Presbyterian Church suited him for two reasons: it was evangelical in its belief in personal salvation and the infallibility of the Bible, as well as strongly Protestant in that it was not ashamed to protest against "false religions", Roman Catholicism in particular.

For the next eight years, until the Antrim church opened in 1978, he worshipped every Sunday at Martyrs Memorial. In July 1975 he and Jean, whom he had met on one of the church's door-to-door gospel campaigns, were married by Paisley in the church.

For Allister Lucas politics are inseparable from religious belief, since both are tied up with the "spiritual warfare" of the evangelical Protestant's struggle against Roman Catholicism in Northern Ireland and the world. Right from the beginning he says he saw the Civil Rights movement as a coming together of Catholic political forces - whether represented by Gerry Fitt, Sinn Fein or traditional Nationalists - in order "to take our position - not so much our position in the United Kingdom as our Protestant position".

Echoing Ian Paisley, Allister is quick to emphasise that he is not against Catholics as people, but rather against the ecclesiastical and political system - he prefers not to call it a church - of Roman Catholicism:

> I was always aware deep down that Roman Catholicism was wrong . . . it was so obnoxious to me from a religious point of view. I wasn't against the individual Roman Catholics. Many of them had worked in our farm. One Roman Catholic man was always our baby-minder. Our mother got him to look after us. When we went out on 12th July it was always Roman Catholics who looked after the farm and maybe turned the hay . . . so I wasn't against individual Roman Catholics but against the system of Romanism . . . I could see right from the very start the hand of Rome was in it.

A new Catholic realignment was not the only threat to the Protestant position: one of his earliest memories of politics was of discussions in his father's Orange lodge in Tyrone in the mid-sixties about whether the then Prime Minister of Northern Ireland, Captain Terence O'Neill, who had been invited to open the lodge's new hall, should be allowed to carry out the ceremony. There were objections from some Orangemen that he was straying from the path of traditional Unionism.

Later, when Ian Paisley first started to be heard on radio and television, Allister recalled his reaction: "I said - that's right, you're speaking for me. You can put it over very very well, but you're just saying exactly what I feel". He still finds that his instinctive reponse to a statement by a government minister or a Nationalist politician turns out to be exactly the same as Paisley's.

In August 1968 Allister, then a boy of 16, was in the front line of a group of Loyalists, led by the local branch of the Paisleyite Ulster Protestant Volunteers, who tried to block Northern Ireland's first Civil Rights march from Coalisland to Dungannon. He recalled lying in bed less than ten years earlier and hearing the sound of a bridge being blown up on the border during the IRA's abortive 1956-62 campaign: for him, as for his neighbours, the Civil Rights movement was just "a continuation of what the IRA had done then, only in a different form".

He admits that there had been abuses in Northern Ireland: gerrymandering in Derry and bad housing in Belfast. But he lays the blame for the "Troubles" squarely on the Catholic Church and its followers' refusal to recognise the Northern Ireland state and political system. He believes that "anybody who doesn't accept the status quo of this country should not be given the liberties and the rights of the person who does".

However, he concedes that his political ideas have changed dramatically during the years of the "Troubles" - to the point where he has even stopped believing in democracy. Like Paisley, he lists Oliver Cromwell as one of his heroes - and Cromwell, he says, did not believe in democracy:

> He was a dictator - I don't like to call him that, but that's what he was. He was God's man. And I feel that's what we need today: men of God who are dictators of nations, men to direct them in the right way. And how was the English Parliament and Bill of Rights established? It was King Billy - William, Prince of Orange - and to all intents and purposes he was a dictator too.

Allister believes that Ian Paisley is a modern-day Oliver Cromwell for Northern Ireland - "a man raised up of God" like Moses, Elijah and King David to lead his people in a time of great spiritual and political turbulence.

He points out that these great Old Testament leaders also had their faults - all three committed murder and David was an adulterer. But despite the "Big Man's" faults, he believes that the power of Paisley's preaching comes from "the anointing of God upon him". Allister claims that his divine backing has been proved both by the steady growth of the Free Presbyterian Church and the spectacular rise in the Democratic Unionist leader's personal and political following.

As he has done again and again throughout the interview Allister supports his contention with a reference from the Bible: Peter and the other apostles being brought before the Jewish religious leaders, who were on the point of ordering them to be killed to stop them preaching - "but Gamaliel the great Jewish lawyer said 'If it's of God we can't stop it, but if it's not of God it will stop anyway.' It's the same with Dr Paisley - if his work was of man, of himself, it wouldn't have lasted when he started preaching in the Ravenhill Road over 40 years ago. So we believe that God is behind it, prospering the work".

This means that God is also behind Paisley's political leadership, Allister believes. For him the conflict in Northern Ireland is "a spiritual battle with political connotations". He goes on:

And I believe there's only the few that can really take up the battle. And the Free Presbyterian Church is basically that few. God never worked with majorities, with big numbers. Gideon was left with only 300 men to fight the battle against the Midianites.[2] We believe we are the salt of the earth and we're leading this campaign under Dr Paisley's guidance and leadership, both politically and spiritually. If we could get the people of this land - no matter who they are, Romanists or Protestants or Jews - to turn back to the word of God and repent of their sin, and God would break forth in revival, then our problem would be solved here.

Allister, like most Free Presbyterians, looks back to a golden age of Protestantism in the 16th and 17th centuries when the puritanism of John Knox and Oliver Cromwell governed the rulings of parliaments as well as pulpits. He concedes that banning the Catholic Mass, as Knox persuaded the Scottish Parliament to do, is not a feasible political option in the late 20th century.

But he still hopes that the revival he dreams of will mean the end of Catholicism, at least in Britain: "If the Lord came with revival to our nation, if 90 per cent of the people of the UK as a whole were to come back to the Lord and become evangelical and see the Mass for what it is, you wouldn't have to put a ban on it."

However, all this emphasis on a heaven-sent revival does not mean that Protestants should not be politically active. Allister believes that the influence of Roman Catholicism can be found in every war and political conflict since the Reformation. He cites as contemporary examples the war in Vietnam - which he calls "Spellman's War" after the then Archbishop of New York - and the overthrow of President Marcos in the Philippines, which he claims was orchestrated by the local cardinal Sin to put a more devout Catholic into power.

He notices papal influence everywhere: in the pictures he saw on the walls of the European Parliament in Strasbourg when he was there as a member of a DUP delegation; in the visit by the Pope's Irish chaplain to see Bobby Sands during the 1981 Maze Prison hunger strike; and in "the politicians running to the Vatican" before the signing of the Anglo-Irish agreement.

Not surprisingly he belongs to the traditional wing of the DUP which sees it "first and foremost as a Protestant party". He is a conservative, a follower of Margaret Thatcher on social and economic issues, disagreeing with the more radical ideas put forward by younger, more urban leaders like Peter Robinson and Sammy Wilson. But ultimately he is confident that they will all line up behind Ian Paisley "to defend our Protestant position". For him Paisley is "not a politician in the true sense of the term" and would not be involved at all were it not to lead the defence of Ulster Protestantism.

It is that Protestant way of life - "Christian", they would call it - that determines Allister and Jean Lucas's every attitude and action. They devote a short time every day to "family worship" - bible reading and prayer - with their four children, aged from five to nine. They emphasise that for them this is a time of enjoyment - "Man's chief end is to glorify God and enjoy him for ever", says Allister,"and you can't enjoy the Lord unless you spend time getting to know him".

On the farm, Allister maintains that he survived the atrocious summer of 1985 only with God's help. He believes God sent him the buyer who turned up when he badly needed to sell off some of his overstocked herd. Allister says that when he is with other farmers, for example at meetings and trips with the Northern Ireland British Friesian Breeders Club, he finds that he is able quickly to recognise fellow "born again" Christians - "they have that special contentment about them" - and fall into conversation with them.

Allister and Jean's friends and social acquaintances tend to be Free Presbyterians or other evangelical Protestants who hold the same basic beliefs as they do. But they put the biblical commandment to love God before the subsidiary command to love one's neighbour, which they claim is the message wrongly favoured by "the ecumenists and peace-lovers". "You can't love your neighbour if you don't love the Lord first because you haven't got that perfect love within you that the Lord imparts in order to love your neighbour", says Allister. As a "born again" believer he stresses that his first concern is that his neighbour should also be "saved'.

Both he and Jean say they feel they have to talk to everybody they meet, Protestant, Catholic and atheist, about their beliefs in order to try to convert them. They don't have any Catholic friends, although Jean nurses with Catholic girls, is friendly with them, and finds that they object less than many Protestants to her talking about her religion. "In Northern Ireland you're soon aware that a person is a Roman Catholic", she says. "Maybe not so much with Allister since he grew up in Tyrone and mixed with them. But growing up in Bangor I didn't know what a Roman Catholic was."

Jean admits that some of her non-evangelical neighbours might consider them narrow-minded - she, for example, never wears trousers because of the biblical command to women not to wear men's clothes, and would not go to the cinema or theatre because it would be seen as "a bad testimony".

The Lucases, like most Free Presbyterians (and other Northern evangelicals), do not smoke or drink, and Jean does not wear make-up. However, they are at pains to emphasise that this is not laid down in any Free Presbyterian code of rules, but is a question of individual conscience, guided by the teachings of the Bible.

Jean, for example, would go to a classical music concert, although many Free Presbyterians would not. On the other hand she would prefer not to have a television. Twenty years ago it was virtually taboo for a member to own a television set - Paisley's mother was particularly strong on this - but with the advent of the "Troubles" the need to keep up with the news allowed a certain licence. The strong discouragement of smoking and drinking is based, as is everything else in the Free Presbyterian canon, on a biblical exhortation to look after the body as "the temple of the Holy Ghost".

The Lucases are also strong Sabbatarians: they go to religious services every Sunday morning and evening, with Jean usually away from home in the evening fulfilling engagements as a solo singer at evangelical services all over Northern Ireland.

They stress that keeping God's day is a biblical commandment, and praise local councils like Ballymena for closing their leisure centres on a Sunday. "If we're ever given a position where we can influence such decisions, the Lord will bless it, and Ballymena will be blessed financially for doing it - even though it might seem unfair and discriminating to other people who want to go", says Jean. "I believe it's a false economy to bring in money by stealing God's day - for Sunday is God's day and he's so good to give us a day to rest on".

They are convinced Calvinists, believing in the élitist - and to outsiders often contradictory - doctrine that a chosen few are "predestined" to be "saved" and thus to go to heaven. "Even before Jean was saved she was the elect of God, she was chosen", says Allister. "If she hadn't been saved at 14, she would have been saved at 64. God has foreknowledge of everything. You're not talking to us here because of your will to be here. It's all in God's plan that you are talking with us".

Both of them are sad to see the decline of religion in Britain - "turning away from the Book", they call it. But Jean is comforted a little by seeing the Queen on television, and recalling her decision not to allow Prince Charles to go to Mass during a recent visit to the Pope in Rome.

She worries about such inclinations in the future king of England - speculating whether perhaps the Queen might live long enough to keep him off the throne. She is unhappy at similar tendencies in the Queen Mother: "she just loves to be in the company of Cardinal Hume - it's very sad that she's looking for peace there, that she has forsaken the faith".

They claim to feel little animosity towards the South of Ireland, where they both used to spend their holidays before the "Troubles". They see it as a foreign country with different standards and a different culture. However, they honestly believe that evangelical ministers are still persecuted there, and have the standard stock of extreme Protestant stories about priests drinking and gambling and going with women.

Allister does not totally rule out the possibility that a future united Ireland might be part of "God's plan". He speculates that it could come about as part of the movement towards a one-world church and government under the rule of the man he sees as the "antichrist', the Pope. Many Free Presbyterians believe that such a movement is already taking place with the formation of the World Council of Churches, the European Economic Community and other international bodies. They claim this is a sign of the imminent "Second Coming" of Christ to earth, as prophesied in the Bible's Book of Revelation.

However, a united Ireland as part of this movement would not stop Allister continuing to fight against Catholicism:

> I have to do good and oppose evil, and as I see it if there was a united Ireland, the Roman Catholic system would be the dominant system. And that being an evil and an anti-Christian system, I've got to oppose it, not only in the Free Church from a religious point of view, but also in my political activity.

However, despite such forebodings, both Allister and Jean still believe that Ulster Protestantism will win the day. And if it requires violence and force? "God works in different ways in each age", replies Allister. "Gideon took the Midianites without a shot being fired; Elijah had to take a sword to slay the false prophets of Baal; with Oliver Cromwell it was again the sword, together with faith and godly generals".

He is impatient with people who tell Unionists to sit down and talk with their enemies: "Cromwell fought a civil war - he didn't sit down and talk; America had to fight a civil war to get rid of Britain - it wasn't through diplomacy; we didn't sit down and talk to Hitler."

They are not at all worried that their children are being brought up in the middle of the Northern Ireland conflict - in fact, quite the contrary. "There's nowhere else in the world I'd want them to be brought up", says Jean. "I think it's God's privileged country. For some reason He's chosen this place - it's such an evangelical country, there are mission halls and every variety of Christian saved people you could get".

Their real fear - "the worst thing that could ever happen to me", Jean calls it - is that their children would not be "saved", and would not go to heaven. "My only ambition for them would be that they would bring honour to God", says Jean. "If they brush the streets that they'll bring honour to God; if they're doctors that they'll bring honour to God".

* * *

Two years ago Alistair and Jean Lucas decided to take their children away from the local state primary school and send them to the recently-opened "independent Christian school" attached to Newtownabbey Free Presbyterian Church eight and a half miles away on the outskirts of Belfast. They did this for two reasons: firstly because their children would be taught "the right things scripturally by Christian teachers - so that the school would be an extension of the home"; and secondly they would be punished, if necessary with the cane, for offences like using bad language, a habit their eldest boy had picked up at his primary school.

There are currently four Free Presbyterian "independent Christian" schools in Northern Ireland: at Kilskeery in South Tyrone, Newtownabbey and Ballymoney in County Antrim and Bangor in County Down. Two more are being planned by the Free Presbyterian congregations at Clogher Valley in Tyrone and at Portadown, while at Kilkeel in South Down and at Ian Paisley's own Martyrs Memorial church there are also groups of people discussing school projects. Thus the makings are already there for a third division in the North's already segregated education system, alongside the present Catholic schools and the largely Protestant state schools.

Education has always been a sectarian bearpit in Northern Ireland. Throughout the twenties, thirties and forties Protestant clergymen fought a bitter rearguard action to safeguard Bible instruction and the Protestant ethic in the schools they had handed over to the state. They appeared to have lost the fight in 1947 when the Stormont Government fell in with the British practice of non-denominational religious instruction in all state schools.

Within a decade Ian Paisley had resumed the struggle. He had been deeply influenced by the experience of American fundamentalists who had opted out of their state system so that they could prevent their children being taught Charles Darwin's pernicious and anti-biblical Theory of Evolution - that man was not made by God, as described in the Book of Genesis, but was

311

descended from the apes.

Among the leaders of this movement were, of course, the Bob Jones family of Bob Jones University. They not only offered higher education at their complex in South Carolina, but kindergarten, elementary and high schools as well. Some families had moved thousands of miles across the United States so that their children could receive a "Bible-centred" Bob Jones-style education.

The battle against the teaching of the Theory of Evolution, first fought out in the American courts in the 1920s, reached Northern Ireland in the late 1950s. The first skirmish was in the County Antrim town of Ballymoney where Paisley's first lieutenant, John Wylie, caused a small furore by using a hammer to attack a figure representing Piltdown Man, believed then to be the fossilised remains of a primitive human, in a local grammar school.

Two decades later the front line moved 20 miles down the road to Paisley's home town of Ballymena, which in 1977 had become the first local council to fall into DUP hands. There the council voted, with no dissenting voices, to demand that the area education board remove all mention of Darwin's evil theory from religious education in Ballymena's schools."If you believe you come from a monkey you'll act like a monkey," said former DUP mayor John McAuley.

Inside the Free Presbyterian Church the demand for separate schools fitted in with its separatist theology and was being voiced with increasing regularity. If the "vile atheistic fictions" of Darwinism were their first concern, Free Presbyterian parents were also watching with growing alarm the liberalisation of syllabuses in Northern Ireland's state schools in line with their British counterparts.

The 1978 DUP conference unanimously passed a resolution condemning "the inclusion of reading matter of a blasphemous or pornographic nature on secondary school examination syllabuses". One of the worst offenders, according to a handbill circulating at the conference, was John Steinbeck's comic classic *Of Mice and Men,* which was on the syllabus for 14-16 year olds. It contained "16 blasphemous sentences'; 26 mentions of "bastard" or "son of a bitch'; 29 mentions of hell in a slang reference; one mention of rape; one mention of attempted rape - this and more within 113 pages".

As if that was not enough, a new programme of religious education for primary schools proposed telling eight and nine-year-olds about Buddhism and Mohammedanism. The party's vice-chairman, David Calvert, accused the education authorities of aiming to "de-Protestantise children's belief and thinking".

The previous year the Free Presbyterians had made an abortive attempt to start their alternative system. Residents of the plush North Down coastal suburb of Seapoint objected angrily and successfully to a plan by Paisley to open a fundamentalist secondary school in their area. The following year Ivan Foster and his schoolteacher wife started an altogether more modest project, a 13-strong primary school attached to the Free Presbyterian church in the village of Kilskeery on the county line between Tyrone and Fermanagh.

In 1983 the Newtownabbey Free Presbyterian minister, Reggie Cranston, together with his colleagues in Ballymoney and Bangor, followed the Fosters' example. At first few families responded, worried, like the Lucases, about the academic standards in a tiny makeshift two-teacher school based in a portakabin and the upstairs room of a church, with few if any modern teaching aids.

They were soon reassured. The Lucases believe that the small classes and greater teacher attention have meant that their seven, eight and nine-year-old boys (now joined by their five- year-old sister) are now about a year ahead of their contemporaries at their former school. They are already studying history and science and, as a result, says Allister Lucas, using a phrase that he admits he does not like, "their minds are being broadened more".

To the outside observer this is the one thing the four independent Christian schools are patently not doing. The Newtownabbey school's explanatory notes for potential parents set out its educational and moral objectives as:

> to provide an academic institution in which the teachers, pupils, teaching methods and subject matter are all subservient to the word of God, the Bible. Every book, every notion of man, every philosophy shall be evaluated by the principles and ideals of the Scriptures. They will be our reference book and ultimate criterion. In such an institution children will be prepared for a life of Christian usefulness and

influence, exercising that wisdom which begins with the fear of the Lord.

To this end all members of staff have to be "born again" Christians (all are, in fact, Free Presbyterian church members), and must subscribe to a strict puritan code of dress, appearance and behaviour. There is no long hair, sideburns or jeans for the men; and no trousers, skirts above the knee, make-up or "garish or obtrusive jewellery" for the women. The code concludes: "Staff members are at all times to so act and look as becomes the gospel of Jesus Christ".

There are similar rules for the children, also based on St Paul's commands about modesty, appropriate dress and length of hair. There were 23 children, aged between four and twelve, at Newtownabbey in the 1985-86 academic year. They all wear identical grey uniforms over white shirts and blue ties, with the school badge - the burning bush motif of traditional Presbyterianism over the motto "The Lord giveth wisdom" - sown onto their pullovers. The girls wear neat grey berets over the long uncut hair that Paul thought so suitable for women.

The English Protestant Bible, the authorised 17th century version of King James 1, is in evidence in every aspect of the school's daily routine. The children start the day with a 35 minute service of hymns and Bible teaching. They put their hands up and request the hymns they want to sing, short choruses with catchy tunes and refrains like "I've been redeemed by the blood of the lamb" and "Ireland needs a Saviour".

After their mid-morning break they say prayers for Free Presbyterian missionaries around the world. After lunch they gather in their classrooms for ten minutes of Bible study before the afternoon's classes. The children will study and eventually become familiar with the whole Bible from Genesis to Revelation. One of the first tasks set to four and five-year-olds on their arrival is to learn the names of the books of the Bible. The learning by heart of biblical passages continues throughout their school careers.

The lessons too are influenced by the teachings of an infallible Bible. There is no nature study for the primary children, but "creation studies", a concept imported from fundamentalist America. This teaches that evolution is just one theory among many, and emphasises the literal teaching of the old Bible that the earth and all its inhabitants were created by God in six days. Biblical verses are used to illustrate ideas in English, biology, geography and history.

When they move into the senior school classroom above the church at eleven, pupils do a history course that starts with Henrys the Seventh and Eighth of England, and continues with the Stuart monarchs. Under the Stuarts, say the study notes prepared by the teacher which are used in place of books, "people could be fined if they didn't go to church on Sundays". Next come the puritan Pilgrim Fathers and their struggles with the religious establishment; the English Civil War between the "high church" King Charles I and his puritan Parliament, led by Oliver Cromwell; and the "Glorious Revolution" against the Catholic King James II by the Protestant King William of Orange.

The teacher, Alison Herron, a daughter of the treasurer of the DUP, says that this concentration on English history was how she was taught, and allows the children "to understand their own country first". In addition, the minister takes the 12-year-olds for half an hour of church history each week, starting with the Protestant Reformation.

Academically it seems to work. The children pass automatically from primary to secondary levels without taking any examination. The problem of small teaching staffs dealing with older pupils taking advanced examination subjects is being tackled by Mrs Foster, who has put together correspondence courses and teaching packages containing notes, films and tapes. Kilskeery has already seen two of its pupils, including the Fosters' eldest son, pass G.C.E. "O" levels in eleven subjects.

In 1985-86 the four schools between them had an enrolment of over 120 pupils. The only complaint from the Department of Education inspector who visited Newtownabbey was the rather unusual one that the pupils were "too quiet".

Rev Cranston is confident that when parents get over their fears about academic standards, there will be an even greater influx: there are already children from seven Protestant denominations, including the mainstream Presbyterian and Baptist churches, on his rolls. One family drives 16 miles four times a day from the far side of Belfast in order to leave their children to the school.

All this happens without a penny of government funding - the

Free Presbyterian Church's education board decided not to apply for government assistance similar to that given to Catholic schools, on the grounds that it would involve Department of Education nominees sitting on school committees. These nominees, points out the Newtownabbey school's information leaflet, could even turn out to be Catholic priests. All finance comes from school fees - running from £315 per year for the first child in a family to nothing for the fourth - and from church collections, covenants and other gifts.

For Cranston the establishment of the independent Christian schools is an integral part of the Free Presbyterian Church's campaign to return to traditional Presbyterian values. Before the Northern Ireland state took over the education of the children of the Protestant majority in the 1920s, many Presbyterian churches had schools attached to them. Here children were taught the three Rs and the Bible, untainted by anti-biblical ideas like the Theory of Evolution. They were under the strict disciplinary code of Victorian morality, enforced if necessary by the cane.

"That used to be the accepted thing", says Cranston. "Just like the Free Presbyterian Church itself is what Presbyterianism used to be. We're just treading the old paths in education, the old-fashioned way of teaching from a biblical standpoint". The school lays a strong emphasis on the children growing up in the evangelical faith - Cranston says that all but four or five of the children are "saved", eight of them through the school's own efforts.

As for the church, so for the schools. For the Free Presbyterians of Ulster the temporary triumph of Presbyterian "modernism" dates from the failure of the Davey heresy trial in 1927. For believers in old-fashioned Protestant values in education, the biggest defeat was the failure of the fundamentalists to force Darwin off the American school syllabus at the Scopes trial in Tennessee two years earlier.

Over sixty years later the Free Presbyterians are re-fighting both those battles. Paisley's educationalists are working overtime in their small but expanding alternative system to turn the clock back to the 19th century for children who will come of age in the 21st.

Part 3

CHAPTER ELEVEN

The Politics of the Wee Protestant Hall

He's much more the representative of the people than their leader.
He's not going to lead them through the wilderness like Moses.
He's too responsive to the feelings of the people in the wee Protestant hall
in Ballymena and simply will not go too far ahead of his supporters.
Clifford Smyth, former DUP Assembly and Convention member.

The Ian Paisley who made his spectacular double entry onto the parliamentary stage in 1970 was already a familiar face. For nearly a decade and a half he had been engaged in back-room politicking and street agitation against the Northern Ireland establishment. Since the mid-sixties his stand as the defender of "not an inch" traditional Unionism and the scourge of the slightest deviation from Protestant ascendancy had made him that establishment's most detested bogey-man.

Thus his victories in Bannside and North Antrim were only the triumphant culmination of a period in his career which had started in an upstairs room of the Unionist Party's headquarters at a meeting of Ulster Protestant Action 14 years earlier. His weapons were the ones he had used so effectively in six years of campaigning against Terence O'Neill: the Orange-style march, the mass rally, the charge of weakness on the Border and the Constitution, the populist accusations of neglect by out-of-touch upper class leaders, the appeals to Protestant solidarity in the face of Republican encroachment.

Another irony, in view of his recent record of rabble-rousing and jail sentences, was that he was now posing as the hard-line defender of Unionist law and order. This was to be a recurrent theme as the violence of the summer of 1969 spread and intensified into the opening of the new decade.

His denunciations found many a ready ear among a defensive and confused Protestant population. Many of them agreed that O'Neill and his successors had weakly allowed the civil rights movement, in their eyes just the latest manifestation of the age-old IRA conspiracy, to take over the streets and put the Northern state under threat. They too were disgusted at the Stormont government's capitulation before Westminster's demand for the disbandment of their favourite anti-Catholic deterrent, the "B" Specials, and the disarming of the RUC.

In this, Paisley's attacks on the Unionist establishment were no different from those of the fifth columnists within it - William Craig, Harry West and Desmond Boal. But unlike them he did not have to moderate his invective because of any membership of that establishment's party. He could revel in the role of the Jeremiah who had prophesied doom and been proved right.

He was able to rub salt in the wounds by invoking the victories of an earlier and more heroic Unionism. No speech was complete without a reference to Carson's stand against Home Rule. To justify taking to the streets to oppose both the civil rights movement and the Stormont Government's failure to suppress it, he recalled another of his personal heroes: William Johnston of Ballykilbeg, the 19th century populist Orange leader, who went to jail to protest against a British government ban on Orange parades and was subsequently elected to Parliament.

Thus firmly placed in the tradition of a hundred years of "not an inch" Unionism, Paisley was able to reassure his audiences that the reforms imposed on O'Neill and Chichester-Clark by a British Labour government were only a temporary aberration. "There are many people in this city who think that all the Protestants are dead, but I will assure them that the Protestant cause is as strong as ever", he told a rally in Derry. "We will do a surgical operation on the body of Unionism and expel from it the cancerous Lundys who have betrayed us, and rejuvenate and revitalise traditional Unionism in the march onward to final victory".[1]

However, Paisley had another face which people outside his church had not seen before: that of the pragmatist, the vote and power-seeking political opportunist. He first showed this face as a new MP at Westminster. The day before his maiden speech in the British House of Commons in July 1970, he was still causing as much havoc in the chamber at Stormont as he had ever done on the streets outside. There had been a row over election literature, and he had stormed out with the Cromwellian jibe that if the serjeant-at-arms would lend him his sword he would "decapitate" a few of the members before he went.

However, there was nothing Cromwellian about his appearance at Westminster. He did not modulate his voice, which boomed out across the chamber as if he were at any small-town Loyalist rally. But his words were carefully chosen: he appealed for a hearing as the representative of a minority - "those Protestants who are against the present policies of the Ulster Unionist Party".

Like Bernadette Devlin 15 months earlier he reserved his harshest condemnation for that Unionist government: he claimed that his own equal treatment of Catholics and Protestants in his Antrim constituencies was the reason "the Unionist Party fear the Protestant Unionists more than they fear anyone else at the present time in the province".

It was a clever speech, pro-law and order yet anti-establishment enough to appeal to both sides of the Commons. But where Devlin's first speech had been welcomed by all sides as one of the most electrifying ever heard in the House, Paisley's was met by indifference and silent hostility.

If he had hoped to win MPs over by the force of his oratory, as close friends said he did, he must have been bitterly disappointed. "The House of Commons is pretty short of characters and in those days it would fill, both to hear a character and to hear about Northern Ireland, which had loomed a year or so before", recalls former Northern Ireland Secretary Merlyn Rees. "But Paisley's arrival began the effect of people saying 'Oh God, what on earth are we supposed to do about this place'. He quickly learned that as important as you are in Northern Ireland, you're not very important at Westminster."

Having made his speech Paisley walked straight out of the chamber, took a taxi to the airport and caught the first plane back to Belfast. Despite Edward Heath's prediction that the Commons would wear him down,[2] he was not going to allow himself to be caught up in the cosy atmosphere of an exclusive club that had been the undoing of so many provincial radicals before him.

What he did learn was to adapt himself to this hostile new audience. "He is a person who is very responsive to atmosphere and environment and he quite quickly picked up the vibrations of the House of Commons and learned to handle it", remembers Enoch Powell. He had an unsuspected aptitude for mastering complex rules and procedures, and his near-photographic memory enabled him to reel off passages from the manual of parliamentary procedure, Erskine May, with a facility he usually reserved for the Bible.

Westminster also taught him the politician's lesson of using different voices to speak to different audiences. In the Commons he soon learned not to bellow his speeches or pepper them with religious exhortations. In April 1971 a former Tory minister, Hugh Fraser, noted that while his Commons speeches were mild enough, they were a far cry from what he said to his working class followers in Belfast.[3]

The publisher of the *Daily Mirror,* Cecil King, who was to become a rare friend in London's political circles over the next few years, noted that he was "moving over to a more responsible attitude", but queried whether he could bring his followers with him.[4]

King, whose dinner guests included most of the senior members of the Tory Government, took a strong liking to Paisley, whom he insisted on seeing as a man who could lead the Protestants into a united Ireland. "He has a big personality, and as politician and orator knocks spots off any member of our present Cabinet", he wrote in September 1971.

Over the next two years King would meet the big preacher at least once a month, sometimes picking him up at the airport, and often bringing him home for dinner. King's wife, who had made the original contact, was particularly fond of Paisley, calling him "a warm and humble man of prayer" - itself an indication of the Dr Jekyll-like transformation that overtook him whenever he landed at Heathrow.

Paisley enjoyed this surprising new friendship and the chance to talk politics with someone who was on intimate terms with the most powerful men in the country. He valued Cecil King's advice on and intimate knowledge of the workings of Westminster. King for his part was urging Heath and his fellow ministers, future Northern Ireland Secretary William Whitelaw and Defence Secretary Lord Carrington, to ditch Brian Faulkner, who had replaced James Chichester-Clark as Northern Ireland Premier in March 1971, and sound out Paisley about heading a new Stormont administration.

Back at home Paisley was preparing to broaden his appeal away from his fundamentalist grass roots in the best tradition of the pragmatic politician. The man who would help him do this was another unlikely associate: the freethinking barrister, Desmond Boal.

Boal was generally recognised to be the most brilliant mind in the Unionist Party. In other ways he was a contradictory figure: he was a hard-line right winger on law and order (although he was against the death penalty); but on social issues he reflected the left-of-centre concerns of his working class constituents in the Shankill Road.

The relationship between Boal and Paisley went back to Ulster Protestant Action in 1956. Boal was one of only two contemporaries Paisley ever admired - the other was Bob Jones Jnr. He was also the only man who could ever control Paisley's huge ego and violent rages."I've seen Paisley in one of his ranting, raving moods standing on the staircase in the City Hall, surrounded by a crowd of his supporters. That's Paisley at his worst, with his own crowd round him, sycophantically chanting 'Yes, Dr Paisley' and 'No, Dr Paisley' - he feeds on that. And Boal went into the middle of that tantrum and put his head down and wagged his finger and lectured Paisley and completely deflated him", recalls one former Unionist politician.

Paisley recognised that Boal had the sharpest brain in Northern Ireland politics, and over the years had come to rely on his political as well as his legal advice. On the rare occasions Boal spoke at Stormont the chamber filled in the hope of witnessing some hapless Unionist minister being savaged by his brilliant and destructive logic.

He spoke for a huge Paisleyite constituency when he condemned the chaos and street violence caused by the civil rights movement, and the inability of "a supine, cowardly and fumbling government" to do anything about a situation where "lawlessness has been made respectable and sedition profitable."[5]

In March 1970 Boal, along with William Craig, Harry West, Johnny McQuade and Norman Laird, was expelled from the Unionist parliamentary party for refusing to support a confidence motion in Chichester-Clark's government. Boal spent the next 18 months wondering about his own and Northern Ireland's future - he even thought of emigrating to New Zealand at one point.

In September 1971 he left the Unionist Party and the following month joined Paisley in launching the Democratic Unionist Party (DUP). "Up to then Boal felt himself to be the guy who pulled the strings", says a former Unionist colleague at Stormont. "I remember him literally lurking in the shadows - coming out of doorways in the city centre as a Paisley parade passed by. He got his kicks through Paisley fronting for him. Now that phase was over and he felt that rather than orchestrating Paisley from a distance, together they would take on the whole establishment".

Boal's attractions to Paisley were obvious. By the summer of 1971 he was already starting to think of himself as a possible future prime minister of Northern Ireland.[6] To do that he would have to build an alternative to the despised Unionist Party, and would need to broaden his appeal far beyond the narrow rural limits and tiny and totally Free Presbyterian membership of the Protestant Unionists. Boal's secular working class Unionism appeared the perfect complement.

It was not as ideal as it might have seemed. In a climate of escalating violence which saw the birth of the Provisional IRA and the number of deaths rise from 13 in 1969 to 467 in 1972, the overriding issue in the minds of Unionist voters was security. Paisley and Boal both believed in the use of every draconian law available, including the Special Powers Act, to smash the rising revolt in the Catholic ghettoes. In August 1970 Paisley took this a step further by echoing the predictable call of other Unionist leaders for the internment of "IRA men".

But Boal did not agree with internment, believing it to be both unjust and ineffective against a Catholic community containing a large number of people who were opposed to the very existence of the state. In March 1971, five months before Brian Faulkner brought it in, Boal had denounced internment as "the kind of policy that a panic-stricken hysterical government is likely to bluster into."[7]

By the time the Stormont government had blundered into using its most oppressive weapon, Boal had persuaded Paisley to come round to his way of thinking. Six months earlier he had taken a first step by objecting to it on the grounds that the Unionist Government would intern Protestants and Catholics on a 50-50 basis and he would be the first to go inside. Now he came out against it in principle.

This was incomprehensible to most Unionists, who were well-used to internment being used against Republicans in the twenties, forties and fifties. One former Stormont MP remembers the damning comments of ordinary Unionists who had seen Paisley on television three days after internment leading a noisy picket outside Faulkner's office. "Faulkner had tapped into a vein right across the Unionist spectrum. The country was up against it, the smoke was rising from the cities and he was doing his best, while this lout was standing at the gates shouting 'traitor'. It was one argument Faulkner won hand over fist. It was a very low point for Paisley".

That autumn Boal's influence would lead Paisley into even more dangerous territory. But first came another switch in policy, this time dictated not only by Boal but by what Paisley had heard at Westminster. Until then Paisley had been a staunch defender of Stormont's right to rule, echoing William Craig's claim that to suspend it, as the British had been hinting they might do since 1970, would be unconstitutional and undemocratic. Now suddenly he learned that the British were thinking seriously about bringing in Direct Rule.

Paisley knew well enough that such a move would be violently resented in Belfast - "without Stormont we should be forgotten", he told Cecil King.[8] But on 30 October, when he made headlines by forecasting the end of Stormont at the Ulster Hall rally to launch the DUP, he astonished his supporters by giving it a guarded welcome. "Those who favour the British connection will at least see in this that we will be more integrated than ever in the United Kingdom," he told them.

The reason for Paisley's about-turn was twofold: firstly, Boal had decided that if Northern Ireland was to be disenfranchised by the abolition of its separate parliament, the only logical Unionist demand was for complete integration with Britain.

Secondly, Paisley was already thinking like an alternative Unionist leader. He knew that at Stormont the Unionists, however shaky, still controlled an electoral machine developed by the likes of Billy Douglas over half a century of one-party rule. He knew that his little band of Boal, Rev William Beattie and the tough old Shankill Road warhorse Johnny McQuade had little chance of competing with them in the backyard parliament they guarded so jealously.

However, the House of Commons, which would have to scrutinise Direct Rule, was another matter. There Paisley had quickly established himself as the most visible of a group of Unionist MPs remarkable mainly for their almost total invisibility. Three of them owed him favours: Paisleyites had signed Captain Lawrence Orr's nomination papers and stood aside to give Jack Maginnis in clear run in the 1970 election, while Paisley himself had done the same for Stanley McMaster 11 years earlier.

Another, Jim Kilfedder, had publicly thanked Paisley for helping him get elected in 1964. A fifth, Jim Molyneaux, was a right-winger who had spoken out against the first O'Neill-Lemass meeting and had been election agent to his predecessor, Sir Samuel Knox Cunningham, a Paisley sympathiser and contributor to the *Protestant Telegraph*. In what Unionists called the "imperial parliament" Paisley, not the Unionists, would be Northern Ireland's outstanding champion.

But Direct Rule was still nearly five months away. In the meantime Boal was working on a strategy of broad-based opposition to Faulkner's government. In mid-November he and Paisley had talks in his home on the County Down coast with John Hume, Austin Currie and Paddy Devlin of the Social Democratic and Labour Party, formed the previous year by a group of Nationalist, Labour and ex-Civil Rights Association politicians.

They found broad areas of agreement in their opposition to internment, support for state investment to deal with unemployment, and belief in better cross-border relations. "Wolfe Tone is alive and well and leading the Democratic Unionist Party", commented a jubilant Paddy Devlin.

If this was likely to raise further question marks among his supporters, what Paisley did later that month would throw them into total confusion. On the evening of Thursday 25 November Paisley and Boal met three Dublin journalists, Liam Hourican of Radio Telefis Eireann, Henry Kelly of the *Irish Times,* and Vincent Browne of the *Irish Press,* in Belfast's Europa Hotel.

They talked late into the night and at one point Browne said there would be no solution to the Northern problem until a majority of people there supported a united Ireland. Boal agreed. Paisley, always reluctant to take Boal head-on in argument, would not commit himself one way or the other, but started instead to talk about the need to change the 1937 Irish Constitution.

At around three o'clock in the morning Boal persuaded Paisley to give Hourican an interview. After Hourican had recorded an hour-long interview, both Browne and Kelly asked their own questions. Although it was close to six o'clock in the morning by the time they had finished, the journalists remember Paisley being in great humour throughout - "it was an extremely genial atmosphere", recalls Hourican.

In his RTE interview, broadcast that Sunday, Hourican asked Paisley would he consider the prospect of being part of a united Ireland if the South scrapped its constitution and changed certain of its laws. Paisley astounded everyone by replying that in such a situation there would be "an entirely different set of circumstances". "That would be the greatest guarantee to Protestants that they really meant business", he said.

In the newspaper interviews he was even more specific. "The cancer is not the 1920 Act and not the partition of the country," he told the *Irish Times,* "but the cancer is the 1937 Constitution and the domination of the Catholic Church through it."[9]

To the *Irish Press* he said: "If the people in the South really want the Protestants of the North to join them in a united Ireland, then they should scrap entirely the 1937 Constitution and ensure that the Roman Catholic hierarchy could no longer exercise an improper influence in politics. If this were done, then the Protestant people would take a different view - there would be an entirely different set of circumstances. We are not saying that the majority of the South should cease to be Roman Catholic. All we are saying is that they should ensure that rule from Dublin would not be rule from Maynooth".[10]

Paisley stressed again and again in the interviews that he was a "realist", pointing out the 1937 Constitution was not scrapped and was not about to be scrapped. He went on: "If you ask me whether I can see at some time, some way, somewhere in the future a united Ireland, that is a question I cannot answer because I cannot say now what will happen in the future, and anyway, I cannot answer the question because I am too much of a realist and such a question is really not even worthy of consideration now".[11]

Boal, sensing the beginning of British fatigue with the whole Northern Ireland imbroglio, might have thought it was time to discuss the whole range of options open to Unionism. But to most traditional Unionists, Paisley had scored an astonishing own goal.

The line-up of people welcoming his comments only served to confirm this: Provisional IRA leader Daithi O'Conaill said that Republicans and Paisleyites were "allies in the cause of a new Ireland", and praised his social conscience and the equal treatment of his Catholic and Protestant constituents.[12] Fianna Fail Finance Minister George Colley invited him to Dublin to help draft a new constitution. The *Irish Times* made the extraordinary prophesy that one day Paisley would sit in Dail Eireann, the Irish parliament.

In the north he was fortunate that his comments were overshadowed by the reaction to Harold Wilson's 15-year plan for Irish unity, announced the previous week. However a delighted Brian Faulkner dubbed him "the new darling of the Republican press". The bulletin of the paramilitary Ulster Defence Association, noting that "at one time we would have followed Paisley anywhere", now dissociated the organisation from him.[13]

His own followers were totally confused: first opposition to internment, then indifference to Stormont's fate, and now flirting with the Republic. "The reaction was one of hostility and astonishment", according to a leading DUP man at the time, Clifford Smyth. "People didn't understand it; it was far too radical and advanced for their thinking. One minute they were out kicking the Pope, 'Old Redsocks', and the next they're into this 'entirely different set of circumstances'."

It was a set of circumstances Paisley was never to return to. He immediately drew back from the brink, telling a BBC interviewer that he was "opposed absolutely" to any kind of united Ireland. "That's the thing about him - he's much more the representative of the people than their leader", says Smyth. "He's not going to lead them through the wilderness like Moses. He's too responsive to the feelings of the people in the wee Protestant hall in Ballymena and simply will not go too far ahead of his supporters."

It was also the beginning of the end of his political relationship, although not his personal friendship, with Boal, the man who wanted him to play Moses. For Boal the interviews with the Southern journalists were only a first step. William Craig remembers Paisley taking Harry West and him to see Boal in his suite in the Europa Hotel one morning in 1973. Boal told them that the time had come to consider a federal settlement in order to protect the interests of Northern Protestants within Ireland. Paisley said nothing. West was dumbfounded and Craig told Boal, "Even if there was merit in it it could never be sold". Boal then lost his temper and the meeting came to an abrupt end.

In January 1974 Boal proposed an "amalgamated Ireland" under a federal parliament, with a Stormont-style provincial parliament in Belfast. He argued that the connection between Britain and Northern Ireland was in the process of being broken anyway, whatever Unionists thought, and "much of the former sentimental attachment to Britain has recently evaporated, even to be replaced sometimes by bitterness and hostility".

Boal had long ago given up active politics - which even at the best of times he treated with the irreverence of the gifted dilettante - and dropped out of sight completely when he became a QC in January 1973.

By this time Paisley was desperate for a way out of the unpopular cul-de-sac of integration. For the truth was that there was absolutely no chance of any Westminster government integrating the bloody chaos of Northern Ireland into the British body politic. "It became clear that the whole emphasis of British politicians was not to bring Northern Ireland more closely into the UK but to push it further out - integration wasn't going to be an attainable goal", says DUP deputy leader Peter Robinson.

In Northern Ireland the suspension of Stormont in March 1972 had led not to a new integrationist momentum, but to a sullen Loyalist backlash, fuelled by the growing ferocity of the Provisional IRA campaign and led by the DUP leader's main rival inside the Unionist "family", William Craig. Craig, now leading his own militant Ulster Vanguard movement, called a two-day work stoppage in protest at the British Government's action which saw nearly 200,000 people staying at home, and staged two massive rallies of angry Loyalists in Ormeau Park and at Stormont.

In contrast, Paisley's support for integration and early backing for the first Direct Rule Secretary of State William Whitelaw were deeply unpopular among ordinary loyalists. "Unionists can only understand what they have experienced. They were asking for the good old days of Stormont back", says one leading Unionist of the time.

DUP members and Free Presbyterians also flocked to Vanguard rallies, despite their leader's denunciations of Craig and his advocacy of an independent Ulster as "the voice of folly". Former party activist Wallace Thompson remembered that time as the DUP's lowest point. "Vanguard had all the trappings of what the people who followed Paisley wanted. They needed displays of symbolism; they needed to let off steam and Craig's rallies provided it . . . They were regarded by most who attended them as the traditional Ulster way of protesting."

By the end of 1972 Paisley had concluded that it was time to switch direction and get back into the Loyalist mainstream: the hopes he had placed in the first Northern Ireland Secretary William Whitelaw had only led to a government Green Paper recognising the North's "Irish dimension"; and increasingly he believed the House of Commons to be a meaningless charade and its MPs a lot of puppets.[14]

It was the British who gave him the perfect opportunity by calling a plebiscite on the Border for March 1973. This was an issue on which every Unionist could agree. Paisley threw his stupendous energies into the campaign to bring the vote out, using it to reassert his traditional Unionist credentials.

The Boal-induced folly of the previous 19 months was forgotten. "When Paisley changes his mind on these things it's like sloughing off an old skin", says David Trimble, then one of William Craig's lieutenants. "You can't detect any signs of embarrassment - he just goes ahead and if you try to remind him of what he was doing beforehand, he gets most indignant".

Paisley's next move was an astute one. The Unionist party had split into warring factions over Brian Faulkner's willingness to go along with Whitelaw's power-sharing proposals. Craig had turned his Vanguard movement into a hard-line but still disorganised alternative Unionist party. The confused Unionist grass roots were calling for a united front to fight the forthcoming elections to a new Northern Ireland Assembly. The Provisional IRA's violence showed no signs of letting up. In the face of this disarray, Paisley and Craig shrewdly decided to bury their differences and form an electoral pact.

It was the first of several such pacts which Paisley's single-minded drive for domination over his fellow-Unionists, backed by the messianic zeal of his followers, would turn to his advantage. Now, after a decade spent biting at Unionism's tail, he was able to pose for the first time as a champion of Unionist unity. The voters, anxious for strong leadership and deeply unhappy at the secret talks the British had been having with the IRA, welcomed him back in style.

In the elections for the Assembly in June 1973 the DUP emerged as the second largest Unionist grouping after Faulkner's deeply divided party. Paisley was exultant. His rehabilitation as a traditional and uncompromising Unionist was complete. He was set to join Craig's Vanguard and Harry West's rebel Unionists as an equal partner in the campaign to destroy Westminster's first attempt to defuse the Northern Ireland crisis: the Faulkner-led power-sharing executive.

THE DOWNFALL OF WILLIAM CRAIG

Never again would Paisley stray so far from the traditional Unionist fold. For the next decade his star as the outstanding hard-line leader of Ulster Loyalism would rise along with his growing electoral support. Those grass roots supporters, battered by the IRA and constantly on the lookout for betrayal both by the British and their own leaders, would henceforth be his sole reference point in dealing with any scheme to attempt to break the continuing and worsening political deadlock.

After the fall of the power-sharing executive in May 1974, the first of those schemes came from inside the Unionist "family", from the unlikely figure of Paisley's fellow diehard, William Craig. While Paisley had been dabbling in moderation and integration in 1971 and 1972, Craig had been turning up at fascist-style rallies with leather-coated paramilitary outriders and warning that he could mobilise 80,000 Loyalists who were prepared to "come out and shoot to kill".

If to Catholics Paisley was the roaring open mouth of Protestant bigotry, Craig was the cold-eyed rabble-rouser whose menacing speeches had sent out the sectarian murder squads of the reformed UVF and the newer and larger Ulster Defence Association (UDA). Craig was the politician most closely identified with the UDA, which had more than 25,000 members by 1972, and provided the intimidatory muscle both for his Vanguard work stoppages and the 1974 Ulster Workers Council strike which brought down the power-sharing executive.

However, in the following year Craig was starting to have a change of heart. He had always nursed the ambition to be Prime Minister of Northern Ireland. Now, with his confidence high after his leadership role in the UWC strike, he toned down his anti-Nationalist diatribes, and stressed in his speeches that it was only when the people of Northern Ireland could share a common allegiance that the conflict would end.

In May 1975 the government's latest effort to get Northern Ireland's politicians into a talking mood, the Constitutional Convention, got under way. It was totally dominated by the three-party United Ulster Unionist Coalition (UUUC), made up of Harry West's right-wing Unionists, Paisley's DUP and Craig's Vanguard: between them they held 47 out of its 78 seats.

Perhaps that is why they were in a conciliatory mood when it opened. This was articulated by Paisley when he said that the big issue was not the link with Britain but how to get institutions of government working which would help to build a "united Ulster".[15]

At the beginning of June Craig, Paisley's deputy leader Rev William Beattie, Austin Ardill of the Official Unionists and Austin Currie and Paddy Devlin of the SDLP agreed to hold informal weekly meetings to discuss areas of common interest. On the same day, in an interview with the *Irish Times*, Craig first introduced the idea of "voluntary coalition".[16]

What he meant was a Unionist-led coalition of Unionist and SDLP politicians who would govern Northern Ireland for a temporary period on the same basis that had brought the British Conservative and Labour parties into coalition during the emergencies of the Depression years and the Second World War. Craig thought this would avoid the statutory "power-sharing" of the previous year's ill-fated initiative, when the SDLP had places as of right in a Northern Ireland Cabinet.

The informal talks between Craig, Beattie and Ardill for the UUUC, and Currie, Devlin and John Hume for the SDLP continued in a desultory fashion until the inevitable impasse was reached in mid-August over power-sharing. Suddenly Craig produced the voluntary coalition idea. The SDLP men expressed interest. According to Craig the Unionists then reported back to the UUUC Convention party, who told them to go ahead with their talks. On 3 September the two sides went together to the Convention chairman, the Lord Chief Justice, Sir Robert Lowry, and asked him to prepare a paper on how voluntary coalition could be brought into effect.

The scheme even hinted at an Irish dimension: Craig had suggested a treaty relationship with Dublin along the lines of the agreement between the Benelux countries - Belgium, Holland and Luxembourg - on common economic and cultural interests. On security the SDLP recognised that in the aftermath of any deal on voluntary coalition there would be an upsurge in IRA violence which would have to be dealt with. "De Valera had to shoot X number of Republicans and we may have to do the same", one of the Unionists remembers an SDLP man saying.

For a moment it looked as though a totally unforeseen breakthrough was about to take place. Craig said later: "I remember coming out of the final round with the SDLP, and reporting to Paisley first of all, because he was the first of the leaders we met, that the SDLP seemed genuinely interested in finding a solution via voluntary coalition - he took my hand and shook it up and down and said 'Bill, we have saved Ulster'".

However, Craig reckoned without Paisley's susceptibility to grass roots pressure. For on Monday 1 September, after a month in which 28 people, nearly one every day, had been killed in sectarian assassinations, there had been an atrocity in South Armagh which struck at the very heart of the Protestant community. Masked men broke into an Orange Hall at Tullyvallen, near Newtownhamilton, close to the Border, and machine-gunned the group of mainly elderly Orangemen inside, killing four of them and wounding seven others.

Three days later Paisley, without consulting West and Craig, threatened that the majority of Unionist members were prepared to pull out of the Convention unless much tougher security measures, such as the total sealing of the Border, were brought in. "The people at the grass-roots are telling us: 'Don't carry on a charade at Stormont while your constituents are being killed'", he told journalists.[17]

David Trimble, then a Vanguard Convention member, recalls that when Craig's scheme was discussed early that week, the DUP leader was not hostile, but by the end of the week he had turned against it. He claims that Paisley had meetings with groups of Free Presbyterian ministers and elders not normally involved in politics, some of them from the Armagh area, who got "very excited" about him going into Government with Catholics at such a time, warning him that it could split the church.

There was pressure from a different quarter on the following Monday. Ulster Workers Council spokesman Jim Smyth and the Ballylumford power workers leader Billy Kelly, himself a Free Presbyterian, appeared on the steps of Stormont to lobby UUUC Convention members against the Craig scheme before they met to discuss it.

The pressure was already starting to tell: of the 14-strong Vanguard Convention party only three supported Craig. Within the Official Unionists Enoch Powell, in his capacity as Westminster MP for South Down, had already thrown his influential weight against the initiative. But the coup de grace came from Paisley: "Without even allowing the chairman to bring the meeting to order, he launched into a violent attack on having the SDLP and Catholic members in government in any shape or form", recalls Craig.

According to Craig, Lowry's paper was not even discussed. The meeting became very heated and Harry West and Martin Smyth went off to a funeral. Craig said if they were not prepared to consider the document or to continue the discussions with the SDLP, he had no option but to resign as leader of Vanguard in the Convention.

Vanguard split down the middle, with the majority of its Convention members, led by deputy leader Ernest Baird, lining up against their erstwhile leader. In meetings around the country Craig suddenly found he was being heckled and barracked in exactly the same way as Terence O'Neill and Brian Faulkner before their downfalls.

William Beattie, Paisley's man on the team who had been talking to the SDLP, was another casualty. He was caught out in a barefaced lie by Lowry on the floor of the Convention while trying to distance himself from Craig's scheme, and was ditched by Paisley, first as DUP chairman and eventually as deputy leader.

It was the effective end not only of the voluntary coalition idea, but also of the Convention itself, as well as the beginning of the end of Craig's political career. Craig had a reputation for stubbornness, but his erstwhile colleagues were astonished that Unionism's toughest right-winger had suddenly decided to stake his whole future on this one abortive experiment in moderation.

Harry West might have thought that his party, as the fold which Craig had left two and a half years earlier, would be where disgruntled Vanguard supporters would now return. But as usual the Official Unionists were divided over the issue. The maverick former Stormont minister John Taylor claimed that Craig's coalition idea was not inconsistent with the party's election manifesto, and demanded a break with Paisley.

It was left to Paisley to seize on the opportunity to do what he did best: to pose as the incorruptible guardian of the hardest line, and to flay those who strayed from it with vicious and highly personalised campaigns of abuse. In December the DUP circulated thousands of leaflets showing a ten-year-old photograph of Craig with Terence O'Neill and Jack Lynch during the former Taoiseach's visit to Stormont in 1967, and urging loyalists to "join the DUP - the party you can trust".

The following February Paisley asserted that attempts to get a coalition government were "a holding operation for the final victory of the terrorists", and demanded the isolation of the Craigs and the Taylors as "a race of collaborators and quislings who are prepared to deceive and destroy the Ulster loyalist community for their own personal advantage and aggrandisement".[18]

For the best part of the next two years he was accusing Craig of having been tempted into treachery by the offer of the prime minister's job in a voluntary coalition. It was all a plot dreamed up by the British and the SDLP to divide the Unionist "family", he declared.[19]

Craig's supporters got the message: in the 1979 general election they turned his 17,000 majority in East Belfast into the narrowest of wins for the DUP's Peter Robinson. By 1982 he was finished, physically ill and politically irrelevant: in the East Belfast constituency for that year's election to the new Northern Ireland Assembly he finished a humiliating eighth and failed to get elected.

Paisley had not engineered Craig's downfall over voluntary coalition. He was the ruthless opportunist who switched sides at the last moment and exploited it to his own advantage.

With Craig's influence on the wane, and the Convention in ruins, Paisley turned on his erstwhile allies in Harry West's Official Unionist party. They were now the only obstacle to his ambition to become the unrivalled leader of Unionism. He devoted the rest of the decade to working to persuade Unionist voters that the party they had traditionally supported was now weak on security, divided on devolution and untrustworthy on the link with Britain. It was back to the 1960s all over again.

It was not a difficult task. The leaders of Official Unionism were continually at loggerheads. Harry West was a conciliator who bent over backwards to accommodate Paisley's hard-line posturing and personal attacks on his fellow-Unionists in order to keep some form of Loyalist coalition in existence. The head of the Orange Order, Rev Martin Smyth, was keen to maintain contact with the SDLP and detested Paisley both personally and for his long record of attacks on the Order and the Presbyterian Church. John Taylor, who saw himself as a future party leader, was prepared to go almost as far as Craig to get a devolved administration back at Stormont. And Enoch Powell was spinning his integrationist spell over Jim Molyneaux at Westminster.

In the face of this confusion in the Official Unionist ranks, Paisley's party presented a picture of unchanging intransigence which many Unionist voters found immensely reassuring. Paisley was "the greatest leader on earth", DUP chairman James McClure told the 1977 party conference. The leader himself hammered more wedges into his rivals' creaking edifice: the Official Unionists had been "very wobbly" during the Convention period and Harry West had admitted there were still "O'Neillites" in his party, he told delegates. In contrast the DUP was seen by both the British and Irish governments as "the last bulwark to be breached in order to get the Republicans into a Northern Ireland government". Any such scheme, he roared, would be "just the half-way house to a united Ireland ruled from Dublin - the first instalment of the British withdrawal and surrender policy in Ulster".[20]

Integration was also out now, since both the Conservative and Labour parties had as their ultimate aim a united Ireland and so could "not be trusted with the future of Ulster". Similarly any watered-down form of administrative devolution, as favoured by Jim Molyneaux, was "yet another Whitehall plan to help forward the IRA goal - rule from Dublin".[21]

At the same time Paisley used his formidable talent for self-advertisement, with the help of some well-placed police and civil service sources, to upstage them by frequent headline-grabbing statements on the security situation. He alleged that there had been troop reductions as part of a British deal with the IRA. He claimed that the IRA had infiltrated an élite RUC unit. He met the US ambassador to protest about the suspension of arms sales to the RUC. And he charged the Catholic Church with responsibility for guns being hidden and ambushes being mounted on its property.

Official Unionist confusion also allowed Paisley to steal their "devolutionist" clothes. He was able to pose as the strongest advocate of a return to the "good old days" ordinary Loyalists yearned for: to an untrammelled Stormont-type parliament with full control of security.

It did not seem to matter that this was a demand the British had pledged never to concede. It was something a confused and embattled Loyalist population could understand. Ironically, in the light of his earlier antagonism to Stormont, it was also Paisley's first coherent policy since the Boal-inspired integrationism of the early seventies.

In the mid-1970s his Unionist coalition colleagues had hardly known from one day to the next which policy line he would favour: some of them believed him to be still an integrationist at heart; he alternated between boycotting and attending the House of Commons; he attacked Ernest Baird for proposing extra-parliamentary action but later joined him in the Action Council which organised the abortive 1977 Loyalist strike; and he even raised the possibility of independence with his intermittent calls for a referendum to find out if the British people wanted to get out of Northern Ireland.

For someone who claimed to stand for the unchanging principles of Unionism, his practice of them was erratic in the extreme. It was clear that since Boal had departed from the scene he was a politician totally lacking in any vision or strategy. "He reminds me of a corncrake", the young Lord Brookeborough had said in 1974," he makes a tremendous noise but one doesn't quite know which field he'll be in next."

The man who did most to rescue Paisley from this confusion and allow him to present himself as the strong, coherent voice of traditional Unionism was Enoch Powell. Since being invited to take over the South Down seat in 1974, Powell had won a considerable section of the leadership, led by its Westminster spokesman, Jim Molyneaux, over to his integrationist ideas, and to his belief that devolution would only be used by the Foreign Office to bring about a united Ireland by stealth.

This succeeded only in dividing that leadership from its traditional Unionist supporters. They wanted the return of a Stormont-style parliament precisely as a veto on Britain's untrustworthy intentions. These were the people who in 1979 would dramatically switch their allegiance to the DUP leader.

The occasion was the first election to the European Parliament, for which Northern Ireland was treated as one constituency. The Official Unionists had already suffered a setback a month earlier in the general election which saw the arrival of Margaret Thatcher in Downing Street. Peter Robinson and Johnny McQuade overturned sizeable Official Unionist majorities to win seats in East and North Belfast.

But nothing had prepared them for the setback of that June. In the first direct election to the EEC's parliament in Strasbourg Paisley polled nearly 30 per cent of the first preference votes, more than doubling any previous DUP total, and exceeding the combined totals of Official Unionist candidates John Taylor and Harry West. West trailed in fourth behind Paisley, the SDLP's John Hume and Taylor, and resigned as party leader less than a month later. Paisley had added one more Unionist leader's scalp to his growing collection: O'Neill, Chichester-Clark, Faulkner, Craig and now the hapless Fermanagh farmer who had tried so hard to accommodate his seemingly unstoppable ambition.

THE TEMPTATION OF MODERATION

Now for the first time Paisley could with justification call himself "the leader of the Protestant people of Ulster". And for the first time the British Government started to treat him as such. The next 12 months would see a real test of his intransigence, as a genial new Secretary of State, Humphrey Atkins, tried to woo him into becoming involved in yet another attempt to devolve some powers to Belfast, and a new "benign" view of the great bogey-man of Unionism started to be peddled by some of the mandarins in the Northern Ireland Office.

As 1979 turned into 1980 this was the new theory in currency: that Paisley's rabble-rousing anti-Catholicism was a function of his personal insecurity and the political insecurity of the people he represented. After his huge European vote, with Northern Protestants becoming increasingly anti-British, and the level of IRA violence continuing at the lowest level since the early seventies, a new Paisley might emerge, the argument went, a more confident and pragmatic politician who would be able to deliver his enormous constituency in the event of an agreed compromise.

Certainly it seemed to be a new Paisley who agreed in November 1979 to attend Humphrey Atkins' constitutional conference. His surprise decision came after the new Official Unionist leader, Jim Molyneaux, had boycotted it on the "Powellite" grounds that devolution would only weaken the link with Britain. This breathed unexpected new life into what had appeared to be a cynical British exercise in "going through the motions" of once again being seen to be consulting local politicians, largely in order to improve Britain's poor Irish image abroad.

Paisley had also been impressed by Margaret Thatcher. Following the killings of Lord Mountbatten and 18 British paratroopers in August, and her closest political confidant Airey Neave the previous March, she was now talking, unlike any previous prime minister, about the military defeat of the Provisional IRA.

However, there was another more important reason to show his conciliatory face. It was just the latest move in the same internecine campaign he had been running since the mid-seventies. "He's not going into that conference to reach agreement - he's just trying to screw up the Official Unionists", said one politician at the time. "He always sees himself on the outside. Every so often he goes through a phase of being all sweet reason when it suits him, but take my word for it - deep down Paisley doesn't change."[22]

Former Secretary of State Sir Humphrey Atkins agrees: "He wanted to take over the leadership of all the Unionists. The Official Unionists wouldn't come: that's why he was there. He saw the opportunity to represent himself as the reasonable voice of Unionism, with the Official Unionists as the far-out ones." If he was able to make inroads into the one section of the Unionist constituency who had not backed him for Europe, the moderates, he could irrevocably cripple the Official Unionists and make himself the undisputed leader of the whole Protestant community at one stroke.

For the first time the Northern Ireland Office thought they were close to tempting Paisley with the idea of leading a Stormont administration. Over innumerable cups of tea Atkins tried to pry out of Paisley exactly what he wanted: did he want to be prime minister of a devolved government or was he more interested in leading an independent Ulster? Paisley would not be drawn.

They discussed a number of complex and convoluted mechanisms to avoid the dreaded concept of "power-sharing": weighted majorities and co-ordinating groups of committee chairmen and second chambers with a minority veto. Paisley kept hinting privately that he might be open to some form of compromise. But as the conference dragged on from January into the spring of 1980 even Atkins realised there was still not the remotest chance he would share any real power with the SDLP.

Atkins' little initiative was dead by that spring, despite some wild speculation in the press, notably from John Healy in the *Irish Times,* that Mrs Thatcher might be close to springing some Rhodesia-style "breaking the link" and leaving Paisley and Hume to sort out a political solution.[23]

Former DUP man Clifford Smyth has pointed out that such wishful thinking was based on two misconceptions: firstly, that the DUP was a normal political party capable of change and compromise, whereas in fact its supporters were puzzled and alarmed at seeing their leader in talks with the SDLP which the Official Unionists had boycotted. And secondly, that Paisley was a leader in the sense that he could deliver his grass-roots, rather than merely articulate their belligerent brand of Unionism.[24]

Paisley did not need much of a pretext to ditch the benign Unionism so favoured by the pundits for the belligerent bigotry he revelled in. In early May the Fianna Fail Taoiseach Charles J. Haughey, a longstanding Unionist hate figure, came to Armagh for the enthronement of the new Church of Ireland Primate. Outside the cathedral Paisley, accompanied by Peter Robinson and Johnny McQuade, led a 30-strong Free Presbyterian picket.

They pushed and shoved, and he bellowed at the RUC about protecting a man who harboured the gunmen who were shooting their colleagues.

It was a classic piece of Paisley street theatre. He roared at a senior RUC officer, who stood about a foot away from him, shouting that he was the politician with the biggest vote in Northern Ireland and demanding that he be allowed through the police cordon to make his protest. He was told he would have to make it where he stood.

He invited the police to arrest him and his fellow MPs - "if you don't you're only going to cause these people to push again", he blustered. "Come on now", he urged the embarrassed officer. "Be a man, come and take us in." He, Robinson and McQuade pushed again. The officer gave in. The three men were arrested and released again in an hour.[25]

The whole episode appeared on that evening's television news. It brought in a wave of support for the DUP, said Peter Robinson afterwards, with even Official Unionists commenting favourably that Paisley was once again the only man who had the courage to stand up and voice what every Unionist was thinking.

Up in Stormont Castle, wrote the *Guardian* correspondent, Anne McHardy, "Mr Atkins is putting the finishing touches to his plans for the future government of the province, and all the signs are that he envisages a devolved administration which Paisley could head." But in Armagh Paisley had once again opted for the adulation of the "no surrender" people at the Loyalist grassroots rather than the risky business of trying to put himself forward as a potential leader of Northern Ireland as a whole.

A day or two later Official Unionist leader Jim Molyneaux met Atkins in the lobby of the House of Commons. "What do you think of Ian Paisley today?" asked Molyneaux. "That bloody man, that bloody man!" Atkins cried, raising his hands in despair.[26]

It took another eight months for the new-look Paisley to disappear totally. The occasion once again involved Charles J. Haughey. The Taoiseach's December 1980 summit meeting with Margaret Thatcher, and the "totality of relationships" statement which came out of it, provoked him into a blazing row with the British Prime Minister, a series of familiar but still bloodcurdling threats of Protestant backlash, and the beginning of the "Carson

Trail" rallies.

Paisley and his lieutenants could look back on his year of "moderation" with satisfaction. For they had succeeded in their primary aim of further undermining the Official Unionists, who were now totally obsessed with the threat he and his party, organised for the first time into an efficient electoral machine by Peter Robinson, posed to their leadership of the Unionist community.

After more than a decade of being plagued by Paisley, they had still to find a chink in his armour. His political judgement and sensitivity to grass roots Loyalism was consistently better than theirs. And for the first time in nearly 60 years of one-party dominance they faced a real rival: an opponent who owed them nothing - a charismatic leader who had built up his own church, his own party and even his own Orange power base through the Independent Orange Order and the Apprentice Boys of Derry.

Against him they had the colourless and diffident Jim Molyneaux. "Powell works Molyneaux with his foot", a Stormont civil servant had once sneered. The gentlemanly Molyneaux would only attack Paisley obliquely. Powell was blunter, denouncing Paisley's participation in the Atkins conference as "not the first, or the last occasion on which he was to reveal himself as the most resourceful, inveterate and dangerous enemy of the Union".[27] To Powell, the DUP leader was henceforth just another actor, albeit a principal and often unwitting one, in a scenario mapped out for him by the anti-Unionist conspirators of the British Foreign Office and the US State Department.

Powell was right to be worried about the DUP leader, although the reasons had nothing to do with the Foreign Office. For the period between the European election of June 1979 and the local elections of May 1981 saw Paisley and his party going from strength to strength.

After the statesmanlike pose of 1980, early 1981 provided him with a convenient threat from the hereditary enemy so that he could brandish anew his loyalist militancy. The Thatcher-Haughey summit, and the "joint studies" of cross-border and Anglo-Irish issues that came out of it, were perfectly suited to the series of "Carson Trail" rallies he launched against them. They gave him plenty of scope for rhetoric without the risk of violent street action that a real constitutional crisis would involve.

His flamboyant fierceness further served to exacerbate the tensions inside the Official Unionists. Those most in favour of devolution, notably Rev Robert Bradford and John Taylor, saw the merit in Paisley's temperature-raising tactics. Molyneaux and Powell condemned his stunts with marching men on hillsides and his latest call for a British referendum on the link with Northern Ireland as the actions of a man bent on undermining that link.

But once again he had touched a paranoid nerve in the ever-vigilant body politic of Loyalism. When the "big man" cried that Thatcher was sacrificing Northern Ireland to "the baying wolves of the Irish Republic", he did not lose credibility, but was given credit for his eternal vigilance. Paisley had learned one lesson long ago: the voice warning of betrayal was always at an advantage in Northern Protestant politics.

The result was that in the May 1981 local elections, held under the shadow of the Maze Prison hunger strike and the street violence it provoked, Paisley's party did what Paisley the individual had done two years previously in the European election: they doubled their representation on the councils and for the first time ever outpolled the Official Unionists, albeit by the wafer-thin margin of a hundredth of a per cent.

Like the superb tactician he was, Paisley immediately moved to reassure Unionists long used to the comforting monolith of one-party dominance: he emphasised his commitment to the strength and unity of the "Unionist family". Commentators started to wonder if the days of the faction-ridden Official Unionists might finally be numbered: one well-informed observer within its own ranks even speculated that the coup de grâce might be delivered at the next of Northern Ireland's endless series of elections.[28]

That was not to be. A number of factors combined to halt the onward march of Paisley's party, at least two of them due to failings on his part. Firstly, many Unionists were impressed by Margaret Thatcher's tough stand against the Republican hunger strikers in the Maze prison, which led to the deaths of ten IRA and INLA prisoners between May and August 1981.

Following this, more respectable Unionists were unhappy with the paramilitary posturings of Paisley's "Third Force" in the wake of the IRA's assassination of Official Unionist MP Rev Robert Bradford in November 1981. Depending on the seriousness of the current crisis, such people have tended to swing from regarding the Loyalist paramilitaries as a necessary evil to shunning them as hoodlums no decent Protestant would want to be associated with. Many of them put Paisley's 1981 marching men into the latter category.

Then early the following year his claim to the moral leadership of the Protestant community was momentarily shaken when he became embroiled in the Kincora boys' home scandal. The home's three housefathers had been jailed for homosexual offences against the boys in their care, and Paisley was exposed as being less than truthful about why he had not acted upon allegations made nine years previously against one of them, William McGrath, who was a worshipper at his church.

For several months there were serious questions asked about Paisley's role in the affair. How could the great champion of puritan values, who had led the "Save Ulster from Sodomy" campaign against the liberalisation of the North's homosexual laws in the late seventies, have failed to take action in this sordid little episode a couple of years earlier?

The questions remained unanswered. Paisley almost disappeared from view for several months: he played only a marginal part in the South Belfast by-election for Rev Robert Bradford's Westminster seat, in which the DUP candidate came a poor third; and his participation in the protests the following May and June during the Pope's visit to Britain was marked by an uncharacteristic reluctance to become involved in dramatic or disruptive confrontations.

A fourth factor which worked against Paisley and in favour of the Official Unionists was Margaret Thatcher's aggressive stance in the 1982 Falklands War, which convinced many ordinary Unionists that they could rely on Jim Molyneaux's insistence that she was the one British prime minister they could trust.

There was one all-important final reason why the DUP's electoral support was about to level off from its 1981 high point: Paisley was preparing to put on his conciliatory face once again. The occasion was yet another experiment in seeing how the locals could run a few of their own affairs in yet another Stormont Assembly. This one was the brainchild of the latest Secretary of State, James Prior, the former Employment Secretary, who had been exiled to the political Siberia of Belfast because of his leadership of the anti-Thatcher wing of the Tories. He had pledged on his arrival that he would lay his political reputation

Ian and Eileen with daughters Rhonda and Cherith outside Belfast City Hall (*Belfast Telegraph*)

Paisley with sons Ian junior (left) and Kyle (*Belfast Telegraph*)

Paisley and Robinson being led away after their arrest outside Armagh Cathedral in May 1980 (*Belfast Telegraph*)

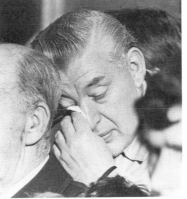

A man of many moods: Six faces of Ian Paisley

Paisley posing beside the statue of Edward Carson outside Stormont (*Bobbie Hanvey*)

Paisley meeting former President Marcos of the Philippines in Manila in 1980 (*Ballymena Guardian*)

Paisley and an admirer during the final "Carson Trail" march to Stormont in March 1981 (*Pacemaker*)

Paisley, Rev William McCrea and colleagues during the gospel meeting at Dublin's Mansion House in September 1978 (*Irish Times*)

Paisley and Official Unionist leader Jim Molyneaux united in Ballymena, Co. Antrim, during the campaign against the November 1985 Anglo Irish Agreement (*Ballymena Guardian*)

Paisley with Allister Lucas, Free Presbyterian elder and DUP activist (*Ballymena Guardian*)

om left: DUP chairman James McClure, UDA leader John McMichael and Peter Robinson arching in front of a Loyalist paramilitary banner in Ballymena in 1984. Third from right is George awright, later expelled from the DUP. (*Ballymena Guardian*).

aisley's brother-in-law, Rev Jim Beggs, leads the singing at Portglenone, Co. Antrim (*Ballymena uardian*)

A Paisley election poster (*Allan McCullough*)

"on the line" in a bid to secure a political settlement in Northern Ireland.

The result was a scheme called "rolling devolution", involving a new Assembly which in the first instance would start off with only consultative and scrutiny powers. If there was sufficient "cross community" support from both Unionist and Nationalist parties in this Assembly - 70 per cent of its members was the figure laid down - it could apply to Westminster to have one or more Northern Ireland government departments transferred to its control.

Throughout the 1970s Paisley had denounced any scheme which fell short of Stormont-style Unionist control as the first step in perfidious Albion's long-term plan for withdrawal and Irish unity. The Atkins conference had seen the first hint of a break in that atavistic stand. Now he turned full circle: he told Unionists that Prior's powerless Assembly could represent the last chance for devolved government in Northern Ireland in his lifetime. Even after the SDLP, under pressure from the Provisional IRA's resurgent political wing, Sinn Fein, decided to boycott it, he still declared that Unionists could muster the necessary "cross community" support to turn it into a local Stormont-style system of legislation and government.

Further evidence of Paisley's latest change of direction came as the new Assembly, with the squabbling Official Unionists still holding on as the largest party, started to meet in November 1982. From the first day it became obvious that there was an unlikely working arrangement in operation between the two parties in favour of making the Assembly work, the DUP and the non-sectarian "moderates" of the Alliance Party.

One of the most striking examples of this was Paisley's behaviour following the sectarian attempt by the Official Unionist deputy leader, Harold McCusker, to block the nomination of Alliance's John Cushnahan as chairman of the Assembly's education committee on the grounds that he was a Catholic. To the astonishment of many of his grass roots members, he made it clear to the Assembly's Speaker, Jim Kilfedder, that he was happy enough with the appointment. Here, it seemed, was the germ of the "cross community support" that Paisley hoped would lead to Stormont-style devolution.

Such flexibility would have been unbelievable had it not been for the fact that for only the second time in his career, Paisley was being significantly influenced by another politician. This was his deputy leader Peter Robinson. Over the previous seven years Robinson's organisational talents had turned the DUP into a sophisticated vote-winning machine. As a consequence he had become the first of Paisley's lieutenants to be essential to his continuing success.

This put him in an unprecedented position of power. British civil servants became aware of Robinson's growing influence over Paisley in early 1981, when the DUP leader had told Humphrey Atkins to disregard his latest outburst about holding a referendum, while his deputy sat beside him grinning broadly. It was clear to the Northern Ireland Office that Robinson had forced Paisley into this climbdown.

Robinson was now supported by a group of even younger men like Jim Allister, Alan Kane, Sammy Wilson and Jim Wells who had joined the party in the late seventies, and now held Assembly seats or high office within that party machine. These ambitious young men, most of them university graduates, were looking forward to making a career out of politics in Northern Ireland.

For that reason they preferred to put aside their leader's forays into confrontational street politics, at least while there was no immediate threat to the Union, in favour of the hard slog of committee work and Assembly debate that might eventually bring them the rewards of office. They were also anxious that Paisley, to many of them a revered father figure, should end his tempestuous career exercising some kind of office. It was a desire also voiced by Paisley, who had never rid himself of the conviction that he was the one politician who could do a deal with the British to return control to the Unionists.

Paisley was at his most statesmanlike as he exercised total domination over an Assembly which boasted not a single Nationalist and only five Catholics among its 60 sitting members. Its 18 SDLP and Sinn Fein representatives stayed true to their pledge to boycott it. In this unreal atmosphere, Paisley was able to leave all the DUP's deep-seated bigotry and blood and thunder vindictiveness to backbench colleagues like William McCrea, Ivan Foster, Alan Kane and David Calvert.

He was the Assembly's most assiduous proposer of motions, and its agriculture committee under his chairmanship became the most effective and publicly-known of its scrutiny committees. "Paisley, in effect, has run the Assembly over the past year", said the BBC's political correspondent, Brian Walker, at the end of 1983. "He's run the Speaker, he's run the business committee, he's run the agriculture committee, and he has kept the Assembly right by acting as father of the House".

But constructive politics was never Paisley's natural ambit. There was a limit to the time he could be well-behaved and reasonable in the hope that the British would think it worth their while to fudge their "cross-community" guarantees to the Catholics and start devolving power to the most anti-Catholic politician of them all.

His conciliatory role in the Assembly won him few votes in the 1983 Westminster election. With the level of deaths and violent incidents at its lowest for 13 years, and with the "iron lady" of the Falklands stronger than ever in Downing Street, the always conservative Unionist electorate turned back in their tens of thousands to the Official Unionists.

It was clear by 1983 that the British Government had again come round to agreeing with the Unionist analysis that Northern Ireland's principal problem was the Provisional IRA and its political wing, Sinn Fein. The latter had won over 100,000 votes in the Westminster election and had seen its leader, Gerry Adams, end Gerry Fitt's career as MP for West Belfast. Its new growth alarmed both the British and Irish governments. The response in Dublin was the agreement of Garret Fitzgerald's government to go along with SDLP leader John Hume's proposal for a constitutional Nationalist New Ireland Forum, which would draw up a new blueprint for peaceful political change to put before the British.

Paisley's response was another mobilisation of the forces of Loyalist paranoia - although this time round the paranoia was to turn, like a self-fulfilling prophecy, into something approaching a real threat.

In early 1984, as he started out on the campaign trail for that summer's European election, Paisley announced that the the enemies of Ulster Protestantism were massing on two fronts and he would fight them on both. He would smash Sinn Fein's Danny Morrison. And he would show the Nationalist architects of the New Ireland Forum "Ulster's determination never to be bought, bartered or bombed into abandoning her British heritage."

His uncanny knack of forecasting, with the help of sympathetic sources in the civil service, what was in the minds of the mandarins at Stormont Castle and in Whitehall, was again put to good use. In March he claimed that Thatcher had given "the green light" to the joint London-Dublin rule of Northern Ireland, an idea which John Hume was known to be pushing energetically in his New Ireland Forum deliberations with the three Southern parties. On the eve of the publication of the Forum Report his gift for the headline-grabbing stunt took him on a midnight jaunt to Dublin to paste up "Ulster is British" posters in O'Connell Street.

The Forum Report's three options - a united Ireland, a federal Ireland and joint sovereignty - came as no surprise to most Unionists. But Paisley was able to keep the level of paranoia high by cleverly linking their suspicion about Dublin's machinations with their outrage at the first mild curbs on their "traditional" right to mount provocative parades through Catholic areas.

As early as May 1983 - on the eve of the Westminster election - he had produced a "confidential" RUC report, claiming it to be a product of the Anglo-Irish "joint studies", which revealed plans to reroute Orange parades away from Catholic areas. The previous summer he had succeeded in making such marches an issue again when he led a parade of "Kick the Pope" Loyalist bands through the until then almost totally peaceful 80 per cent Catholic town of Downpatrick.

In May 1984, on the eve of the launching of his European election manifesto, he led Loyalist bands through a small Catholic housing estate in Cookstown, County Tyrone. Similar exercises in sectarian coat-trailing were to be repeated over and over again during the next two years until they culminated in the bloody violence of the summer of 1986.

Such heightening of the sectarian temperature at election time was not a new tactic for Paisley. He had twice before used the periods before elections to manufacture an atmosphere of crisis in order to encourage voters to turn from more flexible rivals to his own immutable brand of Unionism. In 1977 he had launched an abortive work stoppage on the eve of local government elections, and in 1981 his "Carson Trail" rallies were again timed to climax in the run-up to local elections. Both acted as springboards for successful DUP vote-winning campaigns.

The effectiveness of Paisley's strategy was shown only too clearly in the June 1984 European elections. His sabre-rattling about Sinn Fein, the New Ireland Forum and the Protestant right to march, cleverly mixed with attacks on the EEC as a Roman Catholic conspiracy, won him an astonishing personal poll of more than 230,000 votes, nearly 60 per cent of the total Unionist tally and over 80,000 more than his nearest Unionist rival.

Once again he had shown his uncanny instinct for tapping the deep resistance to change and compromise at the heart of Ulster Protestantism. "I don't like the way he goes about things. I don't like his rough ways, his extreme language, the 'yahoos' he gathers about him", said one middle-class Ballymena housewife, normally an Official Unionist supporter, a week before polling day. "But he's the only man who won't sell us out to Dublin and the Church of Rome. He's the only real leader we've got".

CLOSING THE LAST WINDOW

Just as in the period following his previous European triumph, there was one more "window of opportunity" for Paisley to play the statesman and show that Unionism, even at this late stage, could be magnanimous. In November 1984, following another round of Anglo-Irish talks with Fitzgerald, Margaret Thatcher brutally dismissed all three New Ireland Forum options with the brusque comment that as far as she was concerned they were all "out, out, out".

Unionists of all stripes were delighted. In the next couple of months there was a brief flurry of conciliatory statements from the DUP leader and his acolytes, echoing similar tones among the Official Unionist leadership. Both parties called on the SDLP to take their seats in the Assembly now that, according to Paisley, the New Ireland Forum was "dead and buried in a Sadducee's grave with no resurrection".

Given that it was dead and buried, the DUP leader was now generously prepared to allow it to be on the agenda in any talks between his party and the SDLP - an offer he withdrew two days after making it. The strong impression was that Paisley's conciliatory face this time was merely a cynical exercise to try to convince the British that Unionists were now the reasonable advocates of progress in Northern Ireland, and it was the SDLP who were blocking any movement.

It did not take long, though, for the paranoia and tribal drum-beating to reassert itself. The DUP's ultra-conservative rural grass roots made it clear that they were not keen on even the extremely limited gestures, largely orchestrated by Peter Robinson, which were being made towards the SDLP. They wanted nothing short of the restoration of the pre-1972 "ancien regime" at Stormont.

Paisley's response was the traditional one. He dropped the reasonable mask and upped the noise and the threats. He told the new Secretary of State, Douglas Hurd, that if he was thinking of imposing a solution he would be "in for the hottest summer he has ever experienced." As that summer approached, he warned of a Protestant backlash if the RUC continued to "do Dublin's dirty work" by rerouting Orange parades away from Catholic areas. "It's going to be a battle to the death," he thundered, "but it's better to be dead than green."[29]

The hard-line Paisley, the bloodbath-threatening Paisley, the violent-mouthed bigot who had made his name against Terence O'Neill 20 years earlier, was firmly back in place on the eve of the gravest constitutional crisis of those two troubled decades. In the spring of 1985 he had started a scurrilous little newsletter called the *Protestant BluPrint* to replace the defunct *Protestant Telegraph*. As summer merged into autumn, and it became evident that the British and Irish governments were close to agreeing on their own joint blueprint for the government of the North, Paisley used the new publication to screw up the paranoia of his followers to exploding point.

He accused the media of ignoring IRA attacks on Protestant churches while publicising attacks on Catholic property. He dug up the notorious oath of the early 19th century Ribbonmen - "the forerunners of Hibernianism, Sinn Fein and all the other oath-bound popish societies in Ireland intent on murdering and slaughtering all British Protestants on the island." He claimed the SDLP had thrown down "the gauntlet of war" to Loyalists wanting to march through Portadown. He accused the government of removing the protective escorts of prominent Protestants so as to give "the IRA freedom to murder them".

Months before the signing of the Anglo-Irish Agreement at Hillsborough in November 1985, Ian Paisley had shed any pretence at being the pragmatic leader the British would have to deal with if peace was to return to the North. Once again he was doing what came most naturally to him: acting as the menacing voice of "not an inch" Ulster Loyalism - and hoping that, as had happened so many times before in his confrontations with both

Stormont and Westminster governments, the very ferocity of his call to arms would scare them into a retreat.

His message was again that no-one except he could be trusted. For most of his career Paisley has been more concerned about destroying his rivals than combatting his enemies: just as his religious battles in the fifties and sixties were against fellow-Presbyterians, so most of his later political struggles were against fellow-Unionists. The domination of his own community, not the vanquishing of the enemy's, has always been his first objective. He has presented himself as its strongest leader in a period of deep and recurring crisis, and a huge number of ordinary Unionist men and women have been prepared to follow him on that basis.

It did not appear to matter that the only thing that was consistent about his record was its inconsistency. He has see-sawed from integration to devolution, from sober parliamentary politics to sectarian street protests, from upholding law and order to attacking the police, from moderation to extremism. He has done absolutely nothing to help his people achieve the two objects they most desperately seek: the improvement of their security in the face of Provisional IRA violence, and the making safe, once and for all, of their link with Britain. In fact, many Unionist and British politicians argue that he, more than any other single man, has done most to weaken that link.

Such a catalogue of disaster would have toppled any other Unionist leader long ago. But Ian Paisley has managed to convince a frightened and directionless people that their best hope lies in blindly trusting in him - in his rampaging ego and drive to self-aggrandisement - because of his uniqueness as "God's man for the hour" in a land surrounded by enemies.

CHAPTER TWELVE

The Grand Old Duke of York

*What strikes you about Ian is that he's like the Grand Old Duke of York -
there's a point at which he will always retreat. He'll huff and puff
to bring about a situation and then he'll come back from the edge.
People are in jail for going over the top because they thought
he was leading them there. You can do that sort of thing too often.*
Former senior DUP member.

Ian will fight till the last drop of everyone else's blood.
Former Free Presbyterian Church official.

In 1973, after two years of bloody violence, the British
Government launched the most ambitious political initiative in
Ireland since 1921. The initiative was a victory for Nationalists
and a defeat for traditional Unionism but Loyalists responded in
time-honoured fashion. They organised to defy the will of the
British as their forefathers had and as Paisley had so often
warned they would need to do again to preserve their way of life.

The initiative was a product of British frustration. 1972 had
been the most violent year in Northern Ireland's short history.
467 people had been killed - 103 of them British soldiers - and
there were nearly 1,400 explosions. The unprecedented ferocity
of the Provisional IRA's shooting and bombing campaign had
littered the North's streets with mutilated bodies and had
provoked an equally murderous Protestant backlash. Loyalist
paramilitaries mushroomed and led by the Ulster Defence
Association, struck back with a series of random assassinations
of Catholics.

1973 had been little better - a thousand bombs and 250 deaths.

Internment and harsh security policies had failed to undermine support for the IRA. The Direct Rule Secretary of State, William Whitelaw, turned to politics as a solution.

In October 1972 he announced proposals for a power sharing government, in which Nationalists would serve, and said that an "Irish dimension" would have to be included. A subsequent White Paper endorsed the plan and the SDLP, the main constitutional Nationalist party, gave it a warm welcome as did the new Fine Gael-Labour coalition government in Dublin.

In December 1973, the British and Irish governments together with the new power sharing Executive, which included Brian Faulkner's Unionist Party, the SDLP and the Alliance Party, met at Sunningdale in southern England and after three days of negotiations announced agreement on the "Irish dimension".

The Sunningdale Agreement, as it became known, provided for the establishment of a Council of Ireland, drawn from the Northern and Southern Cabinets which would have a wide range of economic and cultural functions in both parts of Ireland. Arrangements were also made to try to harmonise cross-Border police work and anti-terrorist laws.

They were radical proposals which were sure to attract Loyalist fury - a similar body had been envisaged in 1921 and at the time the British made no secret of their hopes that it would lead eventually to a united Ireland. But the British had reason to believe that they might be able to finesse the deal.

The Unionists were deeply divided and absorbed in mutual recriminations. Paisley was still in the political wilderness after two years of toying with integration and he and Craig, his main rival for hard-line Loyalist support, were at daggers drawn.

Craig had set up Vanguard, an umbrella for Unionist right-wingers which included the largest paramilitary group, the UDA, and workers from the Belfast shipyard and Protestant dominated factories grouped together in the Loyalist Association of Workers (LAW), to oppose direct rule. At Nazi-type rallies he made blood curdling threats of violence and hinted at a campaign to achieve independence if Loyalist demands for the restoration of Stormont were not met.

In February 1973 an attempt at a one-day Loyalist strike, supported by Craig's Vanguard movement, had ended in an orgy of violence. It had been called by the paramilitaries to protest at the extension of internment to Loyalists. By the end of the day five people had been killed in gunbattles between Loyalists and the British Army and there had been rampant intimidation of Protestant workers. Paisley joined in the widespread Protestant condemnations which were reflected in the next day's banner headline in the Unionist daily, the *News Letter:* "Ulster's day of shame".

Brian Faulkner, meanwhile, still led the largest Unionist bloc and his ambition was undiminished. Whitelaw and his advisers reckoned that with other Loyalists divided, Faulkner would be ready and able to make a deal.

Although Loyalists reunited to oppose their proposals, the British could still afford to be optimistic. There were signs before and during the Assembly election campaign in June 1973 of uncertainty and tensions in their ranks. Although Craig and Paisley sank their differences to form an electoral pact it was an alliance that existed only on paper. When the campaigning started, Paisley abandoned his partners and poured all his party's energies into his own party's effort. His DUP ended up with one more seat than Vanguard.

It was the first evidence of what later became an accepted part of Unionist wisdom - that Paisley's ruthlessness gains him more advantage than anyone else when he joins in coalition with other Loyalists. Paisley also made the most gains when the Loyalists escalated their opposition inside and outside the Assembly following agreement in November to set up the Executive and to take office the following 1 January.

In the Assembly, the Loyalist tactics were to disrupt debates with noisy protests and DUP members were to the fore each time. The protests were intensified after the Sunningdale negotiations. During the first Assembly meeting after the agreement, in January 1974, Paisley was forcibly removed from the chamber by the RUC - it took eight policemen to carry him out. The protests earned Paisley and the DUP considerable publicity and the admiration of militants outside.

He was reaping so much benefit from the protests that his allies in the other two Unionist blocs had difficulty persuading him to drop them. Craig complained that Paisley had broken an agreement to boycott the Assembly after the Executive took office: "I think if he'd had his way we would have stayed in the Assembly quite a while; he needed an arena", he said later.

Paisley also had one other major advantage over Craig and

West. He was much more forceful and articulate on TV and radio and as a result the media regularly sought him out for comment. This helped to enhance the impression that he was leading the Loyalist campaign and uniting its previously divided factions. Faulkner also helped by singling him out for attack, on one occasion dubbing him, much to Paisley's annoyance, "the Demon Doctor".

Paisley's skills with the media heightened his profile further when the Loyalists launched a "Save Ulster" campaign in the closing weeks of 1973 in protest at Britain's refusal to invite them to the Sunningdale conference and when at the same time, Harry West's Unionist dissidents broke off from the Official Unionist party and joined with Paisley and Craig in the United Ulster Unionist Coalition (UUUC). Much of the media saw the UUUC and the "Save Ulster" campaign as Paisley creations.

The UUUC was from the start an uneasy alliance and, thanks to Paisley's opportunism, it very nearly broke up at the first hurdle. That came in February 1974 when Ted Heath called a Westminster general election in the wake of a successful coalminers' strike in Britain. The UUUC agreed that only one Loyalist candidate should go forward in each constituency but, inevitably, the three parties squabbled about the share out.

In the end West's party got seven nominations, Vanguard three and the DUP only two. But behind Craig and West's backs, Paisley had afterwards attempted to increase the DUP total by one when he secretly approached the North Belfast Official Unionist nominee, John Carson with an invitation to join the DUP. Carson refused but Paisley's effort, as a contemporary DUP colleague, Clifford Smyth noted, "could have been sufficient to wreck the UUUC" and with it the anti-Sunningdale campaign.

The Westminster poll gave the Loyalists a massive propaganda and political victory. UUUC candidates won eleven of the twelve Northern Ireland seats and just under 51 per cent of the total vote. The Executive and Sunningdale were at a stroke deprived of much moral and political credibility. The election was also a personal triumph for Paisley who increased his own North Antrim majority to a massive 25,000 votes and underlined his growing claim to be included in the first line of Loyalist leadership.

Despite their victory, however, neither Harold Wilson's new

Labour government, which appointed a former schoolmaster, Merlyn Rees as NI Secretary, nor the Faulkner Unionists showed any sign of giving way. While Faulkner had lost the support of the Ulster Unionist Council and resigned as Official Unionist leader he nevertheless retained the support of his Assembly party. The Executive continued to function and plans were made to ratify Sunningdale at Stormont and to implement its provisions. The Westminster results were seen as a temporary setback which could be reversed when Protestants saw the arrangements bringing Catholic rejection of the IRA.

Other Loyalists, however, were working on plans to force Faulkner and the British to yield. The Ulster Workers Council (UWC), the successor to the LAW which broke up in early 1973, had been making plans for a general strike since the summer of 1973 and had held discussions with Craig about its timing and scope. Like many grass roots Loyalists they were angry and frustrated with the politicians' failure and were eager to take their own action.

. The UWC had members, many of them trade unionists, in most major Protestant dominated factories in Belfast and County Antrim but, more crucially, had supporters in the North's two major electricity plants: Ballylumford, near Larne, County Antrim and Coolkeeragh, outside Derry. Between them they generated most of the North's electricity and deprived of it Northern Ireland would literally grind to a halt.

The UWC wanted to launch a strike in December but West talked them out of it on the grounds that the cold weather would cause suffering to their supporters. Another date was set but that was postponed when the British miners' strike started. Finally the UWC and the UUUC chose Tuesday 14 May, the day when the Assembly was due to ratify Sunningdale, as the trigger for the strike. That evening the UWC chairman, shipyard shop steward, Harry Murray told journalists at Stormont that the strike would start immediately; the only thing that could stop it would be fresh Assembly elections.

The strike was slow to take effect. On the first day 80 per cent of the Northern Ireland workforce turned up. The UWC panicked and turned to the UDA leader, Andy Tyrie for help. Loyalist paramilitary groups, including the illegal UVF, Down Orange Welfare, a doomsday outfit led by a former British Army Colonel, Peter "Basil" Brush, the Orange Volunteers and the

Ulster Volunteer Service Corps, had joined Craig, West and Paisley in the UWC's co-ordinating committee to run the strike. But Tyrie, the most important paramilitary leader, had been excluded from the strike planning by the UWC.

A portly, bespectacled and mustachioed figure with a genial, friendly manner, Tyrie's appearance disguised a shrewd, calculating mind. He had started his paramilitary life with the UVF back in the late 1960s where he had been active on the fringes of Paisley's UPV and had risen through the UDA's tough ranks to become its commander in 1973. He agreed to help, and that, together with the increasing impact of power cuts, was the turning point in the strike. During the next few days Tyrie's UDA men were out in force, intimidating workers, forcibly closing factories and shops and placing barricades across major roads.

Those four or five days at the start proved vital to the strike's success but they were nervous ones for Loyalist paramilitaries and politicians alike. Both were worried that the intimidation wouldn't work and they expected the British to strike back - memories of the disastrous 1973 strike were still fresh.

The British response was in fact timid. Attempts to take down barricades were delayed for a fatal week and there were few efforts to confront the strikers. The British Army also signalled, in no uncertain fashion, its reluctance to switch resources from its war against the IRA and its inability to run the power stations. Rees proved to be indecisive and baulked at ordering the Army to take action.

The government also surrendered the propaganda initiative to the strike leaders - after the strike, UWC leaders acknowledged their debt to the BBC in particular for co-operating with the UWC publicity machine. Power cuts eventually reduced electricity output to a mere 30 per cent of normal, closing virtually every major factory and imposing widespread and lengthy blackouts. Fine weather cushioned the hardship and, thanks to a generous gesture by the SDLP Minister for Health and Social Services, Paddy Devlin, the strikers were allowed to collect unemployment benefit.

More significantly though, the strike gathered popular support among Protestants. Nearly everyone had underestimated the strength and solidarity of Protestant hostility towards Sunningdale - even those opposed to the strikers' methods showed no willingness to undermine them.

By the end of the first week the UWC had almost acquired the status of an alternative government. Its leaders co-ordinated the distribution of essential supplies to farmers and hospitals - some UWC leaders were jokingly called "ministers" - and middle class Protestants, some of them civil servants in the government under siege, queued patiently at the UWC offices in Craig's Vanguard headquarters for travel passes and petrol coupons.

The strains inside the power sharing Executive were by then beginning to show. The Unionist members were under intense pressure from their constituents to negotiate with the UWC while the SDLP contemplated resignation in protest at British inaction. Harold Wilson made sure of a UWC victory when, in a TV broadcast, he called Northern Ireland's Protestants "spongers", an insult which solidified their hostility to the British and their support for the strike.

On 28 May, thirteen days after the strike had started and as Northern Ireland was about to face a complete power shut down and the grim prospect of sewage seeping onto the streets, Faulkner and his ministers resigned and the Executive collapsed. The most concerted challenge to Westminster from Ulster Loyalism since 1912 had brought victory and it had been ordinary Protestants who had delivered it.

Paisley had not been around to see the UWC strike turn from uncertainty to success. On Friday 17 May, two days after the strike started, he flew to Toronto, Canada to attend a funeral. There were conflicting versions at the time of whose funeral it was. Some were told an aunt, others an old fundamentalist family friend. Over a decade later the reason for his sudden trip has still not been fully explained.

Paisley could not have chosen a more crucial time to disappear. The bully boys were out on the streets frightening Protestants into joining the strike and there was every chance that even if they didn't resist, the British would. The strike's success hung in the balance.

Within the UWC co-ordinating committee the interpretation of Paisley's absence was virtually unanimous. One of their members recalled: "His decision to go to Canada was noted by all and sundry and most of them believed he'd gone just in case the strike turned out to be a flop". Another commented: "We just accepted that it was Paisley doing his usual thing. When things got hot, Paisley got offside until he saw which way the land was lying".

Few were surprised either because Paisley, like the other two Unionist leaders, had been unsure of the strike's success long before the final decision to launch it was given the go-ahead. When the strike did start, the UUUC leaders didn't give it their approval until the third day. "Paisley thought that the strike wouldn't work and I think he, like the others, had bad memories from the 1973 strike", recalled a strike leader. "It wasn't that he was opposed to the strike in principle, he just had to be convinced that it was worthwhile. Paisley had his doubts as did Craig and West".

Of the three political leaders, West was most nervous about the strike - "he stayed well clear of us until Paisley came back", commented one UWC member - while Craig was the most committed. "Craig said to us at the start 'It's not going to work but I'll stay here and help you out'. To his credit he did and he was the only politician to do so. He let us use Vanguard headquarters and his people helped as well", remembered a paramilitary leader.

Paisley was, in the eyes of the strike organisers, "bouncing about" somewhere between West and Craig but edging more towards West. Two days before the strike he and other UUUC politicians met the UWC and UDA at a hotel in Larne, County Antrim where they were told that the strike was going to go ahead as soon as the Assembly ratified Sunningdale. Paisley, according to *The Times* journalist Robert Fisk's account of the strike, "voiced his disapproval immediately, questioning once again whether the timing was right".

Some in the UWC suspected that Paisley had more pragmatic reasons for questioning the strike tactic. The UWC and the UDA were both close to Craig's Vanguard party and had co-operated closely in the past. The link was symbolised by Glen Barr, the chairman of the co-ordinating committee who was both a member of the UDA and a Vanguard Assembly member for Derry. If successful the strike would probably benefit Craig most.

That would hold whichever way the strike turned out, as one of the more astute UWC leaders appreciated: "Paisley, at that time, was just switching off from integration and didn't know where he was going. The strike would though kill off integration as an option because it was more than just opposition to Sunningdale, it was a challenge to Westminster's authority. Craig on the other hand was in a different position. Vanguard's policies came close to demanding dominion status and if the worst came to the worst and Britain washed its hands of Northern Ireland he would see no dilemma in that. But if the strike was successful then Craig's strong stand from the beginning would be to his benefit".

When Paisley returned from Canada at around the end of the first week of the strike his prevarication had gone. "From the distance of Canada he could perceive that something massive was taking place, that the strike was biting, and when he came back, I have to admit, he came in with his batteries charged", recalled a UWC leader.

From then on Paisley attended every meeting of the UWC co-ordinating committee and was given the task of "stomping the country" whipping up support at Loyalist rallies and meetings. This followed a UWC decision to mobilise rural areas behind greater Belfast, which until then had taken the brunt of the strike.

He is credited in particular with mobilising the farmers and making a dynamic impact in the media - "He really sold the strike to the grass roots and to the world's press", commented the same UWC leader. He also drafted key DUP personnel into the strike headquarters - up to then the DUP, like the Official Unionists, had been noticeably absent - and one of them, Peter Robinson, made a vital contribution.

"Paisley's view on communicating the strike was that it had to be communicated right on down the line to the grass roots", a strike leader remembered. Robinson was given the task of compiling the co-ordinating committee's daily brief - outlining strike plans, dispensation for essential services, plans for the distribution of petrol, feedstuffs and so on - copying it and sending thousands of copies down to the people on the ground. "That whole communication system was down to Robinson", said the same leader.

Paisley's relations with the paramilitaries on the co-ordinating committee were acrimonious, however. Since the 1969 bombings Paisley had steered well clear of any paramilitary associations and groups like the UDA suspected he was resentful of their links with Craig. According to one strike leader, the paramilitaries had no love for him either: "They didn't like his fundamentalist views and were pretty contemptuous because of his Canadian trip. They had nicknames for him in those days like 'God' and 'Papa Doc'."

The hostility, according to one account, showed when Paisley returned from Canada. By that stage UWC morning meetings were so busy that the chairman, Barr, had ordered two tough UDA men to stand guard at the door to prevent interruptions:

> . . . I remember very distinctly looking out the window and seeing Paisley arrive at about 9.30 but he never appeared in the room. We went out for a cup of tea at about 11 and when I came back there was Paisley sitting in Barr's chair, the chairman's chair. Barr said "Ian, that's my chair, would you move round a bit?". "No", he says, "I'm just disgusted. I came here to lend my support and I couldn't get in". So Barr said "What do you mean?". "Those two big fellas outside wouldn't let me in". Apparently they'd stopped him and he'd said "Do you know who I am, I'm going into this office". But they wouldn't budge. He was extremely annoyed, I can tell you. Anyway Barr insisted that he get his chair back, he was the chairman and Paisley would have to move. "Well I've got a sore back, my back's not well", said Paisley. So Barr said "I'll tell you what we'll do. You take my chair and move to the end of the table. You're sitting in the chairman's place. You know the position, you're not as big a man here as you are outside". So reluctantly he took the chair and moved.

There were more jibes later: "We'd knocked off all the public transport and there were no buses moving at all but Paisley wanted special dispensation for his buses on Wednesday nights which took people from behind the City Hall to the Martyrs Memorial. Andy Tyrie said to him jokingly that he'd let him have the buses if Paisley would let Andy lift the collection.

"Then the boys from the airport approached us and said they wanted to join the strike and shut the planes down. Paisley raised such a furore that day: 'We've got to get to Westminster to present the case on behalf of our people and that's the way we travel.' So Tommy Lyttle looked at him and said: 'It's not true then?'. Paisley says 'What do you mean?' and Tommy replies: 'You can't walk on water'. Thirty seconds later Paisley joined in the laughter."

The chair incident convinced Barr that Paisley would try to take control of UWC meetings and the two became intense rivals. Relations reached a low point when Barr ordered the UWC switchboard to stop any outgoing calls made by Paisley or West, who started attending meetings when Paisley returned from Canada.

"We discovered that decisions we were taking in the morning, particularly about releasing feedstuffs to the farmers, were being credited to Paisley and West. They were running out of meetings and phoning up people in their constituencies and telling them: 'I've got you that load of feed now'. They were trying to give the impression that they were running the committee. So Barr told them they weren't allowed to use the phones until all the regional commanders had been told what the committee had decided."

Paisley's most significant contribution inside the co-ordinating committee came at the end when the Executive collapsed. The UWC and many rank and file paramilitaries wanted the strike to continue, either to press on for the demand for new elections or to take advantage of their power by establishing a provisional government. Tyrie and some other paramilitary leaders were under considerable pressure from their members but realised that the strike was a lost cause. But it was left to Paisley to argue successfully that Protestant workers were already voting with their feet to end the strike. Paisley proposed the motion to call the strike off and Tyrie seconded it.

Former DUP colleagues like Clifford Smyth now reckon that Paisley was shocked by the UWC's success and, like other Unionists, was worried that, by mobilising working class Loyalist strength, the UWC might have developed into a serious threat to established politicians.

That threat never materialised and the politicians survived. But of the three UUUC leaders, Paisley probably came out ahead. During the strike his media profile was much higher than either Craig's or West's. At the end, as one paramilitary leader bitterly noted, "He even managed to push us into the background at the Stormont victory rally". His initial caution was noticed only by the strike leaders. To the mass of Loyalists he was once more the familiar forthright Protestant leader, his brief liaison with moderation completely forgotten. Any residual doubts about his Loyalist credentials were gone.

Paisley's return to the first line of Loyalist leadership had been noted with mounting concern by an old discarded ally from the 1960s, Major Bunting. About a week after the strike ended he turned up at the UWC offices, determined to warn them against further involvement with Paisley. The UWC was in conference but he insisted that he speak to somebody important. He was shown into an adjoining room and asked to wait.

A UWC member took up the story:

> We had our meeting and then three of us went to speak to him. There he was sitting, a shell of a man, nervous and almost demented. He explained who he was and begged us, quite literally begged us, to make sure that under no circumstances would we allow Ian Paisley to benefit from the strike.
>
> He was totally obsessed and was quite prepared to damn Paisley with stories of what had happened to him - how he had jeopardised his health and career for Paisley, how he had been made to look ridiculous in public and how, when the activities he'd embraced on Paisley's behalf had brought him into conflict with the authorities, he'd been dropped and left high and dry. We sympathised but we had to explain that there wasn't anything we could do. What happened to Ian Paisley was out of our hands.

TO THE BRINK AND BACK AGAIN

I'm finished if this doesn't work.
Ian Paisley quoted by one of the 1977 Loyalist strike leaders.

The 1974 UWC strike not only rehabilitated Ian Paisley, it convinced him that the strike tactic could be used again to advance his own and the Loyalist cause. Three years after the fall of Sunningdale that conviction led him into the greatest political miscalculation of his career and brought him to the verge of quitting politics altogether.

The Loyalist strike of 1977 - "Paisley's strike", as the public saw it - was an ignominious failure which many thought would help to strengthen Paisley's moderate Official Unionist rivals and thus pave the way for a political settlement between Nationalists and Unionists. The strike in fact had the opposite effect. Although an operational disaster, the strike touched a Protestant nerve, an achievement which was given eloquent expression by substantial DUP gains in the local council elections which immediately followed it.

The gains made by Paisley's DUP in that election were all at the expense of the Official Unionists. They killed off any hope of moderation from that quarter and renewed Paisley's faith in his political instincts. But they also destroyed his last Loyalist political rival - the remnants of Bill Craig's once powerful Vanguard party. From then on Unionist politics would be dominated by a titanic struggle between the DUP and the Official Unionists - the only survivors from a decade of Protestant political turbulence and fractures.

In 1977, Paisley snatched survival from impending obliteration and it was ruthlessness which did it - not his this time, but that of his able and devoted lieutenant, Peter Robinson. As Paisley, for the first time in his career, reeled directionless in the face of defeat, Robinson took charge and rescued him and his party.

A political vacuum and a cynical change in British security policy provided the backcloth to the 1977 strike. On the political front, the collapse of the Executive in 1974 was followed a year later by the Constitutional Convention, an attempt by the British to cajole the political parties into reaching agreement among themselves.

The Convention was a failure - the majority Unionists, still in the UUUC alliance, stubbornly recommended a return to Stormont majority rule, a proposal which was angrily condemned by the SDLP and rejected by the British. When it finally folded up amid uproar in March 1976, the Convention had left one important casualty in its wake - Bill Craig, whose stubborn espousal of Voluntary Coalition split Vanguard apart. The anti-Craigites re-formed themselves under the leadership of Ernie Baird, a right wing East Belfast Presbyterian and the prosperous owner of a chain of chemist shops. The remnants of Vanguard were re-christened the United Ulster Unionist Movement (UUUM).

The Convention's failure marked an end, at least for the foreseeable future, to political experiments - it was back to uninterrupted Direct Rule by British politicians. The British once again turned to a security solution and, aided by a Provisional IRA ceasefire in 1975, followed by protracted and unsuccessful negotiations with Northern Ireland Office officials, used the breathing space to devise an ingenious new security policy.

It had many names - "Ulsterisation", "Normalisation", "Criminalisation", "the primacy of the police" and "the Castlereagh conveyor belt" among them. What it amounted to was this. Internment and all its trappings would be phased out and all terrorist-type cases would be dealt with by the courts. The Long Kesh internment complex would be replaced by a modern H Block-shaped prison. Special Category status, another important element of internment which was regarded by Republican and Loyalist prisoners as recognition of their political status would also be phased out - all prisoners would be treated like ordinary criminals with no special privileges.

The most significant change, though, was in the field. The British Army's leading role in the battle against the IRA would be reduced and their duties would be gradually taken over by local security forces: the 90 per cent Protestant, RUC and the 98 per cent Protestant, Ulster Defence Regiment.

Northern Ireland is still living, and in some cases dying, with the consequences of those changes. Catholic criticism of RUC interrogation methods and of the judiciary intensified but in the jails the attempt to criminalise prisoners was resisted by Republicans, at first by refusing to wear prison uniform but eventually by a hunger strike that cost the lives of ten people inside the H Blocks and sixty-one outside. It also gave the IRA's political wing, Sinn Fein, a springboard to mount a successful entry into electoral politics.

The first and most immediate effect of the new British security policy, however, was felt by the Protestant community. As the RUC and the UDR took over more and more of the British Army's role so their casualty rate increased.

In the early years of the "Troubles", from 1970 to 1974, the British Army had borne the brunt of IRA attacks - deaths of British soldiers accounted for nearly twenty per cent of the 1,380 death toll during that period. "Ulsterisation" of security meant that it was increasingly UDR and RUC men, the vast majority of them Protestants, who were dying in their place. In 1976, the first year of "Ulsterisation" they suffered forty-two deaths, four times more than the British Army. It was also their worst year since the murderous slaughter of 1972 and nearly all the dead were Protestants. The British had reduced the cost of staying in Northern Ireland and released battalions to serve in NATO but at considerable cost in Northern Ireland.

The immediate effect was to intensify Protestant demands for tougher security measures, particularly in rural and Border areas where most of the killings had taken place. In the long term it meant that sectarian antagonisms would be heightened throughout the whole community - Loyalist allegations of an IRA campaign of "genocide" date from this period. The cynicism of the British move was noted by the Orange Order in a wide ranging review of British policy in early 1977: "the 'Ulsterisation' of the security battle represents nothing more than the 'Ulsterisation' of the victims".

The political vacuum and the new emphasis on security were given physical shape by Merlyn Rees' replacement as Northern Ireland Secretary in August 1976. The new man was Roy Mason, a blunt, pipe-smoking, former coalminer from Barnsley in Yorkshire. He came to Northern Ireland, much to the dismay of Nationalists, with a name for being an "Army man", a reputation earned during a spell in the Ministry of Defence. It wasn't long before he signalled his intentions. In his first speech he spoke of the IRA "reeling" under the weight of security pressure. A few months later he candidly told the political parties that he had no plans for a political initiative unless they had.

Mason was popular with the Official Unionists. They liked his commitment to the war against the IRA and they were happy with his reluctance to launch political experiments. Direct Rule was preferable to the uncharted waters of protest and the uncomfortable prospect of alliances with paramilitants and Paisleyites which would inevitably follow another British attempt at partnership government.

Mason also secured extra financial help for Northern Ireland from the Labour Cabinet and at Westminster Harold Wilson's successor, James Callaghan, negotiated a deal with the Official Unionist parliamentary leader, James Molyneaux, under which support for his minority government would be exchanged for extra House of Commons seats - most of which would inevitably go to the Official Unionists. In the respectable, cautious, middle class eyes of Official Unionists, the Union was more secure, Northern Ireland more prosperous and the IRA more resolutely pursued than at any time since the "Troubles" started.

To Loyalists of Paisley's ilk, for whom a state of permanent insecurity is part of the natural order, the relative tranquillity of the Mason era was, by sharp contrast, deeply unsettling. It was this, as much as the rising death toll of RUC and UDR men, which led to the 1977 strike. As one of its leaders put it: "Things were slipping and flagging and people were getting into the way of Direct Rule. We thought we'd give it a wee bit of a jab."

Loyalist political dislocation was shown in various ways. The UDA and Loyalists like John McKeague began espousing the idea of Ulster independence. They were spurred in this direction by the belief, shared by Loyalist politicians like Baird, that Britain was secretly withdrawing. The NIO's talks with the IRA had planted this seed and it was watered during 1976 with decisions to close factories like Rolls-Royce and the Royal Navy's re-fitting yard in Belfast. The pro-independence lobby was not confined to Loyalists - some in the SDLP flirted with it as did elements in the IRA.

The Loyalist mainstream, however, including Paisley, stayed with the traditional and familiar demand to have the old majority rule Stormont parliament returned. The only problem was that there was no chance that any British government would voluntarily grant it.

Many in the Official Unionist Party appeared to give only token support to that demand while others were, under Enoch Powell's influence, beginning a cautious move towards integration. Loyalists, however, wanted action. Following Westminster's rejection of the Convention report in early 1976 they moved to set up machinery to keep the demand alive and kicking.

On the urging of Baird, a Loyalist Action Council, later given the unwieldy title of the United Unionist Action Council (UUAC), technically a sub-committee of the UUUC, was set up to agitate for devolution and better security. The Official Unionists quickly made their disapproval of the Action Council known.

The Action Council soon acquired a semi-paramilitary wing. Loyalists in Counties Tyrone and Armagh, many of them former "B" Specials, set up an organisation called the Ulster Service Corps (USC). In May, following a declaration from Paisley and Baird that they were not prepared "to sit idly by and watch our province being destroyed" by the IRA, the USC announced plans to mount overt and covert patrols, some armed with legal weapons. Their action was also a calculated defiance of the authorities, a challenge to the State's monopoly of security powers.

That autumn, as local security force deaths mounted, the lobby for more direct action intensified. The USC staged more roadblocks and in September the authorities moved against them. Five USC men from County Armagh were arrested - one of them was Robert Murdock, the Portadown Free Presbyterian who had faced UVF explosives charges in 1966 and 1969. The Action Council stuck up posters in Loyalist areas which read: "How long before you join the Direct Rule death toll?". In November, Paisley told MPs at Westminster that he had been out on patrol with the USC in Portadown. The patrols were necessary, he said, "because of the continuing apparent lack of will on behalf of our Government to defeat the terrorists in our midst".

The Action Council, which included the DUP, Baird's party, the UWC, the Apprentice Boys of Derry, the Royal Black Preceptory and the Independent Orange Order began in October and November to seriously discuss plans for a repeat of the 1974 strike. The aims this time were to be radically different. In 1974 the goal was to bring down Sunningdale; this time the strike's objectives were to bring back a majority rule Stormont and to force the British to introduce a new tougher security policy.

Paisley for one was convinced that the tactic could work again. Significantly the Official Unionist leader, Harry West, and the Orange Order chief, Martin Smyth disagreed. They both attended some early Action Council meetings but pulled out as the strike plans were laid, leaving Paisley isolated. The Action Council included some of the paramilitary groups involved in the 1974 strike - the UDA, the Orange Volunteers and Down Orange Welfare - but the absence of the Official Unionists badly weakened it.

These moves were paralleled by signs of increased militancy within Paisley's DUP. According to Clifford Smyth, who was then secretary of the UUUC, Peter Robinson approached him in June 1976 with the suggestion that the party should set up a paramilitary wing. According to a senior UDA figure, his organisation was also approached later that year by a leading DUP member with a request for assistance in setting up the force - in particular the DUP man wanted drawings of home made rocket launchers. The ideas came to nought and the DUP, and Paisley in particular, was forced to go to the UDA, still the largest paramilitary group, to ask for help.

Relations between the three UUUC leaders and the paramilitaries had deteriorated since the 1974 strike. The paramilitaries wanted their crucial role in the strike officially recognised by being given a seat on the UUUC executive but the politicians refused, citing the illegality of some groups. Paramilitary resentment at being dropped after they had outlived their usefulness, boiled over on occasions. During one meeting of UUUC politicians in Craig's Vanguard headquarters in 1975, two armed UDA leaders from North Belfast burst in threatening to shoot them - fortunately for the politicians, a senior UUUC figure managed to calm them down.

Paisley played a prominent role in negotiations with paramilitaries during this period. One senior paramilitant recalled one important and secret meeting in the Martyrs Memorial between Paisley and a group of paramilitary leaders which included two representatives of the illegal UVF - Billy Mitchell and Ken Gibson, both of whom, ironically, were former Free Presbyterians. At the meeting, according to this man: "Paisley gave an undertaking that he would try to get us recognised within the UUUC".

When a few weeks later the UUUC decided to exclude both the UWC and the paramilitaries from membership, the paramilitaries, in particular the UVF, turned against Paisley. "Shortly after that all the groups held a conference to work out our strategy for independence and one group under Mitchell had the job of looking at the military implications. I remember some of them talking about bumping Paisley off because of the way we had been treated."

Paisley's relations with the UDA leader, Andy Tyrie had also soured. The UDA had initially supported Craig's Voluntary Coalition proposal and strongly criticised Paisley and West for their opposition. Paisley replied to the criticism in swingeing terms:

The brazen effrontery and confounded cheek of Mr Tyrie baffles description. He is a man who leads an organisation whose members in the past months have been tried in the courts and have been pleaded guilty or have been found guilty of the most diabolical of crimes.

They have murdered Protestants as well as Roman

Catholics in the most sadistic and inhuman ways and have sought to intimidate decent people who seek to carry out their business in a proper manner.

Stung by his attack, the UDA considered releasing a dossier to the press containing details of "talks Mr Paisley has had with Loyalist paramilitary groups and also the use of Loyalist funds", but stayed its hand.

During 1976, as the plans for strike action hardened, Paisley was forced to eat humble pie and apologise to Tyrie. Unable to create its own paramilitary wing the DUP needed the UDA's skills in intimidating "decent people who seek to carry out their business in a proper manner" to enforce the strike. Lengthy talks took place between Tyrie and Paisley and Tyrie extracted a price for the UDA's co-operation. "We deliberately put Paisley and Baird into the front line; it wasn't going to be another case of the UDA carrying the whole can", recalled a UDA member.

During the last half of 1976 and the spring of 1977 - as the strike plans took firmer shape - Paisley made the first of several mistakes. He alienated the Official Unionists and the Orange Order, two bodies whose neutrality at least during the strike would be crucial. In June 1976 he leaked details of secret meetings between the Orange leader, Martin Smyth and the SDLP. As a result Smyth, whose intense dislike for Paisley dated back to the 1950s, was heckled during Orange demonstrations in July - it was hardly calculated to make him sympathetic to Paisley's plans.

In April 1977, only three weeks away from the start of the strike, Paisley used the DUP conference to launch a vitriolic attack on a whole litany of past Official Unionist traitors from O'Neill to Craig. They included members of Harry West's party who had been tempted during the Convention, he claimed, to make a deal with the SDLP by the bait of "a Government car, a Ministerial office, and so many thousands a year". When the strike started, the active opposition of both the Orange Order and the OUP was a significant factor in its failure.

As 1976 turned into 1977 a decision in principle to launch the strike had been taken - Paisley signalled it by announcing that he was thinking of boycotting Westminster in protest at British security failures. By that stage not only had the UDA committed itself to the strike but the Ulster Workers Council, the people who had organised factory closures and the critical pulling of the plugs in the power stations in 1974, were on board.

The UWC leadership had changed in the intervening years. Some leaders had gone "moderate" and had been sacked while others just drifted away. Loyalist paramilitary leaders suspected that Paisley had had a hand in most of the changes and was trying to take over the UWC. The two most important 1974 veterans left were Jim Smyth, the eloquent, former Rolls-Royce shop steward and Billy Kelly, the small, shy, bespectacled union convenor in one of the small Belfast power stations who, in 1974, had won over the power workers in the key Ballylumford power station. That alone had ensured the strike's success.

Kelly was a strong Paisley supporter and a passionate believer in British-Israelism. After the 1977 strike he joined the Free Presbyterian Church in Omagh, County Tyrone and was involved in a bitter split there when the minister opposed the growing influence of Kelly's élitist and extreme British-Israeli supporters. During the run up to the 1977 strike, he assured the Action Council that he had talked to the Ballylumford power workers and had secured their support for industrial action.

The second and most important mistake made by Paisley and the strike leaders was to believe him. Kelly, in fact, had barely consulted the Ballylumford workers at all - when the strike started their resentment over this denied Paisley and the Action Council the support of the one group of workers who could have stopped the wheels of industry from turning.

When the Action Council discovered that Kelly had misled them and that the promised co-operation of other key sectors, like the petrol tanker drivers, was also fictional, it was too late to stop.

The bearer of the bad news was Jim Smyth who had doubted Kelly's assurances from the start and had decided to check up for himself. "Smyth discovered that Kelly's key man at Ballylumford turned out to be the man who worked at the gate. Smyth met him with Kelly and asked him about the workers' support and he was saying things like 'I haven't asked so-and-so because I don't work on the same shift but I hope to see him before the strike'. This was only four weeks before the strike and none of the 1974 people had been talked to. Smyth couldn't believe it," recalled an Action Council member.

The UDA and the other paramilitaries didn't believe Smyth

and neither, to begin with, did Paisley. Smyth also saw Baird and spent six hours trying to talk him out of the strike. Baird was unmoved: "He said no. We're too committed - we've said too much in statements and have committed our people", said an Action Council member.

A week before the strike Smyth again checked around Ballylumford, the Coolkeeragh power station, the Harland and Wolff shipyard and Shorts aircraft factory and discovered that most of their workers were either opposed to the strike or were deeply confused. "They just couldn't see how a strike would achieve the aims we were after", said one strike organiser.

The UDA insisted that their own intelligence indicated that there was support for the strike and they urged that it should go ahead - in fact the organisation was divided, with some key areas like West Belfast opposed to the strike. Paisley was, however, "shaken" by the news. "He kept insisting that we have support in the grassroots, our people expect us to do something and so do the relatives of the security forces. He knew there was a risk that if he lost the DUP would be pilloried, but if he won, he knew that the Official Unionists would lose badly", remembered one Action Council member.

Paisley's doubts did, though, surface at the Action Council meeting which decided to launch the strike, held in the DUP's Ava Avenue HQ in South Belfast on 23 April. He voted against the strike and only one other significant group, the Belfast UWC, supported him. Everyone else, including the UWC's rural members, voted for it. There were also differences about the strike demands. Paisley was alone in advocating that the demand for majority rule should not be included - "he said British opposition to the Convention report was so adamant that we'd get nowhere and that it would be a liability", recalled one who was at the meeting - while everyone else wanted both tougher security and majority rule as the strike's major demands.

The trigger for the strike came on 19 April when the five Portadown Ulster Service Corps members arrested the previous September appeared in court charged with operating illegal roadblocks. The centre of Portadown was brought to a standstill by hundreds of Loyalists as Paisley, flanked by Baird and Tyrie, told them they were beginning a campaign that would lead to the restoration of Stormont, the return of security to local hands and the "extermination" of the IRA.

On 26 April, the Action Council delivered an ultimatum to Roy Mason. He had seven days in which to show a new determination to defeat the IRA and willingness to implement the Convention report. Otherwise there would be an indefinite strike. The Official Unionists retorted with an appeal to Protestants to ignore the strike and to go on working normally.

As the Action Council well knew, Mason would never grant their demands. So at midnight on Monday 2 May, with the Official Unionists and Orange Order actively hostile, the Action Council itself divided on major issues, the key power workers unconsulted and workers in major Belfast factories confused or in outright opposition, Paisley and his Loyalist allies began the second major challenge to Westminster's authority in three years.

There were other important differences between this strike and 1974. Roy Mason's decisiveness was one. Before the strike started he promised firm action against the strikers, ruled out the possibility of negotiating with them and committed the British Army to underpinning essential services. An extra 1,200 troops were flown in on the eve of the strike.

Mason also ensured that Government policy was consistent and well-informed throughout. A three man committee composed of the NIO's Permanent Secretary, Sir Brian Cubbon, the NIO's Chief Information Officer, David Gilliland and a member of the British Security Services was set up to advise him. It met every morning at 8 a.m. to review overnight events and that day's policy options, and met Mason at 9 a.m. when final decisions were taken. Any Protestants who imagined they might be dealing with another Merlyn Rees were quickly disabused.

The British had also learned important lessons from their 1974 mistakes. One of these was in the crucial area of propaganda and public relations which in 1974 had been virtually surrendered to the UWC. During the 1977 strike, in contrast, the NIO's press office operated 24 hours a day, pumping out hourly statements from 5 a.m. onwards and holding frequent Ministerial press conferences to disseminate the Government's view. Nor was there any repeat of Harold Wilson's disastrous "spongers" jibe.

The unemployment problem, which had worsened considerably since 1974, was skilfully exploited. Mason and his Ministers constantly emphasised the threat to inward investment posed by the strike and other groups, the trade unions, business organisations and some Protestant churches echoed it. The British thus had a PR edge on the strikers throughout the protest and this became particularly evident in disputes with the Action Council over the numbers of people at work.

Paisley's high media profile, which had been his great asset in 1974, inflicted a mortal wound on the Action Council. He dominated its press conferences and pushed all the other participants into the background. On the eve of the strike, in an extraordinarily careless and completely uncharacteristic move, he also staked his political career on the strike's success, declaring: "I am only remaining in public life to see the thing through, and if it fails then my voice will no longer be heard".

The combined effect was to personalise the strike, making it appear as "Paisley's strike". In contrast the 1974 strike had been successful partly because it was viewed as a united and general Protestant protest dominated by no single person. Paisley's dominance succeeded only in highlighting Official Unionist and Orange opposition. This discouraged support from Protestants who might have been sympathetic to the strike's aims but were loath to identify so closely with a strike leader who had built his career by attacking and dividing Protestant institutions. Paisley was incapable by himself of uniting and leading all the disparate sections of Unionism.

On 3 May, the first day of the strike, it became clear that intimidation would be the organisers' principal weapon. Gangs of up to 100 UDA men roamed the streets "persuading" factories and shops to close. Shipyard workers, who had voted against the strike at a mass meeting, were told their cars would be burned if they stayed at work and a bomb damaged the Bangor to Belfast railway line, the main commuter line from East Belfast and the dormitory suburbs.

The next day there was more of the same. The UDA were again out on the streets and the RUC reported 400 complaints of intimidation in Belfast. The UDA were, however, anxious to avoid direct confrontation with the police or Army and no roadblocks were set up. Nevertheless the strike appeared to be biting. A lot of large factories in Belfast closed and commercial life in towns like Ballymena, Coleraine, Lurgan and Portadown came to a standstill. The strikers had also scored a major achievement when the important cross-channel port of Larne closed down.

The turning point in the strike came early in the morning of the third day, Wednesday 4 May, outside the UDA's headquarters on the Newtownards Road in East Belfast when the paramilitaries, frustrated at their lack of success, erected their first road block to prevent shipyard workers getting into work. There at 8 a.m., gangs of UDA men clashed for an hour with the RUC's anti-riot, Special Patrol Group in what appeared to be a confrontation deliberately engineered by the authorities. The riot started when the police moved in to remove a makeshift barricade constructed of beer barrels and ended with the successful clearing of the road of both rioters and obstructions. During the riot the UDA Commander, Andy Tyrie, appeared on the scene shouting angrily at the police and threatening "aggravation" everywhere.

He had, as he later admitted, "fallen into the trap" of confronting the very security forces whose safety the strike was aiming to improve. Furthermore, the RUC had signalled right on the UDA's doorstep its determination to deal firmly with Loyalist roadblocks, one of the most effective weapons of the 1974 strike - by the end of the strike they had taken down a further 700.

Political pressure on the Action Council increased after that. West called for an end to the strike but protected his Loyalist flanks with a parallel demand for better security. Craig also joined in, calling the strike a "debacle". His Vanguard party had summed up Loyalist confusion over the strike tactic with a statement on its eve: "A strike can only bring something down - like the Assembly in 1974 - it cannot build anything up".

Intimidation, though, increased, much to Paisley's embarrassment. In some areas Loyalists stoned police landrovers and in North Belfast a police station was bombed. By Thursday, the RUC had logged 1,000 complaints of intimidation.

Confronted with the allegations and his own association with bully boy tactics and violence, Paisley hopped between bald denials, disassociation and ingenious and extravagant counter-allegations. On the first day of the strike he said: "Whatever happens out there is no responsibility of mine. If the British Army and Mr Mason bring about circumstances in which this [intimidation] happens, that is their business."

On the second day he accused the authorities of intimidating the strikers and maintained, to the astonishment of observers, that if the strikers were engaged in intimidation then that was "an indictment of the RUC" which had utterly failed in its duty. When Mason pointed out that all the Westminster parties had condemned intimidation, Paisley lost his temper: "When I consider the drunkenness, lewdness, immorality and filthy language of many of its [the House of Commons] members, I care absolutely nothing for their opinions." In contrast, Paisley condemned the UDA after the Newtownards Road riot, promised it would never happen again and pledged an end to roadblocks.

Paisley's attitude towards intimidation irritated UDA leaders. They felt that he was distancing himself from it in public while inside the privacy of the Action Council's meetings his DUP members had sanctioned its use.

By the fifth day, Friday 6 May, it was clear that the strike was fast losing ground. More and more people were getting into work, buses and trains were operating normally, petrol was freely available and the RUC was dealing firmly with roadblocks.

All this was possible because the 450 workers at Ballylumford, where two-thirds of Northern Ireland's electricity is generated, had not joined the strike. By refusing to join, the power workers had ensured sufficient power for industry and had forced the organisers to rely more and more on physical intimidation. Billy Kelly had promised that electricity output would be reduced to 30 per cent of normal within three days - not only had that failed to materialise but Kelly himself took ill and was hospitalised two days after the strike started.

At Ballylumford, Paisley was outmanoeuvred by old fashioned trade union wheeling and dealing. One sparsely attended meeting during the first two days had voted for the strike but when it was clear that a majority of the other workers would still be opposed, a delegation, led by some shop stewards, decided to meet Mason and relay the results back to a mass meeting which would take the final decision.

On Thursday 5 May, they travelled up to Stormont Castle where Mason unveiled a security package which he had been working on before the strike started. The RUC's strength would be increased to 6,500 and they would have modern weapons and vehicles, he said. The full-time UDR complement would also be raised to 1,800; there would be ten new RUC Divisional Mobile Support Units (DMSU's) - an updated version of the Special

Patrol Groups - a review of anti-terrorist laws with a view to increasing prison sentences and a greater emphasis on SAS covert operations by the British Army. Mason signed a statement to that effect in the presence of the delegation.

It did the trick. The next day, much to Paisley's chagrin, the Ballylumford workers voted against joining the strike by nearly a three to two majority. Paisley tried to put a brave face on the reversal by claiming that the mass meeting at Ballylumford had been unrepresentative of the key electricity workers who, he maintained, were in favour of the strike. The managing director, senior executives and canteen staff had all been included in the vote, he said. He went on to maintain that the strike had in fact been a success, pointing to Mason's security package as evidence, and he accused the media of "lying propaganda" in their claims that industry and commerce were working normally.

More ominously, he said that the people of Larne were "very sore" with the power workers. Privately, the Action Council let it be known that intimidation of the Ballylumford workforce would be stepped up.

Defeat now stared Paisley in the face. On the Saturday he decided to have one more try at talking the power workers round. If that failed it looked as if his political career was over. He drove down to Larne with Baird and a delegation from the Action Council to speak to the workers for the last time.

It was a grim, depressing journey full of foreboding for Paisley. One of those with him recalled: "On the way down, and I can remember it clearly, he was at a crisis point and he and everyone else knew it. 'I'm finished if this doesn't work', he said and then he started to tell us that he didn't need to be in politics and that he wanted to spend more time in his church work. As we arrived he confided to me that he felt he was on his last legs and had completely lost the will to win. He was at the lowest ebb I've ever seen him".

Paisley's forebodings were well founded. The workers listened politely and then gave him an ultimatum - full power or no power at all. They would only come out *en bloc* - not in support of the strike but because of intimidation and fears of violence - and furthermore it would have to be a total walk out which would result in a complete blackout. There would be no power for essential services; hospitals, old people's homes and the like would be without any heat or electricity and, inevitably, there would be deaths.

Paisley backed down and to all intents and purposes the strike was over. In the middle of the next week he and Baird were arrested at a roadblock in Ballymena in a last desperate attempt to boost the strike by their martyrdom but whatever slim chance of success that had was undermined by the paramilitaries.

Their reaction to Paisley caving into the Ballylumford ultimatum was furious. The UDA said they would have called the power workers' bluff and lived with the consequences. Paisley got the blame: "The rank and file didn't like it at all. We were being led by a man with no balls and from then he was the Grand Old Duke of York to us", recalled one UDA member.

In desperation the paramilitaries intensified the violence and intimidation the following week with disastrous, self-mutilating results. On Tuesday 10 May, the UVF shot dead a Protestant busman in North Belfast and the UDR son of one of the strike leaders was killed when a massive bomb destroyed a petrol station in the same area. Another man was killed as he assembled a fire bomb. Intimidation had failed to stop Ballylumford, fewer and fewer businesses were affected and by this stage even Larne was operating normally.

On Thursday 12 May, after a brief meeting of the Action Council, the strike was called off "to give Mr Mason the opportunity to turn the additional security forces onto the IRA". Paisley moved fast and ingeniously to limit the damage. He withdrew his promise to leave politics, he announced, on the pretext that the strike had been a success in his North Antrim constituency. He also claimed a wider victory, maintaining that Mason's security package would not have materialised without the strike.

The strike's failure was, however, widely seen as a victory for Paisley's rivals in the Official Unionist party. That was expected to be reflected in the local council elections on 18 May, days after the end of the strike. Ironically the strike date had been chosen with the council elections in mind; but instead of having their triumph confirmed at the polls, the DUP were now apparently facing the prospect of a severe bruising.

The results startled everyone. The DUP more than doubled its total of councillors to 74, won outright control of its first council, Ballymena, and gained seats in all the 23 councils contested by the party. The Official Unionist lost 35 seats, nearly all to the

DUP, while Baird's party was all but obliterated. The results were seen as a vindication of the strike and evidence of support for Paisley's forthrightness. More significantly the election had left only two Unionist parties to contend for the Protestant vote. The stage was set for the professionalisation of the DUP in preparation for the destruction of the Official Unionists. The DUP had been hauled back from the edge of defeat.

The truth was that the DUP had been saved by Paisley's young deputy, Peter Robinson. On Sunday 8 May, the day after the ultimatum from the Ballylumford workers, he and Jim Smyth met to discuss the next step. "Smyth told him the strike was all but finished and that the DUP should try to salvage what they could", recalled a strike leader. "Robinson agreed and together with some DUP councillors they decided to use the second week of the strike for the election by switching all their energies to the council campaign and to attack the Official Unionists for undermining the strike. Robinson went to see Paisley and he was so grateful for any ideas by this stage that he immediately agreed".

The DUP took that decision unilaterally, leaving their allies, particularly Baird's party, to fend for themselves. The destruction of Baird's party had been in senior DUP minds long before the strike, as Clifford Smyth, purged from the party in late 1976, could testify: "I remember walking in to headquarters one day and there they were talking about how Ernie Baird's people would be destroyed". The strike headquarters were abandoned by all but the UWC, a few of Baird's people and the odd paramilitary. Apart from an occasional appearance by Paisley, the DUP had discarded the strike for the hustings.

During the second week Robinson "went out with a great deal of gusto on the basis that there were two ways to go - down the plughole or out campaigning. And it worked. Paisley was completely rudderless and Robinson rescued him", said an Action Council leader.

Baird's party was not the only casualty. The UDA was also severely damaged by the strike's failure. In the months following the strike the RUC took advantage of its new initiative and cut swathes into UDA membership by arresting and charging many of its most active middle level leaders. Morale dipped badly and for the next four years the UDA was hard pressed keeping its organisation intact. Of the principal participants in the 1977 strike only the DUP, by ruthless concentration on its self interest, had prospered.

We are now over the brink.
Ian Paisley at Rev Robert Bradford's funeral, November 1981.

If there is one thing Margaret Thatcher will not take, it is being threatened. If there is one thing Ian Paisley cannot stand, it is being contradicted. In December 1980, just six days before Christmas, the British Prime Minister received the DUP leader in her office at the House of Commons to discuss her summit meeting with the Taoiseach, Charles Haughey, in Dublin 11 days before. Humphrey Atkins had told Thatcher that if Paisley appeared in a collar and tie he would probably behave reasonably, but if he had donned his dog collar, he would bang the table and shout at her.

On that occasion Paisley was wearing a tie, but it was the dog collar man who was doing the talking. He was not interested in an exchange of views. He read her a prepared statement in a loud and hectoring voice. He accused her of having given Dublin a "direct involvement" in Northern Ireland's affairs through her joint pledge with Haughey to consider "the totality of relationships in these islands". He alleged that the "joint studies" of Anglo-Irish and cross-border matters of common interest would inevitably threaten the Union. He quoted Lord Carson threatening that if the British Government created "a situation that it is impossible for men in Ulster to bear", then the responsibility for any resulting confrontation would be the government's.

Thatcher was coldly furious. She interrupted him continuously with the retort: "I stand by the guarantee". As Paisley's tirade climaxed, she became angrier. She repeated again and again, hitting the side of her chair, "I stand by the guarantee". She said very little else. Colleagues said she was repelled by his tone, unconvinced by his arguments. That meeting was to form her opinion of the DUP leader in all future dealings with him. He was a bully, and as a bully herself, she took a deep dislike to him.

For Paisley it was the end of a year of conciliatory chats over cups of tea with Humphrey Atkins. It was time to launch another campaign to whip up the fears of the North's Protestants into a menacing street-marching fever that would, he hoped, scare the British out of their dealings with Dublin. Such a campaign would serve the added purpose of throwing his Official Unionist rivals on to the defensive in the run-up to the following spring's local elections.

"No British government could resist the passive disobedience of the Protestant people.It would bring this province to a complete and total standstill", he told one TV interviewer. "Under Lord Carson, our founding father, and Craigavon, the Protestants of Ulster armed themselves and said 'we will resist to the death' . . . I would resist to the death any attempt to subvert the democratic wishes of the Ulster people".[1]

It was an almost Pavlovian response, and one his Loyalist followers understood only too well, for Paisley to appeal for legitimacy to the great 1912-14 Home Rule crisis that led to the foundation of the Northern Ireland state. "It was only fitting", he wrote, "that in 1981, when Ulster again was called to face a serious effort by a British government to edge us out of the United Kingdom, that Ulstermen should revert to the ways of their fathers".[2]

The exaggerated claims of Haughey and his foreign minister Brian Lenihan - the latter said he foresaw a united Ireland within 10 years as a result of the new relationship - had certainly set alarm bells ringing among ordinary Unionists, especially in the countryside. Rural Official Unionists reported larger attendances at political meetings, while previously defunct paramilitary groupings in Tyrone and South Derry started talking about re-forming.

As usual it was Paisley who cashed in most effectively on the popular mood with a piece of paramilitary theatre that was flamboyant even by his standards. On a bitterly cold night in early February 1981 he brought five journalists to a hillside outside Ballymena, where 500 men, some of them dressed in combat jackets and balaclava helmets, were lined up in the dark in military formation. At a command from Paisley they held above their heads pieces of paper which he said were certificates for legally-held firearms. They were not armed.

The midnight parade, it was learned later, included members of the Ulster Defence Regiment and the RUC reserve. One man who had been approached to join the new force said the men involved were "all solid country types". The UDA and UVF were not involved. For the moment Paisley was steering clear of any involvement with the hard young men of such existing paramilitary groups, and they were equally wary of him after his performance during the abortive 1977 strike. Instead, he was launching his first serious attempt since the late 1960s to organise his own paramilitary unit: later that year it would re-emerge under the title the "Third Force".

First, though, he had some more conventional showmanship in mind to raise the sectarian temperature. The following Sunday he preached one of his classic political and anti-Catholic sermons at the Martyrs Memorial church. He told his attentive congregation that in this "hour of crisis", they faced a double threat from the Irish Republic and the IRA's campaign of "Protestant genocide". Roman Catholics had a peculiar advantage when it came to terrorism, he went on - "All they have to do is to go to their priest and get a pardon. Isn't it remarkable that all the worst crimes of republican violence have been committed immediately after Mass?"[3]

Having appealed to his followers' fear of Catholicism, he turned to one of the most potent of their historical symbols: the signing by nearly half-a-million Unionists of the anti-Home Rule Ulster Covenant in 1912. He now produced an "Ulster Declaration", which he invited Loyalists to sign in protest against the Thatcher-Haughey initiative. It was a bizarre document, an ill-spelt attempt to adapt the archaic language of 1912 to the circumstances of the 1980s, and clearly intended to invite comparisons with the most heroic era of Ulster Unionism.

Next he turned to the kind of politics he loved best: he announced a series of eleven rallies around Northern Ireland, again copying Carson's 1912 campaign, to culminate in a massive demonstration of Loyalist solidarity at the foot of Carson's statue outside Stormont.

The "Carson Trail" rallies were typical Paisley affairs. His speeches were aimed at evoking all the gut-fears of rural loyalism. In his attacks on Charles Haughey he used "language which the crowd understood and loved", noted the chronicler of the rallies, Sammy Wilson, later the DUP's first Lord Mayor of Belfast. At Omagh, County Tyrone, he boasted that "our ancestors cut a civilisation out of the bogs and meadows of this country while Mr Haughey's ancestors were wearing pig-skins and living in caves . . . When our forefathers donned the British uniform and fought for their King and Country, Mr Haughey's fellow countrymen used their lights to guide enemy bombers to their targets in Northern Ireland".[4]

At Newtownards, County Down, it was Margaret Thatcher's turn to feel his wrath as he played the role that came most naturally to him - not the leader of, but the spokesman for the inarticulate Loyalist masses. "The wee woman washing the dishes is saying the same things about Margaret Thatcher as I'm saying - 'Let them have it, because that's what I would do'. All I am is your representative - if you want me to say these things I will say them and no-one will stop me, inside or outside of Parliament, even should it bring an even greater volume of abuse, hatred, spite, even physical violence," he told the wildly cheering crowd.[5]

Former colleagues have commented that the larger and the more clamorous the audience, the more Paisley gets carried away with the violence of his own rhetoric, pushing it to new extremes of menace and paranoia. During the "Carson Trail" he excelled himself. At Newtownards the applause was so ecstatic that he produced an astonishing new claim in response to it. He accused no less a party than the Official Unionists of plotting to assassinate him, a claim based on an anonymous phone call to the Belfast *News Letter*.

At rally after rally he fed the faithful with what they wanted to hear. At Newtownards he conjured up a picture of Haughey with "a green baton dripping with blood" in one hand and "a noose specially prepared for the Protestants of Ulster in the other". At Banbridge the crowd spontaneously burst into the DUP anthem - "Paisley is our leader". He told the crowd in Cookstown that "we will have the last word - there will be no structures in our province or no control exercised by anyone of which we do not approve."

After the rally at Enniskillen, County Fermanagh, Paisley and four colleagues drove to Hillsborough Castle to deliver a protest note to Margaret Thatcher, who had flown into Northern Ireland on a hurriedly-arranged mission of reassurance. As they handed it in at the gate of the sleeping castle at 3.45 in the morning, they bawled together at the top of their voices "No surrender". It was a symbolic act of defiance guaranteed to warm the hearts of the Loyalist multitudes.

There were two other elements without which no Paisley

extravaganza would be complete. One was a tantalising hint of mysterious and threatening events to come. Peter Robinson told the crowds that after the rallies there would be third, fourth and fifth phases of the campaign still to come, if necessary, "and no-one but a few know the timing and the details". All they had to do was put their "trust in Dr. Paisley. Times past have proved his advice and warnings to be true. Give him your trust and he, with God's help, will give this country the leadership it needs".[6]

And, with the May local elections in mind, there were the constant attacks on the vacillations of the Official Unionists and "the pathetic spectacle" of their leader, Jim Molyneaux, "falling over himself to excuse the Prime Minister as he blames the civil servants and everyone but the lady who did the dirty deal with Dublin".

There were, of course, no third, fourth or fifth phases. Fewer and fewer people began to turn up as it became apparent that there was no immediate threat to Northern Ireland's Britishness. To make up the numbers devout Paisleyites were bussed in from all over the province. Fewer than 10,000, including two and a half thousand bandsmen, turned up for what was billed as the final triumphant rally at Stormont at the end of March, although Paisley kept doggedly insisting that 100,000 were present.

The faithful waited in the drizzle to be told what to do in the "third phase" of the now cold and mucky Carson Trail. They were to be disappointed. For the moment their only instruction was to go out and vote for the DUP in the May local government elections. These, Paisley said, had a significance far greater than electing councillors and aldermen. They would be the thermometer which measured the temperature of the Loyalist people. Votes cast for the DUP were votes for resistance to Haughey and Thatcher.

And that was exactly what they and tens of thousands like them did. Few showed any disappointment at the unfulfilled promises, the unrealised threats of action, the clear evidence of a crisis manufactured and exaggerated by a master manipulator for his own electoral advantage. It seemed to be enough that Paisley was once again seen to be doing something, seen to be eternally vigilant against the ever-present menace of Dublin. In the May 1981 local elections, with the community more polarized than ever by the Republican hunger strike in the Maze prison, Unionist voters pushed the DUP's vote up for the first time above that of their Official Unionist rivals. The "Carson Trail", despite its abortive finale, and despite the fact that the Anglo-Irish dialogue was still going strong, had served Paisley well.

* * *

It did not serve him so well six months later, when a real crisis blew up following the IRA's assassination of the Official Unionist MP Rev Robert Bradford. A whole range of people, from the UDA to the British Government, were to remember, to Paisley's cost, the emptiness of his "Carson Trail" bluster. Nevertheless the immediate reaction of many ordinary Unionists to the shooting of the MP in one of his South Belfast advice centres on 15th November was that once again Paisley had been proved right. For months before the latest Anglo-Irish summit meeting on 6 November his had been the lone voice warning against the hidden dangers of the dialogue with Dublin. Now Official Unionists like Harold McCusker - bitter critics of his "Carson Trail" - rushed to join him in condemning the Anglo-Irish process as the "the spur the terrorists needed" to step up their own violent push for a united Ireland.

The killing of Robert Bradford came in the middle of a wave of murderous IRA attacks on UDR and RUC men in Border areas. It affected the Unionist community like almost no other atrocity since the beginning of the "Troubles". Unionist politicians were inundated with phone calls from their constituents demanding everything from the laying waste of the Falls Road and the Bogside to the setting up of a Protestant provisional government. Protestants were saying that if there was going to be a civil war "then let's get it over with", said UDA leader Andy Tyrie.

It also had a deep personal impact on Paisley. Robert Bradford, a former Methodist minister, was a close friend and ally who personified the contradictions at the heart of Unionism: he was an ultra-right winger with identical views to the DUP leader, yet was in the Official Unionist party. Three years previously he and Paisley had staged a joint protest at Westminster, walking out of a religious service because a Catholic priest was taking part. He was a fierce campaigner against homosexuality, child pornography and the employment of alleged IRA sympathisers in Belfast's Royal Victoria hospital. He was also known for his sympathies with the "British

Israelites", who believed that Ulster Protestants were descendants of the lost tribe of Israel. Such a bizarre belief, with its emphasis on Northern Ireland as a place specially ordained by God, was not without its attractions to Paisley - he never tired of telling people that Ulster had been "consecrated as holy ground".[7]

Paisley, however, had for once been caught unprepared by events. The Official Unionists had been meeting in their Glengall Street headquarters to discuss the Border killings when the news of Bradford's assassination came through, and they took the initiative. It was the Official Unionist MPs and councillors from Border areas, led by McCusker, who made the running in calling for a one hour work stoppage on the day of Bradford's funeral, and who set in motion a boycott of local councils in pursuit of tougher security measures. Again it was Official Unionists who drew up tentative plans to establish their own alternative government and security structures if their demands were not met.

Paisley's immediate response was a typical piece of one-upmanship: he called for people to come out in mourning for Bradford an hour before the Official Unionist-called work stoppage was due to begin.

At Westminster his antics were even more calculated to grab centre-stage. The previous week he was reported to have called Mrs Thatcher "a traitor and a liar" from an upstairs gallery of the Commons. On Monday 16 November he appeared there again, apparently attracted by its theatrical possibilities, together with Peter Robinson and Johnny McQuade. MPs said they had seen him laughing and joking with his colleagues beforehand.

Half-way through a lengthy and sombre statement on the assassination by the recently appointed Northern Ireland Secretary Jim Prior, Paisley shouted "nonsense", and Robinson and McQuade, as if on cue, also started barracking. When they refused to stop, the Speaker suspended the debate, and then suspended them. They refused to leave. Both Labour and Conservative MPs shouted "Out, get out". The speaker threatened to suspend them for the session. Paisley rose contemptuously to his feet with the words "Amen, there is no use coming here anyway", pulled a reluctant Johnny McQuade after him, and stalked out.

If Paisley was alienating the politicians in Britain, he was dividing the Unionists back in Belfast. He was once again mouthing unspecific threats about making Northern Ireland "ungovernable". When asked what concretely he proposed to do to achieve this, all he could come up with was a threat of more demonstrations and the non-cooperation of already virtually powerless local councillors, with mayors refusing to "wine and dine" government ministers.

The problem was that his party only controlled two councils out of 26, so he needed the Official Unionists to join him to make any protest action effective. His next move, a call for a half-day work stoppage on 23 November, did receive a positive response from ordinary grass-roots Unionists. The DUP leader also promised the first show of strength of his newly-created "Third Force", the fruit of the seed planted on the County Antrim hillside the previous February.

Most of the Official Unionist leadership, though, dismissed all this as a typical piece of bluster and political opportunism. They called a rival demonstration at Belfast's City Hall on the same day. At it Paisley clashed with the barrister Robert McCartney, a rising new star in the Official Unionist firmament, who blamed his "outrageous conduct and irresponsible language" for the divisions in Unionism. In an interview the following day McCartney called Paisley a Fascist who was "more interested in an independent Ulster, a mini-Geneva run by a fifth-rate Calvin" than in the union with Britain.

Just to make matters even more chaotic, the UDA refused to have anything to do with Paisley's "Third Force", and called their own rally outside the Belfast shipyard. Little wonder that the maverick Unionist MP Jim Kilfedder raised a cheer at this last rally when he deplored the previous week's "confusion and disarray" among Unionists.

However, Paisley still had one card to play: his putative loyalist army. That night, in pouring rain, the 6,000 men of the "Third Force" marched through the streets of Newtownards, County Down, to a rally outside the town's handsome 18th century courthouse, where nearly two centuries before the Presbyterian United Irishmen had been despatched to the gallows and the convict ships. The town square was full of foreign journalists and television crews, lured back to Northern Ireland by hysterical rumours of impending civil war.

There was no civil war: instead Paisley was offering them a

piece of paramilitary melodrama, a private army complete with masks and cudgels. The theatre was more impressive than the threat. Peter Robinson asked for two minutes silence "and you'll hear something that will bring joy to your hearts". The crowd hushed in the dreadful hope of hearing gunfire. Nothing happened. Paisley, looking like Lord Carson in a heavy overcoat and homburg hat, strode across the square. There was a tense pause, perfectly stage-managed, followed by a chorus of wild cheers as the first ranks of the "Third Force" spilled into the square.

They were a motley crew. The leading squad wore paramilitary uniforms and carried swagger sticks. Most of the rest came in a mixture of masks, flak jackets and forage caps; a few carried heavy sticks. Others were still in their work clothes; some had donned their Sunday best. There were sallow-faced teenagers and plump, prosperous farmers. They stood awkwardly in lines under the harsh television lights. The crowd revelled in the spectacle but was disappointed by the absence of one vital ingredient - there was not a gun to be seen anywhere.

From the platform Paisley thundered that he wanted to see a force of 100,000 men "on the march in Ulster". He said that recruiting officers would soon be visiting every community, and there would be a women's corps as well.

The "Third Force" never marched again. Little more was heard about it apart from a few desultory gatherings of men in Loyalist housing estates and on country roads in the following few weeks. The RUC Chief Constable, Sir John Hermon, after narrowly surviving a vote of no confidence proposed by Paisleyite policemen at a meeting of their trade union, the Police Federation, attacked "self-appointed armies" whose object was to seize power and dictate to people "whether they should live or die".

Hermon had refused to meet any more local politicians earlier that year after Paisley had told him that if he wanted to stay on as Chief Constable he would have to do what one million Protestants wanted: the Catholics did not matter. It was the beginning of a bitter animosity between the two men, as the DUP leader made the removal of the Chief Constable a key part of his security demands.

Once again, Paisley had brought his people to the edge of the abyss of civil war, and then led them away from it. In a pointless last gesture he offered the "Third Force" as a back-up to the existing security forces - the role he had always seen for such a Loyalist "people's militia" ever since he had first tried to mobilise its predecessor back in 1969. But Loyalists brought up in the tougher school of Belfast's sectarian ghettoes were already sneering at what they called the "Third Farce", and at the calibre of its self-styled "county commanders" - Rev Ivan Foster in his dark sunglasses, and Rev William McCrea with his gospel records.

Some key actors in future Northern Ireland scenarios would never again take the threat of a Paisleyite backlash quite so seriously. Members of the Thatcher government, for example, were known to share the view of the *Daily Telegraph* editorial on the day of Robert Bradford's funeral: "The posturing of Mr Paisley . . . continues to do much to persuade the British people that Ulster is a strange and alien land which tends to inspire not terror, but ridicule".

Nearer home the Official Unionists were more suspicious than ever of any efforts to include Paisley in a broad Unionist front against the Anglo-Irish dialogue. The UDA, whose central role in the 1974 UWC strike had shown that any long drawn-out campaign of loyalist disruption required their muscle to be successful, had also refused to become involved in Paisley-organised protests. The UVF and the Red Hand Commandos had followed suit.

A leading UDA man, Freddy Parkinson, issued a statement from his cell in a Dublin jail, where he was serving a sentence for a firebomb attack in that city, which summed up the feelings of many former paramilitary activists about Paisley. Appealing to "Third Force" members not to become involved in violence, Parkinson wrote: "I remember vividly the parliamentary megalomaniacs of the late sixties and early seventies who beckoned us to follow them but who later left us abandoned to be scorned as common criminals".

Paisley, he went on, "the tarantula who spreads the venom of further conflict around us, has been a major contributor to our prolonged tragedy". He concluded with the words of Major Ronald Bunting about his former master: "He uses words to create violent situations, but never follows the violence through himself". Was the master showman of the "Carson Trail" and the "Third Force" beginning belatedly to be seen as an empty vessel?

It would take another constitutional crisis, a real constitutional crisis this time, to find out.

> *The Anglo-Irish Agreement has pushed us onto*
> *the window ledge of the Union.*
> DUP deputy leader Peter Robinson, April 1986.

His unceasing vigilance - almost to the point of paranoia - about the possibility of a "sell-out" by Britain, often made Paisley sound like a prophet. And sometimes he was. He foresaw the form the first serious weakening of the constitutional link with Britain would take nearly ten years before it happened. "It is eventually going to be a confrontation between the Protestants of Ulster and Westminster", he told a loyalist rally in Omagh in January 1976. Nearly five years later, on the day after Margaret Thatcher first met Charles Haughey at Downing Street, he warned the British Prime Minister that should she dare to give the Republic a say in Northern Ireland, he would "lead the Ulster Protestant people in whatever actions are necessary to thwart and destroy such machinery."

He may have been engaging in his well-tried tactic of scaring governments out of new Northern Ireland policies by threatening murder and mayhem against them. It was a gambit with diminishing returns. By the mid-1980s the British government had a more pressing concern than Paisley's endless threats of violent Protestant backlashes. Worried by the growth in electoral support for the Provisional IRA's political wing, Sinn Fein, Margaret Thatcher and her ministers were feeling their way towards the first major political initiative in Northern Ireland for more than a decade.

First and foremost Thatcher wanted a crackdown on IRA violence. The Taoiseach, Garret FitzGerald, with John Hume in support, was starting to convince her that the way to tackle both the IRA and Sinn Fein was to give the Dublin government an input into the North's affairs. This, they argued, would reduce longstanding Nationalist "alienation" from the police and judicial system in particular, and would lead to a falling off in support for the "men of violence".

The two Unionist parties, already working together to boycott newly-elected Sinn Fein councillors on local councils, desperately tried to pre-empt a deal. In August 1985 a joint Official Unionist-DUP working party was set up to co-ordinate opposition to any agreement which would involve the Irish Government in the North's affairs. Later that month Jim Molyneaux and Ian Paisley wrote to Margaret Thatcher. "The people of Ulster" - which in Unionism's exclusivist language meant the North's Protestants - were "profoundly anxious" about the secret Anglo-Irish talks, they wrote. Their leaders, they went on, were "fearful for the future of constitutional politics" - a coded threat of a Loyalist paramilitary backlash - if Dublin was given any say in the North.

A second letter a month later contained a uniquely Unionist mixture of wild anti-Catholic paranoia and a claim that for once was unerringly accurate. It alleged that "a cardinal from the Vatican" had been briefed by the Irish government on the talks - "the Pope is to know more about your deliberations than Unionist members of the British Parliament", the two leaders complained. But they also claimed that any Anglo-Irish agreement would result in a secretariat, staffed by Irish as well as British civil servants, being set up in Belfast.

That, as it turned out, was exactly what was at the centre of the agreement signed on 15 November between Thatcher and FitzGerald in the old governor's residence at Hillsborough, one of Northern Ireland's most picturesque Georgian villages. An Anglo-Irish Conference was to be set up, serviced by a joint secretariat which, it later emerged, would be situated beside a British Army complex on the edge of East Belfast. This physical symbol of Dublin's input, the Maryfield "bunker", was what incensed Unionists most.

The most striking image on that cold early winter's day was Paisley, his face bloated with suppressed rage, towering over his grim little band of disciples outside Hillsborough Castle's gates. His words, though, were unremarkable. After two decades of blustering and threatening there was little new he could say now that a real deal had been struck with the detested traditional enemy.

Strangely, in the weeks following the Anglo-Irish Agreement his level of rhetoric continued to be noticeably lower than in earlier "crises" largely manufactured by him for his own ends. Even at the massive "Ulster Says No" protest rally outside Belfast's City Hall on 23 November, he kept his fearsome tongue under control, mindful perhaps of the warning in Jim Molyneaux's opening speech that this time the crisis was too serious for fever-pitch oratory.

It was all too clear from the array of faces in that huge crowd that the Unionist people in their hour of need were demanding a united stand from their long-divided leaders. Civil servants and their smartly-dressed wives, tweed-capped farmers and venerable sash-wearing Orangemen mixed with the "boot boys", "Kick the Pope" bandsmen, punks and the pinched-faced men and women of the Belfast ghettoes. Paisley, sensitive as always to the feelings of the Loyalist masses, would not disappoint them.

He had his own reasons for his anxiety to maintain Unionist unity. The fiasco of the 1977 Loyalist strike was a reminder of the impotence of a divided Unionism. He knew too that in the past he had dominated any Unionist coalition, particularly at a time of crisis, through his powerful personality, huge personal appeal to the Loyalist public, and unimpeachable position at the hardest, purest end of the Unionist spectrum.

However, he left to his deputy leader, Peter Robinson, the hard job of starting to spell out what every intelligent Unionist was thinking, that the Agreement was the beginning of the end of the union with Britain as they knew it. "The Union I was taught at my father's knee was nothing like the Union we have today. The Union then was a protection to the people in Northern Ireland who wanted to remain out of a united Ireland. Now the Union forces us towards a united Ireland", was Robinson's verdict. "The Anglo-Irish Agreement has pushed us onto the window ledge of the Union."

Robinson and his following of "Young Turks" in the DUP were by this stage talking privately about independence. But they knew that the only man who could sell such a radical prescription to grassroots Loyalists was the man those people had come to worship almost as their messiah, "God's man for the hour", Ian Paisley.

When the House of Commons endorsed the Anglo-Irish Agreement by one of the largest majorities in living memory, the logic of the extreme Unionist position became inescapable. However, Paisley refused to face up to it. At post-agreement strategy meetings Unionist politicians of both parties asked the inevitable question : what would a militant campaign of civil disobedience, political strikes and violent street protests lead to if not a serious weakening of the link with Britain?

Paisley, however, was the first to throw up his hands in horror at any suggestion of independence, said Unionist colleagues. He would often say that the leaders of Unionism had to face up to swallowing "a dose of unpleasant medicine", but would recoil when it was suggested to him that there were only two kinds of medicine - to deal with the British on their terms in order to stay inside the United Kingdom, meaning some role in government for the SDLP and some relationship with Dublin; or to go it alone in an independent Ulster.

Many Official Unionists believed they had finally found Paisley out. The deep contradiction which had been at the heart of his politics for most of his career was now a crucial factor in the confusion in the Unionist camp. As long ago as 1973 senior Northern Ireland Office officials had pointed out that the DUP leader could not have it both ways: he could either go along with Brian Faulkner and remain inside the United Kingdom on the terms dictated by the British Government and Parliament, or he could follow the logic of William Craig's arguments and go for independence.[8]

Thirteen years later, in the middle of the most serious constitutional crisis of the "Troubles", he was still trying to have it both ways. He seemed incapable of telling his blinkered supporters the plain truth: that the relationship with Britain would never be the same again. He was still clinging to the vain hope that another bout of sabre-rattling, this time in concert with the Official Unionists, would force the British to renege on their deal with Dublin.

"He has the leadership ability to take Northern Ireland out of this crisis - he could save the province from absolute mayhem if he used his tremendous abilities for good", says one leading Official Unionist. "But I don't think he will. At the end of the day he's a weak man, and a scared man - he's always scared of losing his support - it's the weakness of the politician".

Another colleague puts it even more bluntly. "It's a case", he says, "of I am the leader, there is the mob, I must follow". Paisley was now the prisoner of the "no surrender" instincts of that mob - instincts to which he had done so much over the previous 20 years to give expression and credibility.

However, for the moment he resisted the pressure from the mobsters of militant Loyalism to up the tempo of street protests and prepare for industrial action - measures he knew would push Northern Ireland even further out onto the UK's window ledge. Not having a strategy of his own, he fell in behind the Official Unionists in their campaign to exhaust all constitutional avenues of protest.

They were quickly exhausted. After all 15 Unionist MPs, including an extremely reluctant Enoch Powell, were persuaded to resign their seats, a "mini-referendum" was called for late January. Although the object of this was to demonstrate the solidity of Unionist opposition to the Agreement, it actually did more to reinforce the arguments of the pro-Agreement side. 418,000 Unionists turned out - not enough to worry the British, who were more impressed with the swing in the Nationalist community away from Sinn Fein, which resulted in SDLP deputy leader Seamus Mallon winning a seat. It appeared that the Agreement really was starting to reduce the alienation of the minority.

In contrast, the Unionists' constitutional strategy seemed to be in disarray. Tensions within the Unionist "family" increased. The Official Unionists were unhappy at Paisley's inevitable eclipse of Molyneaux on shared platforms, and accused their leader of having been taken in by Enoch Powell's assurances the previous year that the Anglo-Irish discussions would lead nowhere. DUP militants, on the other hand, muttered darkly about Molyneaux's moderating influence on Paisley, and complained about the lack of the promised strategy for boycotting councils, boards and government institutions.

Loyalists were also beginning to express their hostility to the Agreement in a more traditional and violent fashion. A four-day protest march from Derry to Belfast over the New Year, organised by the youth wings of the two parties, was joined by paramilitaries from the UDA and UVF and by militants from the new grassroots Loyalist organisation, the Ulster Clubs. When the marchers arrived at the gates of the Anglo-Irish Conference secretariat's offices at Maryfield - a name which had not gone unnoticed by countless anti-Catholic Paisleyite conspiracy theorists - its gates were torn down and there were vicious assaults on the lines of RUC men guarding it.

Paisley had pulled out of speaking at the end-of-march demonstration on the pretext that he was officiating at the wedding of a close friend. Molyneaux, whose speech was rowned out in the commotion, denounced the attacks as the work of thugs. Robinson refused to condemn them.

Robinson was more in touch with the frustrations of ordinary grassroots Loyalists. For the first time Paisley's usually infallible Loyalist antennae were about to let him down. His commitment to Unionist unity, plus the demands of a crippling schedule as party and church leader, Westminster, Strasbourg and Stormont parliamentarian, had left him out of touch with those grassroots for the first time since the early 1970s. He was about to make one of the most serious mistakes of his political career.

The occasion was the long-requested meeting at Downing Street between the two Unionist leaders and Margaret Thatcher on 25 February. They went with two messages from the joint DUP-Official Unionist working party: firstly an offer of a two-tier conference on devolution and a new relationship with Dublin if the Anglo-Irish agreement was put into cold storage; and secondly a threat that if the Prime Minister was not interested in this a one-day strike would be mounted, and the protest campaign would be stepped up, increasing the likelihood of confrontation with the RUC.

Neither message was delivered. Instead Paisley proposed a conference on devolution, a suggestion seized upon by Mrs Thatcher and Northern Ireland Secretary Tom King. At an impromptu press conference in the House of Commons afterwards Molyneaux said they had got away from "a deadlock situation", and he hoped that the organisers of the threatened one-day strike would now not put their plans into action.

Paisley sat beside him leaning backwards and smiling approvingly. In the corner of the crowded room Peter Robinson shook his head after every statement. "That sounds all right", someone said to him as the journalists filed out. "It's all right till we get them home to Belfast", he replied.

Back in Belfast even Paisley's most loyal lieutenants were shouting about a sell-out. Significantly it was his fellow clerics, William McCrea and Ivan Foster, who issued the most angry denunciatory statements. There was an only half-joking proposal to send a DUP delegation to give the two leaders a hot reception when they arrived at Aldergrove airport. One wag suggested they carry placards demanding "Paisley must go".

However, for once Paisley knew when to backtrack. Robinson had quickly convinced him that there would be hell to pay back home. Within an hour of the press conference he was already on the phone to Belfast contradicting Molyneaux and insisting to colleagues that nothing acceptable had come out of the meeting with Thatcher. He finally conceded defeat at a stormy session with senior DUP men early that evening.

When the joint working party met that night at the Official Unionist headquarters in Glengall Street, Paisley went onto the offensive, denying that the government statement issued after the Downing Street meeting had been approved by him and describing it as having been a "very angry" affair. Molyneaux also under pressure from his lieutenants, reluctantly went along with his version. Both men then put their names to a statement rejecting further talks with the Government and announcing an intensification of the protest campaign. It was Peter Robinson's finest hour.

All that was left was for Paisley and Molyneaux to meet representatives of the "1986 Workers Committee", a group of factory and power station workers brought together largely at Robinson's instigation to co-ordinate strike action against the agreement. The two leaders assured them that the "day of action" could go ahead. the following Monday, 3 March.

Suddenly Robinson was the man to watch. British journalists well-briefed by a Northern Ireland Office only too anxious to split Paisley's party, started to speculate about a bid for the DUP leadership.

Robinson had certainly gone out of his way to cultivate the cold, clinical "hard man" image. The Loyalist paramilitaries saw him as a leader who, unlike Paisley, could be ruthless enough actually to lead the Loyalists into armed conflict with the RUC the British Army and Republican groups. He had already made clear that he saw the "day of action" as a dry run for a full-scale repeat of the 1974 Ulster Workers Council strike. He claimed to have gained the agreement of workers' leaders at the North's two key power stations, Ballylumford and Coolkeragh, and was aiming for a date sometime over the next couple of months before the cold weather ended in the spring.

However, Robinson appears to have overplayed his hand. He was at the centre of the events of 3 March. In marked contrast Paisley disappeared to play a marginal role in his North Antrim heartland, and it paid off. His deputy's reputation as the man who could deliver the paramilitaries backfired. The hooded men n the barricades and the violence which marred the protest, articularly in his own East Belfast backyard, did the DUP eputy leader little good among the solid Free Presbyterian ountry folk who still comprised the party's core support. Among hem Paisley's leadership was as strong as ever.

Within six weeks Robinson's position was further weakened. Jn Easter Monday 1986 there was a confrontation in Portadown, County Armagh, between the RUC and Apprentice Boys who vere trying to march through the Catholic Tunnel area of the own. Paisley, inevitably, was not present when the real violence tarted - he had already left on his way to a preaching ngagement in the United States. But he had cleverly identified vith the marchers by leading them in a surprise midnight sally nto a neighbouring Catholic area several hours earlier.

Clashes between the RUC and marching Orangemen in ortadown the previous summer had led to intermittent attacks v Loyalist gangs on policemen's homes. These now became most a daily occurrence. Once again Robinson refused to ondemn them. But this time he had seriously misread the strong ro-law and order current in conservative rural Paisleyism. obinson's young East Belfast sidekick Sammy Wilson had ppeared on television calling the RUC "boot-boys". There was flood of protest phone calls to DUP headquarters. Paisley came ick from the US and "unequivocally and unreservedly" ondemned the attacks on RUC men's homes and families. They opped shortly afterwards.

By the time of the DUP conference in late April Paisley had early seen off Robinson's challenge, at least for the present. It as not the "so-called champions of Protestantism" who tacked police widows in wheelchairs who would save Ulster, he undered. He, Ian Paisley, was in politics to do that. While early bereft of any new ideas to oppose the Anglo-Irish greement, he hammered home the well-worn theme of nionist unity, paid fulsome tribute to Jim Molyneaux, and nted that Margaret Thatcher was beginning to see sense.

A compliant Robinson joined Paisley in putting the lid on any cipient revolt. He had heard one DUP local councillor warning e party's leadership against behaving like the Grand Old Duke York, and backing off from bloody confrontation at the last oment. He had noted the beginnings of a groundswell of hard-e dissatisfaction with Paisley's leadership. The young bloods from East Belfast and Mid Ulster might not be happy. But Pete Robinson could afford to bide his time.

For its part, the British Government was not yet ready to su for peace on Paisley's terms. In late June it closed down th Northern Ireland Assembly, which for the previous six month had been turned into an all-Unionist "grand committee" devote to discussing ways of bringing down the Hillsboroug Agreement.

Paisley was incensed by the Assembly's closure. He showed in his furious attack on the policemen who carried him out of th Stormont chamber at two o'clock in the morning following its las unauthorised ten-hour sitting. "Don't come crying to me if you homes are attacked", he snarled at them. "You will reap wha you sow".

"The removal of the Assembly was a real trauma for him", say one former fellow-member. "He loved it. It was the DUP citadel. They could play at being what they love to be - He Majesty's Loyal Opposition. They could snipe, bully, vilify, wit no possibility of being called to account. They had virtuall moved their party HQ into Stormont".

In Stormont's unreal atmosphere, with not a Nationalist i sight, Paisley had been able to indulge the Dr Jekyll side to h character, the constitutional politician, to the full. There he wa not the disliked oddball he was in the House of Commons, but revered father figure to his inexperienced young party. Man colleagues believed this was the role that increasingly h preferred playing as he got older, in a belated belief that he coul make people love him a little after a career spent destroying bot political institutions and the men who ran them.

With Stormont gone he became the uglier and more familia Mr Hyde of earlier manifestations. "He's schizoid", says on experienced political observer. "While he's happiest being constitutionalist, there is another side of him which clearly reve in sectarian confrontation - it's almost as if he can't stop himsel he loves it, he thrives on it."

Within hours of being dragged out of the Assembly, he wa fuelling the sectarian flames. "There could be hand-to-han fighting in every street in Northern Ireland," he threatened. "W are on the verge of civil war because when you take away th forum of democracy you don't have anything left." That night h told an Ulster Clubs rally in Larne: "Every man in Ulste including every member of the RUC, is now to declare himself whether he is on the side of the lying, treachery and betrayal of the agreement, or whether he stands ready to defend to the last drop of blood his British and Ulster heritage".[10]

Encouraged by this new fierceness, some of his party colleagues went further. The unfortunate William Beattie told the DUP's youth wing that "we must hire assassins and pay them when the job is done", only to find that he had once again gone too far. The press release of his speech was withdrawn, on the thin pretence that he had been misquoted.

Meanwhile Paisley was already having second thoughts. Less than a week later he pulled back from the brink. People who know him say that such volte faces are caused by a combination of political cowardice and occasional bouts of the clergyman's bad conscience. "Ian Paisley, the leader of a church, the 'born again' Christian, the bible-believing Protestant, could not contemplate thousands of deaths in a civil war. That's why he looks over the edge and doesn't like it", comments one colleague.

The excuse he used this time was extremely unconvincing, especially in his mouth. He echoed Jim Molyneaux's claim that, of all things, the massive "NO" vote in the Republic's referendum on the introduction of divorce - strongly reinforcing the South's Catholic ethos - had reduced the likelihood that Britain would push the North towards a united Ireland. A victory for the hated system of Irish Catholicism meant that the possibility of civil war had receded, he declared.

Paisley had always been a reactive rather than a reflective politician: in the past that had been his major strength. Now he was at his most inconsistent and irrational, a split personality zig-zagging from policy to policy, from idea to idea. In one speech in early July he was able to claim in one breath that the government was prepared to see him killed and had him under surveillance by the police's elite E4A "hit squad", while moments later he was rejecting an enquiry into E4A's alleged "shoot to kill" tactics in the early 1980s.

His confused and angry mood matched the frustrated fury of his Loyalist supporters on the eve of the Orange "marching season", the tinder-box which Unionist politicians had been threatening would explode ever since the signing of the Anglo-Irish Agreement. He now started to do everything in his power to make sure it did just that.

The fuse would be lit in "the Protestant citadel" of Portadown, the grey North Armagh town whose Catholic Tunnel area had been barred to Orange marchers the previous summer at the instigation, Unionists claimed, of the Dublin Government. Now, in the wake of the Anglo-Irish Agreement, Portadown had become the most potent symbol of Dublin's power to prevent Loyalists marching their bands and parades through any area they chose. In the days before the 12 July parade in the town, which the RUC had ordered to be rerouted away from the Tunnel's main thoroughfare, Obins Street, Paisley screwed up the sectarian temperature to boiling point.

He called on Loyalists throughout the North to go in their thousands to Portadown to force a way through RUC lines to allow the local Orangemen to march. He fulminated about "facing up to the butchery of the RUC"; about taking on tanks with bare hands like Second World War freedom fighters, and dying for "the inalienable right to walk the roads of Ulster". In a remark that steered close to sedition he also urged RUC members to follow the example of the British Army mutineers at the Curragh in 1914 and resign rather than block the Portadown Loyalists.

The build-up of threats, the menace of Protestant mayhem was a familiar tactic. Paisley had been using it against successive governments and police chiefs for more than a quarter of a century, ever since the ban on an Orange march through the Catholic town of Dungiven back in 1959. He reinforced it with one of his well-tried "show of strength" stunts: several thousand Paisleyites drilled in the streets of Hillsborough in the middle of the night 30 hours before the Portadown parade.

This typical piece of sabre-rattling did the job. Throughout that week British ministers and civil servants had been telling journalists to expect a showdown at Portadown - one civil servant talked about "taking the Prods on". It was to be the much-promised confrontation with and symbolic defeat of militant Loyalism which would pave the way for an acceleration of the process set in motion by the Anglo-Irish Agreement.

Paisley's Hillsborough demonstration convinced the RUC Chief Constable Sir John Hermon that his force could not handle a wave of Loyalist violence at the same time as dealing with the IRA's undiminished campaign. The police had already been involved for over a week in negotiations with Orange Order and Official Unionist leaders to re-route the Portadown parade. On the eve of 12 July, the Chief Constable decided, with the approval of the Northern Ireland Secretary, Tom King, to allow the Orangemen to march along an even more populous Catholic street parallel to the Tunnel.

Unionist politicians were triumphant; Dublin and the SDLP outraged. The militant Loyalists on the streets, perhaps feeling cheated of the confrontation Paisley had promised them, unleashed a wave of attacks throughout Northern Ireland on Catholics, their churches and housing estates, as well as on the police guarding their areas. Over 165 policemen were injured in the week of the "Twelfth", and dozens of families, most of them Catholic, were forced to leave their homes. Three Catholics were shot dead in ten days by the UVF in North Belfast. The first Loyalist car-bomb for nearly a decade exploded outside a Catholic-owned restaurant in Castlewellan, County Down. Sixty masked Loyalists, some wearing combat uniforms, rampaged through a mainly Catholic estate in the village of Rasharkin in Ian Paisley's North Antrim constituency, smashing doors, windows and furniture with axes and cudgels.

Rev Ian Richard Kyle Paisley was not in Northern Ireland to witness the orgy of violence his call to arms had let loose. Two days after the "Twelfth" he had left for a fortnight's holiday abroad. He would go on to South Carolina for the four-yearly gathering of the World Congress of Fundamentalists at Bob Jones University.

He may have had no strategy to deal with the Anglo-Irish Agreement, but Paisley's tried and trusted tactic of bawling threats about Loyalist backlashes had worked very well for the moment. The British and the RUC had climbed down; their re-routing policy, the one tangible gain from five years of Anglo-Irish discussions, had been defied; and Catholics all over Northern Ireland were again being terrorised by Loyalist mobs. The leader of Protestant Ulster could go back to his family and his Bible content with a midsummer's work well done.

CHAPTER THIRTEEN

The Confederacy
of the Beast

When Jesus comes the dominating kingdoms in Europe will be the ten-toed
kingdom, the confederacy that's going to dominate Europe in the end time.
Ian Paisley, May 1984.

In 1984 the British Post Office issued a commemorative stamp to mark the second direct election to the European Economic Community's parliament at Strasbourg. The stamp used figures from ancient Greek mythology to celebrate the birth of European culture: it showed Europa, the daughter of the king of Tyre, being carried off by Zeus, in the shape of a bull, to the island of Crete. Here, according to the Greeks, Zeus resumed his human form and they conceived a son, Minos, the founder of Minoan, and thus European civilisation.

In East Belfast the figures on the stamp took on a startlingly different significance. On the Sunday before the election Ian Paisley, who had topped the local poll in the previous European election in 1979, delivered a sermon at his Martyrs Memorial church entitled "The Woman rides the Beast: a remarkable prophetic fulfillment'.

Europe was not the woman on the stamp, he informed the rapt congregation in his usual thunderous crescendo, but the animal on which she was riding. The woman was meant to represent something far more sinister to devout Bible-believing Protestants: she was none other than "the woman of Babylon - the bride of the antichrist, the Church of Rome herself".

In case his audience had failed to grasp the symbolism he underlined it in the language of immorality they understood only too well: "The woman is an unclean women. The woman is a brazen woman, because her garments are "see through" garments showing her naked breasts and naked legs. It is a whore that is upon the beast. The key to the stamp is the child, for this is the Madonna that is riding upon the beast".

The stamp's designer might protest that the baby represented Cupid, and the fish under them the Mediterranean sea between Lebanon and Crete. In Belfast they knew better. The Pope had made the Virgin Mary the Madonna of the Common Market, declared Paisley, and the fish, when it wasn't representing the fish's tail on the Pope's mitre, was the "trend of Paganism and Popery" which was "polluting the people of the world".

It was a message that found a ready echo in the minds of his listeners, weaned on Catholic conspiracies against Northern Ireland around every corner. But this one had a far deeper significance than just another Catholic and republican plot to undermine what Paisley called "the last bastion of Bible Protestantism in Europe". This sermon, like others they had heard in the previous month and before the 1979 election, was about nothing less than the end of the world and the "Second Coming" of Jesus Christ to earth.

For Paisley had taught his followers that the European Common Market was the final antechamber before the appearance of the antichrist, that terrible amalgam of Catholic pontiff and world dictator who the Bible had prophesied would usher in God's judgement on sinful mankind and the reappearance of Christ on earth.

To them, the biblical evidence for the imminent arrival of what they called the "end time" was unanswerable. This was despite the complicated and often downright contradictory nature of Paisley's explanation of it: in the past he had always steered clear of interpreting biblical prophecy, reluctantly admitting that it was one of his weaker suits. But in 1979 he had good political reasons for devoting a series of four sermons to the biblical significance of the Common Market.

In those sermons he went back to the Old Testament prophecies dating from the period when the people of Israel had been conquered and carried off into the land of Babylon. Daniel, one of their leaders, who had risen high in the service of the

Babylonian king, Nebuchadnezzar, had been called upon by him to interpret a particularly disturbing dream.

Nebuchadnezzar's dream was of a great image with a golden head, breasts and arms of silver, belly and thighs of brass, legs of iron, and feet partly of iron and partly of clay; and of a stone which struck the feet of the image and broke them into pieces. Daniel told him that the four parts of the image represented four present and future kingdoms, of declining powers, and that the last of these kingdoms would be the one represented by the feet and toes partly of iron and partly of clay. Daniel prophesied that God would destroy these kingdoms and set up an eternal dominion of his own.[1]

Later Daniel himself had a dream. It was of four macabre creatures coming up out of the sea, the last of them an all-devouring beast with great iron teeth, ten horns and an eleventh horn with a man's eyes and mouth. Once again, Daniel's interpretation was that these were four kings. The last of them would devour the whole earth, and its ten horns would also be kings, and the eleventh horn would be an all-powerful king who would set himself against God.[2]

Paisley's version of Daniel's prophecy had benefited from 25 centuries of hindsight. He taught that the four kingdoms in the dreams were the empires of Babylon, Medio-Persia, Greece and Rome. He concluded that "the toes of the image that Nebuchadnezzar saw, which grew out at the bottom of that Roman empire, being its final manifestation, represent ten kingdoms which will be in existence, with tremendous power in Europe, when the Lord Jesus Christ comes".

The ten-horned beast was another vision of the same ten European kingdoms, and the eleventh horn was the antichrist. In a huge interpretive leap he then claimed that the Common Market was the beginning of that ten-toed ten-horned kingdom, which would be smashed by the stone of Christ at his "Second Coming'.

So where did the Catholic Church come into all this? For that, said Paisley, turning the pages of the big black Bible in the Martyrs Memorial pulpit, one had to go to the last book of the New Testament, the Book of Revelation. Here he uncovered the ten-horned, ten-crowned beast again - and this time there was also a dragon which gave the beast its power, and the dragon, said Paisley, was the Devil.[3]

Four chapters further on, Paisley came upon the Catholic Church. Once again there was a beast, scarlet-coloured this time, with seven heads and ten horns. However this time there was also a woman sitting on the beast - "woman in Scripture is a type of the church, the wife of Israel, the bride of Christ", said Paisley.

This woman, according to Revelation, chapter 17, was a "great whore...with whom the kings of the earth have committed fornication"; she held a cup "full of abomination and filthiness of her fornication", and upon her forehead was written "MYSTERY, BABYLON THE GREAT, THE MOTHER OF HARLOTS AND ABOMINATIONS OF THE EARTH". The woman was "drunken with the blood of the saints and with the blood of the martyrs of Jesus".

Paisley was exultant:

Here we have a woman - not the true Church of Christ, but the church of the antichrist - this harlot woman. The Church of Christ is pure, the church of antichrist is impure; the Church of Christ is sober, the church of the antichrist is drunk with the blood of the martyrs of Jesus. Here we have the greatest indictment ever made of the Roman Catholic system. It was this chapter that opened the eyes of the Reformers to the real significance of Romanism - it's a chapter that's dodged by the evangelicals of our day.

The woman "riding upon the beast, who has spread herself and her influence and her control and her domination over the beast" was the Catholic Church, he said. And the EEC was the beast which she rode and controlled: the final ten-nation Babylonian empire which "ruined, fallen, corrupted and satanically-inspired man" had been planning to rebuild ever since the fall of "the first great ecumenical temple called Babel" in the Book of Genesis at the dawn of time.

For the less well-informed, Paisley spelled out the exact nature of the nightmare. There were nearly 10 million Catholics in Belgium, 51 million in France, six million in "William Prince of Orange's country", the Netherlands, 32 million in West Germany, 12 million in the UK, nearly three million in the "Southern Republic". All but a tiny fraction of the 54 million Italians, "the seat of the papacy", were Catholic. And now a welcoming hand was being stretched out to Catholic Spain,

Portugal and Greece - "the woman rides upon the beast", he intoned after each dramatic statistic.

"She's riding on the beast today", he shouted at his now spellbound congregation. "We're in the Common Market and there's a hundred million more Roman Catholics in the Common Market than Protestants, so we're in a tiny minority."

Unlike earlier and less shrewd millenarian preachers in the 1950s and 1960s, Paisley was not going be caught out by identifying the EEC in its existing form as the final ten-nation confederacy of biblical prophecy. By 1979, after all, it was already evident that the Community would eventually have more than ten members. Instead he emphasised that because the prophet saw a two-footed kingdom, part of clay and part of iron, this meant that five of the confederacy's "toes" would be from democratic Western Europe and five from the East, including Greece, Turkey and the Communist countries.

He forecast a merger between countries from the EEC, the non-EEC Western European countries and the Eastern Bloc Comecon countries. And of course the Catholic Church was intimately involved in this process: "Anybody who has been studying the tactics of Rome recently will see that Rome is moving away from close affiliation with the Western democracies, and especially with the USA, and is moving towards a greater alignment and affiliation with the Communist countries." He cited the visit of the Polish Pope to his home country, conveniently omitting to tell his followers that Pope John Paul II was the most anti-Communist pontiff since the fifties.

Behind the Pope was the Devil. "What holds the Common Market together?" Paisley asked his congregation rhetorically in 1984. "Satanic power." That was how so many "diverse nations with so many problems, so many difficulties, so many political, economic and military strains upon them can suddenly come together".

Since the EEC was still primarily an economic unit, Paisley was forced to search for an economic prophecy in the Bible to support his case, although this time he must have been stretching the credulity of the less impressionable even among his own followers. He turned to the little-known Old Testament prophet, Zechariah, and uncovered not only a woman - this time representing wickedness - but something called an "ephah".

"This ephah, of course, is a measurement", he assured his non-Hebrew speaking congregation. "And here we have this measurement impregnated with the imprint of the woman who is wickedness. So we have the tie-up between religious Rome and economic Rome".

Perhaps realising that even in Martyrs Memorial this sounded a little far-fetched, he returned to more familiar ground: "Isn't it interesting that the European Community of Nations came into being by the signing of the Treaty of Brussels? No, sir. The Treaty of Luxembourg, where the parliament sometimes meets? No, sir. The Treaty of Strasbourg, where the parliament building is for the Common Market? No, sir. Why?" he asks in a whisper pregnant with significance. "Because this Book's always right", he bellowed, gesturing with his Bible - "it was the signing of the Treaty of Rome - because the woman is in the measurement!" It was gobbledygook, a piece of pure theatre - except for the fact that the leading actor and the audience believed every word of it.[5]

What still needed to be explained was why Paisley wanted to take part in the Parliament of this evolving satanic confederacy. Ever since the 1960s he had been issuing dire warnings against becoming involved in the "greatest Roman Catholic super-state the world has ever known". Two leading Free Presbyterian ministers, John Douglas and Bert Cooke, who were the church's experts in prophecy, had confirmed after careful study that the Common Market was a fulfillment of the visions of Daniel and the Book of Revelation.

So it was not surprising that when Paisley first indicated his desire to run in the forthcoming European election, there was a fierce row in the church's governing body, the Presbytery. Paisley's three most senior lieutenants - Douglas, Cooke and John Wylie - spoke strongly against becoming involved in what the Bible had told them was a political expression of anti-Christianity and Popery.

The issue touched another raw nerve inside Free Presbyterianism: the fanatical application of Paisley's teaching of "separation" - that Free Presbyterians should have absolutely no dealings with any church or religious body which was tainted by contact with the World Council of Churches, with its belief in eventual unity with Roman Catholicism. Now suddenly he was proposing to become part of an institution, the European

Parliament, the creation of an anti-Christian confederacy which was totally dominated by members of the dreaded Roman Church itself. Such a volte-face was difficult to stomach.

However, Paisley the ambitious politician was determined to get his way. Northern Ireland would be treated as a single constituency in a European election, thus providing a heaven-sent opportunity for him to prove once and for all that he was the chosen political leader of the North's Protestants. At a secret meeting of the church's ruling Presbytery in early 1977 he used all his formidable powers of oratory and exhortation to bring his for once doubtful disciples round to his point of view.

And he succeeded. "In the end they would have said 'Paisley's a man of God, God has been with him, God has blessed him, God has used him. We can't understand it but we wouldn't want to hinder the work of God, we wouldn't want to stand in the servant of the Lord's way'", says one former minister.

The argument Paisley used at that meeting he later repeated from the pulpit: "When you come back to the Scriptures you find in every manifestation of the antichrist's kingdom, God has a witness. He never left himself without a voice". The message was that he, Ian Paisley from the Ravenhill Road, would be God's voice in the anti-Christian assembly in Strasbourg, "a firm, strong, unbending Protestant voice to raise the standard".

He likened himself to Daniel, who rose to become prime minister of the Babylonian state that had enslaved his people, but who went to the lion's den rather than stop worshipping his God. He invoked the spirits of the Protestant martyrs whose busts adorned his church walls against those pietistic souls who said he should have nothing to do with Europe - "They took a stand. They didn't chicken out, they didn't say it's none of our business, they didn't say 'let's conform' - they said 'let's fight in Jesus' name'."

The unmistakable implication was that he would be in Strasbourg fighting the cause of true Christianity. But he was also able to answer his critics by stressing, in a typically brazen piece of doubletalk, that it was a "political association" he was aiming to join, not a "religious fellowship" - "there are people I could associate with politically that I wouldn't touch with a barge-pole religiously".

However, for the final clinching argument Paisley invoked the Almighty. God himself had told him to go to Strasbourg "and sit among a lot of frog-eaters and snail-mongers", he told the congregation. Although he would far prefer "to have a nice home life and be a preacher in this church", if he did not go into Europe the battle for Ulster, for Britain and for Christianity would be lost. "As thou hast born witness in this city, so shalt thou bear witness in Rome also - that's the text God gave me". Not for the first time, he was modelling himself on St. Paul, "God's messenger". To the unquestioning minds of the Free Presbyterian faithful, long used to seeing their leader as "God's man for the hour", it was utterly convincing.

In June 1979 Paisley realised his goal. 170,000 Unionists voted for him, a staggering total which gave him the largest poll in Europe. Emboldened by this, he made the fighting, protesting start at Strasbourg his followers expected of him. When the Parliament opened in July he immediately involved himself in three dramatic public confrontations which made headlines all over Europe and marked him out for immediate notoriety. His was the very first voice heard in the new session. Even before its opening ceremony had commenced he was on his feet on a point of order to insist that the Union Jack outside the Parliament building was flying upside down, and to demand an assurance that this would never happen again.

The opening speech was by the assembly's oldest member, an 86-year-old Gaullist called Madame Weiss, who referred to the presence in the chamber of the grand-daughter of the "illustrious De Valera", praised Pope Urban II and Karl Marx and failed to mention the Protestant Reformation. This was too much for Paisley. As she finished he walked out and handed her a note protesting that Ulster Protestants associated the name of de Valera with "murder and blood which is still going on by the IRA".

The following day he went further. As the Taoiseach, Jack Lynch, opened his address as the incoming President of the EEC Council of Ministers with a few words in Irish, Paisley started heckling him: "In the name of Ulster's dead I indict you as harbouring their murderers", he shouted before being drowned out by the boos and jeers of his fellow MEPs. He stalked defiantly out of the chamber. Outside he told journalists that it had been the first opportunity ever for a Unionist politician to attack Lynch in person for allowing his country's territory "to be used to launch IRA attacks upon my people".

The leader of the French Gaullist group, Jacques Chirac, later to become his country's prime minister, said that Paisley should be suspended from the parliament if he continued to interrupt its proceedings. Paisley challenged the authorities to try to silence him - there was nothing he would like better, he said, keenly aware of how he could portray such a move in Belfast as the persecution of the champion of Ulster Protestantism.

As it was, his antics made for wonderfully dramatic headlines in Northern Ireland. To his followers it was confirmation of everything he had been saying in the previous months: the battle lines had been drawn between the anti-Christian, anti-British, anti-Ulster conspiracy in Europe and the outspoken leader of the continent's "last bastion of Bible Protestantism".

In Strasbourg, once the dust from that first outburst had been allowed to settle, the reality was somewhat different. It soon became apparent that the powerless EEC parliament, like James Prior's powerless Assembly at Stormont, was becoming a perfect forum for the most acceptable and attractive face of Ian Paisley: the intelligent, energetic, pragmatic politician.

He had already told his followers in Northern Ireland - those who were not let into the secret of the Common Market as the prelude to the end of the world - that his main purpose in going to Europe was to "milk the EEC cow dry before slitting its throat". Now, like the superb "parish pump" politician he could be, he started to use the EEC Parliament as a platform to air the real grievances of Northern Ireland as one of the Community's most underprivileged and neglected regions.

He was far more effective as a speaker in the chamber of the Parliament than his fellow Northern Ireland members, John Hume of the SDLP and John Taylor of the Official Unionists. The atmosphere, positively gentlemanly after the bullying cockpit of the House of Commons, suited his oratorical powers better. Although he had always been a master of the sharp retort, he did not like the hostility he provoked in the Commons, and was happier in the knowledge that he was unlikely to be interrupted.

One Dutch member who sat near him when he arrived, and who was accustomed to the equable temper of his own parliament, admitted that Paisley's early speeches "more or less terrified him", and he was never able to get used to the Ulsterman's "oratorical violence". The assembly's president once threatened to cut Paisley's microphone off if he did not wind up, to which he retorted, to loud laughter around the chamber, that he was not using the microphone.

One member Paisley was not able to intimidate was the unruly Donegal independent Fianna Fail MEP Neil Blaney. They regularly traded jibes and insults until Blaney's defeat in 1984 - Paisley's barbs usually having to do with the part played by Blaney and the Fianna Fail leader, Charles Haughey, in the 1970 arms trial.

He sat in the back row of the chamber with a small band of left-wing independents and Italian neo-Fascists who had chosen not to join one of the parliament's major groupings: the Socialists, the Christian Democrats, the European Democrats, the Gaullist-Fianna Fail group, the Communists or the Liberals.

He did little committee work, and none of the behind-the-scenes lobbying that Hume, a leading member of the parliament's largest group, the Socialists, was so expert at. Thus it was principally Hume's work which secured extra EEC help for Northern Ireland's farmers, money for Belfast housing, and the setting up of the Haagerup enquiry into the North's political problems.

However, Paisley's speeches, particularly those on farming matters, were carefully researched, well-laced with facts and figures and impressively delivered. This was partly due to his choice of two of the brightest of the new young crop of DUP graduates as his European assistants: firstly Jim Allister, a Ballymena barrister who would later become the party's chief whip; and from 1983 Nigel Dodds, a young Fermanagh customs officer's son who was a highly effective researcher with a first-class honours degree from Cambridge. It was a new experience for the mighty preacher to read speeches written for him by another person, but that was increasingly what he found himself doing with Dodds at his elbow.

The ranting ogre portrayed in the media and seen at the parliament's opening all but disappeared. There was rarely a mention of God or religion, let alone the kind of doom-laden bombast he indulged in from his pulpit. Only twice in seven years did he even mention the Pope: once to put down a motion, which was never debated, opposing John Paul II's 1982 visit to Britain; and secondly to warn that if there was ever a papal visit to the parliament he would stage a protest against it.

Instead he gained a reputation as an assiduous attender and energetic representative of his people. He was well-liked by the parliament's officials, whom he treated with consideration and courtesy. He rarely spoke on subjects which did not affect Northern Ireland. He was most effective when he spoke of the plight of Northern Ireland's farmers, the poverty and bad housing of Belfast, and what he called "the public scandal" of the British Treasury not passing on to Belfast funds received by the European Commission for use in Northern Ireland.

He could be flexible. He was a bitter critic of the Common Agriculture Policy, with its greater benefits to Southern Irish famers - whose government had successfully fought their corner while the British government had all but ignored their Northern counterparts. He vividly remembered the crack of one senior EEC agriculture official in Brussels that the Northern Ireland representatives were "perched on a piece of land with a bunch of guys getting 20 per cent more than you".

However, on several occasions he conceded that he and the Southern MEPs were speaking with a common voice on behalf of farmers throughout Ireland. He went out of his way to thank Southern members for their support on the Hume-inspired resolution on emergency housing for Belfast. In September 1985 both he and Taylor signed a Fianna Fail-initiated resolution on emergency aid for Irish farmers on both sides of the Border who had been badly hit by the previous summer's atrocious weather. He got on extremely well with Irish EEC Commissioner Richard Burke, a man who shared his deep conservatism on family and sexual matters, and twice invited him to Northern Ireland.

He dealt with other "non-contentious" issues in a similarly broadminded, pragmatic and occasionally even humorous manner. He joined Hume and Taylor to lobby the EEC Commission on behalf of Northern Ireland's small farmers, the homeless and the Belfast shipyard. Hume and he were in regular contact on economic matters: "You know where you stand with Paisley in Europe - he's up front, out in the open", says the SDLP leader.

When Paisley invited the German External Relations commissioner, a former trade union leader, to visit Northern Ireland to see the depressed state of its manmade fibres industry, he assembled an impressive array of local trade unionists to meet him. He defended Northern Ireland's tobacco industry, while pointing out that he himself was a convinced non-smoker. He strongly criticised the British government over leakages from the Sellafield nuclear waste plant.

During a debate in 1982 on European soccer he intervened to ask whether in the light of the Northern Ireland team's splendid performance in that year's World Cup his constituents should not get a pre-Christman bonus of cheap EEC butter. This won him laughter and applause from fellow members. Politicians everywhere appreciate a good political operator when they see one.

It was the first time many British and Southern Irish MEPs had seen the DUP leader in action, and they were impressed. No-one, for example, could ever accuse the left wing British Labour MEP Richard Balfe, a strong advocate of a united Ireland, of being on Paisley's wavelength. But to Balfe Paisley at Strasbourg is "an affable, friendly person, someone who argues cogently and well for the people of the North of Ireland. He very seldom attacks Catholics here. His speeches are well thought-out, well put together, with plenty of facts and very little in the way of ideology."

The Dublin Fine Gael MEP Mary Banotti is another whose view of Paisley has been strongly influenced by meeting him in Europe. He was very helpful to her when she started as a new member in 1984. "He can be very charming. He's a rather lonely figure - the only person you ever see him having dinner with is Nigel Dodds. But to many people he's 'sympatico'." She says that he has tailored his delivery to his European audience, and since the arrival in the assembly of the French neo-fascist Jean-Marie Le Pen and his "barking dogs" is no longer ever seen as the parliament's most outrageous extremist.

"There's a sneaking respect for him in Southern Ireland," adds her Fine Gael colleague Joe McCartin, who has several times had tea with Paisley and remembers him cheerfully agreeing to requests by groups of Southern visitors to be photographed with him. "There's a warmth, a humanity about the man. I think a lot of Irish people wish he would show his good side, which many of them believe he has."

The impression of many fellow-members was that he seemed to feel more at home chatting and bantering with Irish MEP's than with his British colleagues, the notable exception being the Northern Ireland born Conservative and evangelical lay preacher, Sir Fred Catherwood.

The story is told of John Hume introducing him to the then Irish Foreign Minister, Brian Lenihan, in the parliament's cafebar. Paisley was very polite: "Glad to meet you, sir", he said. There was a moment's awkward silence. "I wonder you wouldn't get this fellow off the devil's buttermilk," Paisley remarked, pointing at Hume's gin and tonic. Lenihan was nonplussed. "What Mr Paisley means is when are you going to buy him a drink", teased Hume. Lenihan reached into his pocket: "Would you like a drink, Dr Paisley?" "Not at all - I never touch the stuff", replied the DUP man. There was another pause. Paisley was not finished yet - he came back again: "But on second thoughts, since it's you that's buying, I'll have an orange, and a bitter one at that".

Hearing such tales it was perhaps not surprising that many in Dublin who should have known better - including politicians and commentators - made the mistake of thinking that the Paisley they saw in Strasbourg was a man they could do political business with back in Ireland. The truth was that the role of the constitutional politician he enjoyed playing so much in Europe was only one side of his character. It was allowed full rein only so long as it did not conflict with the uncompromising "not an inch" stand on the Britishness of Northern Ireland that his followers back home expected of him.

On the rare occasions the battle between Orange and Green reached the floor of the European parliament, Paisley did not disappoint them. When interrupted by Neil Blaney in the middle of a request to the President of the Commission to reaffirm that the EEC had no competence to discuss the constitution of Northern Ireland, Paisley snapped at him, "Thank God we are not under your crowd - a crowd of murderers".

The report by the Danish liberal MEP, Niels Haagerup, into the political affairs of Northern Ireland - which dismissed the possibility of a united Ireland for the foreseeable future and advocated another attempt at power-sharing - Paisley called an "ill-informed, biased piece of Republican propaganda." His most frequent intervention, even during debates on totally unrelated subjects like East-West relations, was still to denounce the Irish government's failure to extradite suspected Provisional IRA killers to the North.

Only once did the parliament's deliberations reach Irish soil, in

September 1984, and Paisley chose the occasion to reassert his familiar "mad mullah" persona. It was time for some histrionics to keep the backwoodsmen at home happy.

Three months previously he had won an astonishing 230,000 votes to top the poll by nearly 80,000 votes in the second election to the Strasbourg parliament. He had fought a clever three-headed campaign, combining a call to smash the growing electoral threat from Sinn Fein; a claim that he was the only man to defend Northern Ireland against the economic and political depredations of the "Eurocrats"; and a set of extravagant anti-Catholic advertisements in carefully selected Protestant-read local newspapers.

Now, with the memories of that victory still fresh in his supporters' minds, he staged, largely for their benefit, another mock confrontation with the enemies of Protestant Ulster. This time the clash would be with Irish Foreign Minister, Peter Barry, a man who was soon to become synonymous in Unionist eyes with creeping Irish reunification, and it would take place in the lion's den itself, in the Irish capital. The occasion was a meeting of the European Parliament's political affairs committee. After all, he told an interviewer before setting off, if he could go to Rome to make a stand for the people of Northern Ireland, he could go to Dublin.

It was Paisley at his most theatrical. First came a high speed motorcade through the Irish countryside with Garda Siochana outriders. In Dublin Castle a discussion about Central America was interrupted when he accused Barry of "unashamedly" using his position as president of the EEC Council of Ministers to denigrate the security forces in Northern Ireland. He was rebuked by the Italian Christian Democrat chairman - no better man for the folks back home - for breaking the committee's confidentiality by commenting on its proceedings to the press outside. Before heading north again, he accused the chairman of belonging to a party well known for its "skulduggery" and its association with the Vatican Bank scandal.

The newspapers' photographs the next day showed an angry Paisley snarling into a barrage of microphones. The lion of Ballymena was out for show; the lamb of Strasbourg had disappeared. It was a timely reminder where his heart had always lain.

This was no democratic politician, after all, but God's man for

Ulster. Three months earlier, in a sermon at Martyrs Memorial, he claimed to have been the only Northern Ireland MEP to vote against a "monstrous plan" to do away with the veto of individual governments over EEC decisions which, he said, would have made them subject to the two-thirds Catholic majority in Europe.

"That's why God sent me to Europe", he reminded the faithful, and perhaps the odd doubting disciple who might have heard that his bark at Strasbourg had lost a good deal of its bite. "I wasn't sent by votes. I was sent by God to stand up and be counted. That's why I'll be going back to Europe, irrespective of what anybody says - because my job is not yet completed in that parliament".

And what was that job? He had given a clue in an apocalyptic climax to a sermon before the 1979 election. He did not believe God was going to hand Britain or Ulster over to popery, he said. "The God of the martyrs still hears their prayer . . . and they say 'Avenge our blood upon the great harlot system of Babylon and upon this conspiracy of evil in Europe', and the prayers of the martyred dead will be heard and He who is the God of truth and the God of immaculate purity will answer those prayers and give to our nation a great deliverance".[5]

CHAPTER FOURTEEN

A Man out of Season

*I cannot help thinking of him as a man of another century, born as it were
"out of due season". Somehow Ian Paisley seems to belong to the
Age of the Reformation.*
Bob Jones Jnr, in the foreword to Paisley's
"Exposition of the Epistle to the Romans".

The DUP's tenth anniversary dinner was held in November 1981 at a temperance hotel outside the village of Broughshane, four miles from Ballymena in the County Antrim heartland of rural Paisleyism. Three hundred party members sat down to a feast of wholesome plain food washed down with flagons of orange squash.

When the tables were cleared and the after-dinner speeches over, the faithful were treated to some very special after-dinner entertainment. Paisley was presented with a handsome "captain's chair" in recognition of ten years of inspired and unchallenged stewardship. Fourteen-year-old Ian Paisley junior played bass guitar in an evangelical group called The Firmaments. And Sam Houston, a famous 'saved' alcoholic with a powerful tenor voice, contributed some resounding old-fashioned hymns.

Then it was time for the highlight of the evening: a DUP version of the popular television quiz game, "Mr. and Mrs.", in which a husband and wife take turns answering intimate questions about their partner, who is usually locked away in a sound-proofed booth. If both give identical answers to the questions, they win a handsome prize.

The DUP's "Mr. and Mrs." were, of course, Ian and Eileen Paisley, and the show was compered by Peter Robinson. As the audience whispered in delighted anticipation, Ian took the stand while Eileen was banished out of earshot to the nether regions of the hotel. "When did you first hold hands with Eileen? On your first date, the second or the third?" Robinson asked, wearing a grin that was close to a smirk. The women in the room started to giggle. "When did you first cuddle her?" The excitement in the room rose an octave. "When did you first kiss her?" The giggles became near-hysterical squeals. They were an eloquent testimony to a rarely mentioned quality which Paisley has in abundance and which those under him, from Robinson downwards, patently lack. Ian Paisley has sex-appeal.

The DUP leader also has a sense of humour, unlike most of his subordinates. Peter Robinson's idea of a joke was his chilling lament that power cuts during the March 1986 one-day Loyalist strike would make it impossible to send Margaret Thatcher to the electric chair. Paisley, on the other hand, is a master of the quick retort flung across a parliamentary chamber or election platform, and his ability to throw back his head in a great guffaw of laughter is one of his most attractive qualities.

He uses his humour to great effect from the pulpit. Once, when trying to encourage more men to come to the Friday night prayer meetings at Martyrs Memorial, he urged wives to invite their husbands to come out and look at the stars, and then to rush back and lock the door, announcing that they would not be let in until after the prayer meeting. "He will come back refreshed and you will have a night together like you've not had for a long time," he promised the delighted congregation. Latecomers are favourite targets: at one service he called out to a woman with a flowery hat trying to get into a crowded and soberly-dressed pew: "Tell the two crows to move up and let the peacock in."

His wit is not only quick, it is often barbed as well, especially if someone tries to joke about his faith or church. The story is told that on one occasion he and Gerry Fitt met on the way to Westminster after a 1981 assassination attempt on the Pope in the Philippines. Fitt remarked that he had not known there were any Free Presbyterians in the Philippines. If there had been, countered Paisley in a flash, they would have done the job a lot more efficiently.

With friends and allies Paisley can be a most likable and charming companion. "There's a breadth to his personality, he really is a big man," says one Official Unionist politician. "He is capable of going from being brutal and vicious to being your friend. And when you're his friend all else - past rivalries and differences - go out the window. The problem with the small men round him is that they're not capable of that. He is capable of being extremely warm, humorous and kindly. When he turns on you he can be as nasty as they come, but at least he is human."

Paisley's obvious warmth and concern for ordinary people have always set him apart from the ordinary run of Unionist politicians. "I found he took an interest in you as a person," says former DUP finance officer Wallace Thompson. "He took more interest in me than Peter Robinson. He was more of a father-figure - he was interested in your family and never forgot what you told him about them." This, when combined with his humour, "always made him more an Irish than a British figure, someone with the humanity and hearty laugh of a Protestant Irishman."

The same qualities make Paisley a conscientious worker on behalf of his North Antrim constituents, Catholic as well as Protestant. He has a reputation for turning up at all times of the day and night to deal with their complaints and problems. He has taken up the cause of local Catholics like the eel fishermen of Lough Neagh and the tiny and long-neglected population of Rathlin Island off the North Antrim coast.

One islander recalled how, after his brother had been drowned trying to get a boat to the mainland, Paisley, then on his way back from Strasbourg, phoned from London airport to ask if he could be of any assistance. The same man said that if some old lady told him that her lavatory was not flushing, the lavatory would be fixed immediately and on his next visit to the island Paisley would remember her name and inquire about it. "And he never takes any notes. He never brings a notebook. He's the only politician who arrives without a briefcase. He brings a Bible and that's all."

Paisley cites his concern for the less than two dozen Catholic voters of Rathlin as an example of his even-handedness, and he has been a regular visitor to the island at election time. It was not an easy place to get to. Former DUP man Clifford Smyth has vivid memories of one election crossing in the early seventies:

> They had this wee flat-bottomed boat that wasn't designed for the open sea at all. It had been bought for pottering around on the north coast. A local councillor from Rasharkin or

somewhere had this boat and he was going to take us ove
And Paisley doesn't go anywhere on his own - there was
coterie of his supporters along. So we crowded into the bo
and set out for Rathlin. The journey became just dreadfu
The seas mounted up and the mists came down. But Paisle
was in his element. He stood at the front of the boat an
recited to us hymns from seafaring books about 40 yea
before the mast. He created this image of himself as the se
captain braving the elements. He really lived it out.

When they arrived on the island, Paisley the inspiration
leader gave way to Paisley the man of the people.

Everybody was crammed into this little Volkswagen beet
and somebody got a tractor and away we all went all round th
island. "When we came back to one of the wee shops by th
harbour we were given a feed of mashed potato and corne
beef. All the residents were around regaling Paisley wit
Rathlin's problems - apparently no-one had heard of th
island up to that point. But his bonhomie and his charm - th
side of his character which even his enemies find appealin
and hard to come to terms with - all this came out. And ther
he was surrounded by people, the vast majority of whom wer
Roman Catholics. And they all talked away with their bi
mugs of tea and ate their corned beef and mash. And then w
got back into the boat and missed the evening rally. My wif
thought we had been murdered by Republican elements an
was nearly going for the police.

Rathlin and Strasbourg, which in their different ways are bot
beyond the scrutiny of his Loyalist constituency, are among th
few places where Paisley allows himself to appear fair-minde
and non-sectarian in public. He knows that elsewhere and at a
costs he must keep up his hard-line image. In private he can als
show his reasonable side. After Austin Currie squatted in
council house in Caledon, Co. Tyrone in 1968 to protest at i
allocation to a young Protestant woman rather than to
homeless Catholic family, one Free Presbyterian remember
Paisley commenting: "Some of those boys do stupid things
imagine giving a three-bedroomed house to a single girl an
families on the waiting list." Yet, as he told Bernadette Devlin a

celebrated meeting later that year, ultimately he "would rather be British than fair".

In his own comfortable home in East Belfast he is the loving husband and devoted and surprisingly tolerant father. All those who know him are agreed on one thing. He dotes on his wife Eileen and their five children: Sharon, 29, Rhonda, 27, Cherith, 20, and the 19-year-old twins, Ian and Kyle.

None of his children have broken out of their father's religious and political mould. Sharon is married to an East Belfast engineer who is an active Free Presbyterian. Rhonda shocked some straitlaced souls by opting to study art at Bob Jones University and working briefly as a commercial artist. However she then returned to the fold as a Free Presbyterian youth worker, trying to convert the punks, skinheads and glue-sniffing and cider-drinking teenagers "hanging out" in the centre of Belfast. In 1985 she became a DUP councillor and in the following year the city's acting lady mayoress. She is also writing her father's official biography.

Cherith edits her father's magazine, the *Protestant Bluprint*. Ian junior is studying history and politics at Queen's University, and doubles as press officer of the DUP's youth wing and chairman of its Belfast branch. He is obviously being groomed by his father for a political career. His brother Kyle completes the equation: he is studying to be a Free Presbyterian minister at Whitefield College. The Paisley dynasty will live on, at least into another generation.

The young Paisleys, however, have always been allowed a surprising amount of freedom of expression within the strict limits imposed by a puritan and Bible-based upbringing. Like the children of most Northern evangelical Protestants, they were never allowed out to play on Sundays, spending it going to church services and Sunday school in the morning, afternoon and evening. Unlike many rural Free Presbyterian children, though, they were allowed to dress, wear their hair, and choose their careers without overt interference from their parents. The result is that they do not always conform to the Free Presbyterian stereotype. "The typical young Free Presbyterian is plain-faced, wears no make-up, and dresses very plainly, whereas Paisley's children dress fashionably, the girls have their hair styled and Rhonda is an artist," notes Wallace Thompson.

The matronly Eileen, holding court among the teacups, cake

trays and old-fashioned highly polished furniture of her larg
suburban house, fits more closely to everyone's idea of a Fre
Presbyterian wife and mother. But it was not always so. Whe
the policemen came to arrest her husband in 1966 she curse
them angrily as Terence O'Neill's hirelings, and in the month
afterwards overcame her youthful shyness to lead a barnstormin
protest campaign throughout rural Northern Ireland and to stan
for Belfast City Council. She exerts considerable influence ove
her husband. Paisley freely admits that she is "the power behin
the throne". He calls her "the Boss" and refers to himself i
public as "my wife's husband". When he is away from home, say
Wallace Thompson, she is never far from his thoughts. "I mus
ring Mammy," he would say at the end of a busy day.

With his family, he also shows two contradictory traits rarel
seen by the outside world: his insecurity and generosity wit
money. "Ian came up the hard way and he was alway
determined that his family wouldn't," says one former Fre
Presbyterian. "He would feel he should hold onto money and d
the wisest thing with it. I think it likely he would hav
investments - Bob Jones would be a pretty shrewd advisor to hir
on this." On the other hand he can be generous to the point c
gullibility, a soft touch for clever charlatans with a hard-luc
story. When people reproach him for this, he says he prefers t
be taken in than to become hard: "I just pray that God will kee
me sweet. Keep me sweet, Lord - I pray that every day".

Sweetness is probably the last quality most people who hav
known the public Paisley would ascribe to him. His person
insecurity, on the other hand, is an important part of hi
character. "I've always thought this was the key to his rappor
with the more extreme Protestants. His personal insecurit
matches their political insecurity," said one politician in 198C
"Remember him in the early days. He got rid of a whole string o
harmless critters who were his lieutenants because he was afrai
of any of them getting to be his rivals."

Ironically he is relatively unconcerned by the wall of securit
round his home, the policemen who travel everywhere with hir
and the anonymous threats to his life, except for their effect o
his family. It is on his irregular visits to Brussels, where he is me
off the plane by machine-gun toting policemen, that he feels h
life is in most danger, because of what he claims is the stupidit
and inefficiency of the Belgian authorities.

One manifestation of both his insecurity and his huge egotism is an insatiable thirst for publicity and adulation. It is one of the few weaknesses he admits to. In his younger days he would avidly peruse the local papers looking for references to his speeches, and would count the lines in reports on his activities. Fellow Unionist politicians say that in the 70s it was difficult to have a private conversation with him without its choicest passages being released to the press. He threw tantrums, made outrageous statements and leaked other politicians' ideas to reporters in order to grab the headlines. He admitted as much when reproached for his behaviour by his Unionist allies, and told close friends that it was a failing he found difficult to control.

His insecurity emerged in an extraordinary fashion at the most triumphant moment of his whole political career, the announcement of his overwhelming victory in the 1984 European election. As his 230,000 votes were chalked up on the blackboard in Belfast's City Hall, the undisputed leader of Northern Ireland's Protestants devoted the greater part of his 20-minute victory speech to a blistering attack on the BBC's political correspondent, Brian Walker, who had earned his ire by mimicking him on radio. The totally inappropriate vehemence of his outburst stunned even sympathetic Unionist onlookers.

Such paranoia, when coupled with his ruthless drive for self-aggrandisement, has spelled disaster for any potential alternative leader of Loyalism. And he has another weapon in his armoury: his dog-collar. "In a sense the Reverend Paisley concealed Paisley's political drive," remembers Clifford Smyth. "You don't expect a minister of religion to act in a ruthless kind of a way, a driving for power kind of a way, and that's part of the difficulty in dealing with him. You don't immediately associate with him those qualities which you would accept in many an ordinary politician."

With insecurity and ruthlessness goes deviousness and cunning. When there are disputes during meetings of the Free Presbyterian Church's ruling presbytery, says former elder Richard Reid, Paisley lets his lieutenants - Foster, Cairns, Cooke and Douglas - lead the attack. "He plays the fly fellow, letting the ball roll back and forth, until at the end of the day he can choose which side is the most beneficial for him. Once he speaks, all the rest of them close up."

The Free Presbyterian moderator is also a master of the half-truth. One former church member remembers him illustrating a lesson in dissimulation by holding up a glass wrapped in a napkin and boasting that no-one could accuse him of holding the glass itself.

Scores of antagonists have found to their cost that he is just as good at using the same kind of innuendo and unprovable charge against others. An associate from his National Union of Protestants days tells why from a very early stage people would shy away from taking on Paisley when he issued his regular challenges to public debate:

Instead of answering you on the issue, he twists the argument round to you as a person. Even if I knew that you were right and he was wrong, I'd still warn you against debating with him. He would say "Who is this fellow? I must ask So and So about him." And he'd ask that person "Does he drink?" "Oh, an odd time". "Does he belong to any clubs or organisations?" "Yes, he's a member of Such and Such golf club." "That's the golf club where Father So and So is a member?" "That's right." "What else do you know about him - does he go out with women?" "He doesn't mind the odd night out." Then the debate comes up, and you're debating something of a political nature that you have challenged him on. Does he answer your question? Not on your life. He says: "Who is this man? He plays golf with Father So and So, the priest that drinks in the pub owned by Paddy Such and Such." He attacks you on everything he has heard about you, but the one thing he doesn't do is answer your question. The crowd is clapping and cheering. They are Protestants, Loyalists. They want nothing to do with pubs, nothing to do with priests, or with a man who is associated with pubs and priests. You come out disgusted because he never answered the question. But the crowd goes home saying Ian wiped the floor with you. That is the problem with debating Paisley.

The ferocity of his temper is legendary. "He was so irascible. At the slightest provocation he would lose the rag, shouting and yelling and thumping the table in a closely confined room so that not only could you hear the volume through your ears, you could feel it in the pit of the stomach," recalls David Trimble from the days when they worked together in the UUUC coalition.

Wallace Thompson has similar memories: "He was very easily made angry if things weren't going right. He used to eat the face off the wee secretary girl over at Martyrs Memorial. I used to feel very sorry for her. If there was a crossed line or a wrong number it was her fault, not the system's. Everyone took it from him."

Everyone took it from him, that is, except Peter Robinson. "Peter tells the story how he challenged him," remembers Thompson. "Ian could get very angry with you, very gruff and aggressive, demanding that you give in to him. But if you fought back he would become as soft as a youngster and would become very apologetic and apologise to you for days afterwards. Peter was prepared to push - that's what got him where he is now. Jim Allister took him on as well. The result was that Paisley respected and admired them. I remember Peter telling me 'You go forward with your own ideas and don't just meekly stand and accept what he says, you'll stand in higher esteem with him.'"

Paisley cannot tolerate weakness - physical, moral or political - in those around him. "Never admit you're wrong," he told Alan Cairns the first time he went out with him as his assistant, "it's a sign of weakness." He knows only too well that his strength in Unionist eyes lies in his apparently unwavering resolution.

His obsession with strength is partly based on his own personal experience of physical weakness. He had been a sickly young man in his twenties, and at one point a doctor told him he would be dead by the time he was 30 if he went on at the pace he was living. But his physical powers seemed to grow as the demands on him increased, and he expected the same tireless 16-18 hour a day commitment from his subordinates.

The rumours about his mental health when he first went into politics were put about by his political enemies in order to discredit him: a minister in the Chichester-Clark government has admitted to the authors that they were started on the basis of Paisley's frequent visits to the clinic of his friends, the Nesbitts. He dislikes sickbeds, and swears by the herbal remedies of a Newtownards-based company called Scrabo Health Products, which regularly advertised such exotica as Yellow Puccoon - "invaluable for stomach, bowels, catarrh, colic, gall-bladder and many more diseases" - in the pages of the *Protestant Telegraph*.

A non-smoker and non-drinker, his only indulgence is food. He has an enormous appetite, consuming Chinese specialities and Indian curries in London or "tarte flambée" in Strasbourg with as much relish as the huge steaks he loves at home or the solid "meat and two veg." he gets in the rural Ulster farmhouses he visits. During summer election campaigns he drinks Coca-Cola by the crateful. At 60, his weight is starting to become a problem, and he tries belatedly to keep his digestion in order by breakfasting on prunes and glasses of hot water spiced with vinegar.

He rarely takes a day off, and often preaches up to four times on Sundays in different parts of Northern Ireland. Friends say that when he is under pressure he will go away and pray for 20 minutes and come back totally refreshed. His Sunday sermons at Martyrs Memorial have the same effect on him. For non-spiritual relaxation he collects books. From childhood he has been a voracious reader of Protestant church history and martyrology. His favourite secular writers are Kipling, Carlyle and J. M. Barrie. Like UDA leader Andy Tyrie, he has Kipling's poem "If" pinned up on the wall of his office.

He can be superstitious. At one point in the early 1970s he took ill with a painful five-headed carbuncle, which one wit at Martyrs Memorial immediately dubbed the "Calvinistic carbuncle" after the five theological principles of Calvinism. He had been told a short time earlier by a clairvoyant that he was soon going to die, and he was so convinced by this that he summoned David McIlveen to prepare him for taking over the mantle of power at the East Belfast church.

That episode was quickly forgotten, and he went back to confidently predicting that God would grant him a long life. "I am immortal until my work is done," he told a reporter at the opening of his Coragarry church in Monaghan in May 1975. "When you hear I have gone, naturally, in an accident or assassinated, you will know that I did not go one second before God's time. When the weapons of war are unleashed, when storms are gathering, when the night is dark, I have got peace."

His absolute confidence in himself is one of Paisley's most striking attributes. When he prays he is less than humble - he requests God to do great things for the Free Presbyterian Church because of its proven record of faith and devotion. He tries to inspire the same confidence in his congregation by making vainglorious claims about the parallels between the church of Ian Paisley and the church of Jesus Christ: "They do not recognise our imperial royalty as they did not recognise the imperial royalty of our Master. For if the princes of the world had known they would not have crucified the Lord of Glory. Some day, however, our imperial royalty will be manifested before heaven, earth and hell," he told them in one of his prison messages in 1966.

Some disillusioned former associates accuse him of veering towards blasphemy. "He says that if you do something wrong you put it under the Blood of Christ," says one colleague from the early days. "It's by the Blood of Christ that we are forgiven our sins - that to me is a very vital truth. But to come to me and thump me on the back, as Ian did dozens of times when I criticized him, and say 'put it under the Blood of Christ, brother' - that's bordering on blasphemy. But the average Shankill Road Christian likes that sort of thing."

He is justly famous as one of Europe's greatest orators. As a boy he practised projecting his voice in the Mourne Mountains above his parents' summer house in South Down. He has taken to heart the lesson taught by one of his earliest heroes, the Presbyterian preacher W. P. Nicholson, that a minister must become the absolute master of his congregation. He starts every service on a note of confidence and optimism: "I believe great things are coming in this church. I feel it happening in myself," is a typical line.

He asks his congregations not to ask questions, but to trust him, to trust God, to make an act of faith and become "saved". It is an emotional and uncomplicated message guaranteed to appeal to the anti-intellectual instincts of his fundamentalist flock. He puts it over in the plain, straightforward language they feel comfortable with, adapting it to the colloquialisms of whatever part of Northern Ireland he happens to speaking in. If necessary, he can underline his authority by throwing in a little scholarship, a reference to the original Hebrew or some arcane work of theology. He uses alliteration and eye-catching sermon titles to great effect, and is a strong believer in the significance of numerology in interpreting the Bible.

He uses the same techniques in his sermons as in his political speeches. In the latter he pays terrific attention to dramatic detail: the latest leak of information from his RUC sources, the latest accusation of treachery by a Unionist rival. The bigger questions of how to achieve peace and political stability, or where his strategy is leading Northern Ireland, are left unanswered. Similarly he devotes endless sermons to obscure biblical and theological themes such as the significance of the hem of Christ's garment or the mechanics of dead people coming back to life on God's judgement day.

With his intimate knowledge of the vulnerable points in the Northern Protestant psyche, he may mention the Treaty of Rome or the World Council of Churches and allow his congregation's fevered imaginations to conjure up dark conspiracies against all they hold most dear. Everything is left unspecific, mysterious, threatening, with the implication that only he has the key to defeating these multifarious terrors. He devotes large parts of his sermons and announcements to the state of Ulster Protestantism, lashing out at its enemies, political and religious, and recounting humorous and self-promoting stories of his battles on its behalf. He always emerges as the victor, portraying his adversaries more often than not as outmanoeuvred fools.

His heroes are the Protestant rebels of the past: Richard Cameron, the forgotten leader of the Scottish Covenanters, who took up arms against the papal-backed monarchy of James II in the years before the arrival of William of Orange, is a favourite figure. "There is in my heart a wonderful affinity with Richard Cameron," he says in one sermon. The Covenanters were "bold, courageous, strong men…these were not the putty paper men of the 20th century - these were the rugged men of the Reformation." "He never tells them that the Covenanters were defeated," points out one former Free Presbyterian.

His greatest hero, though, is Cromwell: puritan, regicide, dictator and scourge of the Catholic Irish. He has taken the English Civil War leader as his model "because of his rise from obscurity to prominence through rigid adherence to his religious and political conviction." He tells his congregation: "Thank God for Oliver Cromwell! I never go into the House of Commons but I do give his statue a salute and say 'I wish you were down in that parliament today with that sword. I tell you there are a lot of fellows down there you could decap'."

He has a whole pantheon of religious exemplars. As a child he pored over the biblical exploits of men like Moses and David, Samson and Daniel, and often uses the intervention of Old Testament prophets into politics as a rationale for his own political involvement. The Old Testament world of "men of

God" fighting men who were the instruments of evil and corruption was perfectly suited to the black and white, "Christian versus unbeliever" faith he was brought up in.

The Protestant luminaries and martyrs who have given their name to his East Belfast church are his second great reference group. They begin with Luther, Calvin, John Knox and the 16th century English Protestant martyrs. He admires the great popular preachers of the 18th and 19th centuries: John Wesley, the outspoken Baptist evangelist Harold Spurgeon, and George Whitefield - in Paisley's eyes the greatest of them all, who in 34 years preached over 18,000 sermons in Britain, America and the colonies.

From 19th and 20th century Ulster Paisley takes three models: the Presbyterian Tory, Henry Cooke; the maverick Presbyterian preacher W. P. Nicholson and the Unionist politician Sir Edward Carson. He is intensely conscious of the semi-magical quality of Carson's name among the Loyalist faithful. He quotes him endlessly. "In his early Protestant Unionist days he used to wear the same kind of hat as Lord Carson," recalls one associate from the 1950s. "And all his speeches were based on what either Carson or that Presbyterian 'black man' Cooke used to say."

He does not change. At the huge "Ulster Says No" rally in Belfast after the Anglo-Irish Agreement, he wore an overcoat with a velvet collar, exactly like that favoured by Carson. And a portrait of the hero of Unionism, his jaw set in defiance, hangs in the DUP leader's dining-room.

"He is always copying somebody from history," says one former Free Presbyterian. "He had a bonfire and burned Professor Davey's books. He was copying someone. Did Luther do that? That kind of gesture is not something he thinks up. He has read about it somewhere and does it to show that he is still carrying the torch for the Protestant Reformers. It's exactly the same in politics."

Paisley's talent for dressing up in the personalities of the great men of the past is the most striking and theatrical element in his style of leadership. Allied to it is the real fear he instils in his followers. A former church secretary of Martyrs Memorial confessed to friends that every time he went into a meeting intending to take issue with Paisley over something, he became paralysed by fright and said nothing. "I know people who idolised him, and wanted to ask him something, but didn't dare -

I can't imagine that people are even that afraid of the Pope," says another former Martyrs Memorial member.

He has other more positive leadership qualities. His huge physical presence and energy, his appetite for non-stop work, his near-photographic memory, his ability quickly to grasp a complicated brief. "I reckon Paisley is a guy who if he had been about ten per cent less extreme, and had a better way of dealing with his own supporters, would have been the kind of natural-born leader to whom all sections of the community in Northern Ireland could have turned," says one former Official Unionist politician. "He's got all the qualities: charisma, popular appeal, a brilliant mind. You could hand him a sheet of paper, for example on a complex subject like agricultural subsidies, and he could grasp the whole thing very quickly. That's the kind of quality a minister needs to be able to stand at the dispatch box and argue his case."

Paisley has sought political power but always shirked from exercising it. The price of minsterial office - flexibility, compromise, reasonableness - has always been too high. Now it is too late, despite his associates' claims that as he mellows slightly with age he wants to leave something other than chaos behind him.

Even Paisley's claim to be a democrat is riddled with contradictions and hypocrisy. He has been known to concede - for example to the U.S.-based academic Padraig O'Malley in 1981 - that he would accept a united Ireland if 51 per cent of the people of the North voted for it. It is a pledge that is easily made, because it will never have to be honoured in his lifetime.

The real hollowness of his commitment to democracy is shown in the way he has run both his church and party - at least until the rise of Peter Robinson - as the fiefdoms of an old-fashioned autocrat. And for all his talk about liberty, the old Calvinist authoritarianism is never far below the surface. It shows in the treatment he and his followers mete out to those who disagree with them: they demand the right to stage violently provocative marches through Catholic areas; they close the leisure facilities on Sundays in towns they control; they censor art exhibitions and school booklists; they beat up journalists and hecklers at their meetings, while demanding the right to stage abusive pickets at those of their opponents.

One disillusioned former Free Presbyterian says he is less

worried by a united Ireland than by "an independent Ulster with Paisley as political supremo", which he says could lead to "churches which did not conform to Free Presbyterianism being threatened". Another dissident goes even further: "If Paisley took over, people like me would be liquidated," he says bitterly.

Such concerns, however, rarely cross the minds of the Paisleyite faithful. They worry about one thing and one thing only: being swallowed up by a Rome-dominated Gaelic-speaking Fenian republic. "Hell is real to many of these people," comments one distinguished Northern Irish commentator from a Protestant background, "it is a united Ireland". Paisley feeds this by constantly referring in his speeches to what he calls the "genocide" and "annihilation" of the Protestants in the Republic of Ireland: the reduction of their numbers from around 10 per cent of the population at the time of independence to just over 3 per cent now.

One of Paisley's greatest strengths is his intimate knowledge of the peculiarly politico-religious paranoia of Loyalism. He is as skilful as any fanatical Muslim leader in whipping it up in his people. And his methods are similar. "He has brainwashed them into believing that protecting Ulster is a holy crusade," says one prominent ex-follower. "They are fighting for God, and God's a Protestant and an Orangeman, as everyone knows, and so he must want Ulster to stay as it is. Anybody who says anything else is the enemy."

He understands those gut feelings, based in the racist belief that Ulster Protestants are inherently superior to Irish Catholics, because he shares them. Very occasionally he lets his own real feelings slip in public. In one July 1980 sermon, emphasising that the SDLP and the South's political leaders shared the common goal of a united Ireland, he went on: "And why should they not? They are all pigs from the same sow, as we say in North Antrim."

Ian Paisley is a hugely contradictory figure. He is a Christian minister who incites religious hatred and threatens bloody civil war. He is a constitutional politician who leads coat-trailing sectarian street protests. He claims to believe in democracy yet he runs his church like a Protestant pope and his party like a medieval despot. He is a European politician who denounces the EEC as a Roman Catholic plot at home while abroad he works hard to make it serve the people he represents. He is an obsessive publicity-seeker who has instilled into his followers a deep paranoia about the media. He is a warm and humorous companion who can turn almost without warning into a ranting bully. He is a sober Scottish Calvinist on his knees, and a roaring American fundamentalist in the pulpit.

Paisley is now an elderly man. Associates say he is prone to bouts of tiredness. At times during the crisis sparked off by the Anglo-Irish Agreement he has shown signs of losing his previously unerring feel for the instincts of the ordinary Loyalist. Yet he knows that his stubborn refusal to change remains the key to his political survival, in the same way that his leadership of the resistance to change was the key to his original rise from backstreet obscurity. "He won't change now," says an Official Unionist who knows him well. "He's not going to open up any new ground in his lifetime. You have seen all there is to see of him. There are no surprises left."

CHAPTER FIFTEEN

A Prophet Among His Own People

*You've got to take your stand, you know. There's not going to be any compromise.
If you compromise God will curse you. If you stand, God will bless you . . .
why God has blessed this preacher and this church.*
Ian Paisley in a sermon "The EEC prophetically considered", 1979.

A deep and immutable anti-Catholicism among a large section of
Northern Ireland's Protestant population lies at the very heart of
the story of Ian Paisley's remarkable rise from street preacher to
political leader.

Its roots go deep into Irish history, back to the dispossession of
Catholic natives by 17th Century Scottish and English colonists.
It has traditionally expressed itself in insecurity, bigotry, fear and
hostility towards all manifestations of Catholicism, political as
well as religious. In the 19th Century, Ulster Protestantism
created an Orange and Unionist monolith to protect its interests
and to resist the advancement of Irish Nationalism. Out of this
the divided and troubled state of Northern Ireland was born.

The story of Ian Paisley is also the story of the disintegration of
that monolith, of the unwillingness of a large intransigent section
of Unionism to accommodate Catholic demands for equality,
and of the impotence of the Protestant establishment in the face
of its own extremists. Ian Paisley personified that extremism
better than any other previous Protestant leader and by
channelling it into politics, he created one of the most powerfully
conservative movements in recent Irish history.

Protestantism always came first in Ian Paisley's life. His
career, like that of his father and countless other fundamentalist

preachers before them, has been based on constant vigilance against attacks on biblical Protestantism, a set of beliefs based on a simple and literal interpretation of the Bible as the only source of the revealed word of God.

It was an extreme version of the Protestant belief that only the Bible could reveal God's will to man. This freedom to commune directly with God was the fundamental Protestant liberty which countless martyrs had gone to the stake to defend.

Ranged against this Biblical Protestantism was Roman Catholicism, in their eyes a vast dictatorial system of law and politics, not a church. Its theology revolved around precisely the opposite idea, that corruptible human agencies - popes, priests, bishops and curias - did have the power to mediate between man and God and to re-interpret, add to and subtract from biblical truths. With this power, Catholicism sought to impose its interpretations of God's word on the world at large, to extinguish Protestantism and to replace it with papal tyranny. Rome was the cunning "fox", ever ready to grasp the slightest opportunity to enfeeble Protestantism.

Between Catholicism and Protestantism there could never be compromise, only conflict. In Ireland, as elsewhere, Catholicism straddled the spiritual and political worlds, constantly seeking new ways to achieve its ambitions. Sometimes it sought to weaken Protestantism in subtle fashions, undermining it from within, as with ecumenism. At other times, it made open alliances with political movements, like the nationalist struggle for political independence, the civil rights movement or the IRA, in an effort to erode and destroy Protestantism's defences.

Because Catholicism used politics to advance its cause, Protestantism also had to be political in defence and counter-attack. For Paisley the defence of biblical Protestantism has always been a political act, requiring eternal watchfulness against attempts to subvert and overthrow its last bastion, the state of Northern Ireland. Defeat would mean an all-Ireland Republic, and the spiritual and political slavery of Catholicism. Paisley's Unionism springs from his Protestantism: "Victory for our enemies would put us under the priestly jackboot of that double tyranny. To submit would be worse than death".

This view was reflected in the Unionism into which Paisley was born. Northern Ireland's first leaders constructed a State built upon the slogan "No Surrender!" It was a slogan which

ymbolised their defiance of Catholicism and Nationalism, but it
lso articulated their fear of the "Lundy", the traitor within - the
rotestant who dealt in any way with the Catholic enemy. Above
ll else it severely inhibited Unionism's ability to modernise and
o reform, for to do so risked the ire of powerful ghosts and their
nodern imitators.

Paisley's career took off when the religious leaders of
rotestantism began to show flexibility. At first this was
nanifested by a less dogmatic, more liberal approach to
heology. At the centre of this movement was an injection of
ntellectual rationality into religious debate and a more open-
ninded interpretation of the Bible by Presbyterian leaders like
rofessor Ernest Davey.

That was followed by the spread of ecumenism, whose aim was
o create a united Protestant church and ultimately a united
Christian church which would include Rome. That could only
appen, Paisley believed, on terms dictated by "modernists" and
Catholics, and in a way which would dilute Bible Protestantism
eyond recognition.

Paisley became the most outspoken opponent of those "selling
ut" the Protestant religion: "This is not the time for the velvet
ongue. It is a day of war and war to the death. The enemy we fear
s the enemy within . . . These are the men we have in Ulster. If
hey want to go to Rome, then let them go, but they are not
aking Ulster with them".

"Come ye out from among them and be ye separate" - the
lominating biblical text of his childhood - became his religious
nd political slogan. His separatism was based on three
rinciples: an absolute opposition to compromise, conflict with
hose who do, and an elitism which claims sole possession of the
ruth.

The Free Presbyterian Church is an example of all three in
ction. Paisley established it as an aggressive breakaway to
ttract fellow dissidents with whose help he would reverse the
compromise" of established Presbyterianism.

He later applied his separatist philosophy to Orangeism and
Jnionism. The resulting conflict with all three pillars of the
Northern Protestant establishment have dominated his life with
harply differing results. While conflict with "weak" Protestant
eaders won him a substantial following, it also severely inhibited
is ability to gain the overall leadership of the Protestant

community. His rigid religious separatism and political elitism ruled out the possibility of co-operation on equal terms with many sections of Protestantism. Protestants and Unionists could only choose Paisley as their leader on the terms dictated by him.

It was when the religious ecumenism of the 1950s and 1960 was repeated in Unionist politics that Paisley was able finally to bond his Protestantism to his Unionism. As one of his liberal Protestant opponents, the Rev John Morrow put it: "Paisley convinced a significant proportion of people that political and theological betrayal were proceeding hand in hand. He convinced many Northern Protestants that their heritage was being sold down the river by an unholy alliance of ecumenists and Lundies."

It had started slowly during Brookeborough's period as Prime Minister but accelerated under the technocratic, modernising premiership of Terence O'Neill. O'Neill's message was the very antithesis of the sort of Unionism that Paisley grew up with because it was based on the need to reconcile Catholics, not to confront them. O'Neillism developed behind the backs of most Protestants and it posed, in their minds, a threat to their whole religious, political and economic status. No-one could voice and manipulate the fears of such frightened and bewildered people as effectively as Paisley, none could better simplify the complexities of O'Neillism and present them as all-encompassing threats.

Paisley represented comforting certitude. To those Protestants reared in Paisley's style of religion and Unionism, he offered a way to re-assert old values. On the one hand he provided religious and political alternatives to the "compromising" establishment, on the other he inspired resistance and reaction within it.

The civil rights movement gave Paisley a new momentum. It forced O'Neill, and then the British, to grant concessions to Catholics. In the process it both confirmed Protestant suspicions and vindicated Paisley's warnings. It also set in motion a Protestant backlash which toppled O'Neill, splintered the Unionist monolith and encouraged an intransigent violence out of which the Provisional IRA was born and the philosophy of violent Republicanism rejuvenated.

That in turn produced massive Catholic violence, an equally violent Protestant backlash, and then a succession of British attempts to discover totally new political structures in Northern reland. It hardened a conviction in the bulk of Protestants that he Union with Britain was indeed being undermined and, in arger and larger numbers, they turned for reassurance to Ian Paisley, the very man whose self-fulfilling prophecies had started he whole process.

Part of the secret of Paisley's success, and the explanation for is widening popularity during the 1970s and 1980s, lay in his ability to hijack and confiscate all the important symbols, customs and heroes of Protestant mythology.

He followed the 19th century Protestant tradition of uncompromising, anti-Catholic preaching represented by clerics like Henry Cooke, Thomas Drew and Hugh "Roaring" Hanna. He emulated one of Orangeism's most celebrated heroes, William Johnston of Ballykilbegs, when he went to jail for mounting street protests in defiance of the authorities and then used his martyrdom to gain election to parliament. Most of all he imitated Carson in politics, defiance, tactics and even dress.

Carson symbolised several recurrent themes in Northern Protestantism. Among these was the tradition of banding together for self-protection and, if necessary, in defiance of awful authority if it threatened their interests. At its heart lies the almost feudal concept of contractual Unionism: that the Union with Britain is a "two way street", a "covenant" between Ulster Protestants and the British Crown which guarantees the Protestantism as well as the Britishness of Northern Ireland.

This explains one great contradiction which mystifies the outsider - Paisley's loud proclamations of loyalty to Britain while he simultaneously leads Protestants into conflict with her. His Unionism is not about being British; he has regularly stressed that his loyalty is to the British Crown only because it is Protestant. He would cease to be a Unionist if a Catholic succeeded to the throne.

There are countless examples of Paisley imitating Carson. His Ulster Constitution Defence Committee, the Ulster Protestant Volunteers and the "Third Force" were all facsimiles of Carson's UVF. The 1981 "Carson Trail" travelled exactly the same route followed by Carson nearly 60 years earlier and began, as did Carson's, with the signing of a Solemn League and Covenant.

By the end of the 60s, Paisley was well on the way to establishing his claim to be the only true representative of traditional Protestantism, Orangeism and Unionism. Long

before the civil rights movement, Paisley had exposed th
weakness of the Unionist Party when faced with loyalis
intransigence. Even during Brookeborough's final years he wa
able to wring concessions from the Stormont government and t
force confrontation with Catholics. O'Neill himself, often laude
as the brave moderate, backed away from Paisley as much as h
faced up to him, while all his successors have, in varying degree
quailed at the prospect of taking him on.

By the end of the 70 s, the IRA's violence and the Britis
government's increasingly irresolute commitment to Norther
Ireland had combined to generate such deep Protestar
insecurity as to make Paisley's claim to lead them virtuall
complete and unchallengeable. His 170,000 votes in the 197
European election were an eloquent confirmation of that.

Despite his defiant resistance to British government policies
he has always stopped short of taking his followers over the brin
into outright armed rebellion. After his perilously clos
association with UVF violence in 1969, he broke all links wit
loyalism's "hard men". In 1974 he re-established those links - bu
only in the safe company of a wide coalition of Unionis
politicians - and then hesitated before joining the UWC'
challenge to Westminster. In 1977 he baulked at pulling the plu
on electricity supplies.

In 1981 his "Third Force" vanished as quickly and as peacefull
as it had materialised, while in 1986 his reluctance to openl
confront the British government has been the most significar
feature of the Unionist campaign against the Anglo-Iris
Agreement. The enduring symbol of Paisley's resistance ar
those gun licences waved by ranks of his followers on the Antrir
hillsides in 1981 - a theatrical but empty gesture.

There is one other vital element in Paisley's character. In bot
political and religious matters, principle has often taken a bac
seat to the pragmatism needed to further his over-weenin
political ambitions.

There is one outstanding example of this - his decision to ru
for the European Parliament. The Common Market was a heres
which went against everything he ostensibly believed in, yet h
was prepared to sit in an assembly which he denounced a
dominated by Rome, if it meant that he could grasp th
opportunity to make himself the leader of the Protestant people

Despite all this, there are limits to Paisley's ability o

willingness to compromise. He cannot compromise in the most fundamental area in Northern Ireland - in the search for political reconciliation and peace - in the way that other politicians might. "There's no such thing as reconciliation," he said in 1981. "When you marry Christ to Beelzebub, then we'll be ready for talks with them (the Republic)." To compromise with Roman Catholicism and Irish Nationalism would be to betray his heritage, his faith, even his God.

He cannot compromise either because he would be destroyed if he tried. The mass of ordinary Loyalists who flock to him do so because he articulates their fears and offers them the certainty of resistance to their all-encompassing Catholic enemies. Despite his own formidable qualities, Paisley is as much the creation of his followers as any other Unionist hero of the past. Should he ever waver, he, like the "Lundies" he has spent a lifetime denouncing, would be consumed - and behind his back these days stands Peter Robinson, a pretender to the crown, albeit one with few of Paisley's special qualities.

Unionism, though, has paid a terrible price for Ian Paisley's uncompromising leadership. His fierce "separatism" has brought disintegration in Unionist ranks which no single leader, least of all him, can now heal. His roaring bigotry has cost Unionism important allies in Britain and abroad where a more rational expression of its case might have evoked greater sympathy. And by presenting the greatest obstacle to reconciliation inside Northern Ireland, he has helped to unleash an awful self-destroying violence and set in motion a search for political solutions which now threatens the very Union he seeks to defend.

He remains, however, one of the most powerful Protestant figures of this century. His expediency, opportunism, ruthlessness and heavy-handed autocracy are tolerated, both by his immediate followers and the wider Protestant community because he has, in the eyes of many of them, one other unique quality.

He is a prophet honoured among his own people, defying authority in the defence of righteousness and persecuted by the people's enemies. Like the Old Testament prophets, he has the gift of foresight and has predicted the ills that would be visited upon Northern Ireland's Protestants. Notwithstanding the large element of self-fulfilment, his power and influence grew as each one came to pass: the birth of the IRA, the fall of Stormont, the Anglo-Irish Agreement.

Among his church and party members he really is "God's man". But even in that large section of the Protestant community less disposed to accept such a literal view, his years of defiance have given him unequalled status in the pantheon of Unionist leaders. His warnings of treachery and forecasts of danger are believed and trusted by a wide layer of normal, peace-loving, respectable Protestants. "Where would we be now without him?" - the rhetorical question asked by a middle-class, professional Protestant woman - finds an echo throughout the entire Unionist population.

Those who attack and criticise him are lost. His Unionist rivals are emasculated by the power of his thunderous denunciations, and rendered powerless to manoeuvre an accommodation with Nationalism. His unique hold over the Protestant psyche has made him the principal obstacle in the way of peace in Northern Ireland, for those who oppose him quickly find that they are taking on more than just Unionism's powerful history.

Ian Paisley has said it himself: "Show me a man of whom is said every evil and wicked slander. Show me a man who becomes the recipient of wave after wave of condemnation: who is condemned out of hand, who is accused of the most outrageous of crimes, and I will show you a man whom God has commissioned, whom God has called, who God has sent to be a prophet to his generation."

NOTES

Chapter One

1. In 1926 the make-up of Armagh City Council was: Catholic Labour 8 seats; Nationalist Combine 4 seats; Unionists 6 seats.

2. According to local historian Oliver Gibson, himself an Omagh DUP councillor, the Republicans had been in two minds about the attempt anyway, believing mistakenly that the barracks was too heavily guarded.

3. *The Baptist Magazine,* 1923.

4. "My Father and Mother" - two sermons preached by Paisley on 22 August 1973 and 9 April 1972.

5. David Taylor, "The Lord's Battle: An ethnographic and social study of Paisleyism in Northern Ireland." PhD. thesis, Queen's University Belfast, 1983. pp. 123-27.

6. Rev R.J.Beggs - "Great is Thy Faithfulness: an account of the ministry of Pastor Kyle Paisley and a history of the separatist testimony in Ballymena".

7. "The Four Windows of Life" - two sermons preached by Paisley, summer 1983.

8. "This is my Life" - taped series of sermons by Paisley, Part 1, 1979.

9. Michael Farrell, *The Orange State,* London, 1976, pp. 85-86.

10. *Belfast Telegraph,* 22 June 1946, church notices.

11. "The Four Windows of Life".

12. Paul Blanshard, *The Irish and Catholic Power,* Connecticut, 1953, p.234

13. *Irish News,* 1 June 1948

14. All examples from John Whyte, *Church and State in Modern Ireland,* Dublin, 1971, pp. 163-93.

15. Interview with "The Voice of Ulster", December 1982.

16. Conversation with Lord Fitt, April 1986.

17. He also had his first writ served on him, to prevent him abusing a Labour election agent whom he was accusing of having tricked a loyalist worker into signing Downey's nomination papers - Conversation with Jack Myers, May 1986.

18. *Belfast Telegraph and Northern Whig,* 14 August 1950, and conversation with Rev John Brown, former County Antrim Grand Master.

19. Conversation with Jim Welsh, May 1986.

20. *Woman's Own,* 24 May 1986, and conversations with former members of Ravenhill Free Presbyterian Church.

21. Reprinted in *The Revivalist,* December 1967.

22. *Northern Whig,* 21 March 1951.

Chapter Two

1. *The Revivalist,* April 1955.

2. *The Revivalist,* August 1955.

3. *Belfast Telegraph,* 15 October 1953.

4. *Belfast Telegraph,* 19 April 1952.

5. *Northern Whig,* 9 June 1954.

6. *The Irish and Catholic Power,* p. 226.

7. *The Irish and Catholic Power,* p. 233.

8. *The Revivalist,* January 1957.

9. *Belfast Telegraph,* 21 December 1956.

10. *Irish News,* 21 December 1956.

11. *Belfast Telegraph,* 11 May 1957.

12. *News Letter,* 13 July 1957.

Chapter Three

1. *Belfast Telegraph,* 18 March 1958.

2. *Irish Times,* 13 August 1959.

3. *News Letter,* 12 April 1954.

4. *News Letter,* 8 October 1959.

Chapter Eight

1. Ian Paisley - *The "Fifty Nine" Revival.* Belfast, 1958.

2. "This is My Life" - series of taped sermons by Paisley, part 2.

3. *The Revivalist,* June 1955.

4. *The Revivalist,* October 1955.

5. *The Revivalist,* November 1961.

6. Apostasy is one of Paisley's favourite charges against other Protestant churches and the World Council of Churches. He explains to his congregation that it is derived from the Greek word for "falling away", and thus means the abandonment of the true Christian faith.

7. *The Revivalist,* February 1959.

8. *The Revivalist,* June-July 1962.

9. *The Revivalist,* July-August 1957.

10. *The Revivalist,* April 1962.

11. *The Revivalist,* September 1959.

12. Alan Bestic, *Praise the Lord and Pass the Contribution,* London, 1971, pp. 85-9. Bestic visited Rockford and talked to Robert Hansen's ex-wife, who said he had been a minister in the Church of Christ, a fundamentalist Baptist sect, but had left to start his own church. She said he was a great preacher but mentally deranged. Also *Christianity Today* (Washington USA), 9 May 1960 - "The Scandal of Bogus Degrees".

13. David Taylor, *The Lord's Battle,* pp. 206-11. Additional information from conversations with former members of Martyrs Memorial.

14. *The Revivalist,* April 1965.

15. *The Lord's Battle,* p. 265.

16. Bob Jones - *Cornbread and Caviar: Reminiscences and Reflections.* Greenville, 1985, p. 24.

17. Jones Senior was also fanatically anti-Catholic, and had been prominent in the sectarian campaigns against Al Smith, the Catholic nominee for the Democratic Party ticket in the 1924 US presidential election and the party's presidential candidate four years later.

18. *Sunday Times,* 16 February 1969; *Irish Times,* 24 August 1979.

19. *Cornbread and Caviar,* p. 192.

Chapter Ten

1. The Pentecostalists are an evangelical sect who, like the Baptists, believe in converts being totally immersed in water. They also believe that people can "speak in tongues" and have healing powers when filled with the Holy Spirit.

2. God told Gideon to reduce his army of Israelites from 32,000 to 300 so that it would be clear that He was responsible for their defeat of the Midianites, the invaders who were laying waste their country (*Judges,* Chapter 7)

Chapter Eleven

1. *Irish Times,* 9 February 1971.

2. *The Cecil King Diary, 1970-1974,* London 1975. p. 22.

3. *Cecil King,* p. 97.

4. *Cecil King,* p. 110.

5. Clifford Smyth - "The Ulster Democratic Unionist Party: A case study in political and religious convergence". PhD. thesis, Queen's University Belfast, 1983, p. 27.

6. *The Times,* 3 August 1971.

7. *Irish Press,* 15 March 1971.

8. *Cecil King,* p. 144.

9. *Irish Times,* 29 November 1971.

10. *Irish Press,* 29 November 1971.

11. *Irish Times,* 29 November 1971.

12. *Sunday Independent,* 12 December 1971.

13. David Boulton, *The UVF 1966-73: An Anatomy of Loyalist Rebellion,* Dublin, 1973, p. 149; *Newsletter,* 1 December 1971; *Sunday Times,* 12 December 1971.

14. *Cecil King,* p. 219, 263.

15. *Irish Times,* 30 June 1975.

16. *Irish Times,* 13 September 1975.

17. *Irish Times*, 9 September 1975.

18. *Belfast Telegraph*, 4 February 1976.

19. For example, his speech at the DUP's annual conference, 15 April 1977.

20. *Ibid*.

21. Speech in Ballymena, 4 July 1977.

22. *Irish Times*, 5 January 1980.

23. *Irish Times*, 8 March 1980.

24. Clifford Smyth - The Ulster Democratic Unionist Party, pp. 149-50.

25. David McKittrick, *Irish Times*, 8 May 1980.

26. *Irish Times*, 18 August 1980.

27. *Irish Times*, 9 January 1981.

28. Clifford Smyth, now back in the Official Unionists. *Irish Times*, 18 June 1981.

29. *Irish Times*, 29 June 1985.

Chapter Twelve

1. LWT Weekend World, 14 December 1980.

2. *The Carson Trail*, foreword. Belfast, 1981.

3. *Irish Times*, 9 February 1981.

4. *The Carson Trail*, p. 35.

5. *Irish Times*, 20 February 1981.

6. *The Carson Trail*, p. 36.

7. For example at the 1979 DUP Christmas dinner, quoted in David Taylor, *The Lord's Battle*.

8. Simon Hoggart, The *Guardian* - "A stone's throw away from independence?" 4 June 1973.

Chapter Thirteen

1. *Daniel*, Chapter 2.

2. *Daniel*, Chapter 7.

3. *Revelation*, Chapter 13.

4. Quotes, except where stated, from "The EEC Prophetically Considered", a series of sermons preached by Paisley in May-June 1979.

5. *Ibid*.

BIBLIOGRAPHY

Akenson, D. H. *Education and Enmity: The Control of Schooling in Northern Ireland 1920-1950*. David & Charles, 1973

Bardon, Jonathan. *Belfast: An Illustrated History*. Blackstaff Press, 1982

Barkley, John M. *A Short History of the Presbyterian Church in Ireland*. Presbyterian Church in Ireland, 1959

Barrington, Ruth and Cooney, John. *Inside the EEC*. The O'Brien Press, 1984

Bell, J. Bowyer. *The Secret Army: the IRA, 1916-1979*. The Academy Press, 1970

Bestic, Alan. *Praise the Lord and Pass the Contribution*. Cassell, 1971

Blanshard, Paul. *The Irish and Catholic Power*. Greenwood Press, 1953

Boulton, David. *The UVF: 1966-1973*. Torc Books, 1973

Boyd, Andrew. *Holy War in Belfast: A History of the Troubles in Northern Ireland*. Grove Press, 1969

Brown, Terence. *Ireland, A Social and Cultural History, 1922-79*. Fontana, 1981

Browne, Vincent (ed). *The Magill Book of Irish Politics*. Magill Publications Ltd, 1981

Buckland, Patrick. *A History of Northern Ireland*. Gill and Macmillan, 1981
   The Factory of Grievances: Devolved Government in Northern Ireland 1921-1939. Gill and Macmillan, 1979

Budge, Ian and O'Leary, Cornelius. *Belfast: Approach to Crisis, A Study of Belfast Politics 1613-1970*. Macmillan, 1973

Coogan, Tim Pat. *Ireland Since the Rising*. Pall Mall, 1966
   The Irish - A Personal View. Phaidon, 1975

De Paor, Liam. *Divided Ulster*. Penguin, 1970
   Portrait of Ireland. Rainbow, 1986

Deutsch, Richard and Magowan, Vivien. *Northern Ireland 1968-73: A Chronology of Events*. Blackstaff Press, 1974

Devlin, Bernadette. *The Price of My Soul*. Pan, 1969

Dillon, Martin and Lehane, Denis. *Political Murder in Northern Ireland*. Penguin, 1973

Farrell, Michael. *Arming the Protestants: The Formation of the Ulster Special Constabulary and the Royal Ulster Constabulary 1920-1927*. Brandon, 1983

   Northern Ireland: The Orange State. Pluto, 1976

Fisk, Robert. *The Point of No Return: The Strike Which Broke the British in Ulster*. Andre Deutsch, 1975

Flackes, W. D. *Northern Ireland: A Political Directory 1968-1983*. BBC, 1980

Fulton, Austin. *Biography of J. Ernest Davey*. Presbyterian Church in Ireland, 1970

Gray, Tony. *The Orange Order*. The Bodley Head, 1972

Harbinson, John F. *The Ulster Unionist Party 1882-1973*. Blackstaff Press, 1973

Heskin, Ken. *Northern Ireland: A Psychological Analysis*. Gill and Macmillan, 1980

Holmes, Finlay. *Our Irish Presbyterian Heritage*. Presbyterian Church in Ireland, 1985

Jones, Bob. *Cornbread and Caviar*. Bob Jones University Press, 1985

Kelly, Henry. *How Stormont Fell*. Gill and Macmillan, 1972

King, Cecil. *The Cecil King Diary 1970-1974*. Jonathan Cape, 1975

Knight, Derrick. *Beyond the Pale: The Christian Political Fringe*. Kegan Paul, 1981

Marrinan, Patrick. *Paisley: Man of Wrath*. Anvil Books, 1973

McBride, Paula J. *A Geographical Analysis of the Free Presbyterian Church 1951-78*. Unpublished dissertation, Department of Geography, The Queen's University of Belfast, 1978

Millar, David W. *Queen's Rebels: Ulster Loyalism in Historical Perspective*. Gill and Macmillan, 1978

Murphy, Dervla. *A Place Apart*. Penguin, 1978

Nelson, Sarah. *Ulster's Uncertain Defenders*. Appletree Press, 1984

O'Malley, Padraig. *The Uncivil Wars: Ireland Today*. Blackstaff Press, 1983

O'Neill, Terence. *The Autobiography of Terence O'Neill*. Granada Publishing Ltd, 1972

Patterson, Henry. *Class Conflict and Sectarianism: The Protestant Working Class and the Belfast Labour Movement 1868-1920*. Blackstaff Press, 1980

Paulin, Tom. *Ireland and the English Crisis*. Bloodaxe Books, 1984

Rees, Merlyn. *Northern Ireland: A Personal Perspective*. Methuen, 1985

Smyth, Andrew Clifford. *The Ulster Democratic Unionist Party: A Case Study in Political and Religious Convergence*. Unpublished PH.D thesis, The Queen's University of Belfast, 1983

Stewart, A. T. Q. *The Narrow Ground: Aspects of Ulster 1609-1969*. Faber and Faber, 1977

   The Ulster Crisis: Resistance to Home Rule 1912-1914. Faber and Faber, 1967

Sunday Times Insight Team. *Ulster*. Penguin, 1972

Taylor, David Frank. *The Lord's Battle: An Ethnographic and Social*

Study of Paisleyism in Northern Ireland. Unpublished PH.D thesis, The Queen's University of Belfast, 1983

Whyte, J. P. H. *Church and State in Modern Ireland.* Gill and Macmillan, 1971

Winchester, Simon. *The Holy Terror: Reporting on the Ulster Troubles.* Faber, 1974

PAISLEYITE PUBLICATIONS

Beggs, R. J. *Great is Thy Faithfulness.* Ballymena Free Presbyterian Church

Calvert, David. *A Decade of the DUP.* Crown Publications, 1981

Cooke, Ronald. *Ian Paisley: Protestant Protagonist Par Excellence.* Manahath Press, 1984

McCrea, William and Porter, David. *In His Pathway: The Story of Rev William McCrea.* Marshall, Morgan and Scott, 1980

Paisley, Ian R. K. *These Twenty-eight Years.* Martyrs Memorial Productions, 1974

The Four Windows of My Life. 1983

My Father and Mother. Martyrs Memorial Publications, 1973

Richard Cameron: The Lion of the Covenant

God's Ultimatum to the Nation

The Ulster Problem (Spring 1972), Bob Jones University Press, 1972

An Exposition of the Epistle to the Romans. Martyrs Memorial Free Presbyterian Church, 1968

Messages from the Prison Cell. 1969

No Pope Here. Martyrs Memorial Publications, 1982

The Man and His Message. Martyrs Memorial Publications, 1976

Northern Ireland: What Is the Real Situation? Bob Jones University Press, 1970

W. P. Nicholson: Tornado of the Pulpit. Martyrs Memorial Productions, 1982

The "Fifty Nine" Revival. The Free Presbyterian Church of Ulster, 1958

This is My Life. Tape Recordings, Martyrs Memorial Productions, 1979

Wilson, Sam. *The Carson Trail.* Crown Publications, 1981

Ulster Democratic Unionist Party Yearbooks

The Protestant Telegraph, 1966-1982 (Protestant Unionist/DUP newspaper)

The Revivalist, 1955-1986 (Free Presbyterian Church Magazine)

Voice of Ulster, 1982-1983 (DUP newspaper)

The Protestant Bluprint (Martyrs Memorial news sheet)

PAMPHLETS AND ARTICLES

Belfast Workers Research Unit. *Belfast Bulletin 8: The Churches in Northern Ireland.* Belfast, 1980

Brown, Terence. *The Whole Protestant Community: The Making of a Historical Myth.* Field Day, 1985

Egan, Bowes and McCormack, *Vincent*. Burntollet LRS Publishers, 1969

Elliot, Sidney. *Northern Ireland: The First Election to the European Parliament*. The Queen's University of Belfast, 1980

Smith, Peter. *Why Unionists Say No*. The Joint Unionist Working Party, 1986

Wallis, Roy; Bruce, Steve and Taylor, David. *"No Surrender!" Paisleyism and the Politics of Ethnic Identity in Northern Ireland*. The Queen's University of Belfast, 1986

Wright, Frank. *Protestant Ideology and Politics in Ulster*. European Journal of Sociology, volume XIV, (1973) pp. 213-80

NEWSPAPERS AND PERIODICALS

The Belfast Telegraph
The News Letter
The Northern Whig
The Irish News
The Irish Times
The Irish Press
The Irish Independent
The Ballymena Guardian
The Ballymena Observer
The Lurgan Mail
Loyalist News (John McKeague publication of the early 1970s)

INDEX OF NAMES